Understanding Women's Entrepreneurship in a Gendered Context

Women entrepreneurs are indeed a formidable force of economic growth and social change, though we still often question the "how" and "why." For the readers who seek to understand the spectrum of gender influences in the context of entrepreneurship, *Understanding Women's Entrepreneurship in a Gendered Context: Influences and Restraints* widens the contextual focus of women's entrepreneurship and entrepreneurship research by providing powerful insights into the influences and restraints within a diverse set of gendered contexts including social, political, institutional, religious, patriarchal, cultural, family and economic, in which female entrepreneurs around the world operate their businesses. From recognition of a seventh-century businesswoman in Mecca to the construction of a gendered scientific Business Model Canvas, this collection of studies will inspire readers to think differently about theory, patriarchy, trade systems, adoption or transformation and strategies to create inclusive entrepreneurial ecosystems. In doing so, the contributing authors demonstrate not only the importance of studying the contexts in which women's entrepreneurial activities are shaped, but also how female entrepreneurs, through their endeavours, modify these contexts.

This book will be of great value to scholars, students and researchers interested in women's entrepreneurship, entrepreneurial ecosystems, gender hierarchy and the transition to gender equality. It was originally published as a special issue of *Entrepreneurship & Regional Development*.

Shumaila Yousafzai is Associate Professor at Cardiff University, UK. Her research focuses on the contextual embeddedness of entrepreneurship, institutional theory and entrepreneurial orientation. She has published in various international journals and has co-edited a special issue on women's entrepreneurship for *Entrepreneurship & Regional Development*.

Alain Fayolle is Professor of Entrepreneurship and Founder and Director of the Entrepreneurship Research Centre at EM Lyon Business School, France. Alain has published 35 books and over 150 articles. In 2013, he received the European Entrepreneurship Education Award and in 2015, he was elected Wilford L. White Fellow by ICSB (International Council for Small Businesses). He was elected Chair of the AOM (Academy of Management) Entrepreneurship Division for the academic year 2016–2017.

Saadat Saeed is Associate Professor in Entrepreneurship at the Durham University Business School, UK. His past research efforts have included the global study of supportive institutions and women's entrepreneurship, entrepreneurship in adverse conditions, corporate entrepreneurship and firm performance in multi-country contexts.

Colette Henry, FRSA, is Head of School of Business & Humanities at Dundalk Institute of Technology, Ireland, and Adjunct Professor of Entrepreneurship at UiT–The Arctic University of Norway. Colette holds the Diana International Trailblazer award for Female Entrepreneurship and the Sten K Johnson European Entrepreneurship Education Award.

Adam Lindgreen is Professor of Marketing and Head of Department of Marketing at Copenhagen Business School, Denmark, and he is Extraordinary Professor with Gordon Institute of Business Science, University of Pretoria, South Africa. He has published in *California Management Review, Journal of Business Ethics, Journal of Product and Innovation Management, Journal of the Academy of Marketing Science, Journal of World Business* and *Organization Studies*, amongst others.

Understanding Women's Entrepreneurship in a Gendered Context

Influences and Restraints

Edited by
Shumaila Yousafzai, Alain Fayolle, Saadat Saeed, Colette Henry and Adam Lindgreen

LONDON AND NEW YORK

First published 2021
by Routledge
2 Park Square, Milton Park, Abingdon, Oxon OX14 4RN

and by Routledge
52 Vanderbilt Avenue, New York, NY 10017

Routledge is an imprint of the Taylor & Francis Group, an informa business

Chapters 1–6, 9 and 10 © 2021 Taylor & Francis
Chapter 7 © 2018 Mirela Xheneti, Shova Thapa Karki and Adrian Madden.
Originally published as Open Access.
Chapter 8 © 2018 Annie Roos. Originally published as Open Access.

British Library Cataloguing in Publication Data
A catalogue record for this book is available from the British Library

ISBN: 978-0-367-68879-0 (hbk)
ISBN: 978-0-367-68880-6 (pbk)
ISBN: 978-1-003-13945-4 (ebk)

Typeset in MyriadPro
by Newgen Publishing UK

Publisher's Note
The publisher accepts responsibility for any inconsistencies that may have arisen during the conversion
of this book from journal articles to book chapters, namely the inclusion of journal terminology.

Disclaimer
Every effort has been made to contact copyright holders for their permission to reprint material in this
book. The publishers would be grateful to hear from any copyright holder who is not here acknowledged
and will undertake to rectify any errors or omissions in future editions of this book.

Contents

Citation Information

The chapters in this book were originally published in *Entrepreneurship & Regional Development*, volume 31, issue 3–4 (2019). When citing this material, please use the original page numbering for each article, as follows:

For any permission-related enquiries please visit:
www.tandfonline.com/page/help/permissions

Notes on Contributors

Kent Adsbøll Wickstrøm, Department of Entrepreneurship and Relationship Management, University of Southern Denmark, Kolding, Denmark.

Hammad Akbar, Management School, University of Liverpool, UK.

Haya Al-Dajani, Plymouth Business School, University of Plymouth, UK.

Sara Carter, Hunter Centre for Entrepreneurship, University of Strathclyde, Glasgow, UK.

Maryam Cheraghi, Department of Entrepreneurship and Relationship Management, University of Southern Denmark, Kolding, Denmark.

Nathalie Duval-Couetil, Department of Technology Leadership and Innovation, Purdue University, West Lafayette, IN, USA.

Caroline Essers, Department of Business Administration, Nijmegen School of Management, Radboud University, Nijmegen, the Netherlands.

Alain Fayolle, Strategy & Organization, EM Lyon Business School, Lyon–Ecully, France.

Vishal K. Gupta, Culverhouse College of Business, The University of Alabama, Tuscaloosa, AL, USA.

Colette Henry, Dundalk Institute of Technology, Ireland; UiT–The Arctic University of Norway.

Markus Kemmelmeier, Interdisciplinary Social Psychology, University of Nevada, Reno, NV, USA.

Kim Klyver, Department of Entrepreneurship and Relationship Management, University of Southern Denmark, Kolding, Denmark; Entrepreneurship, Commercialisation and Innovation Centre (ECIC), University of Adelaide, Australia.

Adam Lindgreen is Professor of Marketing and Head of Department of Marketing at Copenhagen Business School, Denmark, and he is Extraordinary Professor with Gordon Institute of Business Science, University of Pretoria, South Africa. He has published in *California Management Review, Journal of Business Ethics, Journal of Product and Innovation Management, Journal of the Academy of Marketing Science, Journal of World Business* and *Organization Studies*, amongst others.

Ye Liu, Department of Public Administration, Zhejiang Sci-Tech University, Hangzhou, China; Department of Entrepreneurship and Relationship Management, University of Southern Denmark, Kolding, Denmark; Sino–Danish Center of Education and Research, Beijing, China.

Adrian Madden, Department of Human Resources and Organisational Behaviour, University of Greenwich, Old Royal Naval College, London, UK.

William McKelvey, Anderson School of Management, University of California, Los Angeles, CA, USA.

Annie Roos, Rural Entrepreneurship Group, Department of Economics, Swedish University of Agricultural Sciences, Uppsala, Sweden.

Saadat Saeed, Durham University Business School, Durham, UK.

Thomas Schøtt, Department of Entrepreneurship and Relationship Management, University of Southern Denmark, Kolding, Denmark.

Eleanor Shaw, Hunter Centre for Entrepreneurship, University of Strathclyde, Glasgow, UK.

Shova Thapa Karki, School of Business, Management and Economics, University of Sussex, Brighton, UK.

Hayfaa A. Tlaiss, College of Business, Alfaisal University, Riyadh, Saudi Arabia.

María Villares-Varela, Department of Sociology, Social Policy and Criminology, University of Southampton, UK.

Mandy Wheadon, Department of Technology Leadership and Innovation, Purdue University, West Lafayette, IN, USA.

Alice M. Wieland, College of Business, University of Nevada, Reno, NV, USA.

Mirela Xheneti, School of Business, Management and Economics, University of Sussex, Brighton, UK.

Shumaila Yousafzai, Cardiff Business School, Cardiff University, UK.

Chuqing Zhang, Department of Innovation, Entrepreneurship and Strategy, Tsinghua University, Beijing, China.

The contextual embeddedness of women's entrepreneurship: towards a more informed research agenda

Shumaila Yousafzai, Alain Fayolle, Saadat Saeed, Colette Henry and Adam Lindgreen

'For the modern man the patriarchal relation of status is by no means the dominant feature of life; but for the women on the other hand, and for the upper-middle class women especially, confined as they are by prescription and by economic circumstances to their "domestic sphere", this relation is the most real and most formative factor of life'. (Veblen 1899, 324 as quoted in Van Staveren and Odebode 2007, 903)

Introduction

Entrepreneurship is positioned within contemporary scholarship as a noun that describes the 'world as it is' (Calás, Smircich, and Bourne 2009, 561). Krueger and Brazeal's (1994, 91) definition of entrepreneurship as 'the pursuit of an opportunity irrespective of existing resources' is consistent with the common assertion that entrepreneurship offers gender-neutral meritocratic career opportunities. In practice, however, interaction with the environment determines the future of women's entrepreneurship, that is, women are never just women, but also are located within a specific context (Ahl and Marlow 2012; Calás, Smircich, and Bourne 2009; Mirchandani 1999; Yousafzai, Saeed, and Muffatto 2015).

Feminist philosophers argue that the constitution, development, critique and application of knowledge is profoundly gendered (Butler 1993; Harding 1987, Hardiong 1991; Marlow and McAdam 2013). Even though gendered institutions have long been recognized as exemplary for how historical and cultural contexts influence the economic process of provisioning (Veblen 1899; Van Staveren and Odebode 2007), they have received considerably less attention in the institutional analysis of the 'gendered terrain' of the women's entrepreneurship landscape (Brush, de Bruin, and Welter 2009; Tedmanson et al. 2012; Welter, Brush, and de Bruin 2014). Indeed, a critical shortcoming of research on women's entrepreneurship is that instead of pursuing a more reflexive, theoretically informed and holistic understanding of the embedded context, it tends to focus on a direct relationship between general conditions and arrangements in the overall entrepreneurial environment (for both male and female entrepreneurs) and women's entrepreneurial activity (Ahl 2006; Brush, de Bruin, and Welter 2009; Hughes et al. 2012; Tedmanson et al. 2012). Such 'all are alike' (Aldrich 2009) and 'extreme decontextualisation' (Welter, Brush, and de Bruin 2014) approaches ignore research, which suggests that gender-differences should be conceptualized as fluid processes and rooted within a historical context that informs and sustains the normative, hierarchical subordination shaping women's life chances (Marlow and McAdam 2013). This is important because 'a mismatch between theory and context can result in false leads and inconclusive findings' (Zahra 2007, 445). Accordingly, researchers have pointed out that a gender-neutral approach may have accounted for the failure of research on women's entrepreneurship to unravel the complex web of intertwined socio-economic and politically framed realities constructed by gendered institutions (Ahl and Marlow 2012; Lansky 2000; Marlow and Swail 2014).

Although the impressive expansion of scholarly interest and activity in the field of women's entrepreneurship within recent years has done much to correct the historical lack of attention paid to female entrepreneurs and their initiatives, scholars consistently are being asked to take their research in new directions. Most importantly, the need for greater gender consciousness has been highlighted in the women's entrepreneurship literature, with calls for future research to 'contextualize' and enrich the 'vastly understudied' field of women's entrepreneurship (de Bruin, Brush, and Welter 2006, 585) by going beyond biologically essentialized identities and questioning gendered hierarchies and structural constructions embedded within highly informed conceptual frameworks (Ahl 2006; Ahl and Marlow 2012; de Bruin, Brush, and Welter 2007). Such changes in direction help shift the focus towards the 'more silent feminine personal end' of the entrepreneurial process (Bird and Brush 2002, 57), with significant implications for women's entrepreneurship research, policy and practice (Brush and Cooper 2012; Carter, Anderson, and Shaw 2001; Hamilton 2013; Minniti and Naudé 2010).

Hughes et al. (2012, 431), quoting Ahl (2006), note that the entrepreneurship literature 'by excluding explicit discussion of gendered power structures, [and discussing] the apparent shortcomings of female entrepreneurs … reinforce[s] the idea that explanations are to be found in the individual rather than on a social or institutional level'. These perilous suppositions are counterproductive, as they tend to perpetuate the 'hierarchical gendered ordering' in which femininity is associated with deficit in a context of masculinized normality (Marlow and McAdam 2013). Furthermore, such suppositions challenge the importance of balancing different perspectives on women's entrepreneurship by inferring that individual attributes alone result in entrepreneurial success. Thus, regardless of the varied contextual settings in which entrepreneurs operate, all ultimately are alike. Consequently, our partial understanding of the construction of the gender gap – rather than being grounded in a gendered perspective and based on a female norm – is developed, measured and evaluated in terms of how women's entrepreneurship deviates from the yardstick that is the male norm (Achtenhagen and Welter 2011; Ahl 2006; Bird and Brush 2002; Mirchandani 1999). Accordingly, the patriarchal economies and societies, along with their gendered power structures that not only shape the context of entrepreneurs (men and women alike), but privilege men over women, remain unchallenged (Vossenberg 2013). This has considerable consequences for research and policy-making and may well explain why the gender gap continues to exist and, more importantly, why real reform for women's entrepreneurship has not yet occurred (Ahl 2006; Calás, Smircich, and Bourne 2009). Consequently, as Hughes et al. (2012, 545) suggest, research on gender and entrepreneurship is reaching an epistemological 'dead end'.

In light of the above, this special issue is timely, encouraging both a change in research direction and a move away from traditional yardsticks towards a deeper understanding of the influence of context on women's entrepreneurship. In our call for papers, we sought contributions that offered valuable and novel perspectives on the contextual embeddedness of women's entrepreneurship, papers that were informed by robust theoretical or empirical research and employed qualitative, quantitative or mixed methods to critically explore the phenomenon in different countries, cultures and industry contexts. We received 45 manuscripts and, following an initial review by the editorial team, a shortlist of papers was subjected to a double blind, peer-review process. After a series of review-and-revision rounds, nine papers were finally selected for inclusion in this double special issue.

Our final selection has a strong international dimension. The selection comprises both conceptual and empirical papers, employs a mixture of methodological approaches and adopts a range of gender perspectives. While each paper offers its own unique perspective, collectively, the papers offer a contemporary view of the contextual embeddedness of women's entrepreneurship at the global level that should contribute usefully to extending scholarly debates and pave the way towards a new research agenda for the field.

In the next section, we categorize the papers according to their overarching theme, and discuss them in the context of extant literature. We subsequently draw on this discussion to map out a more informed future research agenda, which, if implemented, could potentially offer a more theoretically holistic and empirically informed understanding of the contextual embeddedness of the phenomenon that is women's entrepreneurship.

Defying contextual embeddedness

While entrepreneurial practices and processes are evolving, models of entrepreneurship remain embedded in advanced economies, are masculinized and still widely associated with beliefs of individual agency and heroism. Consequently, defiance through entrepreneurship is rarely considered (Al-Dajani et al., Forthcoming). Inherent in Schumpeterian beliefs of 'creative destruction', defiance is the daring and bold disobedience towards authoritarian regimes (e.g. patriarchy) and/or opposition to forces (e.g. established cultural norms). Even though, women's entrepreneurship can be conceptualized as an act of defiance, it rarely has been framed as such. The theme of defiance characterizes our first paper, by Al-Dajani, Akbar, Carter and Shaw (Forthcoming), which explores the collective defiance practices of Palestinian diasphora females operating in the context of a Jordanian patriarchal society. In a longitudinal, ethnographic study, the authors draw parallel between the deeper political connotations of heritage craft production that has kept alive memories of Palestinian traditions with the organizing actions of the socially excluded women in their study. While the women in this study could not change the restraints themselves, they find ingenious ways to circumvent and navigate the boundaries through their highly creative ventures and strategies in hidden entrepreneurial practices. They argue that these actions are instilled within the deeper purpose of defying contextual embeddedness by resisting contractual, social and patriarchal subjugation. The authors uncover the formation of a feminized economy and a secret production network led by the women to defy the supressing boundaries inflicted by their restrictive contractors, community and family members. Their findings on the proactiveness, innovativeness and risk taking actions of Arab women of Palestinian diaspora contradict much of the existing literature that portrays them as subservient, disempowered followers rather than defiant entrepreneurial leaders (Yamin 2013). The authors suggest that regardless of how constrained the context, women entrepreneurs of Palestinian diaspora can thrive and succeed when they take higher levels of risk through 'hidden' entrepreneurial enactment. Thus, their entrepreneurial activities cannot be restrained, and eventually 'finds its way'.

Contextualizing transnationalism and migration

Gender roles are embedded in specific contexts and may stipulate entrepreneurial behaviour (Welter, Brush, and de Bruin 2014). Thus, a thorough consideration of context allows researchers to grasp the effects of the social, spatial and institutional factors that can either restrain or facilitate entrepreneurship (Fayolle et al. 2015, Welter 2011; Zahra, Wright, and Abdelgawad 2014). For example, more traditional gender norms from the countries of origin of migrant women have been shown to affect their entrepreneurial behaviour in their destination countries where they must navigate different social settings (Villares-Varela, Ram, and Jones 2017). In our second paper, Villares-Varela and Essers (Forthcoming) enhance current migrant entrepreneurship accounts by addressing the overlooked gendered structures that shape women's work in the migrant economy.

They argue that while feminist researchers have studied the specific experiences of women entrepreneurs in the migrant economy, it often is circumscribed by specific national boundaries and lacks contextualized insights into the transnational experiences. Accordingly, they adopt a translocational positionality approach by focusing on transnational trajectories and their influence on women's social positions and business strategies. They draw upon the transnational entrepreneurial journeys of females migrant from Latin American in Spain and from Turkey in the Netherlands. The findings explain how female migrant entrepreneurs redefine their social status in different contexts through their entrepreneurial activities and, in this manner, defy or comply with gender relations.

Contextual embeddedness of entrepreneurial career success

Although research on career success has attracted significant consideration in management and organizational studies, the entrepreneurship research seems to examine primarily the objectively measured success of business ventures (e.g. Katre and Salipante 2012; Kiviluoto 2013) or the economic and demographic antecedents of entrepreneurial success (Fisher, Martiz and Lobo 2014). In a context which is already characterized by expectations of female weakness and male normativity and superiority, failure to account for the role of gender has reinforced the gender stereotype of women's inappropriateness for entrepreneurial careers and perpetuated the myth of female deficit and the underperforming female entrepreneur (Ahl 2006; Ahl and Marlow 2012; Marlow and McAdam 2013). In our third paper, Tlaiss (Forthcoming) criticizes the existing research for not questioning the socially embedded gendered assumptions of the so-called female deficiency and their impact on female entrepreneurs' experiences and conceptualizations of their career success. She addresses entrepreneurial success by examining the interplay between gender and culture, the interactions between agency and institutional factors and their specific relationship to women's entrepreneurial experiences as a critical reflexive interrogation of Lebanese female entrepreneurs' 'deficiency' in entrepreneurial competency, ambition and business performance. Tlaiss' study explains how the significant contradictions of masculinity and femininity disadvantage women, further sanctioning their inferior social and entrepreneurial status. While Tlaiss agree that Lebanese females enjoy greater social freedom than their peers in neighbouring Arab countries, the culture retains its masculine, patriarchal structures and endorses rigidly defined gender-specific roles. In such societies, the desirable qualities for success in entrepreneurship, such as aggressiveness, independence and decisiveness, are commonly attributed to men while women are expected to follow the social rules of conduct and prioritize their families' needs and household tasks over their personal career aspirations (Tlaiss 2015). The findings suggest that Lebanese female entrepreneurs draw upon their agency and take the conceptualization of their entrepreneurial careers success into their own hands. They experience it as an act of defiance against socially imposed cultural and gendered mandates by challenging deeply rooted societal and cultural norms and persevering in their entrepreneurial careers. This study also supports the argument that explaining career success using notions and constructs developed and conceptualized in Anglo-Saxon/North American contexts may not be completely suitable for patriarchal societies.

Staying with the entrepreneurial career success theme, but focusing on a slightly different dimension, the fourth paper, by Cheraghi, Jensen, and Klyver (Forthcoming), considers the gender gap in entrepreneurship participation by exploring women's entry into entrepreneurship. Here, the authors contend that low gender egalitarianism results in a gender gap in new venture creation endeavours, presenting both different opportunities and constraints to men and women. Previous research assumed – unrealistically so – that gender-related opportunities and constraints occur evenly throughout an individual's different life stages. In this study, the authors detail an institutional life-course model to explain gender-related patterns in an individual's propensity to engage in entrepreneurship, highlighting contingencies related to the level of gender-egalitarianism in society and an individual's life stages. Their conceptual model is tested on an extensive integrated data set of 71 countries drawn from the Global Entrepreneurship Monitor (GEM) and the World Value Survey. While previous research investigating gender effects in individuals' entrepreneurship participation suggests that gender effects are expected to be centred primarily around women's roles in giving birth and nursing children (Klyver, Nielsen, and Evald 2013; Thébaud 2015), this study observed that the gender gap in entrepreneurship participation was smaller in the launching stage than in the anticipatory stage. Moreover, the gender gap in the launching stage increases with an increase in gender-egalitarianism and is guided by a decrease in men's – not women's – entry into entrepreneurship in countries with low gender egalitarianism. Apart from the generally higher levels of entrepreneurship participation for both women and men in more gender egalitarian countries, this life course dynamic constituted the most significant gendered difference in individuals' entry into entrepreneurship in high and low egalitarian countries, respectively. Building on traditional gender role reasoning (Jayawarna, Rouse, and Kitching 2011), the authors argue that young males are less concerned with future family responsibilities and thus more willing to take risks by performing entrepreneurship at the early stage, while females prepare for future parental roles at a much earlier stages.

Contextualizing women entrepreneurs' business–family negotiations in patriarchal societies

The highest cited motivation for women's pursuit of entrepreneurship has been their need to achieve work-life balance. Yet, research on how women negotiate the boundaries of their work and family roles highlights that entrepreneurship is gendered and the model entrepreneur is characterized with masculinity, while women are expected to fulfil family roles (Ahl 2006; D'Enbeau, Villamil, and Helens-Hart 2015; Özbilgin et al. 2011; Munkejord 2017). Consequently, these struggles shape the processes through which women entrepreneurs 'nurture' the work–family interface (Eddleston and Powell 2012). However, the existing research is skewed towards the experiences of 'ideal work-life balancer' and the psychological and emotional effects of these work–family conflicts on individuals (Özbilgin et al. 2011). In our fifth paper, Xheneti, Karki, and Madden (Forthcoming) argue that despite several scholarly calls for contextualized accounts of women's entrepreneurship, we know little about the negotiating actions taken by women in the context of both livelihood challenges and patriarchal contexts. They further suggest that while women entrepreneurship research has focused mainly on roles such as 'motherhood' (Brush, de Bruin, and Welter 2009) or 'business ownership', it has failed to acknowledge other family-related junctures and the strategies of women entrepreneurs to adapt to changing family needs with regard to income, spare capacity and human resources (Alsos, Carter, and Ljunggren 2014; Poggesi, Mari, and De Vita 2015).

In their study, they highlight how Nepalese female entrepreneurs legitimize their business activities, respond to family/societal expectations and mobilize support for their business. By going beyond existing temporal and spatial strategies of entrepreneurs, the authors shed light on how the patriarchal context and livelihood challenges influence resource mobilization and work satisfaction through three main and interrelated themes – negotiating consent, family resource access and gaining status. By focusing on factors other than gender, this study opens up avenue to recognize how the diverse experiences of responding to business–family demands stem from the paradoxical expectations of different types of institutions.

Challenging existing gender structures through female entrepreneurial networks

While programmes to support women's entrepreneurship play an important role in encouraging more women to become entrepreneurs and in changing the gendered entrepreneurship discourse, Roos (Forthcoming) in our sixth paper argues that such initiatives are determined by masculine foundations and thus comply further with the masculine norm of economy. For example, by stating that women need to network more to become more successful entrepreneurs merely establishes the notion that it is women, and not the structures, that need to change (Mirchandani 1999; Hughes et al. 2012). In line with Marlow and Patton (2005), she agrees that there is a limited discussion on the structural issues surrounding gender and entrepreneurship (Marlow and Patton 2005). To fill these gaps, in her study, Roos (Forthcoming) investigates how a female entrepreneurship network is constructed, and how it simultaneously reinforce**s** and challenge**s** existing gender structures. This paper sheds lights on how embeddedness in context can offer a pathway towards gender equality by looking into the interplay between the gender process (i.e. a dichotomy of either reinforcing or challenging structures) and the embeddedness process (i.e. a process of moving between two extremes; rational market behaviour) within entrepreneurship. Between the two extremes of gender process and embeddedness process lies the entrepreneurship process that is embedded in the social context and enables people to realize the importance of context, become part of it and access resources bound to it (Jack and Anderson 2002; Korsgaard, Ferguson, and Gaddefors 2015). Roos (Forthcoming) further suggests that while embeddedness is associated with positive effects to some extent, at a certain point, a threshold is reached when embeddedness becomes associated with the negative outcomes of over-socialization (Uzzi 1997; Waldinger 1995). To get the most out of being embedded, entrepreneurs need to balance embeddedness through negotiation with the context, being cautious not to cross this threshold (Gaddefors and Cronsell 2009; Kalantaridis and Bika 2006). As Roos (Forthcoming) shows in her study, balancing the embeddedness process within an entrepreneurship process is one way of challenging gender structures. Based on an ethnographic study, Roos (Forthcoming) identifies three processes in the female entrepreneurship network: making proper entrepreneurs, building relationships and engaging in change.

The seventh paper, by Liu, Schøtt, and Zhang (Forthcoming), extends on the inequality dimension of female entrepreneurial networks by exploring women's experiences of legitimacy, satisfaction and commitment in the context of gender hierarchy. As an entrepreneur, when women perceive legitimacy from networks that often are influenced by the gender hierarchy that privileges men over women, they feel encouraged. Using a GEM-derived sample of 5997 female entrepreneurs in developing countries, the authors seek to identify the specific effects of gender hierarchy and networks on the legitimacy female entrepreneurs perceive. They also explore the impact on the women's satisfaction and commitment to their entrepreneurial endeavours. Findings suggest that women entrepreneurs experience legitimacy in their networks both in the private sphere and in the business sphere. Gender hierarchy constrains legitimacy more in the private sphere than in the business sphere. Furthermore, while legitimacy in the business sphere fulfils the need to feel competent and enhances job satisfaction, legitimacy in the private sphere fulfils the need to feel related and enhances job commitment. Findings contribute to a dual contextualization of experiences: micro-level embedding in networks that are nested in macro-level embedding in gender hierarchy.

Gender and technology entrepreneurship: underscoring the token[1]-nature of women

Despite the persistent notion of entrepreneurship as a meritocratic and equally accessible field of gender-neutral opportunities, the historical and cultural masculinity embedded in the concept of entrepreneurship has made it difficult for women to claim symbolically and logistically the position of 'entrepreneur' and this is particularly true when situated within the context of technology. In the eighth paper, Wheadon and Duval-Couetil (Forthcoming) review the literature on gender and entrepreneurship in technology to explore individual and contextual factors maintaining the token status of women in this field. The authors argue that despite extensive work done to generate female participation in entrepreneurship generally and to raise awareness of gender disparities in technology entrepreneurship globally, females in highly developed economies with advanced technological infrastructures remain 'token' or minority players in what is still a fundamentally masculine field. Female entrepreneurs are underrepresented in the more profit-able, faster-growing types of entrepreneurship that are increasingly valued by this new economy (GEM 2010; Kelley et al. 2012). The authors examine how the intersection of gender and context influence participation rates in entrepreneurship, and suggest that the deeply embedded cultural and cognitive associations that frame both technology and entrepreneurship, as masculine con-cepts create barriers for women when these contexts overlap. Given calls for women to participate more fully in high-growth technology ventures, this study highlights the need for research to incorporate broader analytical perspectives that simultaneously examine both the barriers faced by women in these contexts and the factors that systemically sustain them. If research and practice continues to focus primarily on the resources women lack and the improvement of 'female deficits', it may be inadequate for driving significant increases in participation and retention. The authors' proposed framework extends the concept of the 'capital' required for participation technology entrepreneurship beyond that of financial investment and social networks, to human capital and cognitive capital, thereby providing a more comprehensive and descriptive approach to measure the influence of embedded individual and contextual factors influencing intent, outcome and participation.

The ninth and final paper extends the notion of women entrepreneurs' underrepresentation in traditionally male-dominated sectors by bringing us right back to the beginning of the entrepre-neurial process to explore how gender influences entrepreneurial preferences. In their study, Wieland et al. (Forthcoming) explore the social-cognitive factors that lead both women and men to pursue ventures consistent with their gendered social identity, therefore, reinforcing the gender gap in entrepreneurship. Drawing on social role theory, the authors measured the self-assessments of individuals presented with experimentally manipulated entrepreneurial opportunities that were either consistent or inconsistent with their self-reported gender. Findings suggest that a gender match (mismatch) with the entrepreneurial opportunity results in higher (lower) reported self-efficacy, anticipated social resources and venture desirability, and lower (higher) venture risk perceptions. Indeed, self-efficacy and anticipated social resources were found to mediate the effect of gender congruency on perceived risk and venture desirability. The findings from this study offer valuable insights into the insidious barriers that help reproduce the gender gap in entrepreneurial outcomes by 'nudging' women into lower return ventures, and by extension, into possibly less lucrative industries.

Moving forward: where to now?

Our objective with this double special issue was to assemble scholarly contributions that offer valuable and novel perspectives on the contextual embeddedness of women's entrepreneurship, perspectives that could help us better understand the phenomenon of women's entrepreneurship in its myriad contexts. Such new perspectives also could help develop a more informed and relevant future research agenda.

The findings from the included chapters, as well as the insights these chapters provide, suggest that, as scholars, we need to broaden significantly our empirical gaze to accommodate a wider variety of methodological approaches. As Al-Dajani et al. (Forthcoming) highlight, contextual embeddedness takes many different forms, operates on several different levels and can be found in unexpected places and spaces; as such, different methods are needed to capture each. Longitudinal approaches that more deeply explore concepts such as the defiance embedded in entrepreneurship could not only deepen our understanding and theorizing of women's entrepre-neurship but also of entrepreneurship more broadly (Al-Dajani et al. Forthcoming).

More extensive multi-level analytical frameworks are also needed; frameworks that could more effectively explore how social practices and cultural discourses shape women's entrepreneurial preferences, facilitate (or not) access to important support infrastructures, influence experiences and impact (or not) on performance. As Roos (Forthcoming) highlights, context and people can only truly be analysed when considered together because context is not the background to entrepreneurship but a foreground actor in the entrepreneurial process; therefore, women's entrepreneurial experiences need to be fully contextualized if they are to be fully understood (Tlaiss Forthcoming). This means that future research approaches will need to shift from sampling large scale, accessible data sets or convenient, homogenous groups to conducting more in-depth examinations of diverse marginalizsed populations so that we can better understand how to decrease barriers and increase participation sufficiently to carry out more generalizable studies. Sample groups of women entrepreneurs such as migrants, for example, cannot and should not be pigeonholed as one homogeneous group because their experiences are highly diverse and dependent on both their countries of origin and their destinations (Villares-Varela and Essers Forthcoming).

Research objectives must also shift from the development of short-term strategies to help women overcome existing barriers to longer term approaches that focus on discovering how to prevent gendered barriers in the first place. This may require scholars who are willing to apply those more macro-level sociocultural methods traditionally found outside of the discipline – such as case studies, discourse analysis, media content studies and rhetorical framing analysis – to women's entrepreneurship research. Of course, this would require academic entrepreneurship departments to shift their faculty selection criteria to cultivate and/or value more discipline diversity and to ensure that these research methods are rendered acceptable for inclusion in top-tier journals. Most importantly, new approaches to research in this area must be recognized with the award of research funding and be valued in promotion and tenure decisions. Finally, when it comes to the assessment of women entrepreneurs' ventures, support programmes and policies, we must consider including much broader evaluation frameworks as opposed to the existing narrow measurements that are so clearly based on stereotypical forms of masculinity yet have somehow become the embedded yardsticks of success.

Note

1. According to Wheadon and Duval-Couetil (Forthcoming), the term 'token' is used in this article to mean more than just minority status or a problem of numbers and momentum that will resolve itself once more members of the missing group are added to the equation (Kanter, 1977). More significantly, the term is used to highlight the inadequacy of scholarship and policies that superficially addresses inequalities by universalizing diverse experiences into a single social group, identity category or context to simplify the search for causal explanations and concrete solutions (Scott 1986).

Disclosure statement

No potential conflict of interest was reported by the authors.

References

Achtenhagen, L., and F. Welter. 2011. "'Surfing on the Ironing Board' – The Representation of Women's Entrepreneurship in German Newspapers." *Entrepreneurship & Regional Development: An International Journal* 23 (9–10): 763–786.

Ahl, H. 2006. "Why Research on Women Entrepreneurs Needs New Directions." *Entrepreneurship Theory and Practice* 30 (5): 595–621. doi:10.1111/etap.2006.30.issue-5.

Ahl, H., and S. Marlow. 2012. "Exploring the Dynamics of Gender, Feminism and Entrepreneurship: Advancing Debate to Escape a Dead End?" *Organization* 19 (5): 543–562. doi:10.1177/1350508412448695.

Al-Dajani, H., H. Akbar, S. Carter, and S. Shaw. Forthcoming. "Defying Contextual Embeddedness: Evidence from Displaced Women Entrepreneurs in Jordan." *Entrepreneurship and Regional Development.*

Aldrich, H. E. 2009. "Lost in Space, Out of Time: Why and How We Should Study Organizations Comparatively." In *Studying Differences between Organizations: Comparative Approaches to Organizational Research*, edited by B. G. King, T. Felin and D. A. Whetten, 21–44.

Alsos, G. A., S. Carter, and E. Ljunggren. 2014. "Kinship and Business: How Entrepreneurial Households Facilitate Business Growth." *Entrepreneurship & Regional Development* 26 (1–2): 97–122. doi:10.1080/08985626.2013.870235.

Bird, B., and C. Brush. 2002. "A Gendered Perspective on Organizational Creation." *Entrepreneurship Theory and Practice* 26 (3): 41–65. doi:10.1177/104225870202600303.

Brush, C. G., A. de Bruin, and F. Welter. 2009. "A Gender-Aware Framework for Women's Entrepreneurship." *International Journal of Gender and Entrepreneurship* 1 (1): 8–24. doi:10.1108/17566260910942318.

Brush, C. G., and S. Y. Cooper. 2012. "Female Entrepreneurship and Economic Development: An International Perspective." *Entrepreneurship & Regional Development: An International Journal* 24 (1–2): 1–6.

Butler, J. 1993. *Bodies that Matter: The Discursive Limits of 'Sex'*. London: Routledge.

Calás, M. B., L. Smircich, and K. A. Bourne. 2009. "Extending the Boundaries: Reframing "Entrepreneurship as Social Change" through Feminist Perspectives." *Academy of Management Review* 34 (3): 552–569. doi:10.5465/amr.2009.40633597.

Carter, N., S. Anderson, and E. Shaw 2001. "Women Business Ownership: A Review of Academic, Popular and Internet Literature. Discussion Paper." DTI Small Business Service Research Report. Glasgow, Scotland: Strathclyde University.

Cheraghi, M., K. W. Jensen, and K. Klyver. Forthcoming. "Life-Course and Entry to Entrepreneurship: Embedded in Gender and Gender-Egalitarianism." *Entrepreneurship and Regional Development*.

D'Enbeau, S., A. Villamil, and R. Helens-Hart. 2015. "Transcending Work–Life Tensions: A Transnational Feminist Analysis of Work and Gender in the Middle East, North Africa, and India." *Women's Studies in Communication* 38 (3): 273–294. doi:10.1080/07491409.2015.1062838.

de Bruin, A., C. G. Brush, and F. Welter. 2006. "Introduction to the Special Issue: Towards Building Cumulative Knowledge on Women's Entrepreneurship." *Entrepreneurship Theory and Practice* 30 (5): 585–593. doi:10.1111/etap.2006.30.issue-5.

de Bruin, A., C. G. Brush, and F. Welter. 2007. "Advancing a Framework for Coherent Research on Women's Entrepreneurship." *Entrepreneurship Theory and Practice* 31 (3): 323–339. doi:10.1111/etap.2007.31.issue-3.

Eddleston, K. A., and G. N. Powell. 2012. "Nurturing Entrepreneurs' Work–Family Balance: A Gendered Perspective." *Entrepreneurship Theory and Practice* 36 (3): 513–541. doi:10.1111/etap.2012.36.issue-3.

Fayolle, A., S. Yousafzai, S. Saeed, C. Henry, and A. Lindgreen. 2015. "Call Special Issue On: Contextual Embeddedness of Women's Entrepreneurship: Taking Stock and Looking Ahead." *Entrepreneurship and Regional Development* 27 (9–10): 670–674. doi:10.1080/08985626.2016.1099788.

Fisher, R., A. Maritz, and A. Lobo. 2014. "Evaluating Entrepreneurs' Perception Of Success: Development Of a Measurement Scale." *International Journal Of Entrepreneurial Behavior And Research* 20 (5): 478–492. doi: 10.1108/IJEBR-10-2013-0157.

Gaddefors, J., and N. Cronsell. 2009. "Returnees and Local Stakeholders Co-Producing the Entrepreneurial Region." *European Planning Studies* 17 (8): 1191–1203. doi:10.1080/09654310902981045.

GEM. 2010. "Global Enrepreneurship Monitor 2010 Women's Report." Accessed September 2018. www.gemconsortium.org

Hamilton, E. 2013. "The Discourse of Entrepreneurial Masculinities (and Femininities)." *Entrepreneurship & Regional Development: An International Journal* 25 (1–2): 90–99.

Harding, S. 1987. "Introduction: Is There a Feminist Method?" In *Feminism and Methodology*, edited by S. Harding, 1–14. Bloomington: Indiana University Press.

Hardiong, S. 1991. *Whose Science? Whose Knowledge? Thinking from Women's Lives*. Ithaca, NY: Cornell University.

Hughes, K. D., J. Jennings, S. Carter, and C. Brush. 2012. "Extending Women's Entrepreneurship Research in New Directions." *Entrepreneurship Theory and Practice* 36 (3): 429–442. doi:10.1111/j.1540-6520.2012.00504.x.

Jack, S. L., and A. Anderson. 2002. "The Effects of Embeddedness on the Entrepreneurial Process." *Journal of Business Venturing* 17 (5): 467–487. doi:10.1016/S0883-9026(01)00076-3.

Jayawarna, D., J. Rouse, and J. Kitching. 2011. "Entrepreneur Motivations and Life Course." *International Small Business Journal* 31 (1): 34–56. doi:10.1177/0266242611401444.

Kalantaridis, C., and Z. Bika. 2006. "In-Migrant Entrepreneurship in Rural England: Beyond Local Embeddedness." *Entrepreneurship and Regional Development* 18 (2): 109–131. doi:10.1080/08985620500510174.

Kanter, R.M. 1977. Men and Women of the Corporation. New York: Basic Books.

Katre, A., and P. Salipante. 2012. "Start-up Social Ventures: Blending Fine-grained Behaviors from Two Institutions for Entrepreneurial Success." *Entrepreneurship Theory and Practice* 36 (5): 967–994. doi: 10.1111/j.1540-6520.2012.00536.

Kelley, D. J., C. G. Brush, P. G. Greene, and Y. Litovsky. 2012. *2012 Global Entrepreneurship Monitor Women's Report*. Accessed December 2018. https://www.empowerwomen.org/en/resources/documents/2013/8/global-entrepreneurship-monitor-2012-womens-report?lang=en.

Kiviluoto, N. 2013. "Growth as Evidence of Firm Success: Myth or Reality?." *Entrepreneurship and Regional Development* 25 (7–8): 569–586. doi:10.1080/08985626.2013.814716.

Klyver, K., S. L. Nielsen, and M. R. Evald. 2013. "Women's Self-Employment: An Act of Institutional (Dis) Integration? A Multilevel, Cross-Country Study." *Journal of Business Venturing* 28 (4): 474–488. doi:10.1016/j.jbusvent.2012.07.002.

Korsgaard, S., R. Ferguson, and J. Gaddefors. 2015. "The Best of Both Worlds: How Rural Entrepreneurs Use Placial Embeddedness and Strategic Networks to Create Opportunities." *Entrepreneurship & Regional Development* 27 (9–10): 574–598. doi:10.1080/08985626.2015.1085100.

Krueger, N. F., and D. Brazeal. 1994. "Entrepreneurial Potential and Potential Entrepreneurs." *Entrepreneurship Theory and Practice* 18 (3): 91–104. doi:10.1177/104225879401800307.

Lansky, M. 2000. "Gender, Women and the Rest. Part 1." *International Labour Review* 139 (4): 481–505. doi:10.1111/j.1564-913X.2000.tb00529.x.

Liu, Y., T. Schøtt, and C. Zhang. Forthcoming. "Women's Experiences of Legitimacy, Satisfaction and Commitment as Entrepreneurs: Embedded in Gender Hierarchy and Networks in Private and Business Spheres." *Entrepreneurship and Regional Development*.

Marlow, S., and D. Patton. 2005. "All Credit to Men? Entrepreneurship, Finance, and Gender." *Entrepreneurship Theory and Practice* 29 (6): 717–735. doi:10.1111/(ISSN)1540-6520.

Marlow, S., and J. Swail. 2014. "Gender, Risk and Finance: Why Can't a Woman Be More like a Man?" *Entrepreneurship & Regional Development: An International Journal* 26 (1–2): 80–96. doi:10.1080/08985626.2013.860484.

Marlow, S., and M. McAdam. 2013. "Gender and Entrepreneurship." *International Journal of Entrepreneurial Behaviour and Research* 19 (1): 114–124. doi:10.1108/13552551311299288.

Minniti, M., and W. A. Naudé. 2010. "Introduction: What Do We Know about the Patterns and Determinants of Female Entrepreneurship across Countries?" *European Journal of Development Research* 22 (3): 277–293. doi:10.1057/ejdr.2010.17.

Mirchandani, K. 1999. "Feminist Insight on Gendered Work: New Directions in Research on Women and Entrepreneurship." *Gender, Work and Organization* 6 (4): 224–235. doi:10.1111/gwao.1999.6.issue-4.

Munkejord, M. C. 2017. "His or Her Work–Life Balance? Experiences of Self-Employed Immigrant Parents." *Work, Employment and Society* 31 (4): 624–639. doi:10.1177/0950017016667041.

Özbilgin, M. F., A. T. Beauregard, A. Tatli, and M. P. Bell. 2011. "Work–Life, Diversity and Intersectionality: A Critical Review and Research Agenda." *International Journal of Management Reviews* 13 (2): 177–198. doi:10.1111/j.1468-2370.2010.00291.x.

Poggesi, S., M. Mari, and L. De Vita. 2015. "What's New in Female Entrepreneurship Research? Answers from the Literature." *International Entrepreneurship and Management Journal* 12 (3): 735–764. doi:10.1007/s11365-015-0364-5.

Roos, A. Forthcoming. "Embeddedness in Context: Understanding Gender in a Female Entrepreneurship Network." *Entrepreneurship and Regional Development*.

Scott, S. 1986. Why more women are becoming entrepreneurs. Journal of Small Business Management. Winter 47–76.

Tedmanson, D., K. Verduyn, C. Essers, and W. Gartner. 2012. "Critical Perspectives in Entrepreneurship Research." *Organization* 19 (5): 531–541. doi:10.1177/1350508412458495.

Thébaud, S. 2015. "Business as Plan B Institutional Foundations of Gender Inequality in Entrepreneurship across 24 Industrialized Countries." *Administrative Science Quarterly* 60 (4): 1–41. doi:10.1177/0001839215591627.

Tlaiss, H. 2015. "Neither–Nor: Career Success of Women in an Arab Middle Eastern Context." *Employee Relations: An International Journal* 37 (5): 525–546. doi:10.1108/ER-03-2014-0028.

Tlaiss, H. Forthcoming. "Contextualizing the Career Success of Arab Women Entrepreneurs." *Entrepreneurship and Regional Development*.

Uzzi, B. 1997. "Social Structure and Competition in Interfirm Networks: The Paradox of Embeddedness." *Administrative Science Quarterly* 41 (1): 35–67. doi:10.2307/2393808.

Van Staveren, I., and O. Odebode. 2007. "Gender Norms as Asymmetric Institutions: A Case Study of Yoruba Women in Nigeria." *Journal of Economic Issues* 41 (4): 903–925. doi:10.1080/00213624.2007.11507080.

Veblen, T. 1899. *The Theory of the Leisure Class*, 1975. New York: A. M. Kelley.

Villares-Varela, M., M. Ram, and T. Jones. 2017. "Female Immigrant Global Entrepreneurship: From Invisibility to Empowerment?." In *The Routledge Companion to Global Female Entrepreneurship*, edited by C. Henry, T. Nelson, and K. V. Lewis. Abingdon, GB: Routledge.

Villares-Varela, M., and C. Essers. Forthcoming. "Women in the Migrant Economy. A *Positional* Approach to Contextualise Gendered Transnational Trajectories." *Entrepreneurship and Regional Development*.

Vossenberg, S. 2013. "Women Entrepreneurship Promotion in Developing Countries: What Explains the Gender Gap in Entrepreneurship and How to Close It?" Maastricht School of Management. Accessed December 2018. https://ideas.repec.org/p/msm/wpaper/2013-08.html

Waldinger, R. 1995. "The 'Other Side' of Embedded Ness: A Case-Study of the Interplay of Economy and Ethnicity." *Ethnic and Racial Studies* 18 (3): 555–580. doi:10.1080/01419870.1995.9993879.

Welter, F. 2011. "Contextualizing Entrepreneurship. Conceptual Challenges and Ways Forward." *Entrepreneurship Theory and Practice* 35 (1): 165–184. doi:10.1111/etap.2011.35.issue-1.

Welter, F., C. Brush, and A. de Bruin 2014. *The Gendering of Entrepreneurship Context* (February 1, 2014). Working Paper 01/14. Bonn : Institut für Mittelstandsforschung (Hrsg.). doi:10.2139/ssrn.2557272.

Wheadon, M., and N. Duval-Couetil. Forthcoming. "Token Entrepreneurs: A Review of Gender, Capital, and Context in Technology Entrepreneurship." *Entrepreneurship and Regional Development*.

Wieland, A., M. Kemmelmeier, V. Gupta, and W. McKelvey. Forthcoming. "Gendered Cognitions: A Socio-Cognitive Model of How Gender Affects Entrepreneurial Preferences." *Entrepreneurship and Regional Development.*

Xheneti, M., S. T. Karki, and A. Madden. Forthcoming. "Negotiating Business and Family Demands within a Patriarchal Society – The Case of Women Entrepreneurs in the Nepalese Context." *Entrepreneurship and Regional Development.*

Yamin, A. 2013. "Jordan Third Largest Refugee Host Worldwide." *UNHCR Jordan Times*, December 31. Amman–Jordan.

Yousafzai, S. Y., S. Saeed, and M. Muffatto. 2015. "Institutional Theory and Contextual Embeddedness of Women's Entrepreneurial Leadership: Evidence from 92 Countries." *Journal of Small Business Management* 53 (3): 587–604. doi:10.1111/jsbm.2015.53.issue-3.

Zahra, S. A. 2007. "Contextualizing Theory Building in Entrepreneurship Research." *Journal of Business Venturing* 22: 443–452. doi:10.1016/j.jbusvent.2006.04.007.

Zahra, S. A., M. Wright, and G. S. Abdelgawad. 2014. "Contextualization and the Advancement of Entrepreneurship Research." *International Small Business Journal* 32 (5): 479–500. doi:10.1177/0266242613519807.

Gendered cognitions: a socio-cognitive model of how gender affects entrepreneurial preferences

Alice M. Wieland, Markus Kemmelmeier, Vishal K. Gupta and William McKelvey

ABSTRACT

This research explores the social-cognitive factors which lead both women and men to pursue ventures consistent with their gendered social identity, therefore, reinforcing the gender gap in entrepreneurship. We measured the self-assessments of individuals presented with experimentally manipulated entrepreneurial opportunities that were either consistent or inconsistent with their self-reported gender. A theoretical model derived from Social Role Theory is presented and tested. It posits that a gender match (mismatch) with the entrepreneurial opportunity results in higher (lower) reported self-efficacy, anticipated social resources, and venture desirability and lower (higher) venture risk perceptions. The experimental data are tested in a sequential mediation SEM model. We find evidence that self-efficacy and anticipated social resources mediate the effect of gender congruency on perceived risk and venture desirability. The results provide insight into the insidious barriers that play a role in reproducing a gender gap in entrepreneurial outcomes by 'nudging' women into lower-return ventures in less lucrative industries.

Introduction

There are powerful social-psychological forces which guide people's actions. In this work, we explore gendered self-assessments which nudge women and men to pursue entrepreneurial opportunities which are consistent with their gender. One's perceptions of one's abilities and desires are embedded in cultural norms which dictate appropriate social roles given a specific social identity. Within a network of expectations and social interactions, gender is a salient social identity that acts as a lens through which one views the world (Rudman and Glick 2008). Everyday socialization encourages and reinforces gender consistent behaviours (BarNir, Watson, and Hutchins 2011), by biasing perceptions of abilities (self-efficacy) and expectations of access to resources (social support/resources) which influence perceptions of risk in a gender congruent vs. incongruent opportunity. We propose that gender identities orient both men and women disproportionately towards gender-consistent opportunities, which due to differential success rates, may ultimately reinforce existing patterns of inequality.

Women are less likely to become entrepreneurs (Kelley et al. 2013), and when they do, their returns to entrepreneurship are lower than men's (Minniti 2009). These lower returns have been attributed to women starting different types of businesses (Kepler and Shane 2007; Anna et al. 2000), which disproportionately concentrate in lower growth and performance industries, like service and retail (Sullivan and Meek 2012). Occupational sex segregation has been found to be one of the largest contributors to the well-known gender pay gap (Charles and Grusky 2004; Blau and Kahn 2007). Especially in developed countries, women and men exercise greater personal choice in selecting occupations which are personally fulfilling, which also happen to be consistent with traditional gender roles (Charles and Bradley 2009; Charles and Grusky 2004). Much of the difference in the entrepreneurial outcomes of men and women may be due to the specific venture opportunity and industry in which one starts their business. Just as occupations and industries are sex-typed (Glick 1991; Glick, Wilk, and Perreault 1995), entrepreneurial ventures may be similarly sex-typed, affecting the cognitions related to entrepreneurial decision-making.

The purpose of this research is to shed light on processes which reinforce gender differences in entrepreneurship. We explore the social-cognitive factors which encourage gender role conformity (Eagly, Wood, and Diekman 2000), biasing the preferences of entrepreneurs to self-select into traditionally male and female gendered opportunities. Illuminating the decision processes that underlie gender differences in entrepreneurial activity has been identified as a core intellectual question for entrepreneurship research and practice (Jennings and Brush 2013; Sullivan and Meek 2012). Specifically, we ask: Does gender match with the sex-typed valence (gender congruency) of an entrepreneurial opportunity influence one's perceptions of self-confidence at running the venture (self-efficacy), anticipated social support (social resources), degree of risk perceived the venture, and the overall assessment of how desirable a given opportunity is? We present and test a model of how gender match with a venture opportunity influences assessments of self-efficacy, anticipated social resources, perceived risk and their impact on venture desirability.

Theory and hypotheses

A cognitive approach: gender and venture assessments

Researchers have advocated taking a cognitive perspective to addressing questions in entrepreneurship (Baron 2004; Busenitz and Lau 1996; De Carolis and Saparito 2006; Haynie et al. 2010; Wadeson 2008). Social Role Theory (SRT) (Eagly 1987; Eagly, Wood, and Diekman 2000) suggests that pressures to conform to gender roles are based on social norms. Briefly, SRT posits that gender stereotypes are derived from the roles that men and women hold in society, and reflect the sexual division of labour and gender hierarchy in a given society. Gender roles develop as each sex internalizes the roles which society dictates is appropriate for their sex and can induce sex differences in behaviour in the absence of any intrinsic, inborn psychological differences between women and men (Eagly, Wood, and Diekman 2000, 127). Once established, gender roles encompass descriptive norms, which are expectations about what people actually do, and prescriptive norms, which are expectations about what people ought to do (Rudman and Glick 2008). Often others enforce prescriptive gender norms by delivering rewards for conformance and penalties for non-conformance (Deaux and Major 1987). Specifically, non-conforming men are derogated as 'wimps' and undeserving of respect, while women in male-typed domains are derogated and disliked, resulting in lower performance evaluations and organizational rewards (Heilman and Wallen 2010; Heilman et al. 2004). Therefore, SRT suggests that feelings of competency (self-efficacy) and anticipation of social support are more likely for domains which are consistent with one's sex, suggesting that gender-roles map closely onto one's biological sex.

Social Cognitive Career Theory (SCCT) (Lent, Brown, and Hackett 1994, 2000) is also relevant to entrepreneurial opportunity identification and selection, noting the role of gender in the development of self-efficacy and outcome expectations for a given career decision. SCCT suggests that career-related decisions are often based on feelings of self-efficacy, an individual's belief in their own competence, social rewards and sanctions, outcome expectancies (risk) and affect (desirability). Supporting the applicability of these constructs to entrepreneurial decisions, Minniti (2009) notes, 'among perceptual variables, opportunity perceptions, risk tolerance, and self-efficacy have been recognized as being highly correlated to the decision to start a new business for all individuals and among women in particular' (p. 45). In summary, these theories suggest that due to one's relative experience with things associated with one's own gender as opposed to those associated with the opposite gender, a gender-congruent opportunity (as opposed to a gender-incongruent one) will result in greater perceived self-efficacy, greater anticipated social rewards (resources), resulting in lower perceived risk and greater desirability (liking).

Venture desirability

Venture desirability, defined as the perceived desirability as the personal attractiveness of starting a business, is a core pillar in the Entrepreneurial Event formation model (Shapero and Sokol 1982). Much research has established the role of perceived desirability, noting that perceived desirability is an antecedent to entrepreneurial intentions (De Clercq et al. 2009; Krueger, Reilly, and Carsrud 2000; Shinnar et al. 2016).

Research finds that people who identify with their gender role tend to experience more positive self-concepts when they behave in conformance with those identities/ideals (Wood et al. 1997). When observing individuals in various social interactions, Witt and Wood (2010) found that emotion and self-evaluative signals operate as self-regulatory mechanisms, influencing peoples' chronic self-assessments so that people became more positive when they behaved in ways that confirmed personal gender standards. People choose options consistent with their social identities (Leary, Wheeler, and Jenkins 1986; Bem 1981), and gender is the primary social category, for which an identity is developed very early in life (Rudman and Glick 2008). We expect that options representing a gender-congruent activity will be viewed as more attractive or desirable to individuals.

Hypothesis 1: *Individuals prefer gender-congruent to gender-incongruent ventures (find them more desirable).*

Self-efficacy

Self-efficacy refers to the belief in one's own competence (Bandura 1997). Those with greater self-efficacy for a given task are more likely to pursue and persist at the task (Bandura 1997). Self-efficacy influences sex-typed career decisions such that men and women feel greater self-efficacy at pursuing occupations which are consistent with their gender role, to the point where women's lower self-efficacy in masculine domains inhibits them from entering male dominated occupations (Hackett and Betz 1981; Lent, Brown, and Hackett 1994).

Research on Entrepreneurial Self-Efficacy (ESE) typically finds that women report lower ESE than men (Shinnar, Hsu, and Powell 2014; Wilson, Kickul, and Marlino 2007; Zhao, Seibert, and Hills 2005; Minniti 2009). Since prior research has already established that 'entrepreneurship' elicits a masculine image and hence is a masculine-typed occupation (Gupta et al. 2009; Ahl 2006), findings of women's lower ESE are not surprising. We must be careful, however, when describing entrepreneurial tasks and activities in the traditional masculine manner, which may be gender biased. Gupta, Turban, and Bhawe (2008) found that women's entrepreneurial intentions were lower when entrepreneurship was described using the traditional masculine-typed language, yet this sex difference disappeared when the wording was gender neutral. We hypothesize that although entrepreneurship in general may be masculine-typed, specific opportunities may be feminine or masculine-typed due to their similarity with feminine or masculine gender domains. Finally, some argue that ESE is a 'multi-dimensional construct that consists of goal and control beliefs and is *domain specific*' (Drnovšek, Wincent, and Cardon 2010, 334). Therefore, a measure of self-efficacy that captures one's belief in one's ability to run a specific venture successfully is more appropriate for determining if there are gender differences in self-efficacy. Notably, Bandura (1997) originally conceptualized self-efficacy as a context-dependent construct, 'a subjective state that individuals experience with regard to a particular domain or task'. We predict that men and women systematically differ with regard to self-efficacy for masculine-typed and feminine-typed entrepreneurial ventures.

Hypothesis 2a: *Individuals have higher self-efficacy for gender-congruent ventures than for gender-incongruent ventures.*

Self-efficacy is also associated with opportunity recognition and risk-taking. Krueger and Dickson (1994) found that participants with high self-efficacy perceived less threat and took greater risk, while those with low self-efficacy perceived more threats and took less risk. Likewise, Heath and Tversky (1991) reported that people were willing to take risky bets in domains in which they felt competent but were risk-averse in other domains. Cassar and Friedman (2009) found that higher levels of ESE lead to lower risk perceptions in a start-up. To clarify, *risk propensity* is an individual difference variable that signifies how much risk one can tolerate, while *risk perception* is the subjective amount of risk one perceives in a situation. Alternatively, *risk-taking* refers to actually engaging in behaviours which may lead to loss. Another stream of research, SCCT (Lent, Brown, and Hackett 2000, 1994) also suggests that gender consistency with an occupation has a direct effect on one's self-efficacy, which increases the outcome expectances for that occupation, or conversely, reduces perceived risk. Therefore, we expect that self-efficacy is positively related to the gender congruency of the venture, such that increased self-efficacy in gender-congruent ventures reduces perceptions of risk for those ventures.

Hypothesis 2b: *Self-efficacy mediates the effect of gender congruency on risk perceptions.*

According to SRT (Eagly 1987; Eagly, Wood, and Diekman 2000) and SCCT (Lent, Brown, and Hackett 2000) one's self-efficacy in a given domain is influenced by one's gender role causing gender-congruent activities and tasks to be perceived as more desirable and positively influencing the choice to engage in gender-congruent behaviours and activities. Likewise, Bandura (1997) asserts that people prefer endeavours for which they feel more self-efficacious.

Hypothesis 2c: *Self-efficacy mediates the effect of gender congruency on venture desirability.*

Anticipated social resources

Social support is believed to encompass affective support (i.e. liking and respect), confirmation (moral 'rightness' in actions) and direct help (aid, money, information) (Frese 1999). Some researchers make a distinction between emotional support – encouragement, understanding, attention and positive regard – and instrumental support – assistance in problem solving and other tangible assistance (Eddleston and Powell 2012). However, even instrumental support is perceived by receivers to be emotional in nature, signalling caring, understanding and esteem (Semmer et al. 2008). We therefore define *social resources* as emotional support and instrumental support, tangible resources which encompasses time, money, and mentoring from friends and family available to assist with the execution of the venture. Specifically, we use the term *resources*, instead of *support* to delineate that the perceiver views this type of support as a potential resource in venture management.

We expect that social resources are anticipated based on one's conformance to gender stereotypes. Again, gender stereotypes, have a restrictive prescriptive element, which dictates how men and women should behave, and which is enforced through social sanctions, generating social punishments if violated (i.e. 'backlash') (Rudman and Fairchild 2004; Rudman and Glick 1999, 2008). Due to the social approval or reprisals that go along with conformance or non-conformance to these stereotypes, men and women are likely to anticipate access to greater social resources if they embark on an entrepreneurial opportunity that is congruent with their prescribed gender role. We expect that people are sensitive to the subtle messages of support or backlash for conformance or non-conformance with gender stereotypes (Heilman 2001), and will therefore anticipate greater or lesser social resources as a result of how well they conform to others' gender norm expectations.

Hypothesis 3a: *Individuals anticipate greater levels of social resources for gender-congruent ventures than for gender-incongruent ventures.*

The role of social support has been examined at length with numerous studies noting the health and stress reduction benefits that perceived social support provides (Cohen 2004; Cohen and Wills 1985; Lambert, Burroughs, and Nguyen 1999). Notably, the 'buffering hypothesis' suggests that social support acts to alleviate life stress, facilitating one's ability to cope and adapt to challenges (Cohen and Wills 1985). We expect that starting a new venture is a challenge which social support/ resources would attenuate.Backing this link, other research has found that reducing stress, by highlighting available resources to deal with an unfortunate event, also reduced perceptions of risk (Tykocinski 2013). Additionally, the 'cushion hypothesis' (Hsee and Weber 1999) proposes that social support enables greater financial risk taking because of the expectation of financial help if needed. Likewise, corporate managers have also been found to behave more entrepreneurially (take greater risks) when they perceive greater levels of management support (Hornsby, Kuratko, and Zahra 2002). These research findings suggest that social support/resources are relevant to the management of risk inherent in entrepreneurial opportunities. If one expects to receive higher amounts of social resources one may also anticipate the buffering effects that those resources provide, both for stress management and the economic 'cushion' benefits; and that these resources may be useful in mitigating venture risk. Put simply, consideration of one's available social resources, which may be deployed in the mitigation of risk, will reduce the venture's perceived risk.

Hypothesis 3b: *Anticipated social resources mediate the effect of gender congruency on venture risk perceptions.*

Both SRT and SCCT suggest that individuals will expect greater levels of social acceptance for behaviours conforming to gender norms due to self-regulatory processes (Wood et al. 1997). Therefore, higher levels of anticipated social resources for gender-congruent activities will result in those activities being viewed as more desirable.

Hypothesis 3c: *Anticipated social resources mediate the effect of gender congruency on venture desirability.*

Perceived risk

Risk perception is defined as the subjective judgement that people make about the characteristics and severity of a risk (Johnson and Tversky 1983; Slovic and Peters 2006). Optimistic entrepreneurs, those who perceive less risk, are more likely to pursue entrepreneurial activities and persist when faced with challenges (Trevelyan 2008). Simon, Houghton, and Aquino (2000) found that it is the *perception of risk*, and not one's *risk propensity* – an individual difference variable that signifies how much risk one can tolerate – which influences whether one chooses to start an entrepreneurial venture. Therefore, we focus on *perceived* risk, the subjective assessment of the likelihood of sustaining losses, which influences actual decisions.

Byrnes, Miller, and Schafer (1999) contend that the context of a given risk holds different expectancies for different people, such that some contexts promote greater risk-taking in men and others in women. We theorize that different kinds of entrepreneurial opportunities represent contexts that may illicit gender differences in perceived risk. If stereotypes associated with a venture favour men (e.g. technology development), men may feel relatively more competent at running the business, and therefore perceive lower venture risk. Feeling confident about the potential business is a pre-condition to the decision to pursue a new opportunity (Baron 2006). If men and women systematically assess the risks and rewards of various opportunities differently, their pursuits will reflect this bias.

Hypothesis 4a: *Individuals perceive lower risk in gender-congruent ventures than in gender-incongruent ventures.*

Several studies suggest that risk perceptions and the desirability of a venture (and ultimately starting the venture) are inversely related. Forlani and Mullins (2000) provide experimental evidence that entrepreneurs avoid more risky ventures because of the increased of variability of outcomes. Given that both theoretical (Shaver and Scott 1991) and survey research (Simon, Houghton, and Aquino 2000) support the relationship between risk perceptions and venture desirability, we propose:

Hypothesis 4b: *Venture risk perceptions are inversely related to venture desirability.*

Method

Consistent with calls for tightly controlled studies (Colquitt 2008; Gregoire and Shepherd 2012), we conducted an experiment to validate the causal relationships theorized. We choose the experimental method because it allowed us to systematically vary the sex-type of the venture and observe the effects of this manipulation on our dependent variables, while keeping all other influences constant (Hsu, Simmons, and Wieland 2017). Put differently, experiments allow researchers to establish parallel conditions that only vary in terms of the causal variable of interest; if differences in the dependent variable are observed, by necessity they must be the consequence of the variable of interest because the experimental conditions do not differ in any other way, thereby establishing causality.

Three samples (one for the pilot, two for the main experiment) were drawn from Amazon's Mechanical Turk (MTurk), an online labour market, whose appropriateness for behavioural research is well-established (Paolacci, Chandler, and Ipeirotis 2010; Eriksson and Simpson 2010). Aguinis and Lawal (2012, 502) highlight that MTurk can be effectively used in entrepreneurship to conduct the kind of 'experiments' essential to the field's progress. One of the advantages of MTurk is subject-pool diversity (Mason and Suri 2012), representing a wide range of ages, SES classes and geographical locations. Focusing on the American context, we restricted data collection to only those workers located in the US.

Pilot study and scenario selection

Sixty-one participants (33% women) responded to a short survey which listed 44 businesses (e.g. bakery, bookstore, brewery, etc.). Participants indicated if they believed women or men would be more likely to own one of these kinds of business using a 7-point Likert-scale ranging from 1 'Women – much more likely to own' to 7 'Men – much more likely to own.' A series of t-tests determined if mean ratings were significantly different from the scale mean of 4 'Neutral – Men and Women equally likely to own'. If a mean value was significantly different from 4, indicating that owners of this type of businesses were stereotyped to be one gender or the other, subsequent t-tests determined if male vs. female participants perceived the typical sex of the business owner differently. Only if men and women agreed on the probable gender of the business owner for that kind of business (i.e. there was no gender difference) were those businesses considered for inclusion in the main study. Sixteen businesses were classified as feminine-typed (means ranging from 1.87 to 3.79, with each mean significantly lower than 4), three were gender neutral (means not significantly different from 4, ranging from 3.87 to 4.28), and 25 were categorized as masculine-typed (means ranging from 4.37 to 6.33, all significantly greater than 4). Four feminine-typed (florist; direct seller and producer of high quality kitchen tools; nurse supplemental staffing firm; and clothing design and retail [means 2.16, 3.21, 2.95 and 2.36, respectively, all lower than 4, $p < .001$]) and four masculine-typed (strategic and operational consulting; architectural design and construction of home theatre rooms; internet business [e-commerce systems, development and hosting]; and software development for online entertainment [means 4.92, 4.77, 4.57 and 5.61, respectively, all greater than 4 at $p < .001$]) were included in Sample 1. Sample 2 substituted two other feminine-typed (children's book publisher, interior designer [means 2.67 and 2.56, both lower than 4 at $p < .001$]) and two other masculine-typed ventures (bricks and mortar electronics retailer, investment bank [means 5.48 and 5.51, both greater than 4 at $p < .001$]) for two scenarios included in Sample 1. All variances of the mean fell between 0.80 and 1.10.[1]

Main experiment

Participants
A total of 827 US individuals participated. Twenty-two participants were excluded from the analysis because of incomplete data or they took longer than 3 SD's above the mean to complete the survey (mean 10.3, $SD = 4.1$). The final sample includes 805 participants (48% women). Participants were on average between 31 and 35 years old, mostly Caucasian (81.7%) with 48% of the sample possessing a college degree or higher.

Procedure
Using Qualtrics® online survey software, each participant was randomly assigned one of the feminine-typed ventures and one of the masculine-typed ventures (the experimental treatment) with sex-type of the scenario serving as a repeated-measures factor. The order of the sex-typed venture was randomized. After seeing each venture scenario, participants answered several questions that measured the constructs of interest (listed in Measures section). Items were presented in random order to guard against order effects. To control for potential profitability, all scenarios stated that the growth rate of the industry was 15%. Demographic and background information was also collected, such as gender, age, education level, ethnicity and prior entrepreneurial experience. Finally, upon completion of the survey participants received a code to enter into MTurk for payment.

Measures
All scale items were administered twice, in accords with a repeated-measures design; and all items were measured on 7-point Likert scales. Scale reliabilities were high, ranging from Cronbach's $\alpha = .79$ to .96, indicating good internal reliability (DeVellis 2003). Table 1 reports correlations, means and standard deviations.

Gender congruency. The main independent variable is sex-type of the venture, which was coded as 1 if the venture was masculine-typed and the participant indicated their sex as male; or if the venture was feminine-typed and the participant indicated their sex was female. It was coded as 0 if the participant was male and the venture was feminine, or if the participant was female and the

Table 1. Means, standard deviations and correlations.

	Mean	SD	1	2	3	4	5	6
1. Gender congruence	.50	.50	–					
2. Self-efficacy	3.44	1.74	.21**	–				
3. Perceived social resources	4.05	1.57	.11**	.43**	–			
4. Perceived risk	4.23	1.26	−.10**	−.39**	−.37**	–		
5. Desirability	2.97	1.64	.27**	.69**	.47**	−.57**	–	
6. Entrepreneur experience	1.36	1.62	–	.22**	.04	−.01	.08**	–
7. Sex (1 = Male)	.52	.50	–	.11**	.12**	−.03	.08**	.00

Note: **$p < .01$; *$p < .05$.

venture was masculine. This coding reflects whether the venture was congruent or incongruent with the participant's sex.[2]

Desirability. Four items were used to measure venture desirability: 'How attractive is this business to you personally?', 'How interested are you in running a business like this one?', 'A business like this would be a very good fit for me', and 'Would you seek to start a business such as the one described?' (Cronbach's $\alpha_{Male\ Venture} = .94$; $\alpha_{Female\ Venture} = .93$). An exploratory factor analysis from an earlier study showed these items loaded on one factor.

Self-efficacy. General (Chen, Gully, and Eden 2001) and entrepreneurial self-efficacy (McGee et al. 2009; Zhao, Seibert, and Hills 2005) scales assess trait self-efficacy, or constant levels of the construct. We referred to these scales in developing a self-efficacy measure dependent on the venture opportunity evaluated, consistent with Bandura (1997) conception of the construct. Our four-item measure of *self-efficacy* or *self-perceived competence* includes: 'I am confident in my ability to perform the skills and the tasks that would lead to the success of the business', 'I believe I have sufficient education and training to successfully run a company such as this', 'I believe I have the training and competence to make a business like this successful', and 'I am adequately qualified to run a business like this' ($\alpha_{Male\ Venture} = .96$; $\alpha_{Female\ Venture} = .95$).

Social resources. We reviewed relevant scales (Sarason et al. 1983; Timmerman, Emanuels-Zuurveen, and Emmelkamp 2000) and adapted three items from these scales to assess state levels of instrumental social support (consistent with our definition of social resources) dependent on the nature of the business opportunity. Our measure of state social resources includes: 'Would your friends or family provide you with resources, such as mentoring and contacts, to start this business?', 'Would your friends and family support you with time to help you start this business?', 'Would your friends and family lend or give you money to start this business?' ($\alpha_{Male\ Venture} = .84$; $\alpha_{Female\ Venture} = 83$).

Risk perceptions. Drawing on leading research in risk perception measurement (Sitkin and Weingart 1995; Ganzach et al. 2008) we created a four-item measure of venture risk perceptions. This measure in includes the following items: 'How risky do you think this business is?', 'How likely do you think this venture is to be successful (survive more than 2 years)?' (Reversed), 'How likely do you think this venture is to fail within the next two years?' and 'How safe, in terms of investing time and money into, do you think this venture is?' (Reversed), ($\alpha_{Male\ Venture} = .84$; $\alpha_{Female\ Venture} = .88$).

Entrepreneurship experience. We used the Nascent Entrepreneurship scale (McGee et al. 2009) which contains six items of activities related to starting a venture. According to the authors, if respondents answer 'yes' to at least two of the six items, they qualify as an entrepreneur. Since we were mainly interested in entrepreneurial experience as a covariate, we used the total count of 'yes' responses, ranging from 0, indicating no activities, to 6, for participants who indicated 'yes' to all six items. Sample items include: 'Put together a start-up team', and 'Developed a product or service'.

Results

Confirmatory factor analysis

A confirmatory factor analysis (CFA) ensured that the data supported the structure of multiple-item measures (Table 2). Established criteria were used to assess model fit, with good fit being reflected by a Comparative Fit Index (CFI) and a Tucker-Lewis Index (TLI) at or above .90, and the root mean square error of approximation (RMSEA), and the standardized root mean square residual (SRMR) being at or below .05 (Browne and Cudeck, 1993; Kline 2011). CFA fit was satisfactory, CFI = .93, TLI = .92, RMSEA = .044, SRMR = .044. Although significant, $\chi^2(df = 377) = 1560.57$, $p < .001$, the chi-square exceeded the critical value by only a factor of 2.21, which is considered acceptable (Hinkin 1995). To ensure that associations between our measures are not the result of measurement method rather than the underlying constructs, we tested for common method bias using both the common latent factor and the marker variable method (Podsakoff et al. 2003). The marker variable method is the superior method, but only Sample 1 included a marker variable (squared regression coefficient of .047), so we also used the common latent factor analysis (squared regression coefficient of .20). Results indicate that common method variance is unlikely to compromise the results (Podsakoff et al. 2003).

Hypotheses tests

To test the hypothesized model (Figure 1) we employed structural equation modelling (SEM) using Mplus 7.4 (Muthén and Muthén, 2015). The repeated-measures design required multilevel SEM in which responses to each sex-typed scenario were nested within each participant. The fit of the fully saturated model, which controlled for participant sex, age, education and entrepreneurial experience on mean levels of each outcome variable (self-efficacy, social resources, risk and desirability) was

Table 2. Confirmatory factor analysis and reliabilities.

RMSEA = .04, CFI = .93,TLI = .92	Feminine-typed	Cronbach's alpha	Masculine-typed	Cronbach's alpha
Desirability		.93		.94
How interested are you in running a business like this one?	.92		.92	
How attractive is this business to you personally?	.87		.90	
Would you seek to start a business such as the one described?	.86		.88	
A business like this would be a very good fit for me.	.87		.89	
Self-efficacy		.95		.96
I believe I have the training and competence to make a business like this successful.	.94		.92	
I believe I have sufficient education and training to successfully run a company such as this.	.92		.92	
I am adequately qualified to run a business like this.	.90		.94	
I am confident in my abilities to perform the skills and the tasks that would lead to the success of the business.	.88		.90	
Social resources		.83		.84
Would your friends and family support you with time to help you start this business?	.81		.80	
Would your friends and family lend or give you money to start this business?	.75		.76	
Would your friends and family provide you with resources, such as mentoring and contacts, to start a business such as this?	.82		.83	
Risk perceptions		.88		.84
How likely do you think this business is to be successful (Survive more than 2 years)? Reverse Coded	.88		.87	
How likely do you think this business is to fail within the next two years?	.80		.66	
How risky do you think this business is?	.67		.68	
How safe, in terms of investing time and money into, do you think this venture is? Reverse Coded	.83		.82	

Note: Entries reflect standardized loadings.

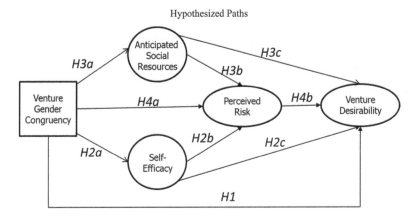

Figure 1. Hypothesized paths.

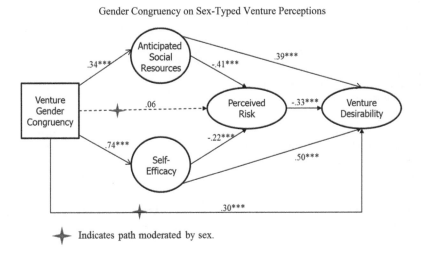

Figure 2. Gender congruency on sex-typed venture perceptions.
***$p < .001$ Controls: Sex, age, education and entrepreneurial experience.

excellent (Table 3). As summarized in Figure 2, the only nonsignificant path in the saturated model was *H4a* (gender congruence predicting perceived risk), so this path was excluded from the final model. All direct path coefficients, significance levels, control variables, and indirect path coefficients are listed in Table 3. For clarity, an indirect path refers to a statistically significant outcome variable which is transmitted through another variable; in this study the mediator variables are the intervening variables. Table 3 specifies through which variables the relationship is transmitted that have an effect on the dependent variable.

We can see from the Direct Model in Table 3 that results support *H1, H2a* and *H3a*; we can also see from the specific indirect paths that *H2b, H2c, H3b* and *H3c* are also supported. Because the results of *H4a* could have been obscured by running the model in SEM (see also Figure 2) – which includes all variables together – a mixed-effects general linear model tested the direct relationship between gender congruency and risk perceptions. This type of analysis allows for testing repeated measures designs such as this. The results of the mixed model did find support for *H4a*, gender congruency predicting lower levels of perceived risk, specifically $F(1596) = 15.33$, $p < .001$. Results from the mixed analysis combined with the significant indirect paths suggest that *H4a*

Table 3. SEM results.

Model fit Indices	χ^2	df	p-Value	RMSEA	CFI	TLI	SRMR
Saturated	.81	.00	.00	.00	1.00	1.00	.00
Unsaturated	2.11	1.00	.15	.03	1.00	.99	.01

Unstandardized path coefficients

Dependent	Direct	Indirect	Saturated
Gender congruency			
Social resources	.34***		.34***
Self-efficacy	.74***		.74***
Risk		−.30***	.06
Desirability	.30***	.60***	.30***
Self-efficacy with			
Social Resources	.72***		.72***
Social Resources			
Risk	−.41***		−.41***
Desirability	.39***		.39***
Self-efficacy			
Risk	−.22***		−.23***
Desirability	.50***		.50***
Risk			
Desirability	−.33**		−.33**

Model controls	Sex	Age	Education	Nascent experience
Self-efficacy	.29***	−.12***	.02	.26***
Social resources	.28**	−.15***	.03	.07*
Risk	−.02	.08***	.03	−.03
Desirability	.17*	−.10***	−.09**	.11***

Specific indirect paths	Saturated
Gender congruency → Social resources → Risk	−.14***
Gender congruency → Self-efficacy → Risk	−.17***
Gender congruency → Social resources → Desire	.13***
Gender congruency → Self-efficacy → Desire	.37***
Gender congruency → Social resources → Risk → Desire	.06***
Gender congruency → Self-efficacy → Risk → Desire	.05***

***$p < .001$; **$p < .01$; *$p < .05$.

Table 4. Hypotheses tested.

Hypotheses	Results	Analysis
Hypothesis 1: Individuals find gender congruent ventures more desirable than gender incongruent ventures.	Supported	SEM
Hypothesis 2a: Individuals have higher self-efficacy for gender-congruent ventures than for gender incongruent ventures.	Supported	SEM
Hypothesis 2b: Self-efficacy mediates the effect of gender congruency on risk perceptions.	Supported	SEM
Hypothesis 2c: Self-efficacy mediates the effect of gender congruency on venture desirability.	Supported	SEM
Hypothesis 3a: Individuals anticipate greater levels of social resources for gender congruent ventures than for gender incongruent ventures.	Supported	SEM
Hypothesis 3b: Anticipated social resources mediates the effect of gender congruency on venture risk perceptions.	Supported	SEM
Hypothesis 3c: Anticipated social resources mediates the effect of gender congruency on venture desirability.	Supported	SEM
Hypothesis 4a: Individuals perceive lower risk in gender congruent ventures than in gender incongruent ventures.	Supported	Mixed Model
Hypothesis 4b: Venture risk perceptions are inversely related to venture desirability.	Supported	SEM

was completely mediated by self-efficacy and anticipated social resources. We therefore report *H4a* as supported in Table 4.

Control variables

Table 3 summarizes the effects of whether the control variables significantly predict mean levels of self-efficacy, social resources, perceived risk or venture desirability. Since participant sex is dummy-coded (0 = female, 1 = male), results indicate that men reported higher overall levels of self-

Table 5. Results of moderation analysis.

Moderator analysis				
Unstandardized path coefficients				
Gender congruency →Risk				
Sex (Male = 1)		.23*		
Gender congruency →Desire				
Sex (Male = 1)		.68***		
Unmoderator paths				
G. Congruency →Self-efficacy		.74***		
G. Congruency →Social resources		.34***		
Self-efficacy →Risk		−.22***		
Social resources →Risk		−.41***		
Self-efficacy →Desire		.50***		
Social resources →Desire		.38***		
Risk →Desire		−.35**		
Self-efficacy with				
Social resources		.72***		
Model controls	Sex	Age	Education	Nascent experience
Self-efficacy	.29***	−.12***	.02	.26***
Social resources	.28**	−.15***	.03	.07*
Risk	−.13	.08***	.03	−.03
Desirability	−.13	−.10***	−.09**	.11***

***$p < .001$; **$p < .01$; *$p < .05$.

efficacy, anticipated social resources and venture desirability. These results are not surprising since entrepreneurship is a masculine-typed occupation (Gupta, Turban, and Bhawe 2008). Equally unsurprising, entrepreneurial experience was related to ratings of self-efficacy, anticipated social resources and venture desirability.

Robustness checks – moderator testing

Prior research suggests that there are sex differences in the decision processes related to evaluating entrepreneurial risk (Dawson and Henley 2015) and the importance of social relationships (Cross and Madson 1997). Others suggest that the decision-making processes of entrepreneurs and non-entrepreneurs are different (McMullen and Shepherd 2006; Baron 2009; Baron and Ensley 2006). As a robustness check, we tested if participant sex, entrepreneurial experience and their interaction term, qualified any paths in the model. The interaction term and entrepreneurial experience did not moderate any paths in the model; though participant sex did moderate two paths (Table 5), such that they were significant for men but not for women. Separate model runs for men and women revealed that the path from gender congruency to venture desirability was significant for men ($b = .62$, $p < .01$), but not for women ($b = −.05, p = .47$); and the path from gender congruency to risk was also significant for men ($b = .17, p = .02$), but not for women ($b = −.07, p = .40$). However, all indirect paths from gender congruency through self-efficacy and social resources, to risk, and through risk on desirability were significant (all p's $< .01$) for both sexes. The lack of direct link combined with the significant indirect paths between gender congruency and perceived risk and desirability for women indicates that other variables in the model completely mediated these relationships for women. However, since these direct and indirect paths were still significant for men, the relationships are only partially mediated for men. These results suggest that the model does a better job of capturing all the relevant cognitions for women.

Overall, there was considerable support for our theorized mediational model (Figure 1). Self-efficacy, anticipated social resources, perceived risk and venture desirability are all a function of venture gender congruency – nudging both genders to pursue stereotypical venture opportunities.

Discussion

Women generally start ventures in less economically rewarding industries than their male counterparts (Anna et al. 2000; Kepler and Shane 2007). In response to recent calls for research to shed light on the role of gender and biases in the entrepreneurial decision-making process (Shepherd, Williams, and Patzelt 2015), the purpose of this research was to test a model of how gendered cognitions affect entrepreneurial preferences; thereby reinforcing the gender gap in entrepreneurship.

We tested several hypotheses related to the effect of gender congruency with a venture opportunity on cognitions related to self-efficacy, anticipated social resources, perceived risk and venture desirability. When the venture opportunity is gender congruent, men and women rate their self-efficacy higher, anticipate greater social resources, perceive lower overall venture risk and ultimately rate the desirability of the venture higher. We found support that feelings of self-efficacy, and anticipated social resources mediate how much risk one perceives in a venture opportunity, and that perceived risk also mediates the relationship between gender congruency and venture desirability. These gender-related self-assessments bias both men and women when evaluating entrepreneurial opportunities coaxing actors to prefer gender-congruent opportunities. This finding, however, can be problematic for women because if women feel less competent in a gender incongruent domain (traditionally masculine-typed domain) they are less likely to start a business in that domain. Since traditionally masculine-typed ventures, such as technology, are associated with greater growth and economic rewards, this preference for gender congruent opportunities can hinder the performance of female owned ventures.

The test of our proposed conceptual model (Figure 1) mainly revealed similarities between men and women, though we observed two interesting differences. Specifically, the hypothesized effects of gender congruency on venture desirability and gender congruency on perceived risk varied between men and women. For women, the relationships between gender congruency and desirability and perceived risk were completely mediated by the other explanatory variables in our model; whereas for men the hypothesized mediators only account for part of the link between a venture's gender congruency and its desirability. That is, our model seems to do a very good job of capturing the relevant processes for women; however, it was unable to fully explain the allure of the gender-congruent venture for men. This implies that there must be other factors shaping men's preferences and risk perceptions, which were not included in our model. For instance, the present model considered social support and its mitigating effect on perceived risk, but it did not consider that men are often motivated by status and social reputation (Huberman, Loch, and Önçüler 2004; Vandello and Bosson 2013). Research suggests that men may be willing to accept great risk and even reject any social support in order to 'prove themselves' in the eyes of others (Vandello and Bosson 2013). In light of this, future research may explore other possible variables that might account for men's preferences, including their orientation towards status (Huberman, Loch, and Önçüler 2004) or their stronger preference for 'thing-oriented activities' compared to women's greater preference for 'people-oriented activities' (Lippa 2010). However, in spite of these sex differences, all indirect paths were significant, thereby indicating that the relationships hold: the match between participant sex and sex-type of the venture evaluated predicts increased venture desirability and all the intervening variables.

Men and women make different assessments of objectively similar businesses, however, we do not suggest this is a cognitive bias or distortion. Rather, participants may accurately and rationally perceive that they would be more successful in gender-congruent opportunities. As Kahneman (2003, 1449) suggests, it is useful to unravel the difference between decisions based on heuristics and those informed by 'optimal beliefs and choices assumed in rational-agent models'. Participants may accurately predict that important others will provide or withhold social resources based on how well they conform to prescriptive stereotypes. Many studies find that social punishments are enforced if gender norms are violated (Heilman and Wallen 2010; Heilman et al. 2004; Rudman and

Fairchild 2004; Rudman and Glick 1999). Via the measurement of anticipated social resources we captured participants assessed differences in social resources for conforming or not conforming to gender role norms. To our knowledge, we are the first to examine the role of participants' assessments of the social rewards or sanctions and demonstrate their effect on risk perceptions, thereby contributing to the literature on the consequences of gender norm violations.

Although men report higher self-efficacy overall, we find that women report higher self-efficacy than men for feminine-typed ventures (and lower levels in masculine-typed ventures), consistent with the idea that self-efficacy is domain-specific (Drnovšek, Wincent, and Cardon 2010). Again, participant self-reports may be 'rational' given that they have had a lifetime of training for their prescribed gender role and probably less experience fulfilling the requirements of the opposite gender role. Although these self-reported gender differences may reflect actual ability differences, they may also reflect biased self-assessments. For example, women report their self-efficacy in math to be lower than their male counterparts, even though there are no gender differences in performance (Wieland and Sarin 2012; Correll 2001). Although, much entrepreneurship research finds women to have lower entrepreneurial self-efficacy (Chowdhury and Endres 2005; Wilson, Kickul, and Marlino 2007; Zhao, Seibert, and Hills 2005), this may be due to gender bias in the trait scales used (as opposed to a domain specific scale) for measuring entrepreneurial self-efficacy (Gupta, Turban, and Bhawe 2008).

Most research suggests that women are more risk-averse than men (Croson and Gneezy 2009), and this has been proposed as a factor limiting women's entry into entrepreneurship (Dawson and Henley 2015). Although we examined risk perception (not risk aversion), our results did not reveal any sex difference on this variable. We found that although there is a main effect for the gender congruency of the venture evaluated, there are no significant sex differences in levels of perceived risk when controlling for age, education and entrepreneurial experience (Table 3). Although this seems to go against the consensus that there is a gender difference in risk related measures (aversion, perceptions and taking), there is a growing body of research indicating that risk-taking and risk-assessments are influenced by gender-role norms and subjective assessments, which vary by domain (Wieland et al. 2014; Byrnes, Miller, and Schafer 1999; Sarin and Wieland 2016). Theoretically consistent with our results, Wieland and Sarin (2012) found that both men and women took more risk in gender-congruent domains.

A prominent stream of research in entrepreneurship explores entrepreneurial decision making (Shepherd, Williams, and Patzelt 2015), encouraging researchers to understand how specific cognitive factors influence entrepreneurial decision-making and to look inside the 'black box' of the decision-making process (Haynie, Shepherd, and McMullen 2009, 338). There have been multiple calls to cast light on factors that serve to reinforce the gender gap in entrepreneurship (DeTienne and Chandler 2007; Jennings and Brush 2013). Jennings and Brush (2013) challenge entrepreneurship researchers to explore gender as a variable to explain differences between men and women's exploitation of new opportunities. Although gender is a fundamental means by which a society is structured, surprisingly few studies explain the link between gender and how opportunities come to be pursued (Sullivan and Meek 2012). Our research, answers these diverse calls by both examining the 'black box' of the preference formation influencing entrepreneurial decision-making and also examining the role that gender plays in entrepreneurial cognitions. We provide a socio-cognitive explanation for the clustering of men and women in different types of ventures noted by prior research (Anna et al. 2000), exploring how gender consistent behaviour may hinder women's advancement in entrepreneurship.

Policy implications

This work suggests that there are three possible points of intervention to support female entrepreneurship: increasing feelings of self-efficacy, improving access to social resources, and/or reducing venture risk. Providing basic training for would-be entrepreneurs in masculine-typed endeavours may serve to increase feelings of self-efficacy. Zhao, Seibert, and Hills (2005) found that entrepreneurship training does increase entrepreneurial self-efficacy for MBA students, while Wilson, Kickul, and Marlino (2007) specifically reviewed the positive effects entrepreneurship training has on women's ESE. Another other point of intervention is increasing access to social resources for women pursuing masculine-typed ventures. Again, we find that anticipated social resources mitigate perceived venture risk. Therefore, policies aimed at creating women's entrepreneurial support groups may be an especially important tool for risk mitigation for female entrepreneurs. A final lever is to reduce venture risk (increase its likelihood of success) directly. In the US, there are currently Small Business Adminisration programmes focused on women owned businesses which target this lever. When the rewards outweigh the risks of pursing a gender-incongruent venture, women will be more likely to enter masculine-typed domains.

When embarking on any policy intervention it is important to remember that entrepreneurial endeavours take place within the cultural context, and that cultures change slowly regarding gender norms (Shinnar, Giacomin, and Janssen 2012). Therefore, just encouraging and supporting women to pursue masculine-typed opportunities may not adequately buffer these women against the backlash due to violating prescriptive gender norms. However, as base-rates of successful female entrepreneurs increase, stereotypes may gradually shift overtime, so that entrepreneurship will no longer be masculine-typed, much like the legal and accounting professions, which are now more gender inclusive.

Limitations

Like all research, this research had some limitations. First, our participants had varying levels of entrepreneurial experience, as opposed to consistent levels for a sample of only entrepreneurs. However, the diversity of our sample benefited this research because it allowed for the control and estimation of the effects of entrepreneurial experience, sex, age and education. Further, we used hypothetical scenarios for our experimental manipulations. While these tasks lack optimal levels of realism, they do enable experimental control, allowing us to isolate and measure relevant social cognitions, which is not possible in an applied setting. Experimental manipulation for hypothetical scenarios allows researchers to generate rich theoretical insights that may not be possible otherwise (Gregoire and Shepherd 2012; Sapienza and Korsgaard 1996; Colquitt 2008). Although venture gender congruency is experimentally manipulated, the mediators (self-efficacy, social resources, risk) are not individually manipulated. Experimental manipulation of mediators is the best evidence of their causal role (Spencer, Zanna, and Fong 2005).

Our results are bound by cultural constraints. Our samples are only drawn from the US. Gender roles vary by culture; entrepreneurship as well as venture sex-type is influenced by norms of what is appropriate for each sex in one's culture (Shinnar, Giacomin, and Janssen 2012). Nevertheless, various scholars have documented that there are greater sex differences in developed Western societies than more traditional developing societies (Costa, Terracciano, and McCrae 2001). This may have implications for occupational and entrepreneurial choice. To the extent that Western (at least by comparison with many developing societies) and more gender egalitarian societies provide women more opportunities to express their preferences through entrepreneurial choice, we might observe greater levels of voluntary sex segregation in Western than non-Western societies. With some of the evidence pointing us in this direction (Charles and Bradley 2009), future research should determine whether there are indeed cross-cultural differences to the extent women (and men) are guided by gender consistency (gender-congruency) in their choice of ventures.

Finally, sex is used as a proxy for gender, in determining the gender congruency of the venture. Although not ideal, gender-roles tend to map closely onto one's biological sex (Eagly 2000) and the current measurement of masculinity and femininity is problematic due to shifting norms of typical male and female characteristics (Eagly, Beall, and Sternberg 2004; Twenge 1997, 2001).

Conclusion

This research explores the social-cognitive processes influenced by one's gender role, which may be partly responsible for producing the gender gap in entrepreneurial outcomes so often noted (Anna et al. 2000; Kepler and Shane 2007; Powell and Eddleston 2008). Specifically, drawing from Social Role Theory (Eagly 1987) and Social Cognitive Career Theory (Lent, Brown, and Hackett 1994) we develop a socio-cognitive model specifying how gender role match with the venture opportunity results in higher assessments of self-efficacy, anticipated social resources and venture desirability, and lower assessments of risk. Our results provide insights to the internalized barriers that hinder women's entrepreneurial progress, 'nudging' women into lower-return ventures in less lucrative industries.

Notes

1. Although samples differed in regard to scenarios and other minor methodological details, none of the results reported differed between samples; hence, for the remainder of the analysis, they were collapsed.
2. Our research also measured psychological masculinity and femininity as well (Spence 1991). However, inclusion of these variables yielded few effects and never superseded the effects of biological sex. Because the results are not altered by the exclusion of these variables, psychological gender is not included in the present analyses.

Disclosure statement

No potential conflict of interest was reported by the authors.

References

Aguinis, H., and S. O. Lawal. 2012. "Conducting Field Experiments Using Elancing's Natural Environment." *Journal of Business Venturing* 27 (4): 493–505. doi:10.1016/j.jbusvent.2012.01.002.

Ahl, H. 2006. "Why Research on Women Entrepreneurs Needs New Directions." *Entrepreneurship Theory and Practice* 30 (5): 595–621. doi:10.1111/etap.2006.30.issue-5.

Anna, A. L., G. N. Chandler, E. Jansen, and N. P. Mero. 2000. "Women Business Owners in Traditional and Non-Traditional Industries." *Journal of Business Venturing* 15 (3): 279–303. doi:10.1016/S0883-9026(98)00012-3.

Bandura, A. 1997. *Self-Efficacy: The Exercise of Control*. New York, NY, USA: W. H. Freeman.

BarNir, A., W. E. Watson, and H. M. Hutchins. 2011. "Mediation and Moderated Mediation in the Relationship among Role Models, Self-Efficacy, Entrepreneurial Career Intention, and Gender." *Journal of Applied Social Psychology* 41 (2): 270–297. doi:10.1111/j.1559-1816.2010.00713.x.

Baron, R. A. 2004. "The Cognitive Perspective: A Valuable Tool for Answering Entrepreneurship's Basic "Why" Questions." *Journal of Business Venturing* 19 (2): 221–239. doi:10.1016/s0883-9026(03)00008-9.

Baron, R. A. 2006. "Opportunity Recognition as Pattern Recognition: How Entrepreneurs "Connect the Dots" to Identify New Business Opportunities." *Academy of Management Perspectives* 20 (1): 104–119. doi:10.5465/amp.2006.19873412.

Baron, R. A. 2009. "Effectual versus Predictive Logics in Entrepreneurial Decision Making: Differences between Experts and Novices Does Experience in Starting New Ventures Change the Way Entrepreneurs Think? Perhaps, but for Now, "Caution" Is Essential." *Journal of Business Venturing* 24 (4): 310–315. doi:10.1016/j.jbusvent.2008.04.001.

Baron, R. A., and M. D. Ensley. 2006. "Opportunity Recognition as the Detection of Meaningful Patterns: Evidence from Comparisons of Novice and Experienced Entrepreneurs." *Management Science* 52 (9): 1331–1344. doi:10.1287/mnsc.1060.0538.

Bem, S. L. 1981. "Gender Schema Theory: A Cognitive Account of Sex-Typing." *Psychological Review* 88 (4): 354–364. doi:10.1037/0033-295x.88.4.354.

Blau, F. D., and L. M. Kahn. 2007. "The Gender Pay Gap: Have Women Gone as far as They Can?" *Academy of Management Perspectives* 21 (1): 7–23. doi:10.5465/amp.2007.24286161.

Browne, M. V., and R. Cudeck. 1993. "Alternative Ways of Assessing Model Fit." In *Testing Structural Equation Models*, edited by K. A. Bollen and J. S. Long, 136–159. Newbury Park, CA: Sage.

Busenitz, L. W., and C.-M. Lau. 1996. "A Cross-Cultural Cognitive Model of New Venture Creation." *Entrepreneurship Theory and Practice* 20 (4): 25–40. doi:10.1177/104225879602000403.

Byrnes, J. P., D. C. Miller, and W. D. Schafer. 1999. "Gender Differences in Risk Taking: A Meta-Analysis." *Psychological Bulletin* 125 (3): 367–383. doi:10.1037/0033-2909.125.3.367.

Cassar, G., and H. Friedman. 2009. "Does Self-Efficacy Affect Entrepreneurial Investment?" *Strategic Entrepreneurship Journal* 3 (3): 241–260. doi:10.1002/sej.73.

Charles, M., and D. B. Grusky. 2004. *Occupational Ghettos: The Worldwide Segregation of Women and Men.* Stanford, California: Stanford University Press.

Charles, M., and K. Bradley. 2009. "Indulging Our Gendered Selves? Sex Segregation by Field of Study in 44 Countries." *American Journal of Sociology* 114 (4): 924–976. doi:10.1086/595942.

Chen, G., S. M. Gully, and D. Eden. 2001. "Validation of a New General Self-Efficacy Scale." *Organizational Research Methods* 4 (1): 62–83. doi:10.1177/109442810141004.

Chowdhury, S., and M. L. Endres. 2005. "Gender Difference and the Formation of Entrepreneurial Self-Efficacy." *Entrepreneurship in a Diverse World*, 8.

Cohen, S. 2004. "Social Relationships and Health." *American Psychologist* 59 (8): 676–684. doi:10.1037/0003-066X.59.8.676.

Cohen, S., and T. A. Wills. 1985. "Stress, Social Support and the Buffering Hypothesis." *Psychological Bulletin* 98 (2): 310–357.

Colquitt, J. A. 2008. "Publishing Laboratory Research in Amj: A Question of When, Not If." *Academy of Management Journal* 51 (4): 616–620.

Correll, S. J. 2001. "Gender and the Career Choice Process: The Role of Biased Self-Assessments." *American Journal of Sociology* 106 (6): 1691–1730. doi:10.1086/321299.

Costa, P. T., A. Terracciano, and R. R. McCrae. 2001. "Gender Differences in Personality Traits across Cultures: Robust and Surprising Findings." *Journal of Personality and Social Psychology* 81 (2): 322–331. doi:10.1037/0022-3514.81.2.322.

Croson, R., and U. Gneezy. 2009. "Gender Differences in Preferences." *Journal of Economic Literature* 47 (2): 448–474. doi:10.1257/Jel.47.2.448.

Cross, S. E., and L. Madson. 1997. "Models of the Self: Self-Construals and Gender." *Psychological Bulletin* 122 (1): 5–37.

Dawson, C., and A. Henley. 2015. "Gender, Risk, and Venture Creation Intentions." *Journal of Small Business Management* 53 (2): 501–515. doi:10.1111/jsbm.12080.

De Carolis, D. M., and P. Saparito. 2006. "Social Capital, Cognition, and Entrepreneurial Opportunities: A Theoretical Framework." *Entrepreneurship Theory and Practice* 30 (1): 41–56. doi:10.1111/etap.2006.30.issue-1.

De Clercq, D., T. V. Menzies, M. Diochon, and Y. Gasse. 2009. "Explaining Nascent Entrepreneurs' Goal Commitment: An Exploratory Study." *Journal of Small Business and Entrepreneurship* 22 (2): 123–139. doi:10.1080/08276331.2009.10593446.

Deaux, K., and B. Major. 1987. "Putting Gender into Context: An Interactive Model of Gender-Related Behavior." *Psychological Review* 94 (3): 369–389. doi:10.1037/0033-295X.94.3.369.

DeTienne, D. R., and G. N. Chandler. 2007. "The Role of Gender in Opportunity Identification." *Entrepreneurship Theory and Practice* 31 (3): 365–386. doi:10.1111/j.1540-6520.2007.00178.x.

DeVellis, R. F. 2003. *Scale Development: Theory and Applications* (2nd ed, 26 Vols). Thousand Oaks, CA: Sage.

Drnovšek, M., J. Wincent, and M. S. Cardon. 2010. "Entrepreneurial Self-Efficacy and Business Start-Up: Developing a Multi-Dimensional Definition." *International Journal of Entrepreneurial Behaviour & Research* 16 (4): 329–348. doi:10.1108/13552551011054516.

Eagly, A. H. 1987. *Sex Differences in Social Behavior: A Social-Role Interpretation.* Hillsdale, NJ: Lawrence Erlbaum Associates.

Eagly, A. H. 2000. "Gender, sex, and culture: Sex differences and gender differences." In *Encyclopedia of Psychology* edited by A. E. Kazdin (3 Vols, 436–442). Washington, DC: American Psychological Association.

Eagly, A. H., W. Wood, and A. B. Diekman. 2000. "Social Role Theory of Sex Differences and Similarities: A Current Appraisal." In *The Developmental Social Psychology of Gender.*, edited by T. Eckes and H. M. Trautner, 123–174. Mahwah, NJ: Erlbaum.

Eagly, A. H., A. E. Beall, and R. J. Sternberg. 2004. The Psychology of Gender. New York: Guilford.

Eddleston, K. A., and G. N. Powell. 2012. "Nurturing Entrepreneurs' Work-Family Balance: A Gendered Perspective." *Entrepreneurship Theory and Practice* 36 (3): 513–541. doi:10.1111/j.1540-6520.2012.00506.x.

Eriksson, K., and B. Simpson. 2010. "Emotional Reactions to Losing Explain Gender Differences in Entering a Risky Lottery." *Judgment and Decision Making* 5 (3): 159–163.

Forlani, D., and J. W. Mullins. 2000. "Perceived Risks and Choices in Entrepreneurs' New Venture Decisions." *Journal of Business Venturing* 15 (4): 305–322. doi:10.1016/S0883-9026(98)00017-2.

Frese, M. 1999. "Social Support as A Moderator of the Relationship between Work Stressors and Psychological Dysfunctioning: A Longitudinal Study with Objective Measures." *Journal of Occupational Health Psychology* 4 (3): 179–192. doi:10.1037//1076-8998.4.3.179.

Ganzach, Y., S. Ellis, A. Pazy, and T. Ricci-Siag. 2008. "On the Perception and Operationalization of Risk Perception." *Judgment and Decision Making Journal* 3 (4): 317–324.

Glick, P. 1991. "Trait-Based and Sex-Based Discrimination in Occupational Prestige, Occupational Salary, and Hiring." *Sex Roles* 25 (5–6): 351–378. doi:10.1007/bf00289761.

Glick, P., K. Wilk, and M. Perreault. 1995. "Images of Occupations: Components of Gender and Status in Occupational Stereotypes." *Sex Roles* 32 (9–10): 565–582. doi:10.1007/BF01544212.

Gregoire, D. A., and D. A. Shepherd. 2012. "Technology-Market Combinations and the Identification of Entrepreneurial Opportunities: An Investigation of the Opportunity-Individual Nexus." *Academy of Management Journal* 55 (4): 753–785. doi:10.5465/amj.2011.0126.

Gupta, V. K., D. B. Turban, and N. M. Bhawe. 2008. "The Effect of Gender Stereotype Activation on Entrepreneurial Intentions." *Journal of Applied Psychology* 93 (5): 1053–1061. doi:10.1037/0021-9010.93.5.1053.

Gupta, V. K., D. B. Turban, S. A. Wasti, and A. Sikdar. 2009. "The Role of Gender Stereotypes in Perceptions of Entrepreneurs and Intentions to Become an Entrepreneur." *Entrepreneurship Theory and Practice* 33 (2): 397–417. doi:10.1111/j.1540-6520.2009.00296.x.

Hackett, G., and N. E. Betz. 1981. "A Self-Efficacy Approach to the Career-Development of Women." *Journal of Vocational Behavior* 18 (3): 326–339. doi:10.1016/0001-8791(81)90019-1.

Haynie, J. M., D. Shepherd, E. Mosakowski, and P. C. Earley. 2010. "A Situated Metacognitive Model of the Entrepreneurial Mindset." *Journal of Business Venturing* 25 (2): 217–229. doi:10.1016/j.jbusvent.2008.10.001.

Haynie, J. M., D. A. Shepherd, and Jeffery S. McMullen. 2009. "An Opportunity for Me? the Role of Resources in Opportunity Evaluation Decisions." *Journal of Management Studies* 46 (3): 337–361. doi:10.1111/j.1467-6486.2009.00824.x.

Heath, C., and A. Tversky. 1991. "Preference and Belief: Ambiguity and Competence in Choice under Uncertainty." *Journal of Risk and Uncertainty* 4 (1): 5–28. doi:10.1007/BF00057884.

Heilman, M. E. 2001. "Description and Prescription: How Gender Stereotypes Prevent Women's Ascent up the Organizational Ladder." *Journal of Social Issues* 57 (4): 657–674. doi:10.1111/0022-4537.00234.

Heilman, M. E., and A. S. Wallen. 2010. "Wimpy and Undeserving of Respect: Penalties for Men's Gender-Inconsistent Success." *Journal of Experimental Social Psychology* 46 (4): 664–667. doi:10.1016/j.jesp.2010.01.008.

Heilman, M. E., A. S. Wallen, D. Fuchs, and M. M. Tamkins. 2004. "Penalties for Success: Reactions to Women Who Succeed at Male Gender-Typed Tasks." *Journal of Applied Psychology* 89 (3): 416–427. doi:10.1037/0021-9010.89.3.416.

Hinkin, T. R. 1995. "A Review of Scale Development Practices in the Study of Organizations." *Journal of Management* 21 (5): 967–988. doi:10.1177/014920639502100509.

Hornsby, J. S., D. F. Kuratko, and S. A. Zahra. 2002. "Middle Managers' Perception of the Internal Environment for Corporate Entrepreneurship: Assessing a Measurement Scale." *Journal of Business Venturing* 17 (3): 253–273. doi:10.1016/s0883-9026(00)00059-8.

Hsee, C. K., and E. U. Weber. 1999. "Cross-National Differences in Risk Preference and Lay Predictions." *Journal of Behavioral Decision Making* 12 (2): 165–179. doi:10.1002/(ISSN)1099-0771.

Hsu, D. K., S. A. Simmons, and A. M. Wieland. 2017. "Designing Entrepreneurship Experiments: A Review, Typology, and Research Agenda." *Organizational Research Methods* 20 (3): 379–412. doi:10.1177/1094428116685613.

Huberman, B. A., C. H. Loch, and A. Önçüler. 2004. "Status as a Valued Resource." *Social Psychology Quarterly* 67 (1): 103–114. doi:10.1177/019027250406700109.

Jennings, J. E., and C. G. Brush. 2013. "Research on Women Entrepreneurs: Challenges to (And From) the Broader Entrepreneurship Literature?" *The Academy of Management Annals* 7 (1): 663–715. doi:10.1080/19416520.2013.782190.

Johnson, E. J., and A. Tversky. 1983. "Affect, Generalization, and the Perception of Risk." *Journal of Personality and Social Psychology* 45 (1): 20–31. doi:10.1037/0022-3514.45.1.20.

Kahneman, D. 2003. "Maps of Bounded Rationality: Psychology for Behavioral Economics." *American Economic Review* 95 (5): 1449–1475. doi:10.1257/000282803322655392.

Kelley, D. J., C. G. Brush, P. G. Greene, and Y. Litovsky. 2013. Gem 2012 Global Women's Report. Boston (MA): Babson College.

Kepler, E., and S. Shane. 2007. "Are Male and Female Entrepreneurs Really that Different?" edited by. In *US Small Business Administration*. Washington, DC: Office of Advocacy.

Kline, R. B. 2011. *Principles and Practice of Structural Equation Modeling*. 3rd ed. New York: Guilford.

Krueger, N. F., M. D. Reilly, and A. L. Carsrud. 2000. "Competing Models of Entrepreneurial Intentions." *Journal of Business Venturing* 15 (5–6): 411–432. doi:10.1016/S0883-9026(98)00033-0.

Krueger, N. F., and P. R. Dickson. 1994. "How Believing in Ourselves Increases Risk-Taking – Perceived Self-Efficacy and Opportunity Recognition." *Decision Sciences* 25 (3): 385–400. doi:10.1111/j.1540-5915.1994.tb00810.x.

Lambert, A. J., T. Burroughs, and T. Nguyen. 1999. "Perceptions of Risk and the Buffering Hypothesis: The Role of Just World Beliefs and Right-Wing Authoritarianism." *Personality and Social Psychology Bulletin* 25 (6): 643–656. doi:10.1177/0146167299025006001.

Leary, M. R., D. S. Wheeler, and T. B. Jenkins. 1986. "Aspects of Identity and Behavioral Preference: Studies of Occupational and Recreational Choice." *Social Psychology Quarterly* 49 (1): 11–18. doi:10.2307/2786853.

Lent, R. W., S. D. Brown, and G. Hackett. 1994. "Toward a Unifying Social Cognitive Theory of Career and Academic Interest, Choice and Performance." *Journal of Vocational Behavior* 45 (1): 79–122. doi:10.1006/jvbe.1994.1027.

Lent, R. W., S. D. Brown, and G. Hackett. 2000. "Contextual Supports and Barriers to Career Choice: A Social Cognitive Analysis." *Journal of Counseling Psychology* 47 (1): 36–49. doi:10.1037/0022-0167.47.1.36.

Lippa, R. A. 2010. "Sex Differences in Personality Traits and Gender-Related Occupational Preferences across 53 Nations: Testing Evolutionary and Social-Environmental Theories." *Archives of Sexual Behavior* 39 (3): 619–636. doi:10.1007/s10508-008-9380-7.

Mason, W., and S. Suri. 2012. "Conducting Behavioral Research on Amazon's Mechanical Turk." *Behavior Research Methods* 44 (1): 1–23. doi:10.3758/s13428-011-0124-6.

McGee, J. E., M. Peterson, S. L. Mueller, and J. M. Sequeira. 2009. "Entrepreneurial Self-Efficacy: Refining the Measure." *Entrepreneurship Theory and Practice* 33 (4): 965–988. doi:10.1111/j.1540-6520.2009.00304.x.

McMullen, J. S., and D. A. Shepherd. 2006. "Entrepreneurial Action and the Role of Uncertainty in the Theory of the Entrepreneur." *Academy of Management Review* 31 (1): 132–152. doi:10.5465/amr.2006.19379628.

Minniti, M. 2009. *Gender Issues in Entrepreneurship*. Now Publishers.

Muthén, L. K., and B. Muthén. 2015. *Mplus - The Comprehensive Modelling Program for Applied Researchers: User's Guide, 7*. Los Angeles, CA: Muthén & Muthén.

Paolacci, G., J. Chandler, and P. G. Ipeirotis. 2010. "Running Experiments on Amazon Mechanical Turk." *Judgment and Decision Making* 5: 5.

Podsakoff, P. M., S. B. MacKenzie, J. Y. Lee, and N. P. Podsakoff. 2003. "Common Method Biases in Behavioral Research: A Critical Review of the Literature and Recommended Remedies." *Journal of Applied Psychology* 88 (5): 879–903. doi:10.1037/0021-9101.88.5.879.

Powell, G. N., and K. A. Eddleston. 2008. "The Paradox of the Contented Female Business Owner." *Journal of Vocational Behavior* 73 (1): 24–36. doi:10.1016/j.jvb.2007.12.005.

Rudman, L. A., and K. Fairchild. 2004. "Reactions to Counterstereotypic Behavior: The Role of Backlash in Cultural Stereotype Maintenance." *Journal of Personality and Social Psychology* 87 (2): 157–176. doi:10.1037/0022-3514.87.2.157.

Rudman, L. A., and P. Glick. 1999. "Feminized Management and Backlash toward Agentic Women: The Hidden Costs to Women of a Kinder, Gentler Image of Middle Managers." *Journal of Personality and Social Psychology* 77 (5): 1004–1010.

Rudman, L. A., and P. Glick. 2008. The social psychology of gender: How power and intimacy shape gender relations. In *Texts in social psychology*, edited by S. T. Fiske. (386 Vols). New York: Guilford Press

Sapienza, H. J., and M. A. Korsgaard. 1996. "Procedural Justice in Entrepreneur-Investor Relations." *Academy of Management Journal* 39 (3): 544–574.

Sarason, I. G., H. M. Levine, R. B. Basham, and B. R. Sarason. 1983. "Asessing Social Support: The Social Support Questionnaire." *Journal of Personality and Social Psychology* 44 (1): 127–139. doi:10.1037/0022-3514.44.1.127.

Sarin, R., and A. M. Wieland. 2016. "Risk Aversion for Decisions under Uncertainty: Are There Gender Differences?" *Journal of Behavioral and Experimental Economics* 60: 1–8. doi: 10.1016/j.socec.2015.10.007.

Semmer, N. K., A. Elfering, N. Jacobshagen, T. Perrot, T. A. Beehr, and N. Boos. 2008. "The Emotional Meaning of Instrumental Social Support." *International Journal of Stress Management* 15 (3): 235–251. doi:10.1037/1072-5245.15.3.235.

Shapero, A., and L. Sokol. 1982. "The Social Dimensions of Entrepreneurship." *Encyclopedia of Entrepreneurship*: 72–90.

Shaver, K. G., and L. R. Scott. 1991. "Person, Process, Choice: The Psychology of New Venture Creation." *Entrepreneurship Theory and Practice* 16 (2): 23–45. doi:10.1177/104225879201600204.

Shepherd, D. A., T. A. Williams, and H. Patzelt. 2015. "Thinking about Entrepreneurial Decision Making: Review and Research Agenda." *Journal of Management* 41 (1): 11–46. doi:10.1177/0149206314541153.

Shinnar, R. S., D. K. Hsu, B. Powell, and H. Zhou. 2016. "A Longitudinal Investigation of the Linkage between Entrepreneurial Intention and Actual Start-Up: The Moderating Effect of Gender." In *Babson College Entrepreneurship Research Conference*. Bodø, Norway.

Shinnar, R. S., D. K. Hsu, and B. C. Powell. 2014. "Self-Efficacy, Entrepreneurial Intentions, and Gender: Assessing the Impact of Entrepreneurship Education Longitudinally." *The International Journal of Management Education* 12 (3): 561–570. doi:10.1016/j.ijme.2014.09.005.

Shinnar, R. S., O. Giacomin, and F. Janssen. 2012. "Entrepreneurial Perceptions and Intentions: The Role of Gender and Culture." *Entrepreneurship Theory and Practice* 36 (3): 465–493. doi:10.1111/j.1540-6520.2012.00509.x.

Simon, M., S. M. Houghton, and K. Aquino. 2000. "Cognitive, Biases, Risk Perception and Venture Formation: How Individuals Decide to Start Companies." *Journal of Business Venturing* 15 (2): 113–134. doi:10.1016/S0883-9026(98)00003-2.

Sitkin, S. B., and L. R. Weingart. 1995. "Determinants of Risky Decision-Making Behavior: A Test of the Mediating Role of Risk Perceptions and Propensity." *Academy of Management Journal* 38 (6): 1573–1592.

Slovic, P., and E. Peters. 2006. "Risk Perception and Affect." *Current Directions in Psychological Science* 15 (6): 322–325. doi:10.1111/j.1467-8721.2006.00461.x.

Spence, J. T. 1991. "Do the Bsri and the Paq Measure the Same or Different Concepts?" *Psychology of Women Quarterly* 15 (1): 141–165. doi:10.1111/j.1471-6402.1991.tb00483.x.

Spencer, S. J., M. P. Zanna, and G. T. Fong. 2005. "Establishing a Causal Chain: Why Experiments are Often More Effective than Mediational Analyses in Examining Psychological Processes." *Journal of Personality and Social Psychology* 89 (6): 845–851. doi:10.1037/0022-3514.89.6.845.

Sullivan, D. M., and W. R. Meek. 2012. "Gender and Entrepreneurship: A Review and Process Model." *Journal of Managerial Psychology* 27 (5): 428–458. doi:10.1108/02683941211235373.

Timmerman, I. G. H., E. S. Emanuels-Zuurveen, and P. M. G. Emmelkamp. 2000. "The Social Support Inventory (Ssi): A Brief Scale to Assess Perceived Adequacy of Social Support." *Clinical Psychology & Psychotherapy* 7 (5): 401–410. doi:10.1002/1099-0879(200011)7:5<401::AID-CPP253>3.0.CO;2-I.

Trevelyan, R. 2008. "Optimism, Overconfidence and Entrepreneurial Activity." *Management Decision* 46 (7): 986–1001. doi:10.1108/00251740810890177.

Twenge, J. M. 1997. "Changes in Masculine and Feminine Traits over Time: A Meta-Analysis." *Sex Roles* 36 (5–6): 305–325. doi:10.1007/BF02766650.

Twenge, J. M. 2001. "Changes in Women's Assertiveness in Response to Status and Roles: A Cross-Temporal Meta-Analysis, 1931–1993." *Journal of Personality and Social Psychology* 81 (1): 133–145. doi:10.1037//0022-3514.81.1.133.

Tykocinski, O. E. 2013. "The Insurance Effect: How the Possession of Gas Masks Reduces the Likelihood of a Missile Attack." *Judgment and Decision Making* 8 (2): 174–178.

Vandello, J. A., and J. K. Bosson. 2013. "Hard Won and Easily Lost: A Review and Synthesis of Theory and Research on Precarious Manhood." *Psychology of Men & Masculinity* 14 (2): 101–113. doi:10.1037/a0029826.

Wadeson, N. S. 2008. "Cognitive Aspects of Entrepreneurship: Decision-Making and Attitudes toward Risk." In *The Oxford Handbook of Entrepreneurship*, edited by M. Casson, B. Yeung, A. Basu, and N. Wadeson, 91–113. Oxford: Oxford University Press.

Wieland, A. M., J. Sundali, M. Kemmelmeier, and R. Sarin. 2014. "Gender Differences in the Endowment Effect: Women Pay Less, but Won't Accept Less." *Judgment and Decision Making* 9 (6): 558–571.

Wieland, A. M., and R. Sarin. 2012. "Domain Specificity of Sex Differences in Competition." *Journal of Economic Behavior & Organization* 83 (1): 151–157. doi:10.1016/j.jebo.2011.06.019.

Wilson, F., J. Kickul, and D. Marlino. 2007. "Gender, Entrepreneurial Self-Efficacy, and Entrepreneurial Career Intentions: Implications for Entrepreneurship Education." *Entrepreneurship Theory and Practice* 31 (3): 387–406. doi:10.1111/etap.2007.31.issue-3.

Witt, M. G., and W. Wood. 2010. "Self-Regulation of Gendered Behavior in Everyday Life." *Sex Roles* 62 (9–10): 635–646. doi:10.1007/s11199-010-9761-y.

Wood, W. P., N. Christensen, M. R. Hebl, and H. Rothgerber. 1997. "Conformity to Sex-Typed Norms, Affect, and the Self-Concept." *Journal of Personality and Social Psychology* 73 (3): 523–535.

Zhao, H., S. E. Seibert, and G. E. Hills. 2005. "The Mediating Role of Self-Efficacy in the Development of Entrepreneurial Intentions." *Journal of Applied Psychology* 90 (6): 1265–1272.

Defying contextual embeddedness: evidence from displaced women entrepreneurs in Jordan

Haya Al-Dajani, Hammad Akbar, Sara Carter and Eleanor Shaw

ABSTRACT

Although entrepreneurial practices and processes are evolving and changing globally, models of entrepreneurship remain masculinized, embedded in advanced economies and associated with notions of individual agency, heroism and control. Rarely is defiance considered. In this paper, we explore the defiance practices of displaced women operating in the Jordanian patriarchal economy and society and consider how this enabled their nurturing of entrepreneurship. Indeed, we argue that socially excluded women actually defy their contextual embeddedness through their entrepreneurial activities. In so doing, we respond to calls for research that explores the contextual embeddedness of women's entrepreneurship, and contribute to shifting the focus towards the more silent feminine end of the entrepreneurial process. We consider the defiance of invisible displaced women entrepreneurs operating in the under-researched context of Jordan. Longitudinal, ethnographic investigation revealed the creation of a secret production network led by, and for, displaced women. This paper focuses on the five founders of this network, which they established to mobilize and manage the production of traditional crafts and, by so doing, to defy the stifling limitations imposed by their restrictive contractors, community and family members.

Introduction

At a time when the Middle East region is experiencing significant social, political and economic upheaval, Jordan's small and fragile economy is additionally experiencing the pressure of approximately 30% of its population being comprised displaced persons requiring aid and support which Jordan struggles to provide (UNHCR 2016). To combat rising unemployment, continuous poverty and social marginalization, displaced women accept contracts to make traditional craft products yet their contracting organizations prohibit them from engaging with other clients and collaborating with other producers. This is despite greater economic returns which can be achieved by multiple client contracts shared between collaborative producers. Longitudinal, ethnographic data collection undertaken between 1999 and 2007 revealed that some women circumvented these restrictive conditions, forming a network of pooled labour delivering craft products to a range of contracting clients. This network operated secretly, masked by the social gatherings of women sharing housework and childcare, hidden from contracting organizations, husbands and other family members (Authors 5). In defiance of terms established by contracting organizations and operating without the knowledge of their husbands and wider families, the founders of this secret production network introduced operating efficiencies and generated undeclared surpluses. Just as their heritage craft production has a deeper political connotation in keeping alive a memory of Palestinian traditions lost through displacement, so too their organizing actions are imbued within the deeper purpose of defying their contextual embeddedness by resisting contractual, social and patriarchal subjugation. This paper explores the five founders of a secret production network, and examines the contractual, social and patriarchal defiance exhibited in their proactiveness, innovativeness and risk-taking. We focus upon women's collective defiance utilized to nurture the entrepreneurship of displaced women living in Jordan. As such, we offer an alternative to mainstream masculinized models of entrepreneurship embedded in advanced economies, typically associated with notions of individual agency and control (Hollenbeck, McCall, and Silzer 2006).

Our contribution lies in adding to the growing research on the contextual embeddedness of women's entrepreneurship by extending the theoretical framework of displaced women's entrepreneurship as defiance. We do so by identifying contractual, social and patriarchal types of defiance in the entrepreneurial orientation of displaced women. This is important as present understandings of how displaced women entrepreneurs within patriarchal contexts exercise and exhibit proactive, innovative and risk-taking entrepreneurial behaviours excludes defiance. By forging informal, collaborative secret production networks, the women in our study defy their contextual embeddedness including male domination, authority, institutional norms and barriers, rather than succumb to them.

Following this introduction, the paper starts by reviewing the literature on defiance, resistance and women's entrepreneurship, and the contextual embeddedness of displaced women entrepreneurs. Next we describe the Jordanian context where the research was conducted, and the methodology adopted, before progressing to the research findings relating to the participants' defiance exhibited in proactiveness, innovativeness and risk-taking in founding and maintaining their hidden network and nurturing the entrepreneurship of displaced women. Next we discuss the implications of these findings for advancing entrepreneurship scholarship, before concluding with future research directions focused upon understanding what contextual embeddedness means for invisible, marginalized communities.

Defiance, resistance and women's entrepreneurship

Defiance is the daring and bold disobedience towards authoritarian regimes such as patriarchy, and/or opposition to forces such as established cultural norms. Defiance is active, explosive and volatile and cannot be passive or placid. It is exercised through dismissing prescriptions, challenging and/or contesting imposed institutional norms (Pache and Santos 2010). As such, defiance differs from resistance which involves efforts to oppose or refuse to cooperate with, or submit to abusive behaviour and control (Profitt 1996). While resistance can be active (Kandiyoti 1988) and explosive (see Kark 2004), it can also be passive when the aim is to overcome or circumvent barriers and unfavourable norms (Javadian and Singh 2012). Resistance may not involve rejecting or eliminating constraints, whilst defiance necessarily involves a higher behavioural intensity, such as the downright rejection of constraints (Pache and Santos 2010). Defiance involves a deeper level of action and intensity and represents a more active form of resistance (Welter and Smallbone 2010).

We define entrepreneurship as an act of defiance that can create new opportunites and execute in uncertain and unknowable environments, to generate economic, social and personal value (Neck and Greene 2011). Defiance is implicit in Schumpeterian notions of 'creative destruction', whereby entrepreneurship disrupts the existing equilibrium by shifting economic activity by engaging in innovation which disrupts the status quo. Similarly, women's entrepreneurship can be an act of defiance althouth it has rarely been framed as such. In other research arenas, female defiance has featured within domestic violence (Koss 2000), feminist scholarship and activism (Murphy 2015) and art (Chhiba 2013). Research on women's corporate careers, and pathways to leadership in education, has also focused on defiance. Curry (2000) for example, showed how women con-structed themselves as leaders by defying the traditional, male-dominated cultural norms to move towards self-efficacy in the workplace. Similarly, Basit (1996) highlighted how young British-Asian, Muslim women defied their working class location aspiring for occupations which were unambigu-ously middle class.

We position defiance as implicit and embedded in the entrepreneurial effort of 'breaking up' perceived constraints as well as 'breaking free' from existing authority (Rindova, Barry, and Ketchen 2009), and consider entrepreneurial orientation as an attitudinal mindset manifested in the enact-ment of innovative entrepreneurial ventures. In breaking up constraints, the entrepreneur defies her comfort zone opting for *proactiveness* – defined as an opportunity-seeking and forward-looking perspective, involving acting in anticipation of future problems, needs or changes, to actively exploit environmental opportunities (Bolton and Lane 2012). Welter (2011), for example, showed that women entrepreneurs in the Ukraine use their female identity to mirror tax inspectors' perceptions of them as weak and ensure they paid minimal tax penalties. These women exploited environmental opportunities by acting in anticipation of future need (e.g. to save resources), suggesting that contractual defiance is closely associated with proactiveness. In breaking free from authority, the entrepreneur defies 'existing prescriptions' and instead opts for *innovativeness* – defined as the ability to think imaginatively and engage in new ideas and experimentation to develop novel and useful ideas (Kreiser and Davis 2010). Welter and Smallbone (2010), for example, highlight how women entrepreneurs in Uzbekistan reduced dependency on the assistance from their families by developing their own contacts – a role that widowed and young women are not traditionally expected to play. These women were able to think imaginatively and develop new solutions to enduring problems, suggesting that social defiance is closely associated with innova-tion. The entrepreneur also defies 'risk aversion' and instead opts for *risk-taking* – defined as the willingness to absorb uncertainty in the wake of an unpredictable future by taking bold action by venturing into the unknown (Bolton and Lane 2012). Jamali (2009) showed that in the context of Lebanon, women initiate new ventures in defiance of their husbands who were not entirely convinced of their ability to break through the social and patriarchal barriers and succeed. These women took bold action by venturing into the unknown, suggesting that patriarchal defiance is closely associated with risk-taking. Nevertheless, the implicit and embedded defiance in entrepre-preneurship has yet to be analytically explicated and applied to researching and understanding women's entrpreneurship. We attempt to bridge this gap within our research as we seek to analyse the entrepreneurial innovativeness, proactiveness and risk-taking of displaced women through their contractual, social and patriarchal defiance. In doing so, we offer a novel approach to analysing displaced women's contextually embedded entrepreneurship.

The contextual embeddedness of defiant displaced women entrepreneurs

The literature on women's entrepreneurship and defiance remains small and focused on women who are citizens or nationals, rather than displaced women. For example, Welter and Smallbone (2010) discussed how women in post-Soviet societies actively defied the cultural norms which ascribed them to defined feminine roles hindering their entrepreneurial activities. Similarly, Chamlou (2008) suggested that female-owned firms in the Middle East and North Africa region represent a defiance of the stereotypical societal expectations of women. The defiance of women entrepreneurs was also implicit in the case narratives from Pakistan where women established successful ventures and interacted with male entrepreneurs despite a volley of criticism from relatives and hostile attitudes from male colleagues (Goheer 2003). Similarly, defiance was implicit in Ahmad's (2011) study highlighting how women entrepreneurs in Saudi Arabia were able to compete with male counterparts who regarded them as submissive and docile.

Entrepreneurship among displaced women is more often grounded in the women's empower-ment paradigm (Goyal and Parkash 2011) which argues for greater access to, and control over, economic and social resources (Kabeer 1999). Displaced women in highly patriarchal, restrictive contexts enact their empowerment through defying their contextual embeddedness (Authors 5). For them, entrepreneurship requires defying institutional norms, social barriers and stereotypical attitudes such as social exclusion within the community and restrictions on movement (Ahmad 2011). In so doing, entrepreneurship becomes a catalyst for their defiance and subsequent empowerment, as it facilitates an otherwise unattainable success (Al-Dajani and Marlow 2013). However, given the contextual embeddedness of the structured social and gender relations, limited agency arising from the patriarchal context, and their positioning through social exclusion, impoverishment and displacement, their defiance must be camouflaged, for example through the creation of hidden, secret networks.

Not only is research on women's leadership within business networks scarce, where it has been studied the context has typically been in corporate sectors and the focus on formal networks (Hopkins et al. 2008). An exception is Torri (2012), who studied an Indian, women-led community-based enterprise and women's visible, informal networks. She argued that networks of self-help groups have particular challenges and as such must not become the paradigm in development policies for women entrepreneurs. To date, research on hidden organizing and networks is extremely limited (Stohl and Stohl 2011) and similarly, women's leadership of informal, secret or hidden networks is a rare topic (Authors 5). Given that informal networks in patriarchal contexts are generally gender exclusive, they offer rare opportunities for women's entrepreneurial leadership. A deeper understanding of how women develop and exercise their leadership at individual and organizational levels within informal, hidden entrepreneurial networks, and how this agency compares with existing conceptions of leadership that largely originate from advanced economies and corporate contexts will enhance our understanding of women's entrepreneurship in informal and developing contexts more broadly.

In reviewing influential entrepreneurship journals and their publications on Arab women in the Arab Middle East over the last 10 years, only 14 articles were found, and only 3 addressed displaced women (Al-Dajani and Marlow 2013; Al-Dajani et al 2015). To date, few studies have considered the entrepreneurial behaviours of displaced women or the defiance inherent in these. As such, this paper contributes to the literature on contextualizing women's entrepreneurship (Henry et al. 2015; Yousafzai, Saeed, and Muffatto 2015) by considering the defiance of displaced female entrepreneurs operating in the under-researched context of Jordan; a culture with influential gendered power structures where displaced women entrepreneurs are rarely recognized as entrepreneurs or entrepreneurial leaders. Given the prevalence of displaced and disadvantaged women producing traditional crafts such as embroidery in developing economies (Chamlou 2008), we consider how defiance nurtures this with strong, yet previously unacknowledged links.

The Jordanian context

Jordan ranks within the world's largest five refugee host countries (UNHCR 2016), yet it has neither ratified the 1951 United Nations Convention on the Status of Refugees, nor the 1967 Refugee Convention Protocol (Stevens 2009). However, Jordan continues to accommodate its communities from neighbouring countries that have become displaced through war and violence, offering shelter, safety and security, although its economic resources are extremely limited (Gandolfo 2012). Indeed, in the most recent Legatum Prosperity Index benchmarking wealth and wellbeing Jordan ranked 89th out of 149 countries (Legatum Prosperity Index 2016).

Jordan's population of 9.5 million includes 2.9 million displaced persons – 30.6% of the country's population (Jordan Department of Statistics 2016). Contrary to popular belief, the vast majority of the 1.4 million displaced Syrian nationals (UNHCR 2016), 300,000 displaced Iraqi nationals (Chatelard 2009) and 2 million displaced Palestinians (UNRWA 2014) reside predominantly within the capital and other urban centres such as Irbid, Mafraq and Zarqa, and not in refugee camps (Habersky 2016). All displaced nationals live legally in Jordan, but are denied full citizenship rights including employment and benefits as their residency is categorized as temporary – even when they and their descendants have lived in Jordan for decades (Stevens 2009). Legal restrictions on employment, coupled with Jordan's high unemployment rate (Fanek 2015), have largely confined the economic activity of displaced persons to the boundaries of the informal economy (Al-Dajani et al 2015).

In this paper, we focus on displaced Palestinian women. Displaced Palestinians have resided in Jordan for over 40 years – much longer than any other displaced group. While institutional interest in Palestinians has been diverted to more recently displaced populations such as the recently arrived Syrians, this group do have one remaining support channel – over 2 million Jordanian full citizens of Palestinian origin (UNRWA 2010) who generally arrived in Jordan pre-1967, and their offspring (Gandolfo 2012).

Methodology

Discovering, accessing and infiltrating hidden populations is challenging, with complex ethical research implications (Minkler and Wallerstein 2010). A hidden population is defined by Heckathorn (1997, 174) as a population where 'no sampling frame exists and public acknowledgment of membership in the population is potentially threatening' to members. We define the collaborative secret production network that emerged in this study as a hidden population since there are no available data on its existence, the overall number of women engaged within it as producers and consumers is unknown except to the five founders and leaders of the network and there exist genuine social and economic threats to its participants if they were identified.

Snowballing strategies are often used and recommended (Liamputtong 2006) for accessing hidden populations as is targeted sampling (Goodman 2011). These approaches however are suitable when the existence of the hidden population is already known to the researcher. Approaches for discovering unknown, invisible and hidden populations remain rare in the available exploratory research methodologies literature. As we were unaware of the existence of the collaborative secret production network when we embarked on this research, the adopted long-itudinal approach was fundamental in revealing this as it fostered trust between the participants and the lead researcher. The Arabic-speaking lead researcher conducted the interviews and gained the participants' trust as they became more familiar with her as they progressed from one interview to the next. The existence of the collaborative secret production network was revealed by its five founders 3 years after the initial interviews were conducted. Given the research benefits of long-itudinal methodologies and their limited implementation in entrepreneurship research, especially in developing and emerging economies, there are encouraging calls for their adoption in entre-preneurship research (Al-Dajani et al 2015; Kiss, Danis, and Cavusgil 2012).

The participants

At the start, 27 organizations contracting displaced home-based women producers operating in Jordan were approached to participate in a study exploring women's empowerment and entre-preneurship and to provide access to their home-based displaced, Palestinian women producers. Eight organizations agreed, and to avoid their potential bias in participant selection, the researcher attended each participating organization to greet the home-based producers as they arrived to deliver their products and invited them to participate. This method proved to be most effective in securing agreement to individual interviews from 43 home-based displaced Palestinian women producers of whom 3 were divorced. By the completion of the study in 2007, the participants were aged between 26 and 64 years, and were mothers to an average of three children. Whilst the majority (28) had completed secondary education, 14 participants completed primary schooling only, and one participant was a university graduate. About their home-based production, by the end of the study in 2007, the participants had on average supplied their intermediary organizations for 15 years.

Data collection and the relevant discoveries

The 8-year longitudinal study comprised three consecutive stages of data collection involving semi-structured individual interviews with the 43 displaced home-based women producers culminating in a total of 129 semi-structured interviews. Stage 1 of the data collection revealed that five contracting organizations through which the participants were accessed, restricted their suppliers' engagement with other producers, clients and businesses, even when the contracts they commissioned were minimal. This finding was later verified and justified by the contracting organizations and discussed in Al-Dajani and Marlow (2010) and Al-Dajani et al (2015). While this finding was not anticipated at the design stage of the study, it was accounted for through the inclusion of relevant questions to the interview guide used in the second stage of the data collection. Overall, 28 of the 43 participating displaced home-based women producers were contracted by these five restrictive organizations. Their prospects of simply finding alternative work models were almost negligible due to their 'displaced' sociopolitical status.

By the end of the second stage of data collection, the unanticipated phenomenon of the collaborative secret production network emerged. Five participants; Jalila, Lubna, Muna, Sundos and Ghalia (alias names used) trusted and confided in the researcher by taking the decision to reveal and declare their creation and leadership of a collaborative secret production network that defies the restrictions imposed on them by contractors, families and others.

As a result, Stage 3 of the data collection focused on these women's motivations for establishing and maintaining this secret network, and their evolving defiance through their proactiveness, innovativeness and risk-taking. This shows the benefits of longitudinal research with under-researched and under-reported populations, and for revealing unexpected and emergent phenomena. Our discussion of these findings seeks to contribute to a research gap concerning the role of defiance in displaced women's entrepreneurship in developing economies and within sociopolitically displaced and marginalized populations. The secret network and its dynamics were presented in Al-Dajani et al (2015).

The founders of the secret production network

The relationships between the five network founders predated their marriages and engagement in home-based enterprise, through school, family and friends. All five women lived within the same community and were connected through birth family and friendships. Table 1 shows that Sundos was the eldest of the founders, and completed primary education only, 'to stay at home and look after my younger brothers and sisters while my parents went to work' (Sundos). Similarly, Lubna – the youngest of the founders and Sundos's cousin, also terminated her education at the end of primary school 'to help my mother and sisters with embroidering' (Lubna). In fact, Sundos was taught to embroider at the age of 9 by her aunt and proudly sold her first embroidery item at the age 13.

Table 1. Profiling the network founders and leaders.

Name	Age	Born in Jordan	Education level	Marital status	Husband also displaced person	Children	Years supplying restrictive organization
Jalila	44	No	Secondary	Divorced	Yes	1	17
Lubna	31	Yes	Primary	Divorced	Yes	2	13
Muna	42	No	Secondary	Divorced	Yes	3	18
Sundos	45	No	Primary	Married	Yes	4	13
Ghalia	34	Yes	Secondary	Married	Yes	3	11

Table 1 shows that all five displaced women had supplied their respective contracting organization for over 10 years and planned to continue. They all agreed with Muna's statement that 'through this work, I am able to know what is happening in the market, the events, the trends, the prices, the embroiderers … it helps us to keep an eye on our work and clients'.

Table 1 also shows that three of the five founders; Jalila, Lubna and Muna were divorced. In a society where divorce is both rare and frowned upon, these women faced significant social marginalization within their own communities. As Lubna explained, 'My participation in this circle is not a choice, I have to … as a divorcee where else can I get support from? How will I feed my children if I don't embroider?'

Data analysis

The qualitative thematic analysis undertaken for this paper focused on the data collected from the five displaced women network founders in Stages 2 and 3 of the longitudinal study. This allowed for an in-depth consideration of the evolution of the women's defiant proactiveness, innovativeness and risk-taking in managing and growing their hidden network to nurture the entrepreneurship of other displaced women.

Qualitative analysis software such as NVivo remains unreliable for 'right to left' languages such as Arabic. To overcome this, the Arabic-speaking lead researcher conducted the thematic analysis and first-, second- and third-order coding process (Gioia, Corley, and Hamilton 2013; Miles, Huberman, and Saldaña 2013) manually by utilizing the Arabic interview transcripts. Quotes presented in this paper were translated to English by the lead researcher, and later back-translated into Arabic by another professional bilingual Arabic – English researcher external to the research team. This practice aided the accuracy of the English translations presented in this paper.

Ethical considerations

Protecting the identities of the participants and their collaborators was paramount due to the social and economic threats of exposure. This was achieved by anonymizing all participants' identities, concealing the identities of the contracting organizations and placing an extended time lapse of 10 years between the completion of the data collection and publication. During this period, the vast majority of managerial staff within the restrictive organizations have transferred to other positions and are no longer a threat to the participants of the study. Furthermore, the restrictive organizations are now impossible to identify due to the number of new organizations that have entered the sector. In addition, given the saturation of the sector, exacerbated by the arrival of displaced Syrians in Jordan since 2011, displaced Palestinian women have become increasingly ignored, and are thus able to continue their hidden entrepreneurship away from any spotlight. Indeed, to ensure that this research did not ignite any concerns or doubts among the restrictive organizations, the researchers did not discuss the emergent theme of the hidden network with them. Consequently, while our priority is the well-being of the participants, we remain unaware of the extent of knowledge of the hidden network among the personnel of the restrictive organizations.

Findings

To critically analyse entrepreneurship and defiance amongst displaced women, the findings focus on the five founders of the secret production network, and explore the three dimensions of proactiveness, innovativeness and risk-taking, through the women's contractual, social and patriarchal defiance. In so doing, we contribute a new meaning embedded within the concept of defiance to women's entrepreneurship.

While the results show defiance as an integral characteristic of the displaced women's entrepreneurship, initially the five leaders appeared to conform to stereotypical images of poor, displaced women, subjugated and dominated within a traditionally patriarchal culture, and did not appear to emanate defiance. However, their interviews during Stages 2 and 3 of the data collection revealed unexpected insights. The ensuing results and discussion below demonstrate how entrepreneurship is a process of defiance that evolves over time, rather than a pre-existing characteristic. Table 2 also shows how proactiveness, innovativeness and risk-taking are matched with the participants' demonstrated contractual defiance, social defiance and patriarchal defiance which are embedded in the participants' various actions.

Contractual defiance

The five leaders reported motivations for proactively creating the secret network 2 years after Ghalia began supplying her restrictive organization. These were overcoming the restrictions imposed by the contracting organizations, preserving their lost heritage and providing support to each other. However, none of the women stated leadership as a motivation for establishing their network. Collectively, the stated motivations demonstrate the proactiveness, innovativeness and risk-taking of the participants in breaking the terms of their contracts (contractual defiance). They all agreed that overcoming the imposed restrictions by their contracting organizations, was a key motivating factor for establishing their hidden network. Lubna explained, 'we are the expert embroiderers and their profits depend on our work. Yet, they strangled us with their control, we had to fight back somehow or we would have given up embroidery altogether'.

Not only did the five women break their own contracts with their organizations by undertaking embroidery for other clients and organizations, they recruited other women to do so and grew their secret network. Recruiting members to the secret network was simple and straightforward as described by Sundos:

> it was very natural for me to recruit other women supplying the same organisation as me, we had known each other forever, they all live nearby, we all suffer from the same frustration with the organisation, and we anyway, already helped each other out with some of the contracts.

However, monitoring and managing the growth of the network was challenging and required risk-taking as initially, the women leaders neither expected nor envisioned the apparent growth. 'We just knew that whatever we did, we had to keep our network hidden to keep ourselves and all our members safe' (Ghalia, Stage 3).

In addition to recruiting embroiderers to their secret network, the five leaders were responsible for securing clients and contracts to increase the production and profits for all their members. Given the number of years that Sundos and Muna had been embroidering, they shared an extensive list of contacts and clients and, Jalila, Ghalia and Lubna had access to unique market intelligence as the restrictive organizations they worked for are recognized throughout the Middle East region for their high-quality products. Thus, innovativeness was a critical aspect of their contractual defiance because 'when we approach potential clients, or are approached by them, they are very impressed by the quality of our work but also by how much we know about our market' (Jalila, Stage 3).

All women agreed that heritage preservation was a key motivator for contractual defiance. Ghalia's statement chimed with the four other leaders; 'we were all taught embroidery here by our mothers, aunts, neighbours, and they were taught by their grandmothers, mothers and aunts in their villages in Palestine. This art is our history and our future'. From the time when they established the secret network, the five leaders recognized that the feminised traditional embroidery sector in which they operate remains highly saturated and intensely competitive (Al-Dajani and Marlow 2010). This is explained in Lubna's statement that, 'we cannot compete with them [contracting organisations] openly, they will eat us alive!' Whilst the five leaders were defeating their restrictive organizations through their growing secret network, they were also terrified from their powerlessness, but nevertheless, took the risks. Overcoming this powerlessness through supporting each other was also a motivating factor for contractual defiance. Sundos and Ghalia

Table 2. Demonstrating the links between displaced women's defiance and proactiveness, innovativeness and risk-taking.

Thematic defiance codes	Proactiveness	Innovativeness	Risk-taking
Contractual *Creating the hidden network*	'Without the embroideries we make for them, their business will fail badly. But they are also failing us badly. We had to find another way' (Ghalia, Stage 2)	'It's not like we learnt how to set up our network from being in another network, or being told by someone how to do it. It was our own idea to start with, but as the network grew, we had to create new techniques to manage it, and the members, and the organisations that employed our members … I mean we learnt together along the way … of course we made some mistakes, but we learnt from them' (Lubna, Stage 3)	'Looking back, we definitely did not have a business model for our network. We were not looking to make money from our friends or neighbours or other women like us. That still isn't our business model. We are aware of how much we can be exploited, and our model is to minimise it, definitely not for us to be part of it' (Jalila, Stage 3)
Social *Exploiting socially conventional events for alternative goals and action*	'All the women in the network consider the network as their family … we cannot find the support we give each other anywhere else, really' (Lubna, Stage 2)	'Our homes are our best hiding place as no one suspects anything. After all, we are just visiting each other, just as we are expected to!' (Jalila Stage 3)	'I never expected that I will be the confident business manager that I have become. I keep the records of each woman's work and earnings and once a month, we all meet for a coffee in the morning at someone's house – we take it in turns to host this gathering, and I pay everyone for their month's work in cash at these meetings … in the streets, no one thinks I am carrying all this cash!' (Muna, Stage 2)
Patriarchal *Mutual support between the five displaced women founders and leaders. Leading, managing maintaining and protecting the network*	'These women are my life-line. This is how marriage should be – we not only support each other, but strengthen each other too' (Jalila, Stage 2) 'Between the five of us, we know more about this sector than anyone else because within the network, we have at least 1 or 2 members contracted in each major organisation in this sector' (Muna, Stage 3)	'As our network grows, we must be stricter with quality control for everyone as it's our reputation and income. And as we grow, we become more and more selective of who we include in the network, because of this' (Sundos, Stage 2)	'The network has been my life line. Without the support from these sisters, my children and I could not have survived after my divorce. Through this work I am able to provide for my children independently of my ex or my family' (Muna, Stage 3) 'We have proven to ourselves and to the others who work with us that we can succeed by relying on ourselves only rather than being at the mercy of our husbands, or families, or employers … of course it is worth the risk' (Jalila, Stage 3)

agreed that 'we just knew that whatever we did, we had to keep our network hidden to keep ourselves and all our members safe' (Ghalia, Stage 2).

For the three divorced leaders, obtaining financial independence to provide for themselves and their children, was a key motivating factor for contractual defiance, whilst Sundos and Ghalia who remained married, enhancing their income was cited as a motivating factor for contractual defiance through the creation of their secret network.

Social defiance

Residing and operating within a collective community, the five leaders quickly identified the perfect cover for their secret production network. Each leader developed a schedule for her members, and regularly met at a different member's home. These women's social gatherings were an accepted and expected part of the local culture but the members of the secret production network dedicated this time to shared production rather than socializing. Thus, the women innovatively defied social expectations and exploited the gendered social norms. Sundos explained that

> everyone is used to seeing us going to each other's houses, they think we are preparing pastries, stuffing vine leaves or picking parsley for tabbouleh. There are no suspicions. Anyway, a few of us will be doing these things while the rest of us get on with the embroidery ... I rotate the duties depending on the embroidery stitches, number of items that need to be made and especially the cooking as some women's cooking is not as good as their embroidery!

Through these gatherings, the women shared embroidery production, childcare, cooking, and other chores to ensure that their domestic responsibilities were not overlooked as this could lead to unnecessary curiosity and questioning from the broader community. While there is no evident innovativeness in the women's embroidery since they chose to maintain the authenticity of it, the secret network itself is an indication of the women's proactiveness, innovativeness and risk-taking. Through their network, the women defied the social norms that restricted their mobility, employment, community engagement and wealth creation, and fulfilled their aim of shared financial, emotional and social support between network members. All five leaders reiterated Lubna's (Stage 3) statement that 'our network has become a fundamental of every member's life ... without it, our lives would be terrible ... we now have such strong bonds with each other, its genuine solidarity and friendship, not just work'.

Patriarchal defiance

The five leaders operated their network in a patriarchal community and culture which imposed stringent regulations to maintain the dominant gender norms. These regulations determined the women's mobility within and beyond the community, their education, employment, enterprise, wealth creation, and community engagement. Creating and maintaining a sustainable hidden network of women producers certainly challenged these patriarchal gendered norms, and the potential exposure of the network put the women at great risk. All five women agreed that the prescribed gender roles within their patriarchal community determined their actions as well as others' judgements of them. Ghalia explained, 'if my father-in-law found out that I was organising other women in our neighbourhood and working with them without the contractor's knowledge, he will immediately ask my husband to divorce me because decent and respectable women don't behave like this'. Sundos added, 'they [family members and in-laws] worry that we will challenge them and their power over us too. Of course we do this already, but what they don't know won't hurt them or us!' Thus, in creating and maintaining the secret network, the five leaders were taking a great risk with their livelihoods.

Aware of their risk-taking through their contractual, social and patriarchal defiance, the five women continued to operationalize their hidden network, and grow it secretly through a fragmentation strategy. They crafted measures to minimize the risk of their network's exposure, and continuously risked the potential exposure when recruiting new members, customers and clients. To operationalize the fragmentation strategy effectively, trust between the women leaders was critical as each was responsible for recruiting home-based producers supplying her restrictive organization.

'In this way, the women from each organisation didn't know that there were other "outsiders" involved' explained Lubna. 'This strategy was first suggested by Jalila, but we all agreed because it meant we all had the same responsibility to make it work' (Sundos).

Thus, the leaders' management approach was to fragment the overall network, and for each leader to manage and grow her pool of members. Muna explained that this was not by design:

> we didn't deliberately choose to embroider for different organisations. I'm sure none of us thought about this at the time. Now that you mention it, I guess it was meant to be, because if we all embroidered for the same organisation, we would not have met all the embroiderers and clients that we have now.

Ghalia and Lubna however, agreed that 'at the time, I definitely did not want to embroider for the same organisation as my sister's friends' (Ghalia). Ghalia explained that '... you never know what happens and the last thing I wanted is for Iman [Ghalia's sister] to find out about my work from Jalila or Muna'. Trust between the five women grew over time as they supported each other, and worked closely on establishing and growing the network. Both Ghalia and Lubna agreed that 'now it is different. I love working with all of them, they are sisters to me and we have no secrets between us' (Lubna).

The network fragmentation strategy appears effective for minimizing the risk to exposing the hidden network, for maintaining cover and controlling membership, the network operations, members' interactions with each other, and clients' access to the network. However, it may have also helped to keep the secret production network hidden from others who might be threatened by it. This included other embroiderers who were contracted by the restrictive organizations but not members of the secret production network, as well as some aid agencies operating in the women's local communities. Jalila explained that 'any benefit we receive from [aid agency] will be taken away as they will be suspicious about our income'.

For Jalila, Lubna and Muna, it was also crucial to keep the network and their leadership roles hidden from their families, in-laws and ex-husbands. Reasons given for this were both financial and sociocultural. Initially Jalila, Lubna and Muna's reasoning appeared to be financial, as stated by Lubna:

> by law, my ex-husband has to give me a child support allowance which is based on his income and mine. If he discovers my real income, he will take me to court and I will lose the little he gives me.

However, it quickly became apparent that all three women were more concerned with maintaining their ex-husbands' commitment to their children as Muna explained; 'by paying the little he does every month, he stays connected to his children and his responsibilities towards them. By law and in Islam, he is expected to provide for his children even if we are divorced'.

The fragmentation strategy appears to be effective in minimizing the risk of exposure of the hidden network. To date, none of the 'cells' of the secret production network have been exposed, but if one or more were to be, the fragmentation strategy would limit further exposure and damage. Evidently, the five leaders were extremely aware and knowledgeable of their community's gendered social norms, roles and expectations, and strategically navigated these to protect themselves from any damaging consequences of potential exposure of the network. Not only did they take a great risk in creating and maintaining their hidden network, they also proactively strategized to minimize any risk to the network and its members. For example, the leaders relied on their embroidery expertise when communicating with potential clients, and never disclosed their secret production network. Sundos explained, 'all our clients expect only one embroidery expert working on their items. They all say I want you to do this for me because you are the best', Ghalia (Stage 2) added, 'because we have this specialist reputation to maintain, we have to be very strict with the quality control of all the embroiderers, and that is why we are very choosey about who we include in our network'. Thus, through their effective organizing, fragmentation strategy, leadership, and risk-taking, these women continued to secure their network's positioning, at least for the near future. The continued success of the network is, however, dependent on the leaders' ongoing collective contractual, social and patriarchal defiance through which, their entrepreneurial leadership thrives.

Discussion and conclusion

While the literature on women's entrepreneurship largely neglects defiance, the evidence presented in this paper illustrates that the defiance of displaced women entrepreneurs occurs in various guises and in unexpected contexts. The motivation for defying their contextual embeddedness was a necessity for the displaced women's evolving entrepreneurship and perhaps unexpectedly, their motivation was initially the women's willingness to help each other, and secondly, to resist and defy the restrictive organizations, families and community. The outcome of the defiance of the displaced women entrepreneurs is a feminised economy where the founding leaders and members of the secret production network and their clients as well as their restrictive organizations, involve only women converging through the medium of traditional embroidery to express their heritage. Defiance through entrepreneurship is rarely associated with displaced Arab women (Jamali 2009) and our findings about their proactiveness, innovativeness and risk-taking contradict much of the existing literature that portrays them as subservient, disempowered followers rather than defiant entrepreneurial leaders (Yamin 2013). Our findings, therefore, also contribute to this literature and policy regarding the empowerment of displaced women.

The findings revealed strong evidence of the displaced women's contractual, social and patriarchal defiance, and demonstrated how these impacted upon their proactiveness, innovativeness and risk-taking. Indeed, this evidence provides new and non-traditional meanings to mainstream entrepreneurship notions of proactiveness, innovativeness and risk-taking. The proactiveness of the displaced women entrepreneurs in creating and sustaining the secret network was essential for contractual defiance, and their innovativeness through the creative use of feminised space facilitated their social defiance. Through their fragmentation strategy, management and growth of their secret production network, the women took great risks in defying the patriarchal culture in which they operated by creating economic and social independence for themselves and their members.

These findings show how displaced women can envision and enact a strategic and institutionally defiant solution through the creation and management of their secret production network. At the economic level, they offered high-quality products which maintained client relationships. At the social level, they forged secret relationships which further deepened their trust, collaboration, organizing and friendship. At the institutional level they not only created parallel networks to their existing contracts, but also fragmented the network size to keep it manageable and hidden. The women also used to their entrepreneurial advantage the existing social norms for example by meeting in social gatherings. At the familial level, some did not disclose their secret production network to their husbands, in-laws and family members, and an important part of this was the balance they created between their work and family responsibilities.

We firstly contribute to contextualizing displaced women's entrepreneurship by theorizing it within a deeply patriarchal context. Our theorization shows that displaced women's entrepreneurship exists within unexpected places such as highly constrained, deeply patriarchal and masculinized contexts. Whilst the displaced women could not alter the constraints themselves, they creatively circumvented and navigated them by initiating highly imaginative ventures and ingenious strategies in hidden entrepreneurial practices. This suggests that no matter how constrained the context, displaced women entrepreneurs can flourish and prosper if they are prepared to take higher levels of risk through 'hidden' entrepreneurial enactment. Thus, the displaced women's entrepreneurship cannot be restrained, and eventually 'finds its way'.

Secondly, we contribute to entrepreneurship scholarship by extending current understandings of how displaced women defy their contextual embeddedness through entrepreneurship. The three dimensions of entrepreneurial orientation – proactiveness, innovativeness and risk-taking – are matched with the participants' demonstrated contractual, social and patriarchal, defiance which are embedded in the participants' various actions. Hence, we theorize displaced women's entrepreneurial orientation as an act of defiance to break up constraints and break free from authority, to create and execute new opportunities in uncertain and unknowable environments, and to generate value (economic, social, personal).

Although displaced women in both hidden and visible networks are rarely associated with defiance in the existing discourse (Al-Dajani et al 2015), this paper shows how displaced women can be entrepreneurial, proactively and innovatively defying the institutions that impose limitations and restrictions on them. Doing so raises significant implications for women's entrepreneurship policy and practice. That is, women's entrepreneurship is generally enacted as a strategy to include, embed and rehabilitate socially marginalized women, and to thwart rather than encourage their defiance. As such, recognizing that defiance is an effective catalyst for women's entrepreneurial orientation will require considerable change in mainstream programmes supporting women's entrepreneurship, whether the women are displaced or not.

We are not convinced that the secret production networks, the displaced women's hidden leadership within them, and their defiance, are unique to the displaced women participating in this study (Al-Dajani et al 2015). Rather, these are likely to be established amongst various communities of entrepreneurs, but remain an under-researched phenomenon (Scott 2013) due to the methodological complexities in identifying and engaging 'defiant entrepreneurs' who deliberately choose to remain hidden. Thus, we recommend that future research adopts longitudinal approaches to explore the defiance embedded in entrepreneurship in unexpected places and spaces, to enrich the contextual embeddedness of women's entrepreneurship. Indeed, doing so will not only deepen our understanding and theorizing of women's entrepreneurship, but also of entrepreneurship more broadly.

Disclosure statement

No potential conflict of interest was reported by the authors.

References

Ahmad, S. Z. 2011. "Evidence of the Characteristics of Women Entrepreneurs in the Kingdom of Saudi Arabia: An Empirical Investigation." *International Journal of Gender and Entrepreneurship* 3 (2): 123–143. doi:10.1108/17566261111140206.

Al-Dajani, H., S. Carter, E. Shaw, and S. Marlow. 2015. "Entrepreneurship among the Displaced and Dispossessed: Exploring the Limits of Emancipatory Entrepreneuring." *British Journal of Management* 26 (4): 713–730. doi:10.1111/1467-8551.12119.

Al-Dajani, H., and S. Marlow. 2010. "The Impact of Women's Home-Based Enterprise on Marriage Dynamics: Evidence from Jordan." *International Small Business Journal* 28 (5): 470–487. doi:10.1177/0266242610370392.

Al-Dajani, H., and S. Marlow. 2013. "Empowerment and Entrepreneurship: A Theoretical Framework." *International Journal of Entrepreneurial Behaviour and Research* 19 (5): 503–524. doi:10.1108/IJEBR-10-2011-0138.

Basit, T. N. 1996. "'I'd Hate to Be Just a Housewife': Career Aspirations of British Muslim Girls." *British Journal of Guidance and Counselling* 24 (2): 227–242. doi:10.1080/03069889608260411.

Bird, B., and C. Brush. 2002. "A Gendered Perspective on Organizational Creation." *Entrepreneurship Theory and Practice* 26 (3): 41–66. doi:10.1177/104225870202600303.

Bolton, L. D., and M. D. Lane. 2012. "Individual Entrepreneurial Orientation: Development of a Measurement Instrument." *Education+ Training* 54 (2/3): 219–233. doi:10.1108/00400911211210314.

Chamlou, N. 2008. *The Environment for Women's Entrepreneurship in the Middle East and North Africa Region*. Washington, DC: The World Bank.

Chatelard, G. 2009. *Migration from Iraq between the Gulf and Iraq Wars (1990–2003): Historical and Socio-Spatial Dimensions*. Working Paper 09-68, COMPAS - Centre on Migration, Policy and Society (Oxford University)..

Chhiba, R. D. 2013. "Images of Kali as Reflections of Female Defiance within Selected Examples of Contemporary Asian Arts." Doctoral dissertation, University of the Witwatersrand, Johannesburg.

Curry, B. K. 2000. *Women in Power: Pathways to Leadership in Education*. New York, NY: Teachers College Press.

Fanek, F. 2015. "Economic Growth and Unemployment." *Jordan Times*, December 28.

Gandolfo, L. 2012. *Palestinians in Jordan - the Politics of Identity*. London: IB Tauris.

Gioia, D. A., K. G. Corley, and A. L. Hamilton. 2013. "Seeking Qualitative Rigor in Inductive Research Notes on the Gioia Methodology." *Organizational Research Methods* 16 (1): 15–31. doi:10.1177/1094428112452151.

Goheer, N. A. 2003. *Women Entrepreneurs in Pakistan*. Geneva: International Labour Organization.

Goodman, L. A. 2011. "Comment: On Respondent-Driven Sampling and Snowball Sampling in Hard-to-Reach Populations and Snowball Sampling Not in Hard-to-Reach Populations." *Sociological Methodology* 41 (1): 347–353. doi:10.1111/j.1467-9531.2011.01242.x.

Goyal, M., and J. Parkash. 2011. "Women Entrepreneurship in India – Problems and Prospects." *International Journal of Multidisciplinary Research* 1 (5): 195–207.

Habersky, E. 2016. "The Urban Refugee Experience in Jordan." *Muftah*. Accessed 21 Febuary 2017. http://muftah.org/the-urban-refugee-experience-in-jordan/#.WKxvIG-LTIW

Heckathorn, Douglas D. 1977. "Respondent-driven Sampling: A New Approach to the Study of Hidden Populations." *Social Problems* 44 (2): 174–199.

Henry, C., L. Foss, A. Fayolle, E. Walker, and S. Duffy. 2015. "Entrepreneurial Leadership and Gender: Exploring Theory and Practice in Global Contexts." *Journal of Small Business Management* 53 (3): 581–586. doi:10.1111/jsbm.2015.53.issue-3.

Hollenbeck, G. P., M. W. McCall Jr, and R. F. Silzer. 2006. "Leadership Competency Models." *The Leadership Quarterly* 17 (4): 398–413. doi:10.1016/j.leaqua.2006.04.003.

Hopkins, M. M., D. A. O'Neil, A. Passarelli, and D. Bilimoria. 2008. "Women's Leadership Development Strategic Practices for Women and Organizations." *Consulting Psychology Journal: Practice and Research* 60 (4): 348–365. doi:10.1037/a0014093.

Jamali, D. 2009. "Constraints and Opportunities Facing Women Entrepreneurs in Developing Countries." *Gender and Management: an International Journal* 24 (4): 232–251. doi:10.1108/17542410910961532.

Javadian, G., and R. P. Singh. 2012. "Examining Successful Iranian Women Entrepreneurs: A Exploratory Study." *Gender in Management: an International Journal* 27 (3): 148–164. doi:10.1108/17542411211221259.

Jordan Department of Statistics. 2016. *Annual Statistical Jordan Yearbook*. Amman: Department of Statistics.

Kabeer, N. 1999. "Resources, Agency, Achievements: Reflections on the Measurement of Women's Empowerment." *Development and Change* 30 (3): 435–464. doi:10.1111/dech.1999.30.issue-3.

Kandiyoti, D. 1988. "Bargaining with Patriarchy." *Gender & Society* 2 (3): 274–290. doi:10.1177/089124388002003004.

Kark, R. 2004. "The Transformational Leader: Who Is (S)He? A Feminist Perspective." *Journal of Organisational Change Management* 17 (2): 160–176. doi:10.1108/09534810410530593.

Kiss, A. N., W. M. Danis, and S. T. Cavusgil. 2012. "International Entrepreneurship Research in Emerging Economies: A Critical Review and Research Agenda." *Journal of Business Venturing* 27 (2): 266–290. doi:10.1016/j.jbusvent.2011.09.004.

Koss, M. P. 2000. "Blame, Shame, and Community: Justice Responses to Violence against Women." *American Psychologist* 55 (11): 1332–1343. doi:10.1037/0003-066X.55.11.1332.

Kreiser, P. M., and J. Davis. 2010. "Entrepreneurial Orientation and Firm Performance: The Unique Impact of Innovativeness, Proactiveness, and Risk-Taking." *Journal of Small Business & Entrepreneurship* 23 (1): 39–51. doi:10.1080/08276331.2010.10593472.

Legatum Prosperity Index. 2016. Accessed 27 September 2017. http://www.prosperity.com/rankings

Liamputtong, P. 2006. *Researching the Vulnerable: A Guide to Sensitive Research Methods*. London: Sage.

Miles, M. B., A. M. Huberman, and J. Saldaña. 2013. *Qualitative Data Analysis: A Methods Sourcebook*. London: Sage.

Minkler, M., and N. Wallerstein, Eds. 2010. *Community-Based Participatory Research for Health: From Process to Outcomes*. San Francisco: Wiley.

Murphy, R. 2015. "Elizabeth Barton's Claim: Feminist Defiance in Wolf Hall." *Frontiers: A Journal of Women Studies* 36 (2): 152–168. doi:10.5250/fronjwomestud.36.2.0152.

Neck, H. M., and P. G. Greene. 2011. "Entrepreneurship Education: Known Worlds and New Frontiers." *Journal of Small Business Management* 49 (1): 55–70. doi:10.1111/jsbm.2011.49.issue-1.

Pache, A.-C., and F. Santos. 2010. "When Worlds Collide: The Internal Dynamics of Organisational Responses to Conflicting Institutional Demands." *Academy of Management Review* 35 (3): 455–476.

Profitt, N. J. 1996. "'Battered Women' as 'Victims' and 'Survivors': Creating Space for Resistance." *Canadian Social Work Review/Revue Canadienne de Service Social* 13: 23–38.

Rindova, V., D. Barry, and D. J. Ketchen. 2009. "Entrepreneuring as Emancipation." *Academy of Management Review* 34 (3): 477–491. doi:10.5465/amr.2009.40632647.

Scott, C. R. 2013. *Anonymous Agencies, Backstreet Businesses, and Covert Collectives: Rethinking Organisations in the 21st Century*. Stanford, CA: Stanford University Press.

Stevens, D. 2009. "Legal Status, Labelling, and Protection: The Case of Iraqi 'Refugees' in Jordan." *International Journal of Refugee Law* 25 (1): 1–38. doi:10.1093/ijrl/eet001.

Stohl, C., and M. Stohl. 2011. "Secret Agencies: The Communicative Constitution of a Clandestine Organization." *Organisation Studies* 32 (9): 1197–1215. doi:10.1177/0170840611410839.

Torri, M. C. 2012. "Community Gender Entrepreneurship and Self-Help Groups: A Way Forward to Foster Social Capital and Truly Effective Forms of Participation among Rural Poor Women?" *Community Development Journal* 47 (1): 58–76. doi:10.1093/cdj/bsq019.

UNHCR. 2016. *Global Trends: Forced Displacement in 2015*. Geneva: United Nations High Commission for Refugees.

UNRWA. 2010."Jordan Facts." Accessed 15 January 2014. http://www.unrwa.org/etemplate.php?id=66

UNRWA. 2014. "Where We Work." Accessed 21 Febuary 2017. https://www.unrwa.org/where-we-work/jordan

Welter, F. 2011. "Contextualizing Entrepreneurship—Conceptual Challenges and Ways Forward." *Entrepreneurship Theory and Practice* 35 (1): 165–184. doi:10.1111/etap.2011.35.issue-1.

Welter, F., and D. Smallbone. 2010. "The Embeddedness of Women's Entrepreneurship in a Transition Context." In *Women Entrepreneurs and the Global Environment for Growth: A Research Perspective*, edited by C. G. Brush, A. De Bruin, E. Gatewood, and C. Henry, 96–117. Cheltenham and Northampton, MA: Edward Elgar.

Yamin, A. 2013. "Jordan Third Largest Refugee Host Worldwide — UNHCR." *Jordan Times*, December 31, Amman–Jordan.

Yousafzai, S. Y., S. Saeed, and M. Muffatto. 2015. "Institutional Theory and Contextual Embeddedness of Women's Entrepreneurial Leadership: Evidence from 92 Countries." *Journal of Small Business Management* 53 (3): 587–604. doi:10.1111/jsbm.2015.53.issue-3.

Women in the migrant economy. A *positional* approach to contextualize gendered transnational trajectories

María Villares-Varela ⓘD and Caroline Essers

ABSTRACT

Drawing on the life histories of migrant women entrepreneurs in the Netherlands and Spain, this article explores the influence of transnational trajectories on their social positions and business strategies. A *translocational positional* approach enables us to research the transnational strategies of women entrepreneurs more effectively in addition to examining the changes in social positions and gendered identities between the country of origin and the country of destination. This approach contributes to scholarship on 'context' by offering a transnational gendered dimension in relation to the effects of social, spatial and institutional factors. Our findings demonstrate how female migrant entrepreneurs redefine their social status in different contexts by establishing a business and challenge, contest or comply with gender relations in their transnational entrepreneurial journeys.

Introduction

This paper uses a translocational positionality approach (Anthias 2002, 2008) to understand the business strategies of female migrant entrepreneurs[1] in relation to context (Welter 2011; Welter, Brush, and de Bruin 2014). Connecting the migrant entrepreneurship literature (Kloosterman 2010; Jones et al. 2014) with feminist scholarship (Essers and Benschop 2009; Essers, Benschop, and Doorewaard 2010; Villares-Varela 2017), we propose a *positionality* approach to enhance our understanding of the transnational (Vertovec 2004) trajectories of migrant women entrepreneurs.

While scholarship studying migrant enterprises has focused on the drivers and outcomes of this type of labour incorporation, feminist scholarship has examined the specific experiences of women in the migrant economy (for a detailed review see Villares-Varela, Ram, and Jones 2017). However, this body of research tends to be circumscribed by specific national boundaries and lacks contextualized insights into the transnational experiences of female migrant entrepreneurs. The complexities arising from a transnational approach reinforce the importance of 'context' in research on entrepreneurship by offering a gendered transnational dimension to it. Fayolle et al. (2015) accentuated the need for a 'contextualised' approach to study women entrepreneurs, given the crucial role of historical context in shaping the hierarchies that condition the processes and outcomes in which women are embedded. The core contributions to the studies of 'context' (Welter 2011; Zahra, Wright, and Abdelgawad 2014) have stressed the importance of social, institutional and spatial factors. This focus is particularly challenging when studying female migrant entrepreneurs: their lived experiences relate to a multiplicity of contexts (e.g. country of origin and destination), contradictory social positions (e.g. different class positions in the countries of origin and destination) and shifting references in terms of gender ideologies.

Departing from intersectionality (Crenshaw 1991; Holvino 2010; Cho, Crenshaw, and McCall 2013), a positionality approach helps to understand the transnational character of women's entrepreneurial strategies and the transformation of their social positions in time and space. This transnational perspective responds to the call by Metcalfe and Woodhams (2012) for more research on the implications of the variability of social identities across time and space (Metcalfe and Woodhams 2012, 133) and on integrating accounts on the gendered geographies of power (Mahler and Pessar 2001) into management studies.

Drawing on the life histories of migrant entrepreneurs from Latin American and Turkey in Spain and the Netherlands, respectively, this paper illustrates: (i) the entrepreneurial strategies that migrant women utilize in a transnational space; (ii) the transformation of social and (iii) gendered positions between the country of origin and the country of destination. This article's theoretical contribution is threefold: first, the article contributes to contextualizing the experiences of women in a multiplicity of contexts (spatial and temporal). Second, the paper enhances current migrant entrepreneurship accounts by addressing the overlooked gendered structures that shape women's work in the migrant economy.[2] Finally, it refines intersectionality theory by considering shifting social positions in time and space.

This paper is structured as follows: the next section is concerned with how the literature on migrant entrepreneurship has overlooked gendered structures, approaches from feminist scholarship and the question of transnationalism. After that, we introduce the concept of translocational positionality to examine the relational and power dimensions in entrepreneurship. We then discuss the methodology, followed by the findings section, which showcases how translocational positionality helps analysing the entrepreneurial strategies of female migrant entrepreneurs. Finally, the article discusses the findings and their theoretical implications, followed by conclusions.

Contextualizing transnationalism and the social positions of migrant women entrepreneurs

In an era of increased mobility identified as the 'age of migration' (Castles, de Haas, and Miller 2014), women compose half of the international migrants worldwide (United Nations and OECD 2013). Migrants largely participate in the labour market of their destination countries as employees, but also play a significant role as entrepreneurs, creating on average 1.8 jobs in the OECD countries and with higher overall self-employment rates than nationals (OECD 2011). Migrant women also engage in business ownership, either as the sole entrepreneur or as contributor to family business ventures. However, migrant entrepreneurship literature has rarely considered the gendered social structures that shape this type of labour incorporation (Ram, Jones, and Villares-Varela 2017).

Scholarly research emphasizing the importance of 'context' maintains that considering context allows us to grasp the effects of the social, spatial and institutional factors on entrepreneurship (Welter 2011; Zahra, Wright, and Abdelgawad 2014; Fayolle et al. 2015). Such accounts understand context as both facilitating and constraining entrepreneurship (Welter 2011) and ought to incorporate the specificities of spatial, institutional and social embeddedness in which gender norms hold sway (Welter, Brush, and de Bruin 2014). As rightly noted by Welter, Brush, and de Bruin (2014), gender roles are embedded in specific contexts and may prescribe entrepreneurial behaviour. These authors highlighted how, for example, for migrant women, more traditional gender norms from their countries of origin may affect their entrepreneurial behaviour in their destination countries in which the women must navigate different social settings (Welter, Brush, and de Bruin 2014). Nonetheless, extant accounts conceptualize context confined to particular national/local boundaries and do not consider its transnational nature.

Deconstructing transnational trajectories for women entrepreneurs

Feminist scholarship has emphasized the 'gender-blindness' of migrant entrepreneurship when analysing the nature of the migration processes in supplying a female labour force to work in addition to the gendered nature of work and employment in these firms (Phizacklea 1988). Literature has examined the effects of patriarchal relations on women's contributions to migrant family firms (Anthias and Mehta 2003, Essers and Tedmanson 2014) as well as their paths to integration and empowerment as sole entrepreneurs (Essers and Benschop 2007). Rindova, Barry, and Ketchen (2009) coined the term 'entrepreneuring', which entails bringing about a 'new state of economic, social, institutional and cultural environments through the actions of an individual or group of individuals' (Rindova, Barry, and Ketchen 2009, 4). As such, entrepreneurship can be a pursuit of freedom and independence ('*breaking free* and *breaking up*' in Rindova, Barry, and Ketchen 2009, 9), a manner of disrupting the status quo and changing one's position in the social order (Rindova, Barry, and Ketchen 2009, 6). Although these accounts contribute to our understanding of women entrepreneurs, the stories tend to focus on how gender representations are enacted within particular nation-state boundaries. To enhance this field, we draw on accounts from the sociology of migration and geography examining transnationalism (Glick Schiller 1999; Vertovec 2004; Rouse 1992).

Transnationalism has been understood as '[...] the political, economic, social and cultural processes that extend beyond the borders of a particular state, include actors that are not states, but are shaped by the policies and institutional practices of states' (Glick Schiller 1999, 96). The literature on transnationalism and migrant entrepreneurship has primarily examined the way migrant entrepreneurs engage in economic activities that transcend national borders (Landolt 2001; Portes, Guarnizo, and Haller 2002; Jones, Ram, and Theodorakopoulos 2010) by examining financial services, the import/export of goods, cultural enterprises that reproduce practices from the places of origin and/or the opening of businesses in the countries of origin. However, these accounts have not extensively examined how gender and other social positions are being (re) produced within transnational spaces for migrant entrepreneurs. One notable exception is the use of transnational feminism to grasp the experiences of women entrepreneurs of Indian origin in New Zealand (Pio and Essers 2014).

Considering the manner in which identities are shaped by the experiences of origin and destination has also been reflected in concepts such as 'bifocality' in Rouse (1992) and the 'transnational habitus' in Guarnizo (1997). Vertovec (2004) explained how a transnational perspective sheds light on the orientation of migrants' lives, which are lived 'here-and-there' (Vertovec 2004, 970). Therefore, a transnational lens examining migrant women's entrepreneurship adds new questions regarding the context (Welter 2011; Welter, Brush, and de Bruin 2014) in which migrant entrepreneurs are embedded into countries of destination, origin or both simultaneously.

Power and social positions

Given this complexity, how do we identify the multiplicity of dimensions and social positions in which female migrant entrepreneurs are embedded? The postmodern critique of the theoretical foundations of feminism has contributed to re-thinking categories of difference. 'Intersectionality' was coined by Crenshaw (1991) to elucidate the oppression of black women in the interaction of race and gender. This concept originally sought to do justice to the experiences of women of colour, which cannot be compared with white women's experiences nor understood by white feminism (Holvino 2010, 252).

The case studies of women in the migrant economy have also utilized this theoretical lens to grasp the intersection of multiple alignments of difference (education, religion, gender, ethnicity, disability) (Anthias and Mehta 2003; Valdez 2016), and have also explained how they 'do' entrepreneurship with regard to their various stakeholders (Essers and Benschop 2007; Essers, Benschop, and Doorewaard 2010). However, this lens rarely considers a transnational perspective. A translocational positionality approach departs from an intersectional stance by incorporating a more dynamic approach to difference. As explicated by Anthias (2002), a 'translocational positionality is one structured by the interplay of different locations relating to gender, ethnicity, race and class (among others), and their at times *contradictory* effects' (Anthias 2002, 275). Anthias (2008) argued that:

> [p]ositionality combines a reference to social position (as a set of effectivities: as outcome) and social positioning (as a set of practices, actions and meanings: as process). That is, positionality is the space at the intersection of structure (social position/social effects) and agency (social positioning/meaning and practice). The notion of 'location' recognises the importance of context, the situated nature of claims and attributions and their production in complex and shifting locales [...] The term 'translocational' references the complex nature of positionality faced by those who are at the interplay of a range of locations and dislocations in relation to gender, ethnicity, national belonging, class and racialization. (Anthias 2008, 15–16) – originally underlined

In the following sections, we demonstrate how such an approach can be used to analyse the strategies and experiences of female migrant entrepreneurs.

Methodology, data and context of the research

This paper draws on the life histories of migrant women entrepreneurs in the Netherlands and Spain. Interviews in Spain were conducted with 25 migrant women, from Latin American countries (Argentina, Uruguay, Venezuela and Colombia) as a component of a larger project on families of migrant entrepreneurs.[3] These entrepreneurs are first-generation migrants who ran small businesses in the service sector. The majority of these businesses were cafes, hair salons, laundrettes, clothing shops, grocery stores and bakeries. In the Netherlands, 10 interviews were conducted with female Turkish migrant entrepreneurs as a component of another larger project studying Moroccan and Turkish women entrepreneurs who established their businesses in the Netherlands.[4] The interviews analysed in this paper were obtained from first-generation migrants active in various businesses, such as hairdressers, children's day care facilities and bathing houses; some women were lawyers or consultants.

Although the data analysed were derived from two different projects, the interviewees' characteristics provided consistency to the sample and to the analysis of the data: in both countries, the interviewees were migrant women who had been entrepreneurs for more than a year at the time of the interview. The women were contacted through a wide range of stakeholders such as migrant associations, council services, business owners and informal contacts of the authors, with the goal of diversifying the profiles of the interviewees. After establishing the initial contacts, chain sampling (Penrod et al. 2003) was used to contact new entrepreneurs. This method is particularly useful to access hard-to-reach populations. The trust provided by known contacts of previous interviewees is crucial to provide a safe setting in which to participate in the interview and express the experiences and thoughts linked to the migration and business experiences. Interviewees narrated their lives, migration and family trajectories and focused particularly on the entrepreneurial process (opportunities, challenges, identity, management practices, connections with the country of origin, aspirations for the future).

One female researcher in Spain and one in the Netherlands, of Spanish and Dutch nationality, respectively, conducted the interviews. Interviews were transcribed verbatim and analysed using categorical content analysis. The outsider positions of the interviewers with regard to the migrant origin of the interviewees likely affected the emphasis the interviewees placed on illustrating their past lives in their countries of origin and the current arrangements in their destination countries. The insider position of the interviewers (also women) facilitated the narratives regarding the commonalities of enabling and constraining experiences of being a woman with regard to family and employment for the interviewees.

The content analysis of the entire sample captured patterns regarding transnational trajectories, social positions and entrepreneurship. Both authors discussed their findings of the content analysis carried out separately and compiled a list of emerging themes that were pertinent to the paper's goals. These discussions led to a selection of the two most illuminating and articulate stories per country in which these transnational trajectories and entrepreneurship occurred, highlighting converging and diverging narratives and the importance of context. Both authors evaluated the narratives of one another's cases to assure the cross-comparability of the analyses and discussed the interpretations.

Context

Regarding the contexts of data collection, Spain, and the Netherlands to a lesser extent, are both immigration countries with a colonial past. Although Turkey was not a Dutch colony, it is argued that the acquisition and treatment of Turkish guest workers is in fact a phenomenon that closely resembles certain aspects of colonialism (Essers and Tedmanson 2014). Turkish men emigrated in the 1960s and 1970s to fill jobs at the lower end of the labour market, and later family reunification resulted in women moving to the Netherlands as well. The women interviewed for this article emigrated in the context of this migration system as dependants of guest workers. Initially, because of scant contact between most 'guest workers' and the Dutch population, national opinion regarding these migrants was indifferent. However, in the 1980s, several politicians opposed the so-called multiculturalism policy, arguing that multiculturalism would entrench social divisions. Accordingly, migrants with Muslim backgrounds were attacked in the discourse against multi-culturalism in the Netherlands in the 1990s, and anti-Muslim sentiment propagated negative stereotypes of people from countries such as Turkey (Essers and Benschop 2009).

The Latin American countries the interviewees originate from have strong links with Spain that relate to post-colonial political relations with the region. The demand for Latin American migrant women grew from the 1990s because of the rapid development of the country since democracy. Latin American women conformed to the image of an ideal postcolonial worker as Catholic, Spanish-speaking who would enter domestic and care sectors that were previously occupied by women from Spanish rural areas (Martínez-Buján 2010). This preference is also reflected in more favourable migration policies (Izquierdo-Escribano and Martínez-Buján 2014), accompanied by greater acceptance of migration flows by the Spanish population because of historical migration corridors to and from Latin America, and because of similarities with Spain in language, religion and ethnicity. These ethno-cultural similarities significantly influenced the settlement of Latin American migrants in a welcoming postcolonial setting, particularly compared with other migrant groups in the country (e.g. North African migration). Despite these advantages, discrimination in the labour market persisted, reflected in the strong employment segregation in particular sectors of the economy.

Although we are aware that culturally, Turkish migrants in the Netherlands differ more from the majority population than Latin American migrants in Spain, both migrant groups are substantially different in their heritage and have other institutional and societal backgrounds. To understand the importance of transnational trajectories and context, we present the experiences of migrant women in different migration contexts. Our goal here is not to systematically compare these two cases or to generalize to the population, but to gather new theoretical insights to provide new conceptual tools in the intersection of context, female immigrant entrepreneurship and transnationalism.

Findings

The examples below illustrate how transnational trajectories affect these female migrant entrepreneurs' social positions and the manner in which the women conduct business. Our analysis focuses on three interconnected areas that reflect shifting social positions and their transnational dimension for migrant women entrepreneurs: (i) their transnational business experiences, (ii) the translation of social status and (iii) the manners in which they comply with and contest gender norms and relations.

Transnational business experiences: ties with the country of origin for developing the firm

Tullay (43) is Turkish, an atheist, and was born near the Black Sea in the north of Turkey, in Trapzon. Notably, during her childhood, she lived in the Netherlands for several years with her parents and then moved back to Turkey, married there, and then returned to the Netherlands 15 years before the time of the interview. Tullay was divorced in Turkey and recounted attempting to rebuild her life in Turkey twice. After those efforts failed, Tullay fled to the Netherlands with her three children. After an extremely difficult period, moving from one shelter to the other, she finally got her life back and set up her own sewing and clothing company. Tullay conveyed the transnational character of her business and trajectory more broadly:

> If you live in your own community, then you cannot become an entrepreneur. Then you are only in contact with your own people, but you do not speak to other groups (...) If someone asks me if I am a native or non-native, I say, 'I feel like a cosmopolitan. I don't have a national feeling because I am a Turk' (...) I sometimes speak, for instance, at the Chamber of Commerce, for ethnic minority women. I was a role model [for other non-native single mothers]. Maybe that is why they were so positive about me (...) I used to import from Turkey, but the shop is too small now to do so. (...) It was only necessary, once or twice a year, [to travel]. It is also fun to do business. Not difficult. In Istanbul you call, you are picked up, and then you get a chauffeur and a secretary and they guide you to that place. It is not that I am totally alone there; [I have] guidance from the family (...) I don't have much contact with people with a Turkish background, because Turks here are different from Turks in Turkey.

For Tullay, to be an entrepreneur means to reach out to other nationalities and other cultures, as shown by her contention that one should not confine business relations to one's own community because such a limitation reduces the likelihood of success. Despite the cosmopolitan narrative, Tullay's entrepreneurial practice is shaped by the traditional gender structures in the market exchange in Istanbul in which she must be guided by male chauffeurs and family. Although she would not easily accept being guided by males and relatives in the Netherlands, Tullay accepts such traditional gender practices in her country of origin for the sake of her entrepreneurial positionality. Tullay accepts this tradition despite her statement that she does not have significant contact with Turks because Turks in the Netherlands are different from Turks in her home country. This dichotomy reflects how her relation with being 'Turkish' is emphasized by complex identity positions. Tullay's speaking to other groups relates, moreover, to the realization that entrepreneurship is something that is conducted in its context with various stakeholders, unlike the traditional idea that entrepreneurship is an individual activity.

Natalia (29) also illustrates the importance of transnational connections in the Spanish context. Natalia emigrated from Colombia to Spain to work as a caregiver. She was divorced and left behind two children, who stayed with her mother and brother. After working in Spain for seven years, Natalia managed to save sufficient money to open a hairdressing salon that primarily targeted a Latin customer base. Natalia explained that links with her country of origin are important to supply certain business needs. The transnational contextualization of her operations indicates she activates the support of family members and their networks to purchase products at a good price. Natalia maintained that knowledge of the Colombian diaspora of hairdressing in the US is transferred back to Colombia and later utilized in her business in Spain:

> I have noticed that the diaspora in the US has accomplished very good deals for products in Colombia and the other way around. Some new techniques and products are developed in the US, particularly among African-American hairdressers. They import hair from India and other Asian countries [...]. The Colombian market has copied some of these new trends, and they have started to source some of these [...] This is thanks to the Colombians in the US [...]. Also with nail products [...] So my cousin in Colombia knows two stalls in big

markets where she gets products at a very good price and she keeps them for me, so I can get them when I go back home to visit, or she sends them with someone to Spain [...] In exchange, she keeps some of the products I pay for, and she also does some informal hairdressing at her place for neighbours and friends. [...] Because my salon is small, I don't need large quantities, so I do it through family.

It is revealing that Natalia activates her family ties in Colombia to have a competitive advantage in her business by reverse remittances of goods and knowledge. Natalia is essentially conducting business transnationally, following Portes, Guarnizo, and Haller's (2002) idea of involving family members in the country of origin and by travelling back and forth to Colombia to import goods for her business. Natalia also helps her cousin in Colombia with her informal hairdressing business. The strategies deployed in her small hairdressing salon in Spain cannot be explained without acknowledging cross-national relations, shaped by the extent and the nature of her family ties in Colombia, the supply of products through diasporic networks in the US, market exchanges in the country of origin and the solidarity among the women in Natalia's family.

Transnational space and enterprise: social status 'here and there'

For Natalia (29), opening up her business meant moving up the mobility ladder in the Spanish context and feeling emancipated from strong power relations between employer and employee. Natalia recounts how this step up provided the chance to start the paperwork to reunite with her children and liberate her mother from care duties. Natalia explained the asymmetry of her positions in her countries of destination and origin: years of sending remittances have provided a better status with regard to her family in her country of origin as opposed to strong power relations that occur in private live-in domestic work. These contradictory class positions are explained in this manner:

I send money home because my children are there. That's why it took me longer to save up enough for the business. Things are not easy. You have to pay for school fees, [and] my mother cannot take as much work as she would like to because she is taking care of them. And my brother is also there. He is unemployed, and I notice he now looks up to me, and he mentions he would like to follow my steps [in emigrating]. [...] I used to always be the one in the family deemed the 'black sheep', with being pregnant when I was too young, unlucky with my husband [...] but now I am respected. Being here, getting out of the country and sending money, now they listen to me [...] And then at work, I was tired of going from employer to employer who made very high demands on my time, only Sundays off, for not much money.

For Natalia, changing contexts transformed her social position in both spaces simultaneously: in Spain, she managed to climb the social mobility ladder by abandoning private care work and starting her own business, whereas in Colombia, Natalia reversed her position from being the 'black sheep' to becoming the central actor in a transnational household. Her transnational experience challenged hierarchical relations within her family. As a business owner, Natalia sends remittances to her mother and brother, who look up to his sister.

However, Natalia's change in social position was not achieved without cost. Because her mother cannot take as much paid employment as in the past, she is much more financially dependent on Natalia. Once again, her entrepreneurial trajectory cannot be explained merely by studying the context of the country of destination (Spain); one must look simultaneously at how the negotiation of her social positions in both country of origin and destination relates to the role the firm occupies in her trajectory.

Status is also at the core of Tullay's description of the difficulties of moving back and forth to the Netherlands:

I have led a life in which my ex [ex-husband] was the boss, but I was also my own boss. I was used to having people working for me, the nanny and cleaner (...). But after the divorce, I tried for 2 years to live in Turkey, but under the pressure of my family and my ex, I couldn't build up my own private life.... Eventually I decided to flee with my children to the Netherlands (...). Yes, we were all illegal. We found a women's shelter, stayed with acquaintances. I was entitled to nothing; I took care of my children by informal work, a bit of support from others. That's over now. Under pressure from the family, he [her ex-husband] wanted to see the kids. He was allowed to see the kids and so he kidnapped them. I was illegal so couldn't leave the country. The police were warned, Interpol, [but] they couldn't find him. Only after 5 days… I received a phone call from the Greek police…[saying] I could get the children. After that, we remained 2 years illegally and then we got our residence permit. I was on benefits, nothing for me; you sit at home and do nothing, an aimless life (…). During that time, I participated in a project that tried to emancipate women through fashion (…) Then I started to make a business plan, marketing research, knocked at the local government's door with 'Look, I have a plan. What do you think about it?' I convinced the first contact person, and then I was transferred to another department, and I convinced her too, and then I got other meetings (…). Then I got my loan and then I started.

In Tullay's situation, albeit in quite a different manner from Natalia, her emigrating from Turkey to the Netherlands implied the transformation of a different social position. In Turkey, Tullay had a middle class position, reflected in the fact that other women worked for her ('the nanny, the cleaner') whereas in the Netherlands she had to start from scratch. Although materially Tullay had nothing, what she did obtain throughout the entire process was her independence. However, this freedom was not acquired easily; the pressure from her family remained, which eventually even caused her husband to withhold their children. Starting a company is an immediate result of her wish to be self-sufficient as well as to have a goal in life. Her narrative makes clear that her transnational movements moved her from a middle class to a lower social status. However, her enterprise improved her social positioning in the Dutch context and allowed Tullay more control of her family life.

Transnational space and enterprise: unsettling (unequal) gender relations

The strategies and identities of migrant women entrepreneurs are shaped by the gendered structures embedded in transnational contexts, which occurred with Lidia (32). Lidia was born in Venezuela, worked as an accountant part time and cared for her children. She immigrated with her husband and children to Spain because of a deteriorating quality of life and fears for their safety. A favourable institutional context allowed Lidia to apply for Spanish citizenship on ancestral grounds. This benefit gave her a 'fast-track' to enter the labour market compared with other migrants in the country. However, Lidia realized that her skills were not easily transferable, given the lengthy process of validating her degree. When confronted with the limited opportunities in the labour market, Lidia decided to open up a shop that sold clothes for children. In the meantime, her husband (with a background in economics) invested in getting his degree validated. This strategy meant going to the local university for two years to complete the required credits. Lidia explained this strategy was designed to prevent the family from falling into poorly paid employment but also to maintain the productive–reproductive structure the family had enjoyed in Venezuela: her husband as well-paid bread winner and Lidia balancing child care and part-time employment.

> In Caracas, our life was perfect regarding jobs. My husband was happy; he was earning relatively well. I would do some work, but mainly took care of my children. But things started to get worse, the economy, politics […] We wanted a better place for our children […] You did not know any more if the country was becoming a new 'Cuba' [a socialist government]. There is a lot of pressure on business owners, or those who are high achievers. They are punished; there are fears of expropriation. So this is not sustainable. We want to prosper and not have limits by the government of the time […] Now here [Spain], the employment situation is limited. I have opened the shop, and it provides the basic turnover to get by. But this is temporary. When he gets a good job, I will get someone for the shop part-time, so I can only come when the children are at school.

Here, we see that with the opening of the business, Lidia is attempting to recover the gender arrangements the family had in their country of origin, where the husband was the primary breadwinner and she was working part time and taking care of the children. It is also important to note that Lidia articulates that the socialist government in Venezuela does not provide sufficient stability ('the country is becoming like Cuba') to become a successful entrepreneur. Therefore, understanding Lidia's motivations as a migrant entrepreneur in Spain must include her political positioning regarding the Venezuelan context and the reconfiguring of her family's gender and income-producing arrangements.

Cemille (47) has a consulting company that advises various organizations regarding diversity management. She depicts her background as a Kurdish girl of the Alevi religion, born in eastern Turkey.

> I was born in the Kurdish part, in Tunceli, a wonderful city. Very liberal. Within Turkey, you have various streams of Islam. The liberal stream, the Alevi, is active in Tunceli. In 1979, I moved from Tunceli to the Netherlands, Rotterdam. (...) My father was already an entrepreneur in Turkey. In 1965, he thought, I am done here. It was a small city where he lived. So he came to the Netherlands as a guest worker while he was an entrepreneur in Turkey. In 1978, my mother came and my siblings. And my other sister and I stayed in Turkey because we wanted to study. But then the war broke out there, with the Kurdish movement, and then I had to come to the Netherlands. Because I was a teenager and 15, and my parents said, this is not to be trusted, what they are going to do.... [laughs] And I was a teenager, and I was already against injustice; back then I already wanted to stand up for minorities. (...). I then learned the language... after a year I already started teaching minority women. I picked things up very quickly, I come from a very dynamic city; then you don't sit at home. I followed an education. I first did my intermediate vocational education and then polytechnic university. And in addition to this, many trainings and courses. Worked in welfare, and in 2002, I started my own company.

Notably, Cemille speaks much more positively about her hometown, her region of origin and her family than Tullay did. Cemille experienced much more freedom than Tullay, emphasizing the liberalism of her hometown, the Alevi, and her family situation. However, Cemille reported experiencing much injustice, referring to the repression of Kurdish people in Turkey, which forced Cemille to leave Turkey. In Turkey, Kurdish people compose a minority, and because of their different ethnic identity, which is expressed in different cultural and religious values and practices, as well as the quest for (more) independence, Kurds are often discriminated against and even perceived as all being terrorists by the formal government (Inquiries 2014). Her narrative indicates a continuity of social position preserving the values of liberalism and gender equality. Within her business context, Cemille capitalized on her minority background in her country of origin, Turkey, and her country of destination, the Netherlands. Notably, she acknowledges the gendered relationships in her own family: the entire family followed their father, the paterfamilias. However, Cemille also emphasized the Alevi value of gender equality, which obviously had a great effect on her family and the manner in which Cemille was able to stand up for herself and become an entrepreneur. These excerpts demonstrate we cannot understand the decision to start a business and the way entrepreneurs establish a firm only by observing the situation and context in the destination country; we must consider the multiplicity of social positions with regard to status, ethnicity, gender and family hierarchies.

Cemille, for example, referred to gender and ethnicity more explicitly:

> My father was an entrepreneur. My mother a housewife in Turkey. We lived in a very liberal city; thus the man-woman equality was very high there. But it was a very small city, so there wasn't a lot of work. Most men worked, women didn't. Yeah, it was a city in which the Turkish government doesn't invest. Because of the Kurdish background. (...)Nationalism I find a bit scary. I don't think this is necessary [...] Like, I live in the Netherlands, but tomorrow I could be in Paris! (...) When we came to the Netherlands, my father still wanted to be an entrepreneur; I have my own company, my sister has a hairdressing salon. My sister is now in Turkey; she also has a company. So it really runs in the family. Particularly the freedom is very important for me. (...) I like taking risks; that could have something to do with my Turkish background. There was some repression of course back then... I don't know. (...) We moved to a real African neighbourhood, nice, quite dynamic. You would see it is a neighbourhood in which there are no investments happening. Perhaps that's why I started my own company in this social area.

According to Cemille, the status quo was that most men worked and women did not. Cemille accepted this situation as a given because of the shortage of labour in that country at that time. However, when situations and contexts changed, she argued, women and men had identical possibilities, which should be realized. According to Cemille, freedom is an extremely important value inherited from her ethnic and religious origins and is manifested in her firm.

Discussion

This paper examined the importance of context in the transnational trajectories of female migrant entrepreneurs in Spain and the Netherlands. We observed that, entrepreneurship gave them status, although their transnational trajectories replaced one social class position with another more than once. Within these trajectories, these women challenged, contested or complied with the gender relations in their families during their transnational journeys. These different positions relate to how gender and status operate within a multiplicity of spaces, as analysed by the framework of 'gender geographies of power' (Mahler and Pessar 2001). This idea is consistent with Rindova, Barry, and Ketchen (2009) re-conceptualization of entrepreneurial activity as a means of emancipation, which views entrepreneurial endeavours as change-creating efforts by which people seek to break free from (and potentially break up) existing constraints (Jennings, Jennings, and Sharifian 2016, 81). In other instances, entrepreneurship emerges as a means of restoring gender arrangements in the country of origin and adjusting to the opportunity structure in the contexts in which they settle (Villares-Varela 2017). We synthesized the experiences of these case studies in the following perspectives of gender and social positionalities. These 'ideal types' can be identified as references to manners in which spatial and temporal contexts affect entrepreneurial strategies.

(i) *Entrepreneurship as liberation from patriarchal structures*. This experience is reflected in Tullay's narrative. Her becoming an entrepreneur was a powerful tool for reshuffling unequal gender relations with her husband and other male relatives in Turkey. Concerning social status, Tullay referred to having a good middle class position before divorcing and moving to the Netherlands, which was lost with migration. In her destination country, Tullay had to start over, beginning with nothing. Eventually, migration and entrepreneurship shifted her social positioning to greater power and equality than she had experienced in the Turkish context.

(ii) *Entrepreneurship as a means of upward social mobility and the re-configuration of gender*. Natalia's narrative shows how starting her business truly meant changing her social position in the Spanish context in which she first had to address unequal power relations at work and the financial demands of her relatives in Colombia. Her enterprise not only resulted in a stronger economic and more powerful position in Spain, but also in a more independent position in her family.

(iii) *Entrepreneurship as re-establishing social status and compliance with gender relations from the country of origin*. Unlike the previous case studies, Lidia's entrepreneurship is temporary, helping her husband regain a certain social status in Spain to enable their gender and social class positions to be restored to the more traditional arrangements the couple enjoyed in the Venezuelan context. In this case, their social status was sacrificed to restore the class-based masculinity of the husband.

(iv) *Entrepreneurship for continuity of gender equality and embracing diversity*. Finally, for Cemille, entrepreneurship appears to be a' natural', predestined position. Entrepreneurship runs in her family, and entrepreneurship is a vehicle to preserve her freedom and gender equality, two values this migrant clearly ascribes to her Alevi religion and Kurdish background. Historical and spatial contexts are crucial to her trajectory. Because these values are so important, Cemille sought to stimulate gender and ethnic equality by her diversity con-sultancy and standing up for other minorities. This type of entrepreneurial strategy can be considered a tool to safeguard and defend gender and ethnic equality.

Conclusion

This paper used a translocational positionality approach to analyse the influence of transnational trajectories on women's social positions. Using a *positionality* approach, we addressed those perspectives that stress the importance of context in entrepreneurship research. We argued that these perspectives should incorporate a transnational point of view, accounting for the multi-faceted nature of entrepreneurship for migrant women.

Using a translocational positional approach, our contribution to theory is threefold. First, the findings help advancing the conceptualization of the historical, spatial, institutional and temporal contexts of transnational women's entrepreneurship. We demonstrated how the lived experiences of women entrepreneurs ought to supersede nation-state boundaries and account for the trajectories and aspirations in both the countries of origin and the destination countries. We analysed various social positions, at times contradictory, that entrepreneurs experience in different contexts. Second, our paper enhanced the current approaches to migrant entrepreneurship by accounting for gendered structures. Thus far, the mixed embeddedness approach has examined migrant entrepreneurship in a rather gender-neutral manner and has not acknowledged how gender interferes with structures at macro, meso and micro levels (Jones, Ram, and Villares-Varela 2017). Third, this paper endeavoured to refine the theory of intersectionality by dynamically demonstrating how social positions change over time and between spaces. Intersectionality, although highly valued as a means of grasping how people are positioned in social categories of inclusion and exclusion, is occasionally criticized for addressing these issues somewhat statically (see Essers and Benschop 2009). A translocational posi-tionality approach (Anthias 2008) allowed us to address how these intersections change according to the ways in which women entrepreneurs move between a multiplicity of spaces and times.

Finally, our paper has a practical, societal contribution. Migrants are generally perceived in the global North as employees in large organizations or as dependent on welfare support. Often, women are perceived as being dependent on their male counterparts and/or as victims in their countries of origin. However, the women interviewed in this study were highly emancipated and independent, something often considered incompatible with the mainstream victimization of migrant women. Our insights indicate that migrants cannot and should not be pigeonholed as one homogeneous group and that their experiences are highly diverse and dependent on their social positions in their countries of origin and destination . In these journeys, the women often take control of their own labour market incorporation in their new societies by establishing their own businesses.

Notes

1. We use female migrant entrepreneurs as an umbrella term for women business owners who were born in a different country from where they currently live.
2. By 'migrant economy', we refer to those spaces in the market in which migrant enterprises operate, irrespec-tive of whether these take place in the countries of origin or destination.
3. This research was supported by the Spanish Ministry of Education and Science FPI grant 'Ethnic Entrepreneurship as a means of Social Integration for Migrants. Second Generation and Gender Relations', project reference SEJ 07750/SOCI. The interviews analysed in this paper were carried out by the first author.
4. This research was financed by the Dutch Ministry of Living, Quarters and Integration. The interviews analysed in this paper were carried out by the second author.

Disclosure statement

No potential conflict of interest was reported by the authors.

Funding

This research has been supported by the Spanish Ministry of Education and Science FPI grant 'Ethnic Entrepreneurship as a means of Social Integration for Migrants. Second Generation and Gender Relations', project reference SEJ 07750/SOCI; and the Dutch Ministry of Living, Quarters and Integration.

ORCID

María Villares-Varela ⓘ http://orcid.org/0000-0002-0137-7104

References

Anthias, F. 2002. "Beyond Feminism and Multiculturalism: Locating Difference and the Politics of Location." *Women's Studies International Forum* 25 (3): 275–286. doi:10.1016/S0277-5395(02)00259-5.
Anthias, F. 2008. "Thinking through the Lens of Translocational Positionality: An Intersectionality Frame for Understanding Identity and Belonging." *Translocations: Migration and Social Change* 4 (1): 5–20.
Anthias, F., and N. Mehta. 2003. "The Intersection between Gender, the Family and Self-Employment: The Family as a Resource." *International Review of Sociology* 13 (1): 112–135. doi:10.1080/0390670032000087014.
Castles, S., H. de Haas, and M. J. Miller. 2014. *The Age of Migration*. Basingstoke: Palgrave McMillan.
Cho, S., K. W. Crenshaw, and L. McCall. 2013. "Toward a Field of Intersectionality Studies: Theory, Applications, and Praxis." *Signs* 38 (4): 785–810. doi:10.1086/669608.
Crenshaw, K. W. 1991. "Mapping the Margins: Intersectionality, Identity Politics, and Violence against Women of Color." *Stanford Law Review* 43 (6): 1241–1299. doi:10.2307/1229039.
Essers, C., and D. Tedmanson. 2014. "Upsetting 'Others' in the Netherlands: Narratives of Muslim Turkish Migrant Businesswomen at the Crossroads of Ethnicity, Gender and Religion." *Gender, Work & Organization* 21 (4): 353–367. doi:10.1111/gwao.12041.
Essers, C., and Y. Benschop. 2007. "Enterprising Identities: Female Entrepreneurs of Moroccan or Turkish Origin in the Netherlands." *Organization Studies* 28 (1): 49–69. doi:10.1177/0170840606068256.
Essers, C., and Y. Benschop. 2009. "Muslim Businesswomen Doing Boundary Work: The Negotiation of Islam, Gender and Ethnicity within Entrepreneurial Contexts." *Human Relations* 62 (3): 403–423. doi:10.1177/0018726708101042.
Essers, C., Y. Benschop, and H. Doorewaard. 2010. "Female Ethnicity: Understanding Muslim Immigrant Businesswomen in the Netherlands." *Gender, Work & Organization* 17 (3): 320–339. doi:10.1111/j.1468-0432.2008.00425.x.
Fayolle, A., S. Yousafzai, S. Saeed, C. Henry, and A. Lindgreen. 2015. "Call Special Issue On: Contextual Embeddedness of Women's Entrepreneurship: Taking Stock and Looking Ahead." *Entrepreneurship and Regional Development* 27 (9–10): 670–674. doi:10.1080/08985626.2016.1099788.
Glick Schiller, N. 1999. "Transmigrants and Nation-States: Something Old and Something New in the U.S. Immigrant Experience." In *Handbook of International Migration*, edited by C. Hirshman, P. Kasinitz, and J. Dewind, 94–119. New York: Russel Sage Foundation.
Guarnizo, L. E. 1997. "The Emergence of a Transnational Social Formation and the Mirage of Return Migration among Dominican Transmigrants." *Identities Global Studies in Culture and Power* 4 (2): 281–322.
Holvino, E. 2010. "Intersections: The Simultaneity of Race, Gender and Class in Organization Studies." *Gender, Work & Organization* 17 (3): 248–277. doi:10.1111/j.1468-0432.2008.00400.x.
Inquiries 2014. "The Turkish-Kurdish Conflict in Theory and Practice." Accessed 2nd March 2017 http://www.inquiriesjournal.com/articles/862/2/the-turkish-kurdish-conflict-in-theory-and-practice.
Izquierdo-Escribano, A., and R. Martínez-Buján. 2014. "Permanence and Mobility of Latin American Immigration in Spain during the 21st Century." *Canadian Ethnic Studies* 46 (3): 103–120. doi:10.1353/ces.2014.0038.
Jennings, J. E., P. D. Jennings, and M. Sharifian. 2016. "Living the Dream? Assessing the "Entrepreneurship as Emancipation" Perspective in a Developed Region." *Entrepreneurship Theory and Practice* 40 (1): 81–110. doi:10.1111/etap.12106.
Jones, T., M. Ram, and M. Villares-Varela. 2017. "Injecting Reality into the Migrant Entrepreneurship Agenda." In *Critical Perspectives on Entrepreneurship. Challenging Dominant Discourses on Entrepreneurship*, edited by C. Essers, P. Dey, D. Tedmanson, and K. Verduyn, 125–145. Abingdon, GB: Routledge.
Jones, T., M. Ram, and N. Theodorakopoulos. 2010. "Transnationalism as a Force for Ethnic Minority Enterprise? The Case of Somalis in Leicester." *International Journal of Urban and Regional Research* 34 (3): 565–585. doi:10.1111/j.1468-2427.2010.00913.x.
Jones, T., M. Ram, P. Edwards, A. Kiselinchev, and L. Muchenje. 2014. "Mixed Embeddedness and New Migrant Enterprise in the UK." *Entrepreneurship and Regional Development* 26 (5–6): 500–520. doi:10.1080/08985626.2014.950697.
Kloosterman, R. 2010. "Matching Opportunities with Resources: A Framework for Analysing (Migrant) Entrepreneurship from a Mixed Embeddedness Perspective." *Entrepreneurship and Regional Development* 22 (1): 25–45. doi:10.1080/08985620903220488.
Landolt, P. 2001. "Salvadoran Economic Transnationalism: Embedded Strategies for Household Maintenance, Immigrant Incorporation, and Entrepreneurial Expansion." *Global Networks* 1 (3): 217–242. doi:10.1111/glob.2001.1.issue-3.

Mahler, S. J., and P. R. Pessar. 2001. "Gendered Geographies of Power: Analyzing Gender across Transnational Spaces." *Identities: Global Studies in Culture and Power* 7 (4): 441–459. doi:10.1080/1070289X.2001.9962675.

Martínez-Buján, R. 2010. *Bienestar Y Cuidados [Welfare and Care]*. Madrid: Centro Superior de Investigaciones Científicas (CSIC).

Metcalfe, B. D., and C. Woodhams. 2012. "Introduction: New Directions in Gender, Diversity and Organization Theorizing–Re-imagining Feminist Post-Colonialism, Transnationalism and Geographies of Power." *International Journal of Management Reviews* 14 (2): 123–140. doi:10.1111/j.1468-2370.2012.00336.x.

OECD. 2011. "Migrant Entrepreneurship in OECD Countries – Part II." International Migration Outlook. SOPEMI 2011. OECD Publishing, Paris.

Penrod, J., D. Preston, R. Cain, and M. Starks. 2003. "A Discussion of Chain Referral as A Method of Sampling Hard-to-Reach Population." *Journal of Transcultural Nursing* 14 (2): 100–107. doi:10.1177/1043659602250614.

Phizacklea, A. 1988. "Entrepreneurship, Ethnicity and Gender." In *Enterprising Women: Ethnicity, Economy, and Gender Relations*, edited by S. Westwood, 20–33. London: Routledge.

Pio, E., and C. Essers. 2014. "Professional Migrant Women Decentring Otherness: A Transnational Perspective." *British Journal of Managemen* 25 (2): 252–265.

Portes, A., L. E. Guarnizo, and W. J. Haller. 2002. "Transnational Entrepreneurs: An Alternative Form of Immigrant Economic Adaptation." *American Sociological Review* 67 (2): 278–298. doi:10.2307/3088896.

Ram, M., T. Jones, and M. Villares-Varela. 2017. "Migrant Entrepreneurship: Reflections on Research and Practice." *International Small Business Journal* 35 (1): 3–18. doi:10.1177/0266242616678051.

Rindova, V., D. Barry, and D. J. Ketchen. 2009. "Entrepreneuring as Emancipation." *Academy of Management Review* 34 (3): 477–491. doi:10.5465/amr.2009.40632647.

Rouse, R. 1992. "Making Sense of Settlement: Class Transformation, Cultural Struggle, and Transnationalism among Mexican Migrants in the United States." *Annals of the New York Academy of Sciences* 645 (1): 25–52. doi:10.1111/j.1749-6632.1992.tb33485.x.

United Nations and OECD. 2013. "World Migration in Figures." A joint contribution by UN DESA and the OECD to The United Nations High-Level Dialogue on Migration and Development, 3–4 October 2013; Accessed 2nd October 2016, https://www.oecd.org/els/mig/World-Migration-in-Figures.pdf

Valdez, Z. 2016. "Intersectionality, the Household Economy, and Ethnic Entrepreneurship." *Ethnic and Racial Studies* 39 (9): 1618–1636. doi:10.1080/01419870.2015.1125009.

Vertovec, S. 2004. "Migrant Transnationalism and Modes of Transformation." *International Migration Review* 38 (3): 970–1001. doi:10.1111/j.1747-7379.2004.tb00226.x.

Villares-Varela, M., M. Ram, and T. Jones. 2017. "Female Immigrant Global Entrepreneurship: From Invisibility to Empowerment?" In *The Routledge Companion to Global Female Entrepreneurship*, edited by C. Henry, T. Nelson, and K. V. Lewis, 125–145. Abingdon, GB: Routledge.

Villares-Varela, M. 2017. "Negotiating Class, Femininity and Career: Latin American Migrant Women Entrepreneurs in Spain." *International Migration*. doi:10.1111/imig.12361.

Welter, F. 2011. "Contextualizing Entrepreneurship. Conceptual Challenges and Ways Forward." *Entrepreneurship Theory and Practice* 35 (1): 165–184. doi:10.1111/etap.2011.35.issue-1.

Welter, F., C. Brush, and A. de Bruin. 2014. "*The Gendering of Entrepreneurship Context*." IfM Working Paper, 01/14, Bonn: IfM Bonn.

Zahra, S. A., M. Wright, and G. S. Abdelgawad. 2014. "Contextualization and the Advancement of Entrepreneurship Research." *International Small Business Journal* 32 (5): 479–500. doi:10.1177/0266242613519807.

Contextualizing the career success of Arab women entrepreneurs

Hayfaa A. Tlaiss

ABSTRACT

Drawing on institutional theory, this study gives voice to Arab women entrepreneurs. Through contextualization and in-depth, semi-structured interviews, I examine Lebanese women entrepreneurs' conceptualizations of career success, the mechanisms they use to realize it and their overall awareness of it. According to the findings, the entrepreneurs experience career success as an act of disobedience against socially imposed cultural and gender mandates. Furthermore, career success evolves as a contextual, dynamic process that is culturally dependent but individually negotiated, interpreted and constructed using external and internal conceptualizations. In turn, these conceptualizations are intertwined with agency and unfold as a process at the intersection of gender, patriarchy and cultural values. Accordingly, I argue against reducing career success to static, objective and subjective criteria. Doing so undermines the complexity and processual nature of the construct and neglects the importance of cultural values in shaping the understanding and experience of career success in different societies. I also stress the importance of contextualizing women's entrepreneurial experiences and demonstrate that Lebanese women entrepreneurs' conceptualizations of career success reflect both Arab social-cognitive and normative institutions and their own agency.

Introduction

The unfolding and conceptualizations of career success (CS) of organizational careerists have attracted considerable attention in management and organizational studies (Dries 2011; Hall 1996; Ituma et al. 2011; Tlaiss 2013, 2015a). However, the current entrepreneurship discourse seems to primarily investigate the success of business ventures (e.g. Katre and Salipante 2012; Kiviluoto 2013) or the economic and demographic antecedents of entrepreneurial success (Fisher, Maritz, and Lobo 2014). Advancing our understanding of how entrepreneurs, especially women entrepreneurs (WE), experience and conceptualize CS has received minimal attention (Buttner and Moore 1997; Fisher, Maritz, and Lobo 2014). In a context characterized by expectations of female weakness (Bruni, Gherardi, and Poggio 2004) and male normativity and superiority (Calás, Smircich, and Bourne 2009), the contemporary entrepreneurship discourse appears consumed with attempts to explain the lower rate of success attributes among WE and the how and why of underperformance of their entrepreneurial ventures (Buttner and Moore 1997; Marlow and Swail 2014). This problematic preoccupation risks becoming counterproductive as it perpetuates the myth of female deficits (Marlow and McAdam 2013) and fails to critically question the socially embedded gendered assumptions of the so-called female deficiency and their impact on WEs' experiences and conceptualizations of CS.

Furthermore, the entrepreneurship literature is Western-centric and geographically biased in favour of developed economies. Few studies go beyond these contexts (Welter 2011; Zahra, Wright, and Abdelgawad 2014), especially to the countries of the Arab Middle East (AME) (Al Dajani and Marlow 2010; Tlaiss 2015b, 2015c). Neglecting the experiences of WEs in non-Western contexts results in an incomplete understanding and contributes to gaps in the literature on women in entrepreneurship, leading to the decontextualization of entrepreneurship research. Furthermore, studies suggest that gender is socially created and constructed differently across time, place and culture (Ahl 2006; Mirchandani 1999) and that women's entrepreneurship cannot be examined in isolation from its interactions with other social categories, such as gender and socio-cultural values (Calás, Smircich, and Bourne 2009). Scant research, though, investigates what roles do patriarchal socio-cultural values and gendered social forces and power structures play in women's entrepreneurial experiences and CS in the AME context.

Against this background, the current study investigates CS from the perspective of entrepreneurs (Fisher, Maritz, and Lobo 2014), in this case, Lebanese women entrepreneurs (LWE). The main objective of this study is to answer the following questions: How do LWEs experience and conceptualize CS in entrepreneurship? What roles do gender and culture play in their experiences and conceptualizations of CS? To overcome the salient under-theorization of context (Welter 2011; Zahra, Wright, and Abdelgawad 2014; Tlaiss 2013, 2015c) and the Anglo-Saxon orientation in the prevailing entrepreneurship discourse (Ahl 2006), this research draws on institutional theory (Scott 2014) and contextualizes WEs' experiences unfolding among the many institutional, cognitive-cultural and normative systems in Lebanon in which human agency is embedded. In doing so, I attempt to understand the social construction and reproduction of gender and consider the influence of Arab socio-cultural values and gender ideologies on LWEs' experiences of CS. Viewing the construction of gender as a series of individual acts and daily interactions with others within the cultural frameworks and norms that establish socially acceptable gender behaviour (Ahl 2006), I am interested in understanding how gender is performed and how the gendered self of the LWEs is produced and reproduced (Ahl and Marlow 2012). I also draw on intersectionality theories (Calás, Smircich, and Bourne 2009) to help grasp the interplay between gender and culture and the interactions between agency and institutional factors.

Attempting to better understand these core constructs and their specific relationships to women's entrepreneurial experiences serves as a 'critical reflexive interrogation' of the female deficiency in entrepreneurial competency, ambition and business performance (Marlow and McAdam 2013, 115). This investigation is intended to narrow the knowledge gap concerning WEs' experience of CS in non-Western economies and gives special attention to the importance of contextualization and the roles of culture and gender in women's overall entrepreneurial experiences. It is also aimed at providing opportunities for women in other non-Western economies to learn from and be inspired by the entrepreneurial experiences of women elsewhere in the world.

To fulfil these objectives in this paper, I first present a review of the current literature on entrepreneurship in the Lebanese context and salient socio-cultural values and gender ideologies. I then move to the main concepts pertaining to CS and the influences of gender and culture on it. Next, I explain the research method and review the empirical insights emerging from the data in relation to the relevant literature. Afterwards, I discuss the empirical data and the implications and contributions of this study. Finally, I shed light on the study's limitations and offer suggestions for future research.

Literature review

To address the challenge and necessity to integrate context into entrepreneurship and CS studies, I commence by reviewing the societal and cultural factors that affect gender, its reproduction and LWEs' careers. In accordance with previous studies aimed at understanding women's entrepreneurship in non-Western contexts (e.g. Yousufazi, Saeed, and Muffatto 2015), I draw on Scott's (2014) institutional theory, giving special emphasis to the cultural-cognitive and normative pillars of institutions. Next, I discuss CS and the role of cultural values and gender in its conceptualizations by careerists.

Socio-cultural values, gender ideology and entrepreneurship in Lebanon

According to Scott (2014), institutions consist of (1) cultural-cognitive, (2) normative and (3) regulative systems that provide meaning and stability to social life. *Cultural-cognitive systems* refer to the patterns of beliefs, assumptions and ideologies shared at the national level. These systems comprise the taken-for-granted understandings of how a society works and the role women play within it. *Normative systems* introduce an evaluative and obligatory dimension into social life by defining the values contrary to desirable behaviour and the norms that prescribe the legitimate means to achieve the desired behaviours. These normative expectations regarding individuals' behaviour impose constraints on social behaviour. To ensure conformity to the normative systems, the *regulative systems* offer rewards and punishments. In short, to attain social rewards, avoid sanctions and maintain legitimacy, individuals must abide by shared norms and values (Scott 2014).

Although women in Lebanon enjoy greater social freedom than their peers in neighbouring Arab countries, the Lebanese culture remains masculine, with patriarchal structures that promote firmly defined gender-specific roles (Tlaiss 2015a). The culture is thus saturated with polarized gender stereotypes and strict gendered expectations of what women may and may not do. Males continue to be the head and the ultimate source of power and authority in the family, while females are frequently limited to the home and constrained to the roles of mother, wife and homemaker (Tlaiss 2015a).

Women and men in Lebanon are expected to behave according to the social roles assigned by these normative systems. Women should be feminine, communal and maternal and display caring behaviours appropriate for mothers and wives. Those women whose occupational choices lead them outside the home violate gender expectations and are perceived as socially deviant. Society attributes to men the qualities commonly held by entrepreneurs, such as aggressiveness, independence and decisiveness, and expects women to abide by the social rules of conduct and prioritize their families' needs and domestic tasks over their personal career aspirations (Tlaiss 2015a). Women's very competence at entrepreneurship is questioned by the salient beliefs that entrepreneurship is a male's domain and that women are rarely equipped with the skills and attributes needed by entrepreneurs (Ahl and Marlow, 2012; Marlow and McAdam 2013). Indeed, when Arab women do choose to have careers outside the home, they are expected to enter professions socially perceived as suitable for women, such as education and nursing, and to avoid the masculine career of entrepreneurship (Tlaiss 2015b, 2015c).

This patriarchal cultural-cognitive system and its normative elements are deeply rooted in traditions that promote male privilege and result in the uneven distribution of power, which (re) produces inequality and constitutes the most fundamental barrier to women's entrepreneurial careers (Tlaiss 2015a). The negative role of socio-cultural values and traditional gender ideologies in women's entrepreneurial careers recurs thematically throughout the academic discourse on Arab women's entrepreneurship. However, knowledge of whether and how these values and ideologies influence women's experience and conceptualizations of CS is limited. The entrepreneurship research conducted in the region has explored the challenges and barriers faced by Arab WEs (e.g. Al Dajani and Marlow 2010) but has left unanswered questions concerning the role and impact of the salient gender ideology and institutional systems on LWEs' self-reported perceptions and conceptualizations of CS. It, therefore, is important to review the literature on the various conceptualizations of CS and the impact of gender and culture on these conceptualizations.

Career success, gender and culture

Traditionally, CS is defined as an externally oriented construct conceptualized through a set of objective measures or criteria observable to others (e.g. job status, organizational progress and financial rewards) (Dries 2011; Hall 1996; Hall and Mirvis 1996). This objective perspective of CS entails a shared social understanding of the external indicators of individuals' career situations. It also accords with social comparison theory (Ng et al. 2005), which holds that individuals evaluate their achievements in comparison to others' or to other-referent criteria (Heslin 2005).

However, with globalization and changing workforce demographics (Hall and Mirvis 1996), subjective approaches to CS have gained prominence (Baruch 2006; Hall 2004). The conceptualization of CS has shifted from objective, external criteria towards a more internal view that people hold different CS values and perceptions, frequently based on personal evaluations rather than external references. Accordingly, subjective CS conceptualizations arise from self-referential criteria, important to the careerists themselves (Heslin 2005), including personal accomplishment (Hall 2004), self-fulfilment (Ituma et al. 2011), work-life balance (Tlaiss 2013), happiness and good family relations (Baruch 2006). The CA conceptualizations in the literature and this study, therefore, incorporate both objective, external measures (e.g. financial rewards and business growth) and subjective, internal measures (e.g. personal satisfaction, independence, work-life balance and fulfilment and achievement in family life).

Although the complexity of the multifaceted CS construct has received substantial interest (Dries 2011; Ituma et al. 2011), the generalization of the objective/subjective dichotomy to individuals across genders and cultures remains controversial (Bruni, Gherardi, and Poggio 2004; Ituma et al. 2011). Scholars have criticized CS research for failing to integrate gender or even acknowledge the daily reproduction of gender in work activities and CS conceptualizations (Tlaiss 2013, 2015a). Furthermore, the experiences of women who achieve CS are often ignored as men's behaviour continues to be perceived as the norm in organizational and entrepreneurial research (Bruni, Gherardi, and Poggio 2004). Failure to account for the role of gender in CS conceptualizations is problematic as it reinforces gender stereotypes of women's unsuitability for entrepreneurial careers (Ahl 2006; Ahl and Marlow 2012) and feeds the myth of the underperforming female entrepreneur (Marlow and McAdam 2013). Accordingly, several scholars (Ahl 2006; Dries 2011) have called for integrating gender into research on women's careers to better understand the approach women often take, evaluating their careers in the context of their relationships.

Moreover, the influence of cross-cultural differences on CS has been underestimated, leading to an overemphasis on Western career measures (Tlaiss 2015a) and the projection of Western values onto careerists in non-Western economies without accounting for cultural differences (Dries 2011). For example, in a cross-cultural investigation in three Arab countries, Karam, Afiouni, and Nasr (2013) found that women academics assessed the legitimacy of their careers based on external judgments (e.g. the opinions of their children, spouses, families, friends, colleagues and society) and on the alignment of their behaviour with women's roles and responsibilities as mandated by the institutional cultural and normative pillars. Whereas this finding suggested that Arab women evaluated their careers relative to other-referent criteria or other people, Tlaiss (2015a) argued that Lebanese women managers subjectively conceptualized CS based on personal criteria, including feelings of personal satisfaction, independence and autonomy. Taking into account these limitations, this study explores how LWEs experience and conceptualize CS and what roles gender and culture play in these entrepreneurial experiences. The following section presents the methods used.

Method

Semi-structured interviews provide a crucial instrument for good qualitative research 'to obtain both retrospective and real-time accounts by those people experiencing the phenomenon of theoretical interest' (Gioia, Corley, and Hamilton 2012). Face-to-face, semi-structured, in-depth interviews, therefore, were conducted in this study to explore LWEs' experiences of CS and to better understand these women in their own right. According to grounded theory (Glaser and Strauss 1967; Strauss and Corbin 1990), such interviews give the participants a voice (McGowan et al. 2012, 56) while capturing the complexity and richness of local contexts. I approached the interviewees as individual cases and compared them to understand *how* LWEs perceived themselves relative to CS and *why* they formed these perceptions and the accompanying conceptualizations (Patzelt, Williams, and Shepherd 2014). Thus, this study explored not only the similarities and differences in CS's conceptualizations but also the situational contingencies leading to or explaining these conceptualizations. Following Tlaiss's (2013, 2015b) recommendations, the *entrepreneur* was operationalized as a self-employed individual who owns and manages a business.

Data sample

Data collection in Lebanon and the Arab world is challenging for various reasons, including the difficulties identifying and accessing research participants and the lack of information about some populations, including WEs (Tlaiss 2015a, 2015c). Purposeful sampling (Neergaard 2007) was used to overcome these challenges and to answer the research questions. It combined network and reference sampling (Patton 2002). The main strategy was network sampling, in which the researcher used her personal circle of connections, networks, friends and family to identify information-rich WEs. Reference sampling targets experts or key informants who are 'ideal' and have 'the specialized knowledge that the researcher needs' (Neergaard 2007, 265). I followed Corley and Gioia (2004) guidelines and initially chose the WEs best able to answer the research questions concerning CS and its conceptualizations. The data collection started with the expert/key informants selected based on their impartiality and their willingness and ability to communicate and cooperate (Tremblay 1957).

Keeping the study's objectives in mind and using these two sampling strategies, I conducted in-depth interviews with 20 LWEs with diverse personal profiles and business activities. I did not purposefully construct the sample on any particular criteria, basis or focus. The participating WEs operated for-profit businesses that employed at least eight workers and were based in Beirut, the capital of Lebanon. The variations in the participants' demographic characteristics (e.g. age range: 30–60 years) and businesses (see Table 1) made this sample comparable to a sample resulting from the maximum variation sampling strategy, which is 'by far the most popular strategy with entrepreneurship researchers' (Neergaard 2007, 263). An advantage of such a diverse sample was that 'any common patterns that emerge[d] from great variation [we] re of particular interest and value in capturing the core experiences and central, shared aspects' (Patton 1990, 172).

Iterative data collection involves gathering and analysing data simultaneously while recruiting new informants based on information considered important by earlier interviewees (Corley and Gioia 2004). Accordingly, data collection continued until it yielded no further clarification, and theoretical saturation was reached (Glaser and Strauss 1967). The sample of 20 LWEs was considered to be adequate as the significance and validity of qualitative research is determined not by the sample size but the 'information-richness of the cases' (Patton 1990, 185).

Data collection

The interview protocol included a variety of open-ended questions on the participants' personal and business demographic characteristics, self-reported CS perceptions, CS conceptualizations and the factors (if any) influencing these conceptualizations. The questions included: *Tell me about your entrepreneurial career. Do you perceive or feel that you have a successful entrepreneurial career? Do you perceive your entrepreneurial career as successful? Why or why not? How do you conceptualize*

Table 1. Overview of participants' personal and business backgrounds.

Personal profile	Frequency	Enterprise profile	Frequency
Age		*Form of the Enterprise*	
30–40	5	Sole Proprietorship	
41–50	9		20
>50	6		
Marital Status		*Number of Employees*	
Single	3		
Married	13	8 or 9	7
Divorced	4	10, 11, or 12	8
Mothers	15	≥13	5
Number of Children		*Years in Business*	
1 or 2	10	≤10	10
3 or 4	5	>10	10
Educational Level		*Nature/Line of Business*	
College	4	Nurseries/Hair Salons/Beauty and	20
Bachelors	4	Aesthetics Centres/Events Planning	
Masters	10	Firms/Travel Agencies/Furniture	
PhD	2	Galleries/Real Estate Agencies/Public Relations Firms/Pharmacies and Drug Distribution/Marketing Research/Clothes Boutiques/Educational Centres	

your CS? Why do you conceptualize your CS this way? What factors have influenced your CS and your conceptualization of it?

The interviews, which lasted 60–120 min, were tape-recorded and were conducted in various locations in Beirut based on the interviewees' choice and preferences. Confidentiality and anonymity were promised to the participants at the beginning and the end of every interview. The interviews were conducted in Arabic, French or English based on the interviewees' preferences, with the majority in English. The remaining interviews involved a significant amount of code-switching, or switching back and forth, between English and Arabic or French, which necessitated translation. To eliminate translation-related problems, back translation, consultation and collaboration were practiced (Birbili 2000). In back-translation, the researcher translated French and Arabic material into English, and an independent academic fluent in all three languages translated the resulting English manuscripts back into the source languages. The researcher and the independent academic also compared the two versions in the source language to clarify any ambiguities in meaning. Other trilingual academicians (Brislin, Lonner, and Thorndike 1973) who understood the local culture were also consulted. Combining these methods is seen as the most efficient way to deal with translation problems (Birbili 2000) as 'the weakness of one method c[an] be offset by the strengths of the other' (Brislin, Lonner, and Thorndike 1973, 51). Equivalence in translation could not be achieved in terms of sameness (Bassnett 1991), so the main focus was capturing the actual meaning. The local academicians who understood the local culture and the subtleties of the languages provided great assistance in reducing the bias resulting from translation.

Data analysis

Following Gioia, Corley, and Hamilton (2012), the analysis followed the established procedures of inductive research (Miles and Huberman 1994; Strauss and Corbin 1990) and constant comparison (Glaser and Strauss 1967). I attempted to work between the data and the emerging theory. These approaches facilitated not only rigorous qualitative data collection and analysis, but also the emergence of themes through the comparison of informants' ideas (Corley and Gioia 2004). Following the recommendations of seminal studies (Corley and Gioia 2004; Gioia, Corley, and Hamilton 2012; Patzelt et al. 2014), a three-step analysis process was used (Strauss and Corbin 1990).

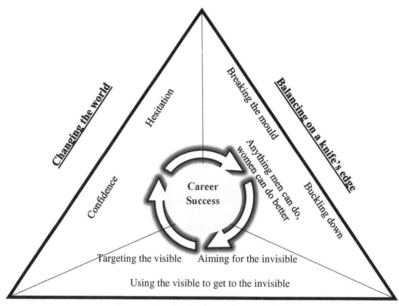

Succeeding in the face of adversity

Figure 1. Proposed theoretical model.

First, open coding was used and it helped identify and categorize initial concepts in the data (Corley and Gioia 2004; Strauss and Corbin 1990). This step exposed the thoughts and meanings contained in the data as I looked for first-order codes. Using constant comparison techniques (Glaser and Strauss 1967), I loosely identified recurring themes as I read and reread the transcripts and coded and recoded the data several times in an iterative process (Patzelt at al. 2014). Gradually, I uncovered the first-order codes and continued this 'recursive, process-oriented, analytic procedure' until codes were assigned to the text of the transcripts (Locke 1996, 240).

Second, I moved to axial coding through developing theoretical categories and subcategories (Strauss and Corbin 1990). I compared the interviewees' responses to identify similarities and differences (Gioia, Corley, and Hamilton 2012). I searched for relationships between and among the first-order codes to reduce their number and classify them into different, higher-order themes or courses of action (Locke 1996; Corley and Gioia 2004). Third, in selective coding, I grouped similar themes into overarching dimensions (Corley and Gioia 2004) and integrated and refined the theoretical categories and subcategories generated in the second step to create a larger theoretical scheme (Strauss and Corbin 1990). Figure 1 illustrates the process used to arrive at the overall themes.

Findings

By examining how LWEs' CS unfolds from conceptualizing to building to accomplishing their endeavours, this research expands the understanding of CS in entrepreneurship. In the following section, I elaborate on the three dimensions pertaining to the LWEs' CS: (1) balancing on a knife's edge; (2) succeeding in the face of adversity and (3) changing the world. To maintain the participants' anonymity, they are referred to by their initials. Table 2 provides a summary of the main findings.

Table 2. Summary of responses.

ID	Marital status	Visible measures	Invisible measures	Mechanisms leading to CS	Awareness of CS
AA	S	Finance	Personal	G	Hesitant
BB	S	Growth + Finance	Personal	E2 + E3	Confident
CC	S	Growth + Finance	Personal	E1 + E3	Confident
DD	D	Growth + Reputation	Personal	E1 + E2 + E3	Confident
EE	D + 1	Growth + Finance	Personal	E1 + E2	Confident
FF	D + 2	Growth	Personal + Family	E1 + E3	Confident
GG	D + 3	Growth + Finance + Reputation	Personal	E2 + E3	Confident
HH	M + 0	Growth	Personal	E2	Confident
II	M + 1	Finance	Personal + Family	E2	Confident
JJ	M + 2	Growth + Finance + Reputation	Personal + Family	E2	Confident
KK	M + 2	Reputation	Family	E2	Confident
LL	M + 2	Finance	Family	F	Hesitant
MM	M + 2	Reputation	Personal + Family	E1	Confident
NN	M + 2	Growth + Finance	Family	E1	Confident
OO	M + 2	Finance	Personal + Family	G	Hesitant
PP	M + 2	Growth + Reputation	Personal + Family	E3	Confident
QQ	M + 3	Finance	Personal + Family	E1 + E2 + E3	Confident
RR	M + 3	Growth + Reputation	Family	E1 + E3	Confident
SS	M + 3	Growth + Finance	Personal + Family	E1 + E2 + E3	Confident
TT	M + 4	Growth + Finance	Family	F	Hesitant

Note:
(1) Marital status: S: Single; D: Divorced; M: Married; + Number of Children
(2) Visible measures; Finance: Making money/being profitable; Growth: Sustain and grow the business; Reputation: Businesses' good reputation
(3) Invisible measures; Personal: Personal/internal satisfaction, fulfilment, achievement, feeling happy, etc.; Family: Being good wives, mothers, and house makers/having good, happy family/well-behaved children/work-life balance.
(4) Mechanisms leading to CS; E1: Breaking the mould; E2: Buckling down; E3: Anything that men can do, women can do better; G: Wants the business to further grow and develop; F: Fear of being perceived as negligent to their duties and responsibilities as mothers and wives
(5) Awareness of CS; Confident: The interviewee acknowledged having CS; Hesitant: The interviewee hesitated acknowledging their own CS.

Conceptualization of CS: balancing on a knife's edge (personal, business and family needs)

The themes in this dimension link notions of challenging the dominant social patriarchy to conceptualizations of CS. The quotations in Table 3 illustrate how the LWEs conceptualized their CS using both visible extrinsic and invisible intrinsic criteria.

Targeting the visible

Given the social norms that inform Arab women's roles and responsibilities, the LWEs were expected to use mostly subjective criteria related to motherhood to conceptualize their CS (Tlaiss 2013). However, as demonstrated in Table 3, they did not; instead, they conceptualized their CS using extrinsic outcomes visible to others, primarily (1) financial rewards, (2) business growth and (3) business reputation. The importance of financial rewards can be partly explained by the high unemployment levels and the difficult economic situation in Lebanon, further supporting the need to contextualize women's entrepreneurial experiences. As one participant stated: *'I am making great money for a woman working in Lebanon. ... To be able to make money in Lebanon is really hard'* (JJ). Business growth and good reputations were also important. The participants' emphasis on financial success and business development is consistent with a small but growing stream of entrepreneurship research (e.g. Marlow and McAdam 2013; Marlow and Swail 2014) suggesting that the financial rewards and growth of entrepreneurial ventures are important not only to male entrepreneurs but also to WEs.

Aiming for the invisible

The LWEs also conceptualized their CS using criteria intrinsically experienced and individually important but not necessarily recognizable by others. Their conceptualizations of intrinsic CS

Table 3. Excerpts of data supporting interpretations of balancing on a knife's edge.

Sub-category	Representative quotes
Theoretical category 1: Targeting the visible	
Financial rewards through making money and high profits	I am now making money... the business is making money, a lot more than what we did in the past and this makes it a successful business... (GG)
	The business is not only covering costs but also making profit in this economic situation, which is great...of the course the financial rewards are important and they prove that I am successful... (EE)
Business growth through making the business bigger and having more employees	How do I measure the success of my entrepreneurial career? Easy, by how big my company is now ...I have more than 15 employees...I started this business as a hair salon only and now, I have a beauty centre and am waiting to hear from the bank for a loan to make the business bigger and add a nutrition centre to it (HH)
Sub-category	Representative quotes
Theoretical category 2: Aiming for the invisible	
Personal satisfaction through feeling satisfied and happy	I am satisfied with what I have accomplished...my business is still young and I can do more and I want to do more, but I am happy... (OO)
Personal control through being independent, achieving what you want, and being in control	I feel good about myself...I achieved what I wanted to do ...despite the resistance of everyone, my family...I made it and now I am independent and in control of my life and my business... (RR)
Motherhood through being good mothers and having successful children	Being a good mother for me is success...it also contributes to my personal satisfaction because I know that I raised good children with whom I have a wonderful relationship...(SS)
Seesawing between the roles through building a family while building a business	I think that I am lucky because I created a good balance...I was not willing to sacrifice my family for my business or the other way around...today I have both (SS)
	I have a good business but I also have a great family...I did not want to build my business on the expense of my family...I have a great family and a great home... (TT)
Theoretical category 3: Using the visible to get to the invisible	
Financial rewards, business growth, business reputation, and personal satisfaction	Yes for sure I have a successful entrepreneurial career... I am making great money for a woman working in Lebanon and at my age...I have a big business, a big clientele base, and my business has a great reputation... all this makes me feel very successful, satisfied and that makes me feel even better. (JJ)
Business growth, personal satisfaction, and financial rewards	I measure my entrepreneurial career success by looking at how far I came since my beginnings and how satisfied I am...I challenged everyone who told me that I cannot make it...look at me now, my business is making profit and I am wealthier than I used to be. All of this makes me happy, it makes me proud with what I have made despite the barriers. (CC)

encompassed (1) feelings of personal satisfaction, (2) feelings of personal control, (3) motherhood and (4) achievement of work-life balance. Whereas personal satisfaction was strongly related to satisfaction with one's career advancement and feelings of happiness, personal control was achieved through independence amid societal restrictions. The LWEs' use of these intrinsic, personally based conceptualizations to explain CS demonstrates their importance to LWEs and the instrumentality of entrepreneurship in helping women experience success. These conceptualizations also reveal the individual agency of the LWEs who did not accept those paralyzing stereotypes but instead, challenged them by building entrepreneurial careers that gave them happiness and self-satisfaction. This finding supports previous studies, including Tlaiss (2013), shedding light on the importance of agency in helping Arab women move past imposed socio-cultural and normative institutional mandates.

Given the cultural-cognitive and normative pillars in Lebanon, the importance of motherhood and work-life balance to conceptualizations of CS was unsurprising. To demonstrate legitimacy as mothers, wives and homemakers, the LWEs emphasized their children's success and their status as good mothers. This finding confirms the claims of Karam, Afiouni, and Nasr (2013) that Arab women legitimized their careers with the external judgements of important others (e.g. their children and husbands) and their compliance with the roles and responsibilities mandated by the cultural and normative pillars of society.

Despite the difficulty of moving between the culturally progressive role of entrepreneurs and the traditional roles of wives and mothers, the LWEs identified work–life balance as a key aspect of CS. They also emphasized their central role within their families as parents to demonstrate their familial commitment while growing their businesses. Their conceptualizations of CS stressed their struggle to balance the obligations of their traditional and progressive roles.

Accordingly, I argue that the LWEs' emphasis on their roles as mothers, wives and homemakers must be interpreted as their attempt to challenge a society that questioned their ability to be both entrepreneurs and the backbone of their families. By focusing on their success in building their families, the interviewees responded to their society's gendered, stereotypical expectations and outperformed them. Although this conceptualization of CS is based on visible rather than invisible criteria, it should not be perceived as an end. In other words, the visible criteria were the bridge and the instrument to the individual, invisible experience of CS.

Mechanisms leading to CS: succeeding in the face of adversity

The themes in this dimension link reluctance to adhere to conventional norms, resistance of female subordination and agency to the building of entrepreneurial careers and CS. The quotations in Table 4 illustrate how the LWEs created their CS by breaking the mould, buckling down and believing that anything men can do, women can do better.

The first mechanism the LWEs used to succeed in the face of adversity was *breaking the mould* and challenging social and gender stereotypes. By pursuing their career choices and succeeding in growing their businesses, the LWEs indeed challenged their society, questioning the female deficiency myth and demonstrating entrepreneurial competency and ambition. Accordingly, I argue against the notion that women are lacking as entrepreneurs. The LWEs did not perceive themselves as deficient. Instead, they responded to social doubts about their entrepreneurial ability by persevering and defying societal constraints to create thriving entrepreneurial ventures, resulting in CS.

The LWEs' second mechanism to achieve CS was *buckling down*, focusing on their objectives and putting in hard work to achieve those objectives. Without a supportive culture welcoming WEs and granting them social legitimacy (Tlaiss 2015b), the LWEs demonstrated agency by believing in themselves. They also displayed agency by keeping their eyes on the big picture and not allowing social rejection to negatively influence their goals or prevent them from achieving their dreams of owning their own businesses.

The third mechanism to achieve CS unfolded through the belief that *anything men can do, women can do better*, in other words, belief in the supremacy of women. The LWEs achieved CS through competing with and outperforming male competitors. In response to their unsupportive environment and ridicule from male competitors, the LWEs constructed CS by comparing their businesses' performance and size to those of their male competitors. In this mechanism, the women found their agency, created an us-versus-them competition and saw CS as achieved when the 'us' was bigger and better than the 'them'. This us-versus-them approach catalysed the women's motivation to focus on their entrepreneurial careers and overcome attitudinal barriers. This claim is supported by social comparison theory (Ng et al. 2005) and demonstrates the LWEs' entrenched internalization of the normative notions of male entrepreneurship (Calás, Smircich, and Bourne 2009; Ahl and Marlow 2012), viewing male entrepreneurs and their businesses as the norms and standards of success (Bruni, Gherardi, and Poggio 2004; Marlow and McAdam 2013).

Table 4. Excerpts of data supporting interpretations of succeeding in the face of adversity.

Sub-category	Representative quotes
Theoretical category 1: Breaking the mould	
Risk taking and persistence in the face of social rejection	My whole society was against me...my husband and my family...but I was adamant to open my own hair salon...I took the risk and created my own business... but I persevered and proved them wrong...yes my entrepreneurial career is successful (FF)
Challenging the society and breaking the gender-role stereotypes	Everyone discouraged me...everyone said that a travel agency is not for women... I continued to work hard and now I have one of the biggest travel agencies...I have a successful thriving business...I was right (NN)
Theoretical category 2: Buckling down	
Having a dream and pursue it through hard work	I have a successful entrepreneurial career because when I started my business I was young and I had a dream... (QQ)
Dismissing the discouragement of others and persevering	Everyone told me not to...everyone said that interior design offices are too masculine but I wanted it... its my baby and I was not willing to allow anything to prevent me from having it... (KK)
Sub-category	Representative quotes
Theoretical category 3: Anything that men can do, women can do better	
Building a business bigger and better than those of male competitors	My business is strong and big...bigger than some of the businesses owned by men and that is why I know that I have a successful entrepreneurial career (SS)
Overcoming ridicule by male competitors	After many years of being ridiculed by my male competitors, my business is better than theirs... (PP)

Awareness of CS: changing the world

The themes in this dimension link the gender mandates shaping social expectations regarding women's career choices to their awareness and experience of CS. The quotations in Table 5 illustrate how mindful and cognizant the LWEs were of their CS.

When asked to assess their careers, most LWEs were *confident in* and proud of their CS as they built entrepreneurial careers despite the outright challenges of institutional barriers and the normative expectations of their culture. By not backing down from their career choices and by practicing determination, persistence and hard work, the LWEs were able to accomplish their entrepreneurial ambitions. The respondents believed they had created agency and gained control over their environment through their CS and entrepreneurship.

A few LWEs were *hesitant* to acknowledge their CS. For AA and OO, their reluctance arose from their desire to grow their businesses even further. These two LWEs' focus on growing their businesses can be explained by recent discussions (e.g. Marlow and Swail 2014) arguing against the claim that WEs' prefer small, stable businesses. As well, the hesitation by LL and TT was driven by their fear of being perceived as socially deviant women and negligent of their families. Consequently, they were eager to emphasize their roles as mothers and their responsibilities in their homes.

Thus, the need to fulfil the strict gender roles and cultural expectations ascribed to women as mothers and wives might have negatively influenced the LWEs' self-confidence and experience of CS. Their doing of gender unfolded as they reproduced social expectations by perceiving their entrepreneurial careers as secondary to their responsibilities in the home and to their children.

Discussion

Before looking more closely at the three dimensions emerging from our analysis, it is important to reflect on the socio-cultural barriers faced by the LWEs. Although the intention of this study is not to examine them, these obstacles are fundamentally tied to the research questions. It is therefore imperative to note that the entrepreneurship discourse in Lebanon in the LWEs' descriptions was indeed masculinized. Women's involvement in entrepreneurship was perceived as problematic for

Table 5. Excerpts of data supporting interpretations of changing the world.

Sub-category	Representative quotes
Theoretical category 1: Confidence	
Achieving goals albeit social objections and obstacles	Of course, my entrepreneurial career is successful...my husband rejected the idea of me having my own business...I was criticised by my own society for setting a bad example for my daughters...my mother-in-law said having a business is a man's thing and not the place of woman...the owners of the real estate offices always remind me that this business is a man's thing... but I did not allow their words to influence me...I worked hard and kept pushing until I created the business that I want ...(MM)
Overcoming bullying by male competitors	Definitely...having a business is for men is this country...my competitors make fun of me behind my back, laugh at the events that I plan, and try to steal my employees (BB)
	I have no doubt whatsoever... it was an industry of only men...they (male competitors) did not like having me around...I worked day and night to make my business successful and to prove to them that I, as a woman, can have my own travel agency and that it will be a successful one (II)
Sub-category	Representative quotes
Theoretical category 2: Hesitation	
Growing the business furthermore	...I am not sure...maybe my entrepreneurial career is a bit successful but I want my business to grow more...I aim to make the nursery bigger and add other sections to it... (AA)
Avoiding being perceived as careless mothers and homemakers	...well I am not sure...you know I am a wife and a mother of two and I have responsibilities towards my family... my business is important and so is my family... (LL)

their families, unsuitable from a socio-cultural perspective and in violation of the socially situated gender roles restricting women to the domestic sphere. Accordingly, the interviewees did not receive any support and were frequently ridiculed and told go home to attend to their domestic responsibilities as mothers and wives. However, these contextual cultural and gendered barriers did not prevent these Arab women from building their entrepreneurial careers through various mechanisms. Each woman, in her own way, resisted female subordination and fought to achieve CS.

The processes that the LWEs used to build and explain their CS, therefore, prove that these entrepreneurial experiences could not be separated from the environment in which they unfolded. They also demonstrate the importance the Arab women placed on entrepreneurship and how their desire to be successful entrepreneurs motivated their development and deployment of mechanisms to overcome their restrictive environment and achieve meaningfulness and success in their lives outside traditional gender roles. Hence, the LWEs' overall experience of CS shows how women's entrepreneurship is intertwined with socio-cultural values and the masculinization of entrepreneurship. Their entrepreneurial journeys also speak to their social experiences of gender and confirm the complexity of adhering to entrepreneurship as a career choice. Thus contextualized, the studied LWEs' stories of entrepreneurship and CS were clearly rooted in the normative and cultural systems that shaped their career choices.

In their conceptualizations of CS, the LWEs responded to the socially imposed biases portraying women as deficient entrepreneurs by using visible, measurable criteria, such as profits. These criteria, which were comparable and observable to others (Heslin 2005), provided concrete evidence that the claims of their society were incorrect. Facing societal rejection of their career choices, the LWEs sought to legitimize their careers and businesses by deploying the most common conceptualizations in the masculinized entrepreneurship discourse. They conceptualized their CS with standardized, factual criteria widely used in their society. This, however, should not to be mistaken for their acceptance of these gendered expectations. To the contrary, the LWEs confronted many barriers to prove their entrepreneurial legitimacy and invoked various forms of agency to legitimize their entrepreneurial careers. These conceptualizations, based on other-referent criteria (Heslin 2005), have significant implications for improving the overall understanding of how context influences entrepreneurship by demonstrating how culturally prescribed femininity pushed WEs to behave contrary to gender beliefs and use masculine means to conceptualize CS.

The LWEs also cited subjective measures related to their success as mothers and the satisfaction of their internal goals. This focus can be understood as another demonstration of the impact of gender stereotypes and the LWEs' internalization of these expected roles. The use of subjective measures, however, can also be understood as a means to silence external criticism, increasing the complexity of how CS unfolds. In other words, the LWEs' references to success in motherhood and home-making can also be seen as an attempt to reduce the tension they experienced with society. Their efforts to comply with salient gender ideologies can thus be seen as a means to avoid further social sanctions and to express their success in the terms socially expected from and accepted for women.

Collectively, these conceptualizations of CS mostly built on other-referent criteria paved the way for the LWEs to experience their CS internally. In other words, one might be tempted to perceive profits, for example, as an end goal. However, the interviewees did not pursue measures generally perceived as masculine normative measures of success as end goals. Instead, they used these measures as a process to achieve personal goals, such as personal satisfaction, fulfilment and, ultimately, CS. Overall, the findings highlight the complexity of LWEs' CS and the need to understand the totality of these conceptualizations from a processual perspective instead of merely describing CS with subjective and objective criteria. Accordingly, unlike previous studies portraying the success of Arab women in mostly subjective terms or on a continuum between the objective and the subjective (Tlaiss 2015a), I emphasize the instrumentality of extrinsic, visible criteria and their processual role in assisting women achieve intrinsic CS. The women used these external measures as a bridge to achieve internal success. I, therefore, argue that the measures used in this study were not an end but a means for the women to achieve what was important to them based on their specific life experiences. Accordingly, for the LWEs, CS, just like entrepreneurship, was socially constructed and conceptualized within the constraints of gender based on idiosyncratic criteria.

Together, these three dimensions demonstrate the complexity of Arab WEs' experience of CS and the interplay between context and agency in shaping their career choices. Accordingly, I argue against the over-simplified approach and understanding of CS using static objective and subjective dimensions. Alternatively, based on the specific conceptualizations of CS that emerged and as demonstrated in the proposed theoretical model, I propose a conceptualization of entrepreneurial CS as a dynamic, evolving process, centrally embedded at the juncture of three-dimensional interrelatedness. This dynamic complexity of interrelatedness also entails the interaction of the women and their agency with their contexts and the constraints within. In addition to the contributions to entrepreneurship and CS, these three dimensions, viewed holistically, are both an expression of and significant contributors to women's empowerment, identity development and greater self-efficacy.

In this case, through the experience of acknowledging, building and conceptualizing CS, the LWEs demonstrated self-efficacy and developed identities as successful WEs. Recognizing their own CS, they claimed their rightful position in society rather than accepting the restrictions imposed on them. Furthermore, by utilizing these three various CS mechanisms, the Arab women entrepreneurs empowered themselves and sought a dynamic purpose for their lives outside the restrictions and limitations of traditional gender roles. Finally, by conceptualizing their CS as a process and grounding it in their personal priorities, they demonstrated their agency and legitimacy as entrepreneurs. The results, therefore, reveal a deepened gender understanding among the Arab WEs resulting from their struggles with their societies and families. The LWEs also demonstrated personal growth, deploying a variety of mechanisms to overcome social and normative restrictions rather than accepting and internalizing them. Accordingly, I argue that entrepreneurial CS should be perceived as a highly negotiable and flexible process, highlighting the living dynamic of the three-dimensional model presented below.

Contributions and concluding remarks

This study demonstrates that the prevailing gender norms and entrepreneurship discourse shaped the LWEs' views of CS. It also illustrates the discursive construction of CS at the complex intersection of the Arab entrepreneurs' agency and the dominant socio-cultural norms and gender ideology. These findings have manifold implications and contributions.

First, this study demonstrates how the salient dichotomies of masculinity and femininity disadvantaged women and endorsed their inferior social and entrepreneurial status. Despite changes in Lebanon, in particular, in terms of women's increased freedoms and growing participation in economic activity, the country's social structure remained dominated by strict, traditional expectations of what was acceptable for women. Accordingly, the LWEs took their entrepreneurial careers and conceptualizations of CS into their own hands. Drawing on their agency, they challenged deeply rooted societal and cultural norms and persevered in their entrepreneurial careers.

Second, contextualizing the LWEs' experiences supports the argument that explaining CS using notions and constructs developed and conceptualized in Anglo-Saxon/North American contexts might not be completely suitable for the Arab societies. The LWEs were gendered entrepreneurial subjects whose conceptualizations of CS could not be understood in isolation from their contexts and the embeddedness of their entrepreneurial experiences. This embeddedness took on paramount importance as the LWEs' self-perceptions and CS conceptualizations evoked their agency and evolved in reaction to and defiance of institutional constraints. Accordingly, I argue that Arab women's entrepreneurship is not a gender-neutral experience but, rather, contextually crafted around gendered institutions informing and sustaining the gender hierarchy. A strong wave of change also deeply affected it as women challenged societal expectations, reshaped their workforce participation and redefined their lives and roles in society. Although this study stresses the importance of conceptualization, the need for more county-specific research is also clear as these findings cannot be generalized across the Arab world's varied economic and political environments.

Third, so far, this study is the first to examine WEs' CS, which has not been researched elsewhere in the Arab world. By taking an interest in Arab women's entrepreneurship, I not only give them a voice and put gender, women and the Arab world on the map of entrepreneurship studies but also inform the broader debate on gender and entrepreneurship. I also respond to the growing number of scholarly calls to use institutional theory to advance the understanding of women's entrepreneurship in non-Western contexts. Furthermore, this study contributes to research on intersectionality by exploring the embeddedness of LWs' entrepreneurship within the gendered biases of their local contexts and by understanding the unfolding of CS at the intersection of gender, institutional systems and contextually situated agency. Nevertheless, more research is needed to better understand the entrepreneurial experiences of WEs across the AME.

Conclusions

This study provides valuable insights into the complexity of women's entrepreneurial experiences and the influence of various cultural and normative structures on their CS in an Arab context. However, I am also conscious of its limitations. It was conducted in one country with a single group of entrepreneurs with the same gender. Given the exploratory nature of this study and its objective to achieve a broader understanding, all the interviews took place in Beirut, the capital of Lebanon. Future studies could explore the similarities and differences in the experiences of LWEs living in major cities and more traditional, rural villages. I also did not compare and contrast the interviewees' responses based on their demographic characteristics (e.g. age or education) or their field of business.

Entrepreneurship studies, therefore, are needed to extend the notion of gender embeddedness to developing contexts, especially in the AME. For example, it would be interesting to explore whether entrepreneurs' experiences of CS are related to or influenced by their entrepreneurial motives and gender. Future research could also explore Arab men's entrepreneurial motives and intentions. Undoubtedly, cross-cultural investigations are needed to compare Arab women's entrepreneurial experiences across national contexts. Moreover, amid the macro-political changes in the AME, it would be especially interesting to investigate the impact of political systems and economic climates on both entrepreneurial activities and conceptualizations of CS. The role of Islam and Islamic teachings in supporting or discouraging the entrepreneurial careers of men and women and their influence on entrepreneurial CS also warrants further study.

Disclosure statement

No potential conflict of interest was reported by the author.

References

Ahl, H. 2006. "Why Research on Women Entrepreneurs Needs New Directions." *Entrepreneurship Theory and Practice* 30 (5): 595–621. doi:10.1111/j.1540-6520.2006.00138.x/full.

Ahl, H., and S. Marlow. 2012. "Exploring the Dynamics of Gender, Feminism and Entrepreneurship: Advancing Debate to Escape a Dead End?" *Organization* 19 (5): 543–562. doi:10.1177/1350508412448695.

Al Dajani, H., and S. Marlow. 2010. "Impact of Women's Home-Based Enterprise on Family Dynamics: Evidence from Jordan." *International Small Business Journal* 28 (5): 470–486. doi:10.1177/0266242610370392.

Baruch, Y. 2006. "Career Development in Organizations and Beyond: Balancing Traditional and Contemporary Viewpoints." *Human Resource Management Review* 16 (2): 125–138. doi:10.1016/j.hrmr.2006.03.002.

Bassnett, S. 1991. *Translation Studies*. London: Routledge.

Birbili, M. 2000. "Translating from One Language to Another." *Social Research Update* 31 (1): 1–7. http://sru.soc.surrey.ac.uk/SRU31.html

Brislin, R. W., W. Lonner, and R. M. Thorndike. 1973. *Cross-Cultural Research Methods*. New York: John Wiley.

Bruni, A., S. Gherardi, and N. Poggio. 2004. "Entrepreneur-Mentality, Gender and the Study of Women Entrepreneurs." *Journal of Organizational Change Management* 17 (3): 256–268. doi:10.1108/09534810410538315.

Buttner, E. H., and D. P. Moore. 1997. "Women's Organizational Exodus to Entrepreneurship: Self-Reported Motivations and Correlates with Success." *Journal of Small Business Management* 35 (1): 34–46.

Calás, M. B., L. Smircich, and K. A. Bourne. 2009. "Extending the Boundaries: Reframing Entrepreneurship as Social Change through Feminist Perspectives." *Academy of Management Review* 34 (3): 552–569. doi:10.5465/AMR.2009.40633597.

Corley, K. G., and D. A. Gioia. 2004. "Identity Ambiguity and Change in the Wake of a Corporate Spin-Off." *Administrative Science Quarterly* 49 (2): 173–208. doi:10.2307/4131471.

Dries, N. 2011. "The Meaning of Career Success: Avoiding Reification through a Closer Inspection of Historical, Cultural, and Ideological Contexts." *Career Development International* 16 (4): 364–384. doi:10.1108/13620431111158788.

Fisher, R., A. Maritz, and A. Lobo. 2014. "Evaluating Entrepreneurs' Perception of Success: Development of a Measurement Scale." *International Journal of Entrepreneurial Behavior and Research* 20 (5): 478–492. doi:10.1108/IJEBR-10-2013-0157.

Gioia, D., K. Corley, and A. Hamilton. 2012. "Seeking Qualitative Rigor in Inductive Research: Notes on the Gioia Methodology." *Organizational Research Methods* 16 (1): 15–31. doi:10.1177/1094428112452151.

Glaser, B., and A. Strauss. 1967. *The Discovery of Grounded Theory*. Chicago: Aldine.

Hall, D. T. 1996. "Protean Careers of the 21st Century." *Academy of Management Executive* 10 (4): 8–16. doi:10.5465/AME.1996.3145315.

Hall, D. T., and P. H. Mirvis. 1996. "The New Protean Career: Psychological Success and the Path with a Heart." In *The Career Is Dead—Long Live the Career*, edited by D. T. Hall, 15–45. San Francisco: Jossey-Bass.

Hall, D. T. 2004. "The Protean Career: A Quarter Century Journey." *Journal of Vocational Behavior* 65 (1): 1–13. doi:10.1016/j.jvb.2003.10.006.

Heslin, P. A. 2005. "Conceptualizing and Evaluating Career Success." *Journal of Organizational Behavior* 26 (2): 113–136. doi:10.1002/job.270.

Ituma, A., R. Simpson, F. Ovadje, N. Cornelius, and C. Mordi. 2011. "Four 'Domains' of Career Success: How Managers in Nigeria Evaluate Career Outcomes." *International Journal of Human Resource Management* 22 (17): 3638–3660. doi:10.1080/09585192.2011.560870.

Karam, C., F. Afiouni, and N. Nasr. 2013. "Walking a Tightrope or Navigating a Web: Parameters of Balance within Perceived Institutional Realities." *Women's Studies International Forum* 40: 87–101. doi:10.1016/j.wsif.2013.05.002.

Katre, A., and P. Salipante. 2012. "Start-Up Social Ventures: Blending Fine-Grained Behaviors from Two Institutions for Entrepreneurial Success." *Entrepreneurship Theory and Practice* 36 (5): 967–994. doi:10.1111/j.1540-6520.2012.00536.x.

Kiviluoto, N. 2013. "Growth as Evidence of Firm Success: Myth or Reality?" *Entrepreneurship and Regional Development* 25 (7–8): 569–586. doi:10.1080/08985626.2013.814716.

Locke, K. 1996. "Rewriting the Discovery of Grounded Theory after 25 Years?" *Journal of Management Inquiry* 5 (3): 239–245. doi:10.1177/105649269653008.

Marlow, S., and J. Swail. 2014. "Gender, Risk and Finance: Why Can't a Woman Be More like a Man?" *Entrepreneurship and Regional Development* 26 (1–2): 80–96. doi:10.1080/08985626.2013.860484.

Marlow, S., and M. McAdam. 2013. "Gender and Entrepreneurship: Advancing Debate and Challenging Myths; Exploring the Mystery of the Under-Performing Female Entrepreneur." *International Journal of Entrepreneurial Behavior & Research* 19 (1): 114–124. doi:10.1108/13552551311299288.

McGowan, P., C. L. Redeker, S. Y. Cooper, and K. Greenan. 2012. "Female Entrepreneurship and the Management of Business and Domestic Roles: Motivations, Expectations and Realities." *Entrepreneurship and Regional Development* 24 (1–2): 53–72. doi:10.1080/08985626.2012.637351.

Miles, M.B., & Huberman, A.M. 1994. *Qualitative Data analysis: An Expanded Sourcebook* (second edition). Sage Publications, Thousand Oaks, CA:

Mirchandani, K. 1999. "Feminist Insight on Gendered Work: New Directions in Research on Women and Entrepreneurship." *Gender, Work and Organization* 6 (4): 224–235. doi:10.1111/1468-0432.00085.

Neergaard, H. 2007. "Sampling in Entrepreneurial Settings." In *Handbook of Qualitative Research Methods in Entrepreneurship*, edited by H. Neergaard and J. Ulhøi, 253–278. Cheltenham: Edward Elgar.

Ng, T. W., L. T. Eby, K. L. Sorensen, and D. C. Feldman. 2005. "Predictors of Objective and Subjective Career Success: A Meta Analysis." *Personnel Psychology* 58 (2): 367–408. doi:10.1111/j.1744-6570.2005.00515.x.

Patton, M. 1990. *Qualitative Evaluation and Research Methods.* 2nd ed. Newbury Park: Sage.

Patton, M. 2002. *Qualitative Research and Evaluative Methods.* 3rd ed. London: Sage.

Patzelt, H., T. A. Williams, and D. A. Shepherd. 2014. "Overcoming The Walls That Constrain Us: The Role Of Entrepreneurship Education Programs in Prison." *Academy Of Management Learning & Education* 13 (4): 587-620.

Patzelt, H., Williams, T. A., & Shepherd, D. A. 2014. Overcoming the walls that constrain us: The role of entrepreneurship education programs in prison. *Academy of Management Learning & Education*, 13(4), 587–620.

Scott, W. R. 2014. *Institutions and Organizations: Ideas, Interests, and Identities.* 4th ed. Thousand Oaks: Sage.

Strauss, A., and Corbin, J. 1990. *Basics of Qualitative Research: Grounded Theory Procedures and Techniques.* Newbury Park, CA: Sage.

Tlaiss, H. 2013. "Women Managers in the United Arab Emirates: Successful Careers or What?" *Equality, Diversity and Inclusion: an International Journal* 32 (8): 756–776. doi:10.1108/EDI-12-2012-0109.

Tlaiss, H. 2015a. "Neither–Nor: Career Success of Women in an Arab Middle Eastern Context." *Employee Relations: An International Journal* 37 (5): 525–546. doi:10.1108/ER-03-2014-0028.

Tlaiss, H. 2015b. "Entrepreneurial Motivations of Women: Evidence from the United Arab Emirates." *International Small Business Journal* 33 (5): 562–581. doi:10.1177/0266242613496662.

Tlaiss, H. 2015c. "How Islamic Business Ethics Impact Women Entrepreneurs: Insights from Four Arab Middle Eastern Countries." *Journal of Business Ethics* 129 (4): 859–877. doi:10.1007/s10551-014-2138-3.

Tremblay, M. A. 1957. "The Key Informant Technique: A Non-Ethnographical Application." *American Anthropologist* 59: 688–701. doi:10.1525/aa.1957.59.4.02a00100.

Welter, F. 2011. "Contextualizing Entrepreneurship: Conceptual Challenges and Ways Forward." *Entrepreneurship Theory and Practice* 35 (1): 165–178. doi:10.1111/j.1540-6520.2010.00427.x.

Yousufazi, S., Y. S. Saeed, and M. Muffatto. 2015. "Institutional Theory and Contextual Embeddedness of Women's Entrepreneurial Leadership: Evidence from 92 Countries." *Journal of Small Business Management* 53 (3): 587–604. doi:10.1111/jsbm.12179.

Zahra, S. A., M. Wright, and S. G. Abdelgawad. 2014. "Contextualization and the Advancement of Entrepreneurship Research." *International Small Business Journal* 32 (5): 479–500. doi:10.1177/0266242613519807.

Life-course and entry to entrepreneurship: embedded in gender and gender-egalitarianism

Maryam Cheraghi, Kent Adsbøll Wickstrøm and Kim Klyver

ABSTRACT

Prior research has suggested that low gender egalitarianism results in a gender gap in entrepreneurship participation, as it provides men and women with different opportunities and constraints. However, this research has primarily relied on an unrealistic assumption, namely that gender-related opportunities and constraints occur evenly throughout different life stages. This paper details an institutional life-course model that explains gender-related patterns in individuals' propensity to enter entrepreneurship and contingencies related to the level of gender-egalitarianism in society and individuals' life stages. We test our conceptual model on a unique integrated dataset from the Global Entrepreneurship Monitor and the World Value Survey, encompassing a total of 672,781 adults in 71 countries.

1 Introduction

Individuals are embedded in different societies with various levels of gender egalitarianism.[1] Gender egalitarianism is defined as normative societal beliefs about the appropriateness and rightfulness of women and men occupying different roles (Inglehart and Baker 2000). Different levels of gender egalitarianism result in different opportunities and constraints on women's and men's entry into entrepreneurship (Jennings and Brush 2013; Ahl and Marlow 2012). The lower status of women in the business world has been reinforced by cultural status beliefs that impose biases on evaluations of competence and install stereotyped norms for appropriateness in career choices (Ridgeway 2014; Yousafzai, Saeed, and Muffatto 2015). Intuitively, one might expect that women that are embedded in societies with high levels of gender egalitarianism are more likely to enter into entrepreneurship compared to women embedded in societies with low levels of gender egalitarianism. However, recent studies have demonstrated the complex nature of the dynamics of women's entry into entrepreneurship. For instance, policies to secure equal rights in the workplace – e.g. policing paid maternity, parental and paternity leave – seem to raise the opportunity costs for women to enter entrepreneurship (Klyver, Nielsen, and Evald 2013). Also, institutions that are supportive of work-family balance, such as subsidised childcare, is correlated with lower representation of women in entrepreneurship (Thébaud 2015).

Although insightful, previous studies investigating gender egalitarianism/gender equality and gender gaps in entrepreneurship share an important limitation, since the theorising is predominantly derived from a single stage in women's lives, namely motherhood (e.g. Klyver, Nielsen, and Evald 2013; Thébaud 2015). In this way, women and men have been treated as homogenous groups, not accounting for the ways in which gendered differences in opportunities and constraints vary between different life stages. While much is known about the gendering of entrepreneurial activity (Davis and Shaver 2012; Klyver, Nielsen, and Evald 2013; Cheraghi and Schøtt 2015) as well as age effects on entry into entrepreneurship (Lévesque and Minniti 2006; Kautonen, Kibler, and Minniti 2017), surprisingly, age and gender have mainly been studied separately in entrepreneurship. The consequence is a lack of understanding of the contextual interplay between age and gender.

Therefore, our knowledge of how gender egalitarianism at the institutional level impacts upon women compared to men at different life stages is still immature. It has relied on a false assumption of homogeneity: that women's' and men's' experiences of opportunities and constraints do not vary between different life stages. This is problematic because it advices the implementation of policy measures to promote women's entrepreneurship, as if all women entrepreneurs are in the same life stage (e.g. motherhood). It overlooks opportunities to promote women entrepreneurs at other life stages.

We apply life course theory, to enable a theorizing that considers that women and men in different life stages react differently to various levels of gender egalitarianism (Mortimer and Moen 2016). From this perspective, societal norms and expectations mould women's and men's choices in an age-graded fashion that is associated with significant life course events such as education, parental role, work, and entrepreneurship participation. Our conceptual model is graphically illustrated in Figure 1.

To test hypotheses related to this institutional life course model of entry to entrepreneurship, we have developed a unique dataset combining individual level data from the Global Entrepreneurship Monitor (2009–2014) with societal level data on gender-egalitarianism from the World Values Survey (WVS). Our dataset consists of 672,781 adults across 71 countries.

2 Theory and hypotheses

While knowledge of the effects of gender[2] and age on entrepreneurship participation has developed from separate studies, there are notable similarities in the mechanisms used to explain gender and age effects, respectively. First, in both lines of studies, the combination of resources and motivation play a central role. Along these lines, gender studies commonly describe women as being discriminated against in terms of their access to entrepreneurial resources (Carter and Rosa 1998) and describes them as being motivated towards domains other than entrepreneurship

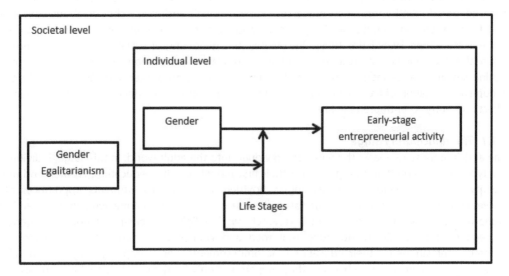

Figure 1. Conceptual model.

(McGovan et al. 2012). Similarly, age studies commonly maintain that entry to entrepreneurship depends on accumulation of resources and risk-willingness; both of these are features that change with age (Lévesque and Minniti 2006).

A second commonality is the emphasis on institutions as an overarching structuring mechanism that moulds access to resources as well as differentially motivating men and women. Institutionalized social norms and values for what is considered appropriate behaviour for women and men, respectively, shape gender roles and affect individuals' decision making with regard to family and career (McGowan et al., 2012).

Using life course theory, we argue that women's and men's resources and their risk-willingness develop differently over various life stages. Moreover, these differences are shaped by normative institutional structures. We specifically focus on the effects of gendered normative institutions as conceptualised by gender egalitarianism, i.e. beliefs or philosophies of what is desirable and right. Gender egalitarianism, in terms of what is desirable and what is appropriate for women and men, respectively, is thus manifested in societal values and norms (Inglehart and Baker 2000). Importantly, this distinguishes this study from prior studies that focus on gender *equality*. Gender equality describes the current states of affairs, and is typically assessed by the current state of formal and regulatory institutions (e.g. number of women in parliament, public childcare, or maternity leave) (Klyver, Nielsen, and Evald 2013; Thébaud 2015). Studies investigating gender egalitarianism, on the other hand, have focused on perceptions of preferred, desirable and appropriate *future* states.

2.1 Life course stages and gendering of entry into entrepreneurship

Life course theory is a multilevel paradigm that considers the effects of individuals' ageing and age in the context of society (Dannefer 2011). There has been a central focus on how age-dependent transitions in individuals' statuses tend to occur in a rather discrete fashion (George 1993). Significant transitions are involved in individuals' decisions to change from bachelor to marriage, from student to employee, from employee to retired, and potentially to becoming self-employed. A basic tenet in life course theory is that societies are structured in a way that normative institutions mould the timing of such transitions.

Early studies by Elder (1977) showed that differing expectations of male and female roles in society affect the ways in which boys and girls form identities and take on roles with regard to responsibilities, rights, and privileges in the family and in school. Later studies have shown that such gendered identity formation processes shape women's and men's choices about education and future profession, family, working careers, and thus their accumulation of resources at any stage in life (Moen 1996; Elder 1999). Presumably, this gendering of social pathways also impacts upon the accumulation of resources and the motivations of women and men to start new businesses in an age-graded pattern. In the next section, using Becker and Moen's (1999) four-group categorization of life course stages, we hypothesize about the effects of age-graded gender effects on entry to entrepreneurship.

2.1.1 The anticipatory stage

The anticipatory stage marks the entry of individuals into the adult world. In this stage, individuals are typically unmarried and preparing for their first job while still in education. Women and men occupy fairly similar statuses such as singles, boyfriends or girlfriends, students, apprentices, etc. However, studies have shown that normative structures at this stage channel women and men into somewhat distinct pathways. Education research has highlighted a persistent horizontal gender segregation (Charles 2011) indicating that men and women have different goals in life and different motivations for their educational accomplishments. For example, young women value security in employment more because they prepare not only for their professional life, but also for their future family life including parenthood. In contrast, young men are more daring and feel less pressure at this early stage with regard to preparing for future family responsibilities (Jayawarna, Rouse, and Kitching 2011). These findings suggest that in the anticipatory stage women are less inclined to develop resources that are useful for more risky career paths such as entrepreneurship (Schoon and Duckworth 2012).

2.1.2 The launching stage

In the launching stage, individuals typically form families; they get married and have children. They typically experience high demands from their new professional careers, as well as from nursing their children. Both work and family responsibilities become greater and the intertwined roles increasingly require negotiation and compromises. Women traditionally face more conflicts between their work and family roles; in particular as they enter motherhood (McGovan et al. 2012).

Normative institutions that emphasise women's responsibilities as the main traditional provider of childcare and care giving in the family place women's careers as the second priority (Pavalko, Elder, and Clipp 1993). This means that women experience more career discontinuity as they take leave from their careers or move to part-time jobs. On the male side, opposite societal expectations tend to dominate. As men enter fatherhood, they typically worry more about the financial aspects of raising a family, and increasingly focus on ensuring the financial independence of the family. This gendered segregation of the breadwinner roles of men and the care giving roles of women is at its greatest in the launching stage (Jayawarna, Rouse, and Macpherson 2014). Because women's risk-willingness and accumulation of resources in the work sphere is particularly low at this stage it is reasonable to expect that differences in women's and men's entry into entrepreneurship are especially pronounced during this life stage.

2.1.3 The establishment stage

In the establishment stage, individuals become more settled in their jobs and the parental roles shift from nursing to raising children. This typically provides individuals with greater levels of freedom in their personal and professional lives (Becker and Moen 1999). In particular, women experience relief from time consuming nursing activities which may accommodate more investments in career opportunities. In addition, as the wealth of the family increases, women experience freer career choices and higher risk-willingness (Jayawarna, Rouse, and Macpherson 2014).

2.1.4 The shifting gears stage

In the shifting gears stage, families typically become more financially established, and their children leave home. In addition, it is in this stage that planning for retirement is initiated. The increased levels of economic freedom, relief from child rearing responsibilities and considerations for retirement affect women and men differently. For example, Moen (1996) demonstrated that the likelihood of women returning to university or the labour market is higher in the second half of their lives. Having prioritized child rearing in earlier life stages, putting professional aspirations, including entrepreneurial aspirations, on hold, we therefore expect to see a delay in the entry of women into entrepreneurship.

Studies have also shown that because women occupy part-time jobs and experience discontinued attachment to the job market in the earlier stages (e.g. because of maternity leave and raising children) they accumulate lower levels of retirement assets than men (Moen 1996). Such shortfalls potentially increase the risk-willingness of women and motivate entrepreneurship; although this is primarily driven by necessity rather than opportunity.

From the theories presented above, we anticipate that the propensity to engage in entrepreneurship will be higher for men than for women across all life stages. However, gendered differences in accumulation of resources and risk-willingness, as the drivers of entrepreneurship participation, likely vary over the four stages. Constraints on women's accumulation of resources increase from the anticipation to the launching stage, and thereafter gradually level off. In a similar way, differences in women's and men's risk willingness increase over the anticipation and launching stages, but decrease over the establishment and shifting gear stages. Therefore, we expect differences in women's and men's participation in entrepreneurship to be more pronounced in the launching stage than in the anticipation stage, the establishment stage, and the shifting gear stage:

Hypothesis 1abc: *Life stages affect men and women differently, such that women are less likely than men to enter entrepreneurship in the launching stage than the other stages: a) anticipatory, b) establishment and c) shifting gears.*

2.2 Gendered life course effects embedded in gender-egalitarianism

The theories presented above share a strong assumption of low gender-egalitarianism. However, beliefs about the appropriateness and rightfulness of women and men occupying different roles vary greatly among societies. In societies with low gender egalitarianism, motherhood and 'care giving' responsibilities are the main roles for women, while men assume the role of breadwinners (Connell 2005). In these societies, life course events such as marriage and motherhood are perceived as having more value for women than education and entering the labour market.

In other societies, with higher levels of gender egalitarianism, norms are less restrictive with regard to women's and men's attainment of particular statuses throughout life. For example, variance in the timing of parenthood has increased, childlessness and divorce have become more normal, and there has been a decline in the number of children born per family, and therefore a decline in women's childcare responsibilities. Such changes have influenced both male and female paths through life (Moen 1996). We maintain that these institutional changes have also influenced women's and men's propensities to enter entrepreneurship.

In the anticipating stage, higher levels of gender egalitarianism provide greater equality in terms of access to education and other important resources for starting a business (Klyver, Nielsen, and Evald 2013). In addition, trends towards greater equality in participation of men and women in child rearing and other family responsibilities, and more equal labour market opportunities in later life stages increase the resource accumulation and the risk-willingness of young women. In turn, this increases young women's entry into entrepreneurship. In contrast, for men, new fatherhood responsibilities and higher expectations for their involvement in the family life (Barnett and Hyde 2001) require a greater balance between work and family commitments (Connell and Messerschmidt 2005).

In the launching stages, for biological reasons, the fact that women and not men give birth is presumably still associated with a reduction in women's propensity to enter entrepreneurship, despite increasing levels of gender egalitarianism. However, we expect that the increased variation in the timing of parenthood, which is correlated with higher levels of gender egalitarianism, will be associated with fewer gendered differences in the launching stage.

Finally, in the establishment and the shifting gear stages, where women no longer take the biologically induced roles surrounding birth, we expect that gender egalitarianism will reduce the gender gap in entry to entrepreneurship. While women have been more constrained in their accumulation of resources in earlier life stages, both women and men are more resourceful at these stages. In addition, women perceive self-employment as a more appropriate and legitimate career choice, together with feeling less burdened by family obligations. It is expected that men experience a relief from family responsibilities (lower than that of women's relief), but it is still greater than that experienced by men in societies with low levels of gender egalitarianism.

Overall, across the four life stages, we expect that gender egalitarianism has the lowest impact on gender gap in entrepreneurship participation in the launching stage (Hypotheses H2abc):

Hypothesis 2abc: *Higher levels of gender egalitarianism in a society reduces the gender gap of entry into entrepreneurship less in the launching stage than in a) the anticipatory stage, b) the establishment stage and c) the shifting gear stage.*

3 Methodology

To create a unique dataset suitable for our purpose, we merged individual level data from the Global Entrepreneurship Monitor (GEM) survey from 2009–2014 with country level data on gender-egalitarianism from the World Values Survey (WVS). The GEM adult population survey data contains individual level data from representative national samples of adults (18–64 years old).

WVS is a '… cross-national, time series investigation of human beliefs' (http://www.worldvaluessurvey.org/wvs, July14, 2016). Several questions in the WVS focus on beliefs about gender roles in society. Pairing GEM data gathered over 6 years with different waves of the WVS we obtained a sample of 672,781 adults from 71 countries around the world (Table 1). Thus, our unit of analysis is multi-level, involving individuals in societies.

3.1 Measures

3.1.1 Dependent variable

'Opportunity-based early-stage entrepreneurial activity' (TEAopp) has been used to measure entry to entrepreneurship (Cheraghi and Schøtt 2015). In GEM, 'early-stage entrepreneurs' are those who are involved in the creation of their own business and/or owner-managers of a firm that have been active in the last 12 months, own at least part of the business, and have not paid salaries or wages, including the entrepreneur's own, for more than 3.5 years. As indicated by Wennberg, Pathak, and Autio (2013) there are several challenges associated with identifying entry to entrepreneurship and firm emergence. Following Baughn, Chua, and Neupert (2006), we have chosen a wide-ranging measurement strategy including many entrepreneurs, rather than a narrow and exclusive measurement strategy, by using early-stage entrepreneurial activities.

We are interested in how gender-egalitarianism impacts men's and women's entrepreneurship entry decisions, and not whether they are forced into entrepreneurship due to economic necessity. Therefore, we limited our focus to opportunity-based early-stage entrepreneurship encompassing '… only those who are pulled to entrepreneurship by opportunity and because they desire independence or to increase their income, not those who are pushed to entrepreneurship out of necessity or those who sought only to maintain their income' (Bosma et al. 2012, 64). The variable opportunity-based early-stage entrepreneurial activity is coded 1 for Yes and 0 for No.

3.1.2 Independent variables

Life course stage. Following Davis and Shaver (2012), we applied Becker and Moen's (1999) four life course stages as follows: Anticipatory stage (18–29 years); Launching stage (30–39 years);

Table 1. Countries, N observation, early stage entrepreneurial activity, and gender-egalitarianism.

	N	Opportunity-based Early-stage entrepreneurial activity (%)	Gender-egalitarianism
Norway	12032	5.6	1.99
Sweden	13107	4.5	1.97
France	14050	3.2	1.58
Egypt	5270	3.4	−2.01
Saudi Arabia	4000	6.5	−2.05
Yemen	2065	13.9	−2.07

Source: GEM(2009–2014) & World Values Survey.

Establishment stage (40–49 years); and Shifting gear stage (50–64 years). Each stage was coded as a binary variable: 1 for Yes and 0 for No. For our sample of countries, the average age of women giving birth was 29 years, the average age of women getting married was 26, and the average age of men getting married was 29 (United Nations Statistics Division 2015). Together this supports a cut-point for the launching stage at approximately 29 years of age. An average total fertility rate of 2.1 (The World Factbook 2013) and considerations of the heaviest child-nursing load from birth until the age of 6 (start of primary school) supports a cut-off point of 40 years for entering the establishment stage. Finally, the average age for girls and boys leaving home was 25 and 28, respectively, making 50 years of age a reasonable average entry-point for the shifting gear stage.

Gender. Gender is coded 0 for male and 1 for female.

Gender-egalitarianism. To measure gender egalitarianism, we constructed an index based on four questionnaire items concerning individuals' attitudes towards women's rights in the public sphere and their role in the family from the WVS (Inglehart, Norris, and Welzel 2002). First, we included two items previously used by Spierings (2014): 'Men make better political leaders than women' and 'University is more important for a boy than for a girl'. We further added two items from the WVS as a proxy for individuals' attitudes towards gender roles in family and social opportunities in the public sphere: 'Being a housewife is just as fulfilling as working for pay' and 'Men should have more right to a job than women'.

Three items use a 4-point Likert scale from 'strongly agree' indicated by 1 to 'strongly disagree' indicated by 4. The last item 'Men should have more right to a job than women' consists of three possible replies: 1 for 'agree' 2 for 'disagree' and 3 for 'neither'. We changed the scale of the latter to 1 for 'agree' 1.5 for 'neither' and 2 for 'disagree'.

Factor analysis of the four items extracted one factor with a Cronbach's Alpha of 0.81. The gender-egalitarianism index was then computed by calculating the mean of the four items (standardised) for each respondent, followed by a calculation of country means. The country means were standardised as a proxy of gender-egalitarianism across the 71 countries. The correlation between our calculated gender-egalitarianism index and the index of Gender Inequality Index (Malik 2013) is .424, indicating some overlap, but also some diversity. Thus, gender equality, defined as achieved measures, and gender egalitarianism, defined as common cultural values and norms, are distinct constructs (Javidan et al. 2006).

3.1.3 Control variables

We controlled for a range of variables to account for alternative explanations as to why women and men enter entrepreneurship. To control for education level (Unger et al. 2011), we recoded the existing education variables to *years of education* as a ratio scale: 'none' to 0 years of education, 'Some secondary' to 8 years of education, 'Secondary degree' to 12 years of education, 'Post-secondary' to 15 years of education, and 'graduate experience' to 19 years of education. To account for financial resources, which is known to impact entry decision (Klyver and Schenkel 2013), we controlled for *household income*. We used a scale where 1 indicates household income at the lowest 33 percentile, 2 indicates household income within the middle 33 percentile, and 3 indicates household income within the upper 33 percentile. These percentiles were calculated per country. We controlled for the current occupational status, which is known to impact entry to entrepreneurship (Klyver, Nielsen, and Evald 2013). Using self-employed as a reference, seven dummy variables were constructed from eight *occupational categories*: full or part time job, part time only, retired, homemaker, student, not working or other and self-employed. Finally, we controlled for the level of economic development (Wennekers et al. 2005) using *gross national income* (GNI) per capita in a country (standardised).

3.2 Analytical technique

Due to the nested data structure (individual in countries), dependence between observations and our dichotomous dependent variable, the most appropriate analytical technique is a hierarchical generalized linear model (HGLM) with a Bernoulli distribution (Raudenbush and Bryk 2002). This analytical technique uses two different equations at the individual and country level, respectively, allowing for estimates at both levels. Variables at individual level are group-mean centred whilst variables at country level are grand-mean centred.

We applied a stepwise modelling approach. Model 1 includes main effects, Model 2 includes the two-way interaction terms for H1abc, and Model 3 includes the three-way interaction terms for H2abc. Testing for the appropriateness of using hierarchical generalized linear modelling techniques, we calculated the intra-class correlation coefficient, which captures the proportion of the total variance contributed by the country level variance for the main effects model. A value of 0.34 indicates that a sufficient proportion of entry to entrepreneurship is explained by country level factors, which justifies the use of multi-level modelling (Snijders and Bosker 2012).

4 Results

4.1 Descriptive analysis

Table 2 shows the descriptive statistics of variables. The highest correlation is between GNI and gender-egalitarianism ($r = 0.54$) indicating that multi-collinearity is not a serious threat to our results. In addition, Variance Inflation Factors (VIFs) calculated for each coefficient for all our models, using ordinary least squares, range between 1.1 and 4.4, which is below the maximum acceptable level threshold of 10 (Kutner, Nachtsheim, and Neter 2004).

4.2 HGLM analysis

Table 3 shows the results from the regression models. Results from model 1 show that females are less likely to enter entrepreneurship compared to men ($b = -0.24$; $p < .0005$) and that individuals in countries with high gender-egalitarianism are more likely to enter entrepreneurship ($b = 0.20$; $p < .005$). Moreover, individuals are more likely to enter entrepreneurship in the anticipatory stage ($b = 0.12$; $p < .0005$) and less likely in the established stage ($b = -0.32$; $p < .0005$) and shifting gear stage ($b = -0.70$; $p < .0005$) compared to individuals in the launching stage. Thus, compared to individuals in the launching stages, individuals in the anticipatory stage, established stage, and shifting gear stage are respectively 12% more likely, 27% less likely (1–0.73), and 50% (1–0.50) less likely to enter entrepreneurship.

In Model 2, we tested hypotheses 1a and 1b and 1c, which test whether gender gaps in entry to entrepreneurship are larger in the launching stage than in the anticipating, establishing and shifting gear stages. While we found no significant differences between the launching stage and the establishing and shifting gear stages (rejecting Hypotheses 1b and 1c), we identified a significant interaction coefficient of anticipatory stage and gender compared to the launching stage and gender ($b = -0.05$; $p < .005$). Surprisingly, and in contrast to Hypothesis 1a, the coefficient was negative, which means that the difference in women's and men's entry into entrepreneurship is larger in the anticipatory stage. The interaction plots in Figure 2 further illustrate this result.

The results are also confirmed in Table 4, which shows the results from the split samples of men and women. Men are 1.14 times (Odds ratio = 1.14; $p < .0005$) more likely to enter entrepreneurship in the anticipatory stage compared to entering in the launching stage, whilst women are only 1.09 times more likely (Odds ratio = 1.09; $p < 0.0005$).

Model 3 (Table 3) tests Hypothesis 2a, 2b, and 2c, which state that increasing levels of gender egalitarianism are associated with reductions in the gender gap of entry into entrepreneurship more in the anticipatory, establishing, and shifting gear stages than in the launching stage. The significant positive three-way interaction term for *gender-egalitarianism and being a woman in the anticipatory stage* ($b = 0.07$; $p < .005$) indicates that the gendering of entry into entrepreneurship

Table 2. Descriptive statistics: means. Standard deviation and correlations of dependent. independent and control variables.

	Mean	S.D.	1	2	3	4	5	6	7	8	9	10	11	12	13	14
1. Early-stage entrepreneurial activity	0.08	0.27	1													
2. Age 18 to 64	39.38	13.07	-0.07*	1												
3. Gender (female)	0.51	0.50	-0.06*	0.02*	1											
4. Gender-egalitarianism	0.35	0.93	-0.02*	0.12*	0.04*	1										
5. GNI	0.24	0.94	-0.09*	0.17*	0.00*	0.54*	1									
6. Education In year	11.02	4.84	-0.03*	-0.10*	-0.04*	0.06*	0.25*	1								
7. Household income	2.11	0.81	0.08*	-0.02*	-0.09*	0.04*	0.02*	0.27*	1							
8. Occupation (full time)	0.37	0.48	-0.04*	0.00	-0.16*	0.05*	0.13*	0.22*	0.20*	1						
9. Occupation (Part time)	0.09	0.28	-0.03*	-0.03*	0.07*	0.05*	0.07*	0.02*	-0.03*	-0.24*	1					
10. Occupation (Retired)	0.11	0.31	-0.09*	0.36*	0.01*	0.08*	0.12*	-0.07*	-0.13*	-0.27*	-.11*	1				
11. Occupation (Homemaker)	0.11	0.31	-0.07*	0.06*	0.30*	-0.13*	-0.13*	-0.20*	-0.08*	-0.27*	-0.11*	-0.11*	1			
12. Occupation (Student)	0.06	0.25	-0.05*	-0.35*	-0.01*	-0.04*	-0.03*	0.05*	-0.00	-0.20*	-0.08*	-0.09*	-0.09*	1		
13. Occupation (No work)	0.10	0.30	-0.05*	-0.10*	-0.01	0.02*	-0.03*	-0.04*	-0.12*	-0.26*	-0.10*	-0.12*	-0.12*	-0.09*	1	
14. Occupation (Self-employed)	0.16	0.378	0.28*	0.04*	-0.09*	-0.05*	-0.17*	-0.08*	0.03*	-0.34*	-0.13*	-0.15*	-0.15*	-0.12*	-0.15*	1

*p < 0.05;**p < 0.01

Table 3. Two-level logistic regression predicting opportunity based early-stage entrepreneurial activity.

	Model 1 Main Effects Coefficient (odd ratio)	Model 2 Two way Interactions Coefficient (odd ratio)	Model 3 Three way interaction Coefficient (odd ratio)
Anticipatory [18–29]	0.12*** (1.12)	0.14*** (1.15)	0.15*** (1.16)
Launching [30–39]	Ref	Ref	Ref
Establishment [40–49]	−0.32*** (0.73)	−0.33*** (0.72)	−0.33*** (0.72)
Shifting gears [50–64]	−0.70*** (0.50)	−0.70*** (0.79)	−0.65*** (0.52)
Gender	−0.24*** (0.79)	−0.23*** (0.80)	−0.21*** (0.81)
Egalitarianism	0.20* (1.22)	0.20* (1.22)	0.19* (1.21)
Anticipatory [18–29]*Gender	-	−0.05* (0.95)	−0.07** (0.93)
Launching [30–39]*Gender	-	Ref	Ref
Establishment [40–49]*Gender	-	0.02 (1.02)	0.02 (1.02)
Shifting gears [50–64]*Gender	-	0.004 (1.00)	−0.03 (0.97)
Gender*Egalitarianism	-	-	−0.07*** (0.94)
Anticipatory [18–29]*Egalitarianism	-	-	−0.06*** (0.94)
Launching [30–39]*Egalitarianism	-	-	Ref
Establishment [40–49]*Egalitarianism	-	-	−0.01 (0.99)
Shifting gears [50–64]*Egalitarianism	-	-	−0.13*** (0.88)
Anticipatory [18–29]*Gender *Egalitarianism	-	-	0.07** (1.07)
Launching [30–39] * Gender * Egalitarianism	-	-	Ref
Establishment [40–49]*Gender *Egalitarianism	-	-	0.02 (1.02)
Shifting gears [50–64]*Gender *Egalitarianism	-	-	0.12*** (1.12)
Education	0.05*** (1.05)	0.05*** (1.05)	0.05*** (1.05)
Income	0.26*** (1.29)	0.26*** (1.29)	0.26*** (1.29)
Full-time employee	−1.59*** (0.20)	−1.59*** (0.20)	−1.59*** (0.20)
Part-time employee	−1.68*** (0.19)	−1.68*** (0.19)	−1.68*** (0.19)
Retired	−2.57*** (0.08)	−2.57*** (0.08)	−2.58*** (0.08)
Homemaker	−2.45*** (0.09)	−2.45*** (0.09)	−2.45*** (0.09)
Student	−2.63*** (0.07)	−2.63*** (0.07)	−2.63*** (0.07)
No work	−2.10*** (0.12)	−2.10*** (0.12)	−2.10 (0.12)
Self-employed	Ref	Ref	Ref
GNI	−0.32*** (0.72)	−0.32*** (0.72)	−0.32*** (0.72)
Intercept	−2.88***	−2.88***	−2.88***
Random Part estimates			
Number of observation	672.781	672.781	672.781
Number of countries	71	71	71
%ICC	0.31	0.31	0.31

+$p < 0.10$;*$p < .05$; ** $p < .005$; *** $p < .0005$ (significant levels are reported: one-tailed for independent variables and two-tailed for control variables).

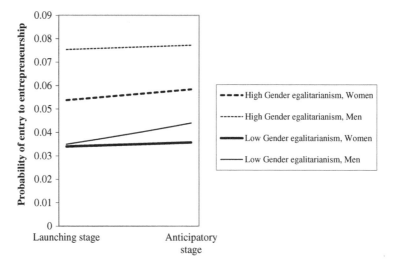

Figure 2. Three-way interactions plot: anticipatory stage (versus launching stage), gender and gender-egalitarianism.

Table 4. Two-level logistic regression predicting Early-stage entrepreneurial activity: Split sample between men and women.

	Men Sample		Women Sample	
	Main Effects	Two way Interactions	Main Effects	Two way Interactions
Anticipatory (18–29)	0.13***	0.14***	0.09***	0.09***
	(1.14)	(1.15)	(1.09)	(1.09)
Launching (30–39)	Ref	Ref	Ref	Ref
Establishment (40–49)	−0.32***	−0.32***	−0.31***	−0.32***
	(0.72)	(0.72)	(0.73)	(0.73)
Shifting gears (50–64)	−0.69***	−0.64***	−0.71***	−0.70***
	(0.50)	(0.53)	(0.49)	(0.49)
Egalitarianism	0.15*	0.15*	0.28*	0.27*
	(1.17)	(1.16)	(1.31)	(1.32)
Anticipatory (18–29)*Egalitarianism	-	−0.05**	-	−0.01
		(0.95)		(0.99)
Launching (30–39)*Egalitarianism	-	Ref	-	Ref
Establishment (40–49)*Egalitarianism	-	−0.01	-	0.02
		(0.99)		(1.02)
Shifting gears (50–64)*Egalitarianism	-	−0.13***	-	−0.00
		(0.88)		(0.99)
Controls included	Yes	Yes	Yes	Yes
Intercept	−2.52***	−2.51***	−3.27***	−3.27***

N = 335,639 women and N = 456411 men (71 countries)
+p < 0.10; *p < .05; ** p < .005; *** p < .0005 (significant levels are reported: one-tailed for independent variables and two-tailed for control variables).

for individuals in the anticipatory stage compared to individuals in the launching stages differs dependent on gender egalitarianism.

Somewhat surprisingly, Figure 2 illustrates that men's entry into entrepreneurship takes a much steeper dive from the anticipatory to the launching stage when gender egalitarianism is low. This result contrasts with Hypothesis 2a; namely that men have fewer constraints on entrepreneurship participation compared to women especially at the life stage involving childbirth, nursing and raising children.

The significant positive interaction term for *gender egalitarianism and being a woman in the shifting gear stage* ($b = 0.12$; $p < .0005$) indicates that the gendering of entry into entrepreneurship for individuals in the launching stage compared to individuals in the shifting gear stages differs dependent on gender egalitarianism. Figure 3 shows that this association is similarly attributed to men's

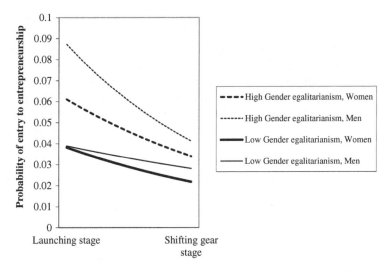

Figure 3. Three-way interactions plot: shifting gear stage (versus launching stage), gender and gender-egalitarianism.

relatively low entry into entrepreneurship in the launching stage when gender egalitarianism is low. Moving from the establishing stage into the shifting gear stage, men's entrepreneurship and the gender gap gradually increase. This pattern is opposite to the expectations of Hypothesis 2c.

The results from the three-way interaction model are confirmed by the results of the split sample analysis (Table 4). Both men's and women's participation in entrepreneurship is greater in the anticipatory stage compared with the launching stage. However, for men, but not women, this difference becomes amplified as gender egalitarianism decreases. Also, for men, but not women, the reduced level of participation in entrepreneurship in the shifting gear stage (compared to the launching stage) becomes more pronounced as gender egalitarianism decreases. While women's entry into entrepreneurship also shows age-graded patterns, surprisingly, these patterns were not significantly associated with gender egalitarianism in society. Therefore, it appears that men's age-graded patterns of entrepreneurship participation are more susceptible to changes in gender egalitarianism than women's entrepreneurship participation.

4.3 Robustness test

We completed several tests to examine the robustness of the results. First, the correct number of stages in individuals' life course, and their age range, has been the subject of heated discussions, essentially without any solutions (Levie and Lichtenstein 2010). To check whether our results are sensitive to more fine-grained divisions of life stages, we tested our results on a seven-stage model (Burt 1991). With some variations, the results show similar patterns and confirm our results. We also ran our models and analyses using opportunity-based nascent entrepreneurship as our dependent variable rather than opportunity-based early-stage entrepreneurship. Again, with small variations we identified a similar pattern and can conclude that our results are not driven by our choice of dependent variable.

5 Discussion and conclusion

5.1 Summary

In this study, we developed and empirically tested a life course model of gendered propensities to enter entrepreneurship as embedded in normative institutional structures. Specifically, life course theory provides a theoretical framework to examine the interaction between gender and age as embedded in normative institutional structures (Lévesque and Minniti 2006). Knowledge of the interaction of age and gender as embedded in normative institutions of gender egalitarianism has been unexplored with regards to entry into entrepreneurship.

In contrast to our expectations, this study revealed that the gender gap in entrepreneurship participation is larger in the anticipatory stage than in the launching stage. Surprisingly, this gender gap in the launching stage increases with increasing gender-egalitarianism, and is noticeably driven by a decrease in men's – not women's – entry into entrepreneurship in countries with low gender egalitarianism. Apart from the generally higher levels of entrepreneurship participation for both women and men in more gender egalitarian countries, this life course dynamic constituted the most significant gendered difference in individuals' entry into entrepreneurship in high and low egalitarian countries, respectively.

5.2 Contributions

The contributions of our findings relate to the on-going discussion of age and gender effects on entry into entrepreneurship, as embedded in surrounding institutional structures (Ramadani, Gerguri-Rashiti, and Fayolle 2015). Following previous studies investigating gender effects in individuals' entrepreneurship participation (Klyver, Nielsen, and Evald 2013; Thebaud, 2015), gender effects were expected to be primarily centred around women's roles in giving birth and nursing children. Thus, in contrast to our expectations, we observed that the gender gap in entrepreneurship participation was smaller in the launching stage than in the anticipatory stage.

Although this result is surprising we may invoke arguments from previous studies to explain it. First, building on traditional gender role reasoning, it may be true that young men are less concerned with future family responsibilities and thus more willing to take risks by performing entrepreneurship at this early stage (Jayawarna, Rouse, and Kitching 2011). Meanwhile, women may prepare for future parental roles at much earlier stages than men. Another explanation may be that women's motivation to enter entrepreneurship could increase in the launching stage; seeing entrepreneurship as a way to handle dual and conflicting pressures from the private and public spheres (Buttner and Moore 1997).

However, looking more closely at differences in how the age-graded gender effects play out in the contexts of high and low egalitarian countries, we may have to revise such interpretations. The latter argument proposed above supposes that increasing gender egalitarianism will reduce the gender gap in the launching stage, because proportionally more women will enter entrepreneurship. However, the results of this study support a very different story; namely that in the launching stage gender egalitarianism paradoxically increases the gender gap by promoting men's entrepreneurship more than women's entrepreneurship.

Thus, men in low gender egalitarianism countries are less likely to participate in the launching stage. We suggest this may be because the traditional masculine role of men as breadwinners in combination with women's role as homemakers (Potuchek 1992) becomes a considerable constraint to men's entry into entrepreneurship as they enter family life. This is because in low gender egalitarianism societies, men's entry into entrepreneurship causes large financial risks on the family; especially when their spouses are not expected to make any considerable financial contributions (Bielby and Bielby 1992; Potuchek 1992). From this view, the choices of men (such as becoming entrepreneurs vs. employees) are highly dependent on women's positions as homemakers. In contrast, in more gender-egalitarian societies, more equal gender roles provide greater scope for both women's and men's participation in entrepreneurship; yet, this seems to apply mostly to men.

Previous studies by Klyver, Nielsen, and Evald (2013) and Thébaud (2015) also somewhat counterintuitively found that a higher level of gender equality is associated with a larger gender gap in individuals' entry into entrepreneurship. With a focus on gender equality as promoted by formal institutions (e.g. number of women in parliament; childcare, maternity leave), this effect was explained mainly due to the increased opportunity cost of women's engagement in entrepreneur-ship. Our study adds a complementary explanation based in normative institutions. We show that gender egalitarianism – as normative cultural norms and values of how men and women should behave – also increases the gender gap, and interestingly, this occurs through enabling men's entry into entrepreneurship. Surprisingly, this effect is most pronounced in the life stage where it is least expected, namely the launching stage.

The finding that men's, but not women's, entrepreneurship participation is particularly suscep-tible to gender egalitarianism provides a new understanding of gendered processes in entrepre-neurship as embedded in normative institutions. Previous research has primarily focused on women's behaviour to theorise about the impact of issues related to equality of genders (Klyver, Nielsen, and Evald 2013; Thébaud 2015), and has especially focused on motherhood as the phenomenon driving the differences. This follows an assumption that women's options have traditionally (in societies with low gender-egalitarian) been constrained by the statuses of their husbands (Bielby and Bielby 1992). Nonetheless, in line with a series of other studies (e.g. Potuchek 1992; Moen and Yu 2000), our findings emphasise that gender gap studies should carefully consider that both men and women adapt their roles to changing societal normative structures.

5.3 Limitations

Several limitations apply to this study. First, because of data limitations, we could not determine respondents' life stages based on life events such as educational attainment, marriage, age at the birth of the first child, having children living at home, etc. This meant that we had to rely on theoretically deduced age categorizations of life stages. Because such categorizations are less precise and build partly on theoretical assumptions, this involves the risk of misclassifying respon-dents. Nevertheless, such misclassification tends to decrease life-stage-related variation, and lead to somewhat deflated effect sizes, i.e. more conservative results.

A related limitation relates to the cross-national design of this study. In general, cross national studies investigating institutional effects benefit from large samples of countries as they increase institutional variation at the societal level. However, for life course studies, such variations also impose a challenge when life stages are identified from respondents' ages. This is because life stages take different forms, and have different timings and different lengths in different societies (Blossfeld, Blossfeld, and Blossfeld 2016). Thus, the results in this paper are potentially biased due to the use of Becker and Moen's (1999) life stage categorization. Although this categorization provides a reasonable fit with average indicators of significant life events for the countries included in our sample, our model does not capture all cross-national life stage variances.

5.4 Implications

Several implications that are applicable to research and policy can be made from this study. Our study emphasises the importance of incorporating life course stages into theories of gender differences, as gender differences are age dependent. Although gender differences might not often vary in direction across life course stages, their mechanisms of variation might be distinctly different. For example, more knowledge is needed to explain why cultural norms and values predominantly shape men's, but not women's, entrepreneurial behaviour surrounding the launch-ing stage.

From a policy perspective, this study substantiates the loss of entrepreneurial potential that is associated with low gender egalitarianism. Even more so, and surprisingly too, countries with low gender egalitarianism in particular seem to miss out on a potential for men's entrepreneurship in their prime ages of between 30 and 39 years. This finding should direct future efforts of policy makers in low gender-egalitarian countries towards relieving men as well as families from the constraints and risks that seem to be correlated with men's roles as single breadwinners. So far, however, these constraints have been unexplored, and there is a large potential for future studies to inform policy on these issues.

In countries with high gender egalitarianism, it remains somewhat of a puzzle that gender equality in individuals' entry into entrepreneurship has not been explored further. It appears that gender egalitarianism promotes more normative freedom for both women and men to pursue entrepreneurship. However, to date we have scant knowledge of how this freedom is experienced differently by women and men at different stages of their lives. Attaining such knowledge is part of the key to understand why policy makers, who try to turn ideas of gender egalitarianism into formal measures and policy initiatives, often experience the opposite effects in the context of entrepreneurship (Klyver, Nielsen, and Evald 2013; Thebaud, 2015).

Notes

1. We use terminology of high and low egalitarianism. An alternative terminology could characterise low egalitarianism as inegalitarianism.
2. We follow an empiricist feminist tradition and treat gender – sex – as a variable (Alsos, Hytti and Ljunggren 2013); however, we simultaneously place women and men within a broader gendered institutional environment (Klyver, Nielsen, and Evald 2013).

Disclosure statement

No potential conflict of interest was reported by the authors.

References

Ahl, H., and S. Marlow. 2012. "Exploring the Dynamics of Gender, Feminism and Entrepreneurship: Advancing Debate to Escape a Dead End?" *Organization* 19 (5): 543–562. doi:10.1177/1350508412448695.

Alsos, G. A., E. Ljunggren., and U. Hytti. 2013. "Gender and Innovation: State of the Art and a Research Agenda." *International Journal of Gender and Entrepreneurship* 5 (3): 236–256. doi:10.1108/IJGE-06-2013-0049.

Barnett, R. C., and J. S. Hyde. 2001. "Women, Men, Work, and Family." *American Psychologist* 56 (10): 781–796.

Baughn, C. C., B. L. Chua, and K. E. Neupert. 2006. "The Normative Context for Women's Participation in Entrepreneurship: A Multicounty Study." *Entrepreneurship Theory and Practice* 30 (5): 687–708. doi:10.1111/j.1540-6520.2006.00142.x.

Becker, P. E., and P. Moen. 1999. "Scaling Back: Dual-Earner Couples' Work-Family Strategies." *Journal of Marriage and the Family* 61 (4): 995–1007. doi:10.2307/354019.

Bielby, W. T., and D. D. Bielby. 1992. "I Will Follow Him: Family Ties, Gender-Role Beliefs, and Reluctance to Relocate for a Better Job." *American Journal of Sociology* 97 (5): 1241–1267. doi:10.1086/229901.

Blossfeld, P. N., G. J. Blossfeld, and H. Blossfeld. 2016. "Changes in Educational Inequality in Cross-National Perspective." In *Handbook of the Life Course*, edited by M. J. Shanahan, T. J. Mortimer, and M. K. Johnson. 223–247. Cham: Springer International Publishing.

Bosma, N., A. Coduras, Y. Litovsky, and J. Seaman. 2012. *GEM Manual. A Report on the Design, Data and Quality Control of Global Entrepreneurship Monitor*. Global Entrepreneurship Research Association.

Burt, R. S. 1991. "Measuring Age as a Structural Concept." *Social Networks* 13 (1): 1–34. doi:10.1016/0378-8733(91)90011-H.

Buttner, E. H., and D. P. Moore. 1997. "Women's Organizational Exodus to Entrepreneurship: Self-Reported Motivations and Correlates with Success." *Journal of Small Business Management* 35 (1): 34–46.

Carter, S., and P. Rosa. 1998. "The Financing of Male- and Female-Owned Businesses." *Entrepreneurship & Regional Development* 10 (3): 225–242. doi:10.1080/08985629800000013.

Charles, M. 2011. "A World of Difference: International Trends in Women's Economic Status." *Annual Review of Sociology* 37: 355–371. doi:10.1146/annurev.soc.012809.102548.

Cheraghi, M., and T. Schøtt. 2015. "Reproduction of Gender Gaps Throughout the Entrepreneurial Career." *International Journal of Gender in Entrepreneurship* 7 (3): 321–343. doi:10.1108/IJGE-03-2013-0027.

Connell, R. W. 2005. "A Really Good Husband: Work/Life Balance, Gender Equity and Social Change." *Australian Journal of Social Issues* 40 (3): 369–383. doi:10.1002/(ISSN)1839-4655.

Connell, R. W., and J. W. Messerschmidt. 2005. "Hegemonic Masculinity Rethinking the Concept." *Gender & Society* 19 (6): 829–859. doi:10.1177/0891243205278639.

Dannefer, D. 2011. "Age, the Life Course, and the Sociological Imagination: Prospects for Theory." In *Handbook of Aging and the Social Sciences*, edited by R. H. Binstock and L. George, 3–16. New York, NY: Academic Press.

Davis, A. E., and K. G. Shaver. 2012. "Understanding Gendered Variations in Business Growth Intentions across the Life Course." *Entrepreneurship Theory and Practice* 36 (3): 495–512. doi:10.1111/etap.2012.36.issue-3.

Elder, G. H. 1977. "Family History and the Life Course." *Journal of Family History* 2 (4): 279–304. doi:10.1177/036319907700200402.

Elder, G. H. 1999. *Children of the Great Depression: Social Change in Life Experience*. Boulder, CO: Westview Press.

George, L. K. 1993. "Sociological Perspectives on Life Transitions." *Annual Review of Sociology* 19 (1): 353–373. doi:10.1146/annurev.so.19.080193.002033.

Inglehart, R., and W. E. Baker. 2000. "Modernization, Cultural Change, and the Persistence of Traditional Values." *American Sociological Review* 65 (1): 19–51. doi:10.2307/2657288.

Inglehart, R., P. Norris, and C. Welzel. 2002. "Gender Equality and Democracy." *Comparative Sociology* 1 (3): 321–345. doi:10.1163/156913302100418628.

Javidan, M., P. W. Dorfman, M. S. De Luque, and R. J. House. 2006. "In the Eye of the Beholder: Cross Cultural Lessons in Leadership from Project GLOBE." *Academy of Management Perspectives* 20 (1): 67–90. doi:10.5465/amp.2006.19873410.

Jayawarna, D., J. Rouse, and J. Kitching. 2011. "Entrepreneur Motivations and Life Course." *International Small Business Journal* 31 (1): 34–56. doi:10.1177/0266242611401444.

Jayawarna, D., J. Rouse, and A. Macpherson. 2014. "Life Course Pathways to Business Start-Up." *Entrepreneurship & Regional Development* 26 (3–4): 282–312. doi:10.1080/08985626.2014.901420.

Jennings, J. E., and C. G. Brush. 2013. "Research on Women Entrepreneurs: Challenges to (And From) the Broader Entrepreneurship Literature?" *Academy of Management Annals* 7 (1): 661–713. doi:10.5465/19416520.2013.782190.

Kautonen, T., E. Kibler, and M. Minniti. 2017. "Late-Career Entrepreneurship, Income and Quality of Life." *Journal of Business Venturing* 32 (3): 318–333. doi:10.1016/j.jbusvent.2017.02.005.

Klyver, K., S. L. Nielsen, and M. R. Evald. 2013. "Women's Self-Employment: An Act of Institutional (Dis) Integration? A Multilevel, Cross-Country Study." *Journal of Business Venturing* 28 (4): 474–488. doi:10.1016/j.jbusvent.2012.07.002.

Klyver, K., and M. T. Schenkel. 2013. "From Resource Access to Use: Exploring the Impact of Resource Combinations on Nascent Entrepreneurship." *Journal of Small Business Management* 51 (4): 539–556. doi:10.1111/jsbm.2013.51.issue-4.

Kutner, M. H., C. J. Nachtsheim, and J. Neter. 2004. *Applied Linear Regression Models*. 4th ed. New York, NY: McGraw-Hill Irwin.

Lévesque, M., and M. Minniti. 2006. "The Effect of Aging on Entrepreneurial Behavior." *Journal of Business Venturing* 21 (2): 177–194. doi:10.1016/j.jbusvent.2005.04.003.

Levie, J., and B. B. Lichtenstein. 2010. "A Terminal Assessment of Stages Theory: Introducing A Dynamic States Approach to Entrepreneurship." *Entrepreneurship Theory and Practice* 34 (2): 317–350. doi:10.1111/(ISSN)1540-6520.

Malik, K. 2013. "Human Development Report 2013. The Rise of the South: Human Progress in a Diverse World." *UNDP-HDRO Human Development Reports*, 2013. http://ssrn.com/abstract=2294673.

McGovan, P., C. L. Redeker, S. Y. Cooper, and K. Greenan. 2012. "Female Entrepreneurship and the Management of Business and Domestic Roles: Motivations, Expectations and Realities." *Entrepreneurship & Regional Development* 24 (1): 53–72. doi:10.1080/08985626.2012.637351.

Moen, P. 1996. "Gender, Age, and the Life Course." In *Handbook of Aging and the Social Sciences*, edited by R. H. Binstock and L. K. George, 171–187. 4th ed. San Diego, CA: Academic Press.

Moen, P., and Y. Yu. 2000. "Effective Work/Life Strategies: Working Couples, Work Conditions, Gender, and Life Quality." *Social Problems* 47 (3): 291–326. doi:10.2307/3097233.

Mortimer, J. T., and P. Moen. 2016. "The Changing Social Construction of Age and the Life Course: Precarious Identity and Enactment of "Early" and "Encore" Stages of Adulthood." In *Handbook of the Life Course*, edited by M. J. Shanahan, T. J. Mortimer, and M. K. Johnson, 111–129, Cham: Springer International Publishing.

Pavalko, E. K., G. H. Elder, and E. C. Clipp. 1993. "Work Lives and Longevity: Insights from a Life Course Perspective." *Journal of Health and Social Behavior* 34: 363–380.

Potuchek, J. L. 1992. "Employed Wives' Orientations to Breadwinning: A Gender Theory Analysis." *Journal of Marriage and Family* 54 (3): 548–558. doi:10.2307/353241.

Ramadani, V., S. Gerguri-Rashiti, and A. Fayolle. 2015. *Female Entrepreneurship in Transition Economies: Trends and Challenges*. London: Palgrave Macmillan.

Raudenbush, S. W., and A. S. Bryk. 2002. *Hierarchical Linear Models: Applications and Data Analysis Methods*. Newbury Park, CA: Sage.

Ridgeway, C. L. 2014. "Why Status Matters for Inequality." *American Sociological Review* 79 (1): 1–16. doi:10.1177/0003122413515997.

Schoon, I., and K. Duckworth. 2012. "Who Becomes an Entrepreneur? Early Life Experiences as Predictors of Entrepreneurship." *Developmental Psychology* 48 (6): 1719–1726. doi:10.1037/a0029168.

Snijders, T. A. B., and R. J. Bosker. 2012. *Multilevel Analysis: An Introduction to Basic and Applied Multilevel Modeling*. 2nd ed. Los Angeles, CA: Sage.

Spierings, N. 2014. "Islamic Attitudes and the Support for Gender Equality and Democracy in Seven Arab Countries, and the Role of anti-Western Feelings." *Multidisciplinary Journal of Gender Studies* 3 (2): 423–456.

Thébaud, S. 2015. "Business as Plan B Institutional Foundations of Gender Inequality in Entrepreneurship across 24 Industrialized Countries." *Administrative Science Quarterly* 60 (4): 1–41. doi:10.1177/0001839215591627.

Unger, J. M., A. Rauch, M. Frese, and N. Rosenbusch. 2011. "Human Capital and Entrepreneurial Success: A Meta-Analytical Review." *Journal of Business Venturing* 26 (3): 341–358. doi:10.1016/j.jbusvent.2009.09.004.

United Nations Statistics Division 2015 [Data File]. https://unstats.un.org/unsd/demographic/products/dyb/dyb2015. htm

Wennberg, K., S. Pathak, and E. Autio. 2013. "How Culture Moulds the Effects of Self-Efficacy and Fear of Failure on Entrepreneurship." *Entrepreneurship and Regional Development* 25 (9–10): 756–780. doi:10.1080/08985626.2013.862975.

Wennekers, S., A. Van Wennekers, R. Thurik, and P. Reynolds. 2005. "Nascent Entrepreneurship and the Level of Economic Development." *Small Business Economics* 24 (3): 293–309. doi:10.1007/s11187-005-1994-8.

The World Factbook. 2013. Washington DC: Central Intelligence Agency. https://www.cia.gov/library/publications/the-world-factbook/index.html

Yousafzai, S. Y., S. Saeed, and M. Muffatto. 2015. "Institutional Theory and Contextual Embeddedness of Women's Entrepreneurial Leadership: Evidence from 92 Countries." *Journal of Small Business Managemen* 53 (3): 587–604. doi:10.1111/jsbm.12179.

Negotiating business and family demands within a patriarchal society – the case of women entrepreneurs in the Nepalese context

Mirela Xheneti, Shova Thapa Karki and Adrian Madden

ABSTRACT

The aim of this paper is to advance our understanding of how women negotiate their business and family demands in a developing country context. The highest cited motivation for women's pursuit of entrepreneurship has been their need to attend to these demands. Yet, empirically we know little about the negotiating actions taken by, and the business satisfaction of women in the context of both livelihood challenges and patriarchal contexts, despite several scholarly calls for contextualized accounts of women's entrepreneurship. We explore these issues by employing a qualitative study of 90 women engaged in primarily informal entrepreneurial activities in three Nepalese regions. Our findings highlight three main and interrelated themes – negotiating consent, family resource access and gaining status. These themes allow us to contextualize the process of negotiating business and family demands by highlighting how women legitimize their business activities, respond to family/societal expectations and mobilize support for, and find satisfaction in their business. Overall, our study contributes towards accounts of business–family interface that incorporate the everyday practices of entrepreneurial activities amongst those less privileged in terms of resource access in particular sociocultural contexts.

Introduction

Women's increased participation in the global workforce, including through entrepreneurship (Kelley et al. 2015) has been accompanied by scholarly interest in the work–family interface and in how women negotiate the boundaries of their work and family roles (see Özbilgin et al. 2011). This literature highlights that work/entrepreneurship is gendered; the model worker/entrepreneur is imbued with masculine characteristics while women are expected to fulfil family roles (Ahl 2006; D'Enbeau, Villamil, and Helens-Hart 2015; Munkejord 2017). The conflicts arising through these tensions have contributed to women's experiences of work and the processes by which women entrepreneurs 'nurture' the work–family interface (Eddleston and Powell 2012).

Common to these debates has been a domination of individual-level discourses on how family and work boundaries are negotiated through locational, temporal, behavioural and communicative strategies (Nippert-Eng 1996; Clark 2000). Little consideration has been given to how socio-structural factors influence these individual experiences and strategies, and their eventual outcomes (Piszczek and Berg 2014). Similarly, entrepreneurship studies suggest that women entrepreneurs gain more than men from the relational resources developed and exchanged within the family context (Aldrich and Cliff

2003; Eddleston and Powell 2012; Powell and Eddleston 2013) without exploring how different family structures and cultural values affect how these processes play out in different contexts.

Despite some recognition that regulatory and sociocultural differences in developing countries provide a unique set of challenges to women entrepreneurs when negotiating the work–family interface (Al-Dajani and Marlow 2010; D'Enbeau, Villamil, and Helens-Hart 2015), knowledge of women's entrepreneurship in these contexts (Zahra 2007; Brush and Cooper 2012; Powell and Eddleston 2013) and their actions to negotiate business and family roles (Essers, Doorewaard, and Benschop 2013; Al-Dajani and Marlow 2010) remains limited. Those studies that have dealt with women's diverse experiences have primarily involved women migrants in Western contexts (Essers, Doorewaard, and Benschop 2013; Azmat and Fujimoto 2016). What these studies do show is that women's actions are developed in response to specific structural tensions/contradictions within particular sociocultural contexts.

Our aim in this paper is, therefore, to take these discussions further by focusing on a disadvantaged, yet predominant form of women's engagement in entrepreneurial activities in developing contexts – informal entrepreneurship. We argue that support for work and the resource access for reconciling business and family demands are particularly difficult to negotiate for these women. Thus, our guiding research question concerns how women entrepreneurs negotiate business and family demands in the context of livelihood challenges and patriarchal societies.

We explore our question by analysing informal entrepreneurial activities in three Nepalese regions, drawing on qualitative interviews with 90 women. Nepal is a good empirical site because it is a patriarchal and highly stratified society whereby power relations are not equal and the roles, behaviours and expectations for men and women are socially prescribed (ILO 2015). Unlike other South Asian countries, Nepal has the highest percentage of labour force participation amongst women (ILO 2015), and has undergone a long process of instability and conflict, as well as institutional change, including through challenging caste and gender inequalities in the country. These features offer interesting contextual dynamics, given the tensions that have arisen due to these institutional-level processes.

Our findings highlight three interrelated themes – negotiating consent, family resource access and gaining status that allow us to contextualize the process of negotiating business and family demands by highlighting a number of dynamics at the individual, family and sociocultural level. In so doing, we contribute towards accounts of business–family interface that go beyond existing temporal and spatial strategies of entrepreneurs. We incorporate the everyday practices of entrepreneurship amongst those less privileged in terms of resource access, who also operate in particular familial and sociocultural contexts that inform specific gender constructions. Overall, we respond to calls for contextualizing women entrepreneurship research (Zahra 2007; Brush and Cooper 2012; Powell and Eddleston 2013).

The article is structured as follows. First, we provide an overview of the work–family interface literature in the context of women entrepreneurship, followed by our conception of how gender constructions in developing contexts affect the processes through which women negotiate business and family responsibilities. Second, we use this conception to analyse our empirical data highlighting the variations in which women legitimize their entrepreneurial activities, respond to family/societal expectations and find satisfaction in their work. We conclude with a discussion of our main findings and their implications for the literature on business–family interface and women entrepreneurship.

The work–family[1] interface in the context of women entrepreneurship – a review and critique of the literature

The recent proliferation of literature on work–family interface has emerged in response to the increased participation of women in the workforce and the need to manage the dual-earner family model of most capitalistic societies. This literature has highlighted the tensions between work and family

(Greenhaus and Beutell 1985) and the proactive strategies individuals use to reconcile these pressures (Clark 2000; Nippert-Eng 1996). Individuals are as such involved in 'boundary work' in trying to keep the family and work spheres separate by using behavioural, temporal, physical and communicative tactics (Nippert-Eng 1996). Entrepreneurship, on the other hand, has been assumed to offer a better experience of work–family balance, allowing individuals to better integrate family, work and other responsibilities (Kirkwood and Tootell 2008; Hilbrecht 2016). Women, in particular, have consistently cited their need to balance work and family roles as their main motivation for taking up entrepreneurship in lieu of responsibilities around childcare, household and spousal degree of support (Hilbrecht 2016).

It is claimed that women-run businesses also benefit more than their male counterparts from family or social support, which ameliorate the tension between work and life domains (Voydanoff 2004). Based on the nature of conflicts women experience, Shelton (2006) proposed various mitigating strategies they could pursue to achieve their business-related objectives. Considering these strategies as a function of the external resources women could utilize and the salience of the family role, he highlighted the benefit of role-sharing strategies, involving delegation of family or work roles. While these strategies were directly linked to business success, others have maintained that women choose strategies that intentionally or inadvertently constrain the performance of their businesses (Jennings and McDougald 2007; Annink 2017). Overall, empirical studies suggest that family support enriches women's experiences (Eddleston and Powell 2012; Powell and Eddleston 2013; Hilbrecht 2016), given their lower access to human, social and financial resources compared to men (Morris et al. 2006). Additionally, it is argued that women's synergetic views of work and family (Jennings and McDougald 2007; Jennings and Brush 2013) enable them to successfully use personal resources developed in their family role in their business. Other studies suggest that women find difficulties in attaining spousal support (McGowan et al. 2012; Rehman and Roomi 2012) and their strong identity as 'good mothers' hinders how family and social support can be converted into resources that positively affect work–family balance (Annink 2017).

This literature, however, is skewed towards the experiences of middle class careers and independent professionals, or what Özbilgin et al. (2011) have called the 'ideal work-life balancer' (see also, Warren 2015). This focus neglects the need to understand the diversity of experiences and meanings attached to the work–family interface or the varied nature of family and social support needs. Emphasis on the psychological and emotional effects of these work–family conflicts on individuals has also overshadowed the structural antecedents of this distress and women's differential resource access to achieve work–family balance (Annink 2017; Rehman and Roomi 2012). Whilst research on women entrepreneurship has focused mainly on roles such as 'motherhood' (Brush, de Bruin, and Welter 2009) or 'business ownership', it has failed to acknowledge other family-related junctures (Poggesi, Mari, and De Vita 2015) and, arguably, the strategies of women entrepreneurs to adapt to changing family needs with regard to income, spare capacity and human resources (Alsos, Carter, and Ljunggren 2014). As importantly, because context is not prominent in these debates, the focus has primarily been on the conflicts between family and business roles rather than the more significant structural issues related to the conflicting expectations of institutions such as family, marriage, education and work. Apart from the practical issues of managing time and space commonly discussed, the work–family interface literature has not been representative of all types of entrepreneurs and has been silent on the institutional and sociocultural contexts that affect women's views of what is possible for them and their families and, in turn, the actions they take in response. We discuss below the implications of business and family demands on women in patriarchal societies.

Situating women entrepreneurs' business–family negotiations within patriarchal societies

The economic, political and social impacts of women's entrepreneurship in developing countries are well recognized (Minniti and Naudé 2010). In addition to their income generating potential, women entrepreneurs are also perceived as 'major catalysts for development' in terms of family health, education and investment in human capital (IFC 2011, 15). Most women entrepreneurs, however, operate in highly clustered, niche and saturated informal entrepreneurial spaces, in terms of spatiality and economic sector (i.e. low-profit services and retail) (Bardasi, Sabarwal, and Terrell 2011; Grant 2013). Their engagement in informal entrepreneurial activities is essential for the economic survival of their families, children's education and caring for the elderly (Gough, Tipple, and Napier 2003). They invest their profits in household and subsistence purposes rather than business investment and expansion (Neves and Du Toit 2012). Family support for running entrepreneurial activities is crucial for this group of women (Khavul, Bruton, and Wood 2009), especially considering the lack of efficient and supportive formal institutional structures in developing countries, such as lack of credit or official help (Bardasi, Sabarwal, and Terrell 2011; De Bruin, Brush, and Welter 2007).

As these women combine informal entrepreneurship and family responsibilities, they confront and manage similar logistical, temporal and emotional challenges as women involved in other types of work do (see for example, Backett-Milburn et al. 2008). However, in these contexts, women's businesses are conducted within patriarchal societies that prioritize male attributes and interests (Ridgeway 2011) and subordinate women within the family, education, as well as financial institutions (Zhao and Wry 2016). In the family context, patriarchy acts through hierarchical control structures, whereby age and gender significantly influence the freedom to make entrepreneurial choices and access household labour and resources (Viswanathan, Gajendiran, and Venkatesan 2008). Families reproduce expectations of female roles as carers or mothers, defining women through roles connected with family and household responsibilities (Welter, Smallbone, and Isakova 2006). Together with other enduring social institutions (i.e. caste or religion), they exert direct influence on whether women should work, the occupational choices available to them as a result of the gendered division of labour in productive work and their choices of work locations (Kantor 2009; Mitra 2005).

These factors often limit market access and business expansion opportunities (Bardasi, Sabarwal, and Terrell 2011) and constrain women to remain in the informal sector (Babbitt, Brown, and Mazaheri 2015). Even when women aspire towards success, there is no expectation that they will pursue a successful business career. Doing so is implicitly riskier for women at the family and social level, as in many patriarchal societies, whilst setting up a business for survival purposes is legitimate, growing to be a successful entrepreneur is not respectable because it delegitimizes women's traditional social positions as 'mothers' or 'carers' (De Vita, Mari, and Poggesi 2014).

Not surprisingly, women find ways to negotiate these challenges when attempting to reconcile personal, family and society's demands and expectations. A number of studies have highlighted how women negotiate with patriarchy to legitimize their work by emphasizing religious and culturally acceptable reasons. Al Dajani and Marlow (2010), for example, found that displaced Palestinian women in Jordan considered the passing on of traditional embroidery skills as an obligation embedded in their home-based business activities. In their study of Muslim migrant business owners, Essers, Doorewaard, and Benschop (2013) provide an account of how familial norms and values are negotiated through identity work in order for women to secure and legitimize their identities as business owners; thus, women construct their identities as business owners around both ethnicity and gender. Similarly, Azmat and Fujimoto (2016) in their study of Indian migrant women entrepreneurs in Australia suggest that the variations in the family embeddedness of women-run businesses are mainly explained by the intersection of ethnicity, gender and the host country's institutional and social contexts.

What emerges from these studies is that considerations of women's business–family interface must situate women's actions in and around gendered roles, household structures and the socio-cultural and institutional contexts they inhabit (Backett-Milburn et al. 2008). This would allow for familial, religious and cultural norms within gender constructions in developing country contexts to be incorporated (D'Enbeau, Villamil, and Helens-Hart 2015; Essers, Doorewaard, and Benschop 2013; Al-Dajani and Marlow 2010). Similarly, by focusing on axes other than gender opens up opportunities to understand how the varied experiences of responding to business–family demands stem from the contradictory expectations of different types of institutions. Thus, situating the business–family interface along both individual-level factors and socio-spatial characteristics would capture a more nuanced set of actions/strategies, whereby women mobilize resources and (re)negotiate relationships when responding to business and family demands. These situated accounts would also allow us to capture how changing conditions and circumstances affect the transient nature of some of women's negotiating actions.

Therefore, in this paper, we explore how livelihood challenges and patriarchal conditions affect how informal women entrepreneurs in Nepal negotiate the demands of business and family.

Methodology of the study

Context of the study

Nepal is situated in South Asia. It first became a republic in 2008 having undergone many decades of political instability and turmoil. The Maoist insurgency (1996–2006) motivated by economic inequality and poverty, and ethnic, caste and gender discrimination led to a heavily damaged infrastructure, the slowdown of private sector development and twice as low GDP rates compared to the decade prior to the crisis (Upreti 2006). The Nepalese economy is small, with agriculture being the major contributor followed by wholesale and retail trade and services. The informal economy employs 70% of the active population (CBS 2009). Women (77.5%) are disproportionally employed in the informal sector and mainly operate micro-enterprises due to their lower levels of education and lack of capital (CBS 2009).

Nepal is also a highly patriarchal and caste-based society influenced by Hindu religion, whereby women have a subordinate status. The Gender Inequality Index ranks Nepal 108 out of 155 countries. Traditionally, girls were excluded from education, as they were considered inferior to boys, who were entitled to good education and other familial privileges (Mahat 2003). To date, only 17.7% of adult women have reached at least a secondary level of education compared to 38.2% of their male counterparts.[2] Women have also been barred from inheriting the parental property getting exclusive rights only to their dowry (Scalise 2009). Changes have been made over the years to reduce gender discrimination by furthering the rights of women to parental property and land. However, in almost 80% of the Nepalese households, women still do not own any property and when they do so, the likelihood is that they reside in an urban area (CBS 2012). The lack of property and other assets also affect how women interact with financial institutions. Even when they own property, financial institutions would need a guarantee from the husband or father and would only disburse the loan if approved by them (Bushell 2008).

Another feature of the Nepalese society is the stratified caste system. The country's economic, political and social developments have affected people's attitudes towards the caste system, with traditional divisions of labour inherited by caste and traditional cultural norms associated with caste slowly disappearing in both the urban and rural areas (Subedi 2011). However, the differences in resources such as knowledge, skills and capital are still visible amongst the different caste groups (Villanger 2012). This particular sociocultural environment has contributed to the features of entrepreneurship and gender relations we discuss in this paper.

Research approach

We employ a qualitative interpretivist methodology to understand the experiences of women in negotiating business and family demands. Our approach is informed by social feminism, which considers gender differences related to early and ongoing socialization processes (Calas, Smircich, and Bourne 2009; De Tienne and Chandler 2007). In line with recent calls for studying women in their own right, rather than through comparison with men (McGowan et al. 2012; Poggesi, Mari, and De Vita 2015), we use a women-only sample and semi-structured interviews as our data collection method. Additionally, Nepal is a little researched context in the entrepreneurship discipline, which renders qualitative research as more suitable for understanding complex issues and contributing towards theory building (Eisenhardt and Graebner 2007).

Sampling

The focus of our empirical work involved three different sites – Kathmandu, Pokhara and Biratngar, where we conducted a total of 90 interviews with women entrepreneurs (30 per region). The capital, Kathmandu, is the main migratory destination for people seeking work from all over Nepal. Pokhara's economic activity is based on the tourism sector (hotels, restaurants, guides and crafts). Biratnagar borders India and serves as the main hub for the eastern part of Nepal. We used a stratified sampling strategy designed on the basis of sector of activity in each region and a mix of formal and informal women entrepreneurs. 70% of the sample (23 in each site) worked informally. Some sample characteristics are presented in Tables 1 and 2 below.

Half of the sample is between 31 and 40 years old, of higher secondary education, married and with school-age children. Most women in the sample are married highlighting the highly customary nature of marriage in the Nepalese society. Five women are single and never married, three women are divorced and three widowed. Women mainly operate own account businesses with only seven businesses being a traditional family business and six partnerships outside the family circle. Most women operate businesses in the trade and services sector (i.e. tailoring, knitting, parlours, grocery shops, clothing shops, cosmetics shops) with half of the sample having been in operation for over 5 years (Table 2). Another interesting feature of the sample, reflecting the high internal migration rates in the country, is the number of women (and their households) that are migrants from other parts of Nepal.

Data collection

Interviews were conducted during December 2014–March 2015, in Nepalese and subsequently translated into English and entered in NVIVO for data analysis purposes. Data collection was supported by three research assistants (RAs), who transcribed and translated the interviews. The RAs were local to the study sites ensuring their knowledge of local languages and these localities. Prior to data collection, they participated in a training workshop, which provided them with background information on the project, its main objectives and familiarized them with the topic guide. This was followed by several pilot interviews that involved the RAs observing and being observed by one of the Principal Investigators (PI). The semi-structured interviews lasted between 30 and 100 minutes and were held at the respondents' work premises. The interviews focused on a number of issues, including motivations to start a business and the range of economic, sociocultural and institutional factors that affected women's present choices and future plans, in line with the original project's main research question for understanding women's experiences of entrepreneurship in the informal economy. What we present in this paper has emerged from our further analysis of these interviews.

Data analysis

The data analysis was inductive and proceeded through several steps, moving from the development of 25 first-order codes that adhered strictly to women's own terms to the abstraction of 9 axial codes based on the literature on work–life balance (Gioia, Corley, and Hamilton 2013) and as a basis for the evaluation of contextual differences.

We then developed these second-order codes into the three overarching themes that form the basis of our argument on how women negotiate business–family responsibilities – *negotiating consent, family resource access* and *gaining status* (see Figure 1).

Table 1. Women's personal characteristics and household characteristics.

Family responsibilities	Education					Age				Household size		
	Illiterate	Primary	Secondary	Higher secondary	University	20–30	31–40	41–50	>50	1–2	2–5	5–10
No children[a] (7)	2	3	0	1	1	4	2	1	0	4	3	0
Pre-school children[b] (20)	3	1	1	7	8	12	8	0	0	1[d]	18	1
School-age children (49)	14	7	4	19	5	3	28	13	5	5	41	3
Extended family[c] (14)	3	0	4	7	10	2	8	2	2	0	8	6
Total (90)	14	11	9	34	24	21	46	16	7	10	70	10

[a] four of these women are single;
[b] two of these women are divorced and three widowed;
[c] one of these women is single and one divorced;
[d] this woman's husband has migrated abroad. She lives alone with her son.

Table 2. Business characteristics.

Business share	Sector					Years in operation			Residential status		
	Trade	Food processing	Handicrafts	Services	Agri-business	<1	1–5	>5	Native	Former migrant	Recent migrant
Single founder (77)	24	4	12	33	4	11	31	35	29	22	26
Family business (7)	5	1	0	0	1	1	2	4	1	4	2
Partnership (6)	1	1	0	4	0	2	1	3	2	1	3
Total	**30**	**6**	**12**	**37**	**5**	**14**	**34**	**42**	**32**	**27**	**31**

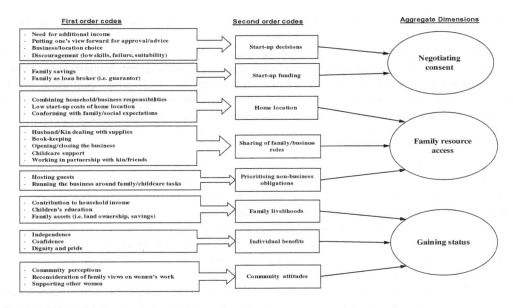

Figure 1. Coding scheme.

Findings

In this section, we explain how the three overarching themes reflect how women respond to experienced contradictions in institutional expectations. We highlight a number of variations when discussing each of these themes. Following Pratt's (2009) suggestion for presenting qualitative research findings, we illustrate our main points with 'power quotes', which provide 'thick description' (Geertz 1994), enabling the contextualization of findings. In addition, we present in Appendix 1[3] representative quotes for each of the first-order codes in order to provide 'proof' (Pratt 2009) of the interpretations of data presented.

Negotiating consent

The institutional changes in the Nepalese society have increased the acceptability of women's participation in the labour market, simultaneously increasing the difficulties for many to access formal jobs. As such, most women considered their involvement in entrepreneurial activities as a path towards gaining access to work and securing an independent income from their family. However, marriage in the Nepalese society still provides women with legitimacy, being the only way through which they can access economic resources, especially considering their subordinate status and lack of rights over parental properties (by custom inherited by sons) (Collinson et al. 2013). Women, thus, are heavily dependent on their husbands and family-in-law more generally, for their livelihoods. Being aware of the Nepalese patriarchal family model, whereby the responsibility for providing family income lies with the man, and the family hierarchies need to be respected meant that most women only started their activities following their families' consent.

Pokhara 2.5.2 said: 'I first talked with my husband. I discussed with him and he also gave me his permission ... I took [doll making] training because my husband told me to do so'. Husbands, their extended families or their parental unit in the case of single women were heavily engaged in the start-up decision-making process. Consent seeking was not uniform throughout the sample as women's life and family experiences were very different. In some cases, when faced with financial difficulties, both spouses had agreed on women's work, which meant that all family members had to contribute towards the family's income. These livelihood challenges were particularly intensified following these families' rural–urban migration and the lack of the necessary skills, education or social networks to facilitate labour market entry.

Consent seeking also led to heavily affected business choices such as setting up home-based businesses or businesses in which there was family experience and tradition. Suggesting the choice of similar-line businesses was justified on the knowledge the family could contribute to the business. Women were discouraged when their ideas were somehow divergent from this family knowledge. Discouragement was the most prevalent constraint in negotiating consent. It took different forms and derived from different sources within the households and wider family networks. It was articulated in terms of fear of failure when women were warned by family that they would not succeed in business given their lack of basic skills; the 'fit' of business activity with the family's spatial contexts/constraints, whereby respondents had to locate the business at their home premises or nearby locations; and the perceived suitability of certain activities ('professions') for women or their compliance (or not) with caste-related associations. Tailoring, for example, as an activity associated with a lower caste was frowned upon by some.

There were some extreme cases when women had undergone familial transitions, such as divorce, being widowed or were single, which 'freed' them from household responsibilities and made them less concerned with family's consent and the legitimacy gained as a result. They took, therefore, a more active role towards ensuring their livelihood. A respondent from Kathmandu engaged in crafting woollen products explained how the main impetus for her to be proactive in terms of learning this skill and running this business successfully was her previous family-based experience, a violent marriage, which she would be able to escape only with the means to sustain herself. As she stated:

> I was physically and mentally abused and he looked down upon my work.... We were married for 12 years and had a difficult time all those years as there was never enough money. That is why I decided to learn knitting, thinking that at least I would be able to survive [by using this skill]. (Kathmandu 1.1.4)

Similarly, 'losing' a husband to international migration and being completely dependent on the family-in-law for their livelihood and for raising their children pushed some women towards making their own decisions. Another respondent, who migrated to Kathmandu following her husband's immigration and her account stated explicitly the inter-generational tensions within patriarchal family contexts.

> Life in the village was difficult. My in-laws didn't treat me well so I came to Kathmandu to educate my children.... My husband didn't approve ... But I insisted and lived here alone. He used to tell me to return home ... Family support also plays a vital role. There should be someone who can support women in their business. Some families do not allow women to work outside home ... Women should be confident in their determination. I was very determined to achieve my dream of starting a business. (Kathmandu 1.5.3)

Being aware of the constraints of their subjugated role in patriarchal families, women also deliberately chose to negotiate consent as it facilitated access to other forms of start-up support such as finance. The family's financial assistance for business activities was highlighted for its interest-free nature or the lack of terms/conditions normally placed by formal institutions and non-formal lenders, thus avoiding institutional pressures such as regulations related to daily/weekly payments and the regular inspection of the business by financial institutions. The family's consent and support thus acted as a 'ticket' to family funding including savings, acting as a guarantor for women who lacked collateral to enable a successful loan application, or in some cases applying for loans to pass on to women.

Other women decided to sell their dowry or use children's savings instead of asking their husbands. Kathmandu 1.2.3, for example, having been engaged in a previous failed business activity decided to sell her golden jewelleries in order to open a parlour against the advice of her husband and friends, who believed there would be no demand for her business. The selling of gold ornaments reflects enormous personal risk in the context of Nepal as it is a form of bride wealth, reflecting the transfer of wealth from a bride's family at her marriage and embodying her social position. Its conversion in this way has great social and symbolic value, as in these contexts, it is often all that many women have by way of security and respect. Converting this dowry to an investment rather than asking for her husband's support highlights the personal risks and the social barriers women face in developing their businesses. What she experienced is representative of a wider family/societal problem related to perceptions about women's work. As she stated: 'everybody had doubts ... the problem is within the family. The family does not fully support women. They think negatively. But now it has improved' (Kathmandu 1.2.3).

Similarly, another respondent, who ran a registered boutique for a long time, problematized the tensions between the governmental discourse of equality between men and women, the lack of formal financial support for women's businesses and other societal expectations about women's roles and opportunities that conspire towards keeping them oppressed:

> If a woman wants to do business there is no support for her. She might have the skill, knowledge and confidence but she lacks capital. How can she start a business? That's why I think women have a backward status in our country. The economic status is very weak. They get skills, training but still are not able to start their own business. Some say 'my husband does not like me doing any businesses' ... Even the government advocates men and women are equal but in practice it's not the same. [Women] are still suppressed. (Kathmandu 1.2.2)

Family resource access

The insignificance attached to women's work was coupled with a strong societal expectation that women's place is in the home taking care of the household. One women involved in handicrafts shared this sentiment when she talked about the constraints women face whereby, 'they have to look after both their business and family. Many people in the society disparage women, who leave the house to start their own businesses' (Biratnagar 3.3.4). When talking about looking after business and family, women discussed issues around flexibility, role sharing and role prioritizing, common to many women entrepreneurs. They mainly referred to the flexibility of home/nearby home locations for taking care of household responsibilities, the sharing of various responsibilities with family and kin, as well as prioritizing family/social obligations to the detriment of their business activities. However, as we explore further in our analysis, the underlying rationales for these strategies reflect variations in resource access for negotiating business and family demands and highlight how family and sociocultural values are embedded in gender constructions.

Home location

Almost half of the sample ran home-based businesses or businesses in a nearby home location. These fulfilled women's need to 'earn a living' and not destabilize family dynamics; women could simultaneously look after their families and businesses. These choices hid several gender inequalities embedded in the family context. They reflected financial dependence on the family, childcare and elderly care expectations taking priority over business activities and family perceptions of women's vulnerability outside the safety of one's home, all with implications for business development. These dynamics are illustrated particularly well in the case of a woman momentarily operating her beauty parlour from home because of negative inter-generational attitudes and failure to mobilize family support with finance and childcare:

> I had to move the parlour at home because my mother-in-law didn't allow me to have it outside home. I couldn't manage time to look after the family. My mother-in-law always complained that I had to pay more attention to home duties ... My in-laws refused to give me any money. ... I am not able to work freely with my own wish because of money and family responsibility...Maybe after we get separated legally and get our part from the property, I will be free and can open my parlour outside my home. (Kathmandu 1.3.3)

When this choice was imposed, or was made for purely economic reasons (i.e. saving on rent), women were vocal about the pros and cons of location choices, particularly being away from central markets as a constraint on their sales or the opportunity to expand their business activities. Nevertheless, they complied with the norm that woman's actual place is in the home, as a way to avoid destabilizing the household and gain legitimacy. Women were also strategic in their choice of home or nearby home locations in order to be able to access free family labour or childcare and to access local markets where they could rely upon personal or family contacts as their customer base. As most women engaged in highly saturated sectors, customer loyalty was essential. Most women reported selling their products in family-members' shops or encouraged their family and social networks to use their services, emphasizing the web of obligations and the importance of reciprocity in subsistence markets.

Prioritizing social obligations

The flexibility the home location provided contradicted the Nepalese social practice of hosting guests at home, which led many women to undermine the business domain in favour of this customary social interaction. Whilst some assertive women asked their family and social circles not to visit during working hours, for others more compliant with social expectations, closing their business at the risk of losing customers or having to work during night time in order to fulfil customer demand was a more obvious choice. The close social bonds of local communities played a part in this dynamic as many of the women that reported this issue were based in Biratnagar, a less urban region with strong community ties. The time pressures women face when negotiating business and family demands, highlight how these pressures are further intensified by social practices as evident below:

> There is a problem when guests come to my house. Neither my husband, nor my children help me. I have to manage time for the guests and for my shop. It hampers my business. I don't even get time to have lunch. (Biratnagar 3.4.7)

This account also clearly illustrates how women postpone 'self' when attending to, or in accommodating, the expectations of family, business and society.

Delegation

Another common strategy which women utilized successfully was sharing the responsibility of running the business with family members. There was a high emphasis on the role of husbands or other male members of the family acting as intermediaries with suppliers. Women often rationalized this choice in terms of their lack of time or lack of social networks but it could arguably be a tacit way in which women's and men's roles are maintained – women being perceived as taking care primarily of household-related roles and men being engaged in male tasks and contact with other men. In this respect, women maintained the legitimacy as wives, mothers and daughters-in-law. Women also ran their business around their household chores and childcare, sometimes working overnight to fulfil client obligations. Some deliberately chose partnerships with other women in order to be able to rotate business around childcare.

Women with children of school age often engaged them in their business activities during holiday time claiming that kids this way 'can practice maths by doing real calculations'. Over half of the sample reported help with business activities or childcare from family and kin which suggests the *co-preneurial* nature of these activities to cope with livelihood challenges despite many not being the traditional family business. The family's collective efforts were intensified in nuclear families, where the intergenerational conflicts of extended families were not a burden to decision-making ability. Nuclear families' internal migration although limited the family and social links they could rely upon, pushed women to take decisions independently, work more cooperatively with their spouses and raise their children free from their families' influence. A woman from Pokhara, who used her experience of running a hotel and a vegetable cart in her native village to manage a vegetable shop with her husband away from her in-laws, illustrates the difficulties of breaking free from intergenerational dependence, educating one's children and meeting business and family demands when faced with resource scarcity:

> We tolerated the trouble my in-laws created. I had two children. My in-laws dominated me on everything, as we were dependent on them. I thought of doing something, I didn't want to be dependent on them.… My father gave me 10,000 rupees.[4] And sisters gave five thousand each. I bought a gas cylinder and benches with that money.… One brother said he will give me a cart. … In order to educate the children, we came here and started the business. It has been 12 years since we left home.… I feel satisfied.… Everyone praises us and say they are happy with our progress. (Pokhara 2.5.4)

Another interesting observation in the data was that women were seen as good at multi-tasking and making things happen through sheer will and determination, as many activities could be undertaken in ways that did not compromise their families and children. Despite problematizing a common view that business and family are in conflict in the case of women, this was often done through complying with gender constructions of women's household roles. Biratnagar 3.3.6, for example, has benefited in her business from a supportive family and access to finance, and she praised women's abilities without reflecting on the barriers many in a less advantageous position than her faced:

> Women can transform the world if they wish.… If a woman is educated all the family is educated is the famous saying … if a woman tries she can be more successful than a man. A woman works at home and also does some business to run the family. If she doesn't have to give time to the family she can achieve even better. (Biratnagar 3.3.6)

The conflicts women experienced in maintaining their roles as wives, mothers and daughters-in-law, and yet progressing in their business domains were also shared with various family members, who offered emotional support and advice and often encouragement with the progress they had made 'against all odds', all factors that led to women feeling the positive value of their work.

Gaining status

The last dimension of our framework related to women's satisfaction with their entrepreneurial activities. Not surprisingly, this reflected various aspects not necessarily related to overall income levels, but instead their family's livelihood, individual confidence and better positioning in the family and community. Being engaged in business activities improved women's value *vis a vis* male members of the household. Women's contribution towards their families' livelihood was central in almost half of the sample. Their work had contributed towards rent or buying a house, land and other living expenses, and most importantly the children's education. The capacity to 'earn a living' gave some women the opportunity to change hostile attitudes towards them from husbands, parents-in-law and the wider community, indicating the transient nature of some of the negotiations of business and family demands. Kathmandu 1.1.4 reflects on her business experience illustrating how her own persistence and positive business outcomes mitigated these negative influences over time: 'In the past, most people, my husband included, used to make fun saying that what I'm doing is a waste of time but now they all think that I have earned my living with this waste of time' (Kathmandu 1.1.4).

As women talked about the difficulties of their hard labour and sacrifices, they saw this as a worthy endeavour because it provided their children with an education and as a result the possibility to live a better life. The value of education was highly emphasized especially as many saw their involvement in these types of activities related to their lack of good education and skills that constrained their waged labour market entry. Thus, they aspired towards more fulfilling lives for their children. Women, whose businesses were more sustainable, hoped that their children would take over these activities and, hence, they were proud of providing them with the means to sustain their livelihoods in the future. Women also perceived their business longevity through the lens of their life-course and other personal circumstances. For example, women who had a successful business experience and supportive families expressed the desire to extend their business by increasing the shop space, diversifying their product range and hiring more women in the future (56 respondents). A former trade union leader being made redundant from a garment factory job, who now designs and produces cushions stated that:

> I want to employ more workers and extend the shop. I want to overtake the market of dolls and cushions in Nepal. I want to export the handmade cushions to foreign countries … I will register and make it bigger…. The trainees are making and selling in their own areas. I have a plan to give work to all my trainees. But I have no money to extend the business. I have a plan to open a cushion factory. So, the fund should be very high. (Biratnagar 3.2.5)

Those at an older age talked about exit (seven respondents) because the business had fulfilled the main objective of educating children. After years of hard labour, they felt it was time for them to reap the benefits of their work. For some, this meant being supported by their sons, as it is customary in the Nepalese culture. In other cases, women saw their spouse's retirement or the expansion of their families as their children got married, as an opportunity to increase the free labour supply in the business. As importantly, this was seen as a source of knowledge/skills brought into the business by younger, more educated people. Another respondent felt sadness in having to exit from a business that had sustained her family's livelihood stating that: 'my modern daughter-in-law does not want to do this business' (Biratnagar 3.5.4). This sentiment indicates how women themselves reproduce gender biases and family hierarchies and clearly emphasizes the intergenerational tensions stemming from processes such as modernity, women's access to education or urbanization that have altered women's expectations about themselves.

At a more personal level, women's business satisfaction related to 'independence', confidence and dignity, having achieved something despite poor education in many cases. The business gave them opportunities to socialize with other women, learn new skills and expand their business, and for many being able 'to give to others instead of asking from them' thus, better fulfilling their caring and nurturing roles. Women also considered values such as courage, determination and self-belief, often not celebrated in a society where women are not encouraged to think for themselves and are constantly framed through their family roles, as essential and worth talking about or shared with other women. Pokhara 2.5.3, who works in partnership with her friend in a tailoring business takes great satisfaction in being able to support women's economic independence through teaching them the tailoring skills. As she stated:

> Many women come. We welcome them and teach them what we know. Many of my trainees have opened their own tailoring shops…I feel very happy that I have taught many sisters [other women] and they have earned their living by this skill. Women should not confine themselves to their homes. They must do something. It is good to be independent…I learned tailoring before marriage. Six months after I opened this shop my husband died. But I didn't lose my confidence. I had to look after my business. (Pokhara 2.5.3)

Whilst these women were doing their share in improving other women's situation, this type of training and involvement clearly leads to the reproduction of women's roles and occupations, pointing to the need for developing a different range of skills and training for women entrepreneurs.

Discussion

Our main concern in this paper is with how women in a developing context negotiate the demands of their entrepreneurial activities and family responsibilities. We aimed to understand how the patriarchal context and their livelihood challenges influence resource mobilization and work satisfaction. We departed from a number of studies that have been concerned with competing business and family demands in the case of women entrepreneurs (Essers, Doorewaard, and Benschop 2013; Al-Dajani and Marlow 2010; Rehman and Roomi 2012), emphasizing that family support enriches women's entrepreneurial experience (Eddleston and Powell 2012; Powell and Eddleston 2013). Our main argument is that in the case of women engaged in informal activities in patriarchal contexts, the support to (and choice of) work, and the resources for reconciling business and family demands might prove particularly difficult to navigate and access. Central to our data analysis was, therefore, the way women occupying (in)formal entrepreneurial spaces exercised agency despite the constraints of their institutional and sociocultural environment. We identified three main and interrelated themes – negotiating consent, family resource access and gaining status that allow us to situate the process of reconciling business and family demands at the sociocultural level (See Figure 2).

As Figure 2 shows through getting support to work and develop their business activities, women gain status. This allows them to re-position themselves and change power dynamics in the household. We contextualize this account by highlighting the conflicts and tensions of institutional expectations – family, marriage, property rights and access to education and credit – which women need to accommodate and (re)negotiate through continuous interaction with their nuclear and extended families, and others in their circles, whilst attending to their family's livelihood challenges. Our first theme of 'negotiating consent' concurs with other studies that have suggested factors such as religion, ethnicity and familial values (Al-Dajani and Marlow 2010; Essers, Doorewaard, and Benschop 2013; Azmat and Fujimoto 2016) to have an influence on perceptions about, and support for, women's work. In fact, choosing to run a business conflicted with predominant views in masculine societies about women's skills and abilities and their societal roles more broadly. As a result, women's engagement in entrepreneurial activities required the consent/approval of the husband, or the household. Most women chose to comply with these gender constructions, primarily to gain business advice and access to family resources and support. Set within a context of difficult economic circumstances, lack of education and formalized state support, women's financial dependence, embedded in institutions such as marriage and family hierarchies, made the process of consent seeking an unavoidable step.

Our second theme of family resource access discusses these dynamics further by highlighting the supporting and conflicting ways in which family-based relationships were negotiated by women for both business and family roles. Not surprisingly, business and family domains were highly intertwined (Aldrich and Cliff 2003) not least because of the nature of women's businesses

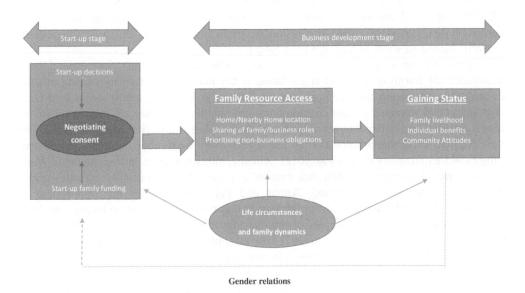

Figure 2. Analytical framework – negotiating business and family demands within a patriarchal society.

(Brush 1992) but also because the livelihood challenges of the developing context blurred the boundaries of business and family in the collective effort of most households to sustain their livelihoods (Webb et al. 2015). Women's family-based relationships allowed them to utilize a number of temporal and locational strategies and to engage in various prioritizations of either business or family/social obligations. Women benefited from the family support (Shelton 2006; McGowan et al. 2012; Powell and Eddleston 2013), but when their strategies are placed in the context of livelihood struggles and patriarchal family contexts, it is evident that they were negotiating more than conflicts between their business and family roles.

On the one hand, the temporal and spatial strategies of reconciling business and family demands, whereby they would choose to work from home or delegate certain work tasks, reflected stereotypical views about outdoor work as imbued with maleness and inside domestic work as feminine (see also Ntseane 2004; Fonchingong 2005). Thus, gendered relations embedded in family and social contexts continue to reproduce gender hierarchies and legitimize female subordination (Ahl and Nelson 2010). Alternatively, many women navigated a complex web of expectations stemming from broader economic choices (such as migration), intergenerational dependence and social practices, and obligations typical of close-knit communities and subsistence markets. Thus, women's negotiating actions reflected these competing demands and, most importantly, what they could achieve based on their available resources.

Our final theme of gaining status demonstrates that entrepreneurship was considered as a positive experience by most women, who saw their position in the family improve as a result of their contribution towards the family income and children's education. Most women talked about their business satisfaction not in terms of profit (see also Viswanathan et al. 2014; De Vita, Mari, and Poggesi 2014) but mainly in terms of reproductive outcomes – sustaining the household and educating children, emphasizing how deeply embedded women are in domestic relationships (Neves and Du Tout 2012; Al-Dajani and Marlow 2010). Making do within particular economic, family and social circumstances, rather than seeking personal advancement through business, characterized many women's strategies to negotiating business and family demands. This reflected not only women's family and caring roles, or the deeply gendered activities – tailoring, knitting and cooking they were involved in and socialized from an early age. It also reflected the affordances and limitations of the saturated markets they were active in. As most relationships with customers and suppliers were based upon communal links and proximity, characterized by 'long-term relationship rather than the short-term transactions' (Viswanathan, Gajendiran, and Venkatesan 2008, 221), typical of the informal economy, women's businesses had limited developmental potential. In fact, considering their circumstances, these women could be easily categorized as 'successful' having survived in business for a long time.

As importantly, the recognition and respect some achieved through their work also led them to problematize the norms of women's space being in the house or their abilities being inferior to men and, thus, increasing their courage and confidence levels. Thus, family values and cultural norms are part of women's gender constructions and relations and they are shaped by women's business activities and family interactions. Several studies have shown that women improve family dynamics and marital relationships as their ability to provide better food, clothing and education for their children increases (Scott et al. 2012). Similarly, migrant women entrepreneurs in Western countries have also improved their standing as a result of their business activities and the consequent identity work performed (Azmat and Fujimoto 2016; Essers, Doorewaard, and Benschop 2013). We take these issues further by pointing out how negotiating business and family demands is also affected by processes of internal migration, or development more broadly. In contexts like Nepal, these processes have led to a number of conflicting demands on women stemming from the varied pace of change in formal and social institutions. They have also affected women's expectations about what they can achieve through their own agency. There is an interesting interaction between gender and internal migration that needs more emphasis in future studies, as internal migration positively influenced women's decision-making ability, when they took decisions away from the influence of the extended family.

Overall, our themes of consent to work, family resource access and gaining status point to the need for conceptualizations of business–family interface that take into account both the nature of women's work and their sociocultural context.

Conclusions

Our main concern in this paper was with how women in developing contexts negotiate their business and family responsibilities. Our interest was both in understanding how these challenges play out in the context of livelihood challenges and patriarchal contexts and to what effect towards women's business satisfaction. We used a qualitative study of 90 women engaged in primarily informal entrepreneurial activities in three Nepalese regions. Our context is unique not least because of its developing nature, but also because not many Asian countries to date have challenged the inequalities embedded in the society as Nepal has done with its Maoist movement. We believe these features of the Nepalese context offer interesting nuances of entrepreneurship, gender and business–family interface. Our study makes two contributions:

First, it has implications for more contextualized accounts of the business–family interface by highlighting what is possible for women within the economic and sociocultural constraints they experience. We contribute towards accounts of work–life interface that go beyond the temporal and spatial issues common to many entrepreneurs to incorporate the everyday practices of work amongst those less privileged in terms of resource access in particular sociocultural contexts. There is value for future research to engage more fully with the nature of conflicts between different institutions rather than between work and family roles. This would help to understand the underlying rationales of individuals' strategies in response to these tensions.

Second, our interrelated themes of consent negotiation, family resource access and gaining status highlight interesting dynamics at the individual, family and sociocultural levels and demonstrate how women's re-positioning through income generation, increased confidence and support provision to other women shapes gender relations in the context of both the patriarchy and livelihood challenges in the informal economy. These findings offer a nuanced account of women entrepreneurship in a developing country context (Zahra 2007; Brush and Cooper 2012; Ahl 2006) by highlighting how gender constructions in these contexts are based on economic circumstances, and family and social values.

Our evidence suggests that both bodies of literature we have engaged with would greatly benefit from intersectional approaches that account for issues of class, race and gender, and how they are experienced by women in particular institutional and sociocultural contexts. Additionally, the nature of women's identity work when trying to fulfil their own expectations and those of their families and society would be interesting to explore longitudinally, thus capturing how their negotiating actions change over time to reflect changes at the individual and sociocultural levels.

Notes

1. We use the term 'work-family' interface although we are aware that most recent literature replaces 'family' with 'life' in order to denote aspects of one's life other than family.
2. http://hdr.undp.org/sites/all/themes/hdr_theme/country-notes/NPL.pdf .
3. Appendix 1 can be found on the corresponding author's University webpage.
4. £1 equals 120 rupees.

Acknowledgments

We thank the Centre for Economic Policy Research and the Department for International Development, UK for supporing the empirical data collection through their Private Sector Development Scheme, Exploratory Research Grant No 2533. We also thank the three Research Assistants who supported the data collection process in Nepal and the three anonymous referees for their useful feedback.

Disclosure statement

No potential conflict of interest was reported by the authors.

Funding

The empirical data collection was supported by the Centre for Economic Policy Research and the Department for International Development, UK within their Private Sector Development Scheme, Exploratory Research Grant No 2533.

References

Ahl, H. 2006. "Why Research on Women Entrepreneurs Needs New Directions." *Entrepreneurship Theory and Practice* 30 (5): 595–621. doi:10.1111/etap.2006.30.issue-5.

Ahl, H., and T. Nelson. 2010. "Moving Forward: Institutional Perspectives on Gender and Entrepreneurship." *International Journal Of Gender and Entrepreneurship* 2 (1): 5-9.

Al-Dajani, H., and S. Marlow. 2010. "Impact of Women's Home-Based Enterprise on Family Dynamics: Evidence from Jordan." *International Small Business Journal* 28 (5): 470–486. doi:10.1177/0266242610370392.

Aldrich, H. E., and J. E. Cliff. 2003. "The Pervasive Effects of Family on Entrepreneurship: Toward a Family Embeddedness Perspective." *Journal of Business Venturing* 18 (5): 573–596. doi:10.1016/S0883-9026(03)00011-9.

Alsos, G. A., S. Carter, and E. Ljunggren. 2014. "Kinship and Business: How Entrepreneurial Households Facilitate Business Growth." *Entrepreneurship & Regional Development* 26 (1–2): 97–122. doi:10.1080/08985626.2013.870235.

Annink, A. 2017. "From Social Support to Capabilities for the Work–Life Balance of Independent Professionals." Journal of Management & Organization, 1–19.

Azmat, F., and Y. Fujimoto. 2016. "Family Embeddedness and Entrepreneurship Experience: A Study of Indian Migrant Women Entrepreneurs in Australia." *Entrepreneurship & Regional Development* 28 (9–10): 630–656.

Babbitt, L. G., D. Brown, and N. Mazaheri. 2015. "Gender, Entrepreneurship, and the Formal-Informal Dilemma: Evidence from Indonesia." *World Development* 72: 163–174. doi:10.1016/j.worlddev.2015.02.019.

Backett-Milburn, K., L. Airey, L. McKie, and G. Hogg. 2008. "Family Comes First or Open All Hours?: How Low Paid Women Working in Food Retailing Manage Webs of Obligation at Home and Work." *The Sociological Review* 56 (3): 474–496. doi:10.1111/j.1467-954X.2008.00800.x.

Bardasi, E., S. Sabarwal, and K. Terrell. 2011. "How Do Female Entrepreneurs Perform? Evidence from Three Developing Regions." *Small Business Economics* 37 (4): 417–441. doi:10.1007/s11187-011-9374-z.

Brush, C. G. 1992. "Research on Women Business Owners: past Trends, a New Perspective and Future Directions. „*Entrepreneurship: Theory and Practice* 16 (4): 5-31.

Brush, C. G., A. de Bruin, and F. Welter. 2009. "A Gender-Aware Framework for Women's Entrepreneurship." *International Journal of Gender and Entrepreneurship* 1 (1): 8–24. doi:10.1108/17566260910942318.

Brush, C. G., and S. Y. Cooper. 2012. "Female Entrepreneurship and Economic Development: An International Perspective." *Entrepreneurship & Regional Development* 24 (1–2): 1–6. doi:10.1080/08985626.2012.637340.

Bushell, B. 2008. "Women Entrepreneurs in Nepal: What Prevents Them from Leading the Sector?" *Gender & Development* 16 (3): 549–564. doi:10.1080/13552070802465441.

Calas, M. B., L. Smircich, and K. A. Bourne. 2009. "Extending the Boundaries: Reframing "Entrepreneurship as Social Change" through Feminist Perspectives." *Academy of Management Review* 34 (3): 552–569. doi:10.5465/amr.2009.40633597.

CBS. 2009. Nepal Labour Force Survey 2008-2009. Kathmandu, Nepal: Central Bureau of Statistics, National Planning Commission Secretariat, Government of Nepal.

CBS. 2012. National Population and Housing Census 2011. Kathmandu, Nepal: Central Bureau of Statistics, National Planning Commission Secretariat, Government of Nepal.

Clark, S. C. 2000. "Work/Family Border Theory: A New Theory of Work/Family Balance." *Human Relations* 53 (6): 747–770. doi:10.1177/0018726700536001.

Collinson, E., N. Habeel, F. Jawaid, L. Jean, and K. Williams. 2013. *Growing Potential: An Analysis of Legal and Policy Barriers Faced by Women in Horticulture in Guatemala, Nepal, Tanzania, & Zambia*. University Minnesota, US: Humphrey School of Public Affairs.

D'Enbeau, S., A. Villamil, and R. Helens-Hart. 2015. "Transcending Work–Life Tensions: A Transnational Feminist Analysis of Work and Gender in the Middle East, North Africa, and India." *Women's Studies in Communication* 38 (3): 273–294. doi:10.1080/07491409.2015.1062838.

De Bruin, A., C. G. Brush, and F. Welter. 2007. "Advancing a Framework for Coherent Research on Women's Entrepreneurship." *Entrepreneurship Theory and Practice* 31 (3): 323–339. doi:10.1111/etap.2007.31.issue-3.

De Tienne, D., and G. N. Chandler. 2007. "The Role of Gender in Opportunity Identification." *Entrepreneurship Theory and Practice* 31 (3): 365–386. doi:10.1111/etap.2007.31.issue-3.

De Vita, L., M. Mari, and S. Poggesi. 2014. "Women Entrepreneurs in and from Developing Countries: Evidence from the Literature." *European Management Journal* 32 (3): 451–460. doi:10.1016/j.emj.2013.07.009.

Eddleston, K. A., and G. N. Powell. 2012. "Nurturing Entrepreneurs' Work–Family Balance: A Gendered Perspective." *Entrepreneurship Theory and Practice* 36 (3): 513–541. doi:10.1111/etap.2012.36.issue-3.

Eisenhardt, K. M., and M. E. Graebner. 2007. "Theory Building from Cases: Opportunities and Challenges." *Academy of Management Journal* 50 (1): 25–32. doi:10.5465/amj.2007.24160888.

Essers, C., H. Doorewaard, and Y. Benschop. 2013. "Family Ties: Migrant Female Business Owners Doing Identity Work on the Public–Private Divide." *Human Relations* 66 (12): 1645–1665. doi:10.1177/0018726713486820.

Fonchingong, C. C. 2005. "Negotiating Livelihoods beyond Beijing: The Burden Of Women Food Vendors in The Informal Economy Of Limbe, Cameroon." *International Social Science Journal* 57 (184): 243-253.

Geertz, C. 1994. "Thick Description: Toward an Interpretive Theory of Culture." *Readings in the Philosophy of Social Science* 213-231.

Gioia, D. A., K. Corley, and A. L. Hamilton. 2013. "Seeking Qualitative Rigor in Inductive Research Notes on the Gioia Methodology." *Organizational Research Methods* 16 (1): 15–31. doi:10.1177/1094428112452151.

Gough, K. V., A. G. Tipple, and M. Napier. 2003. "Making a Living in African Cities: The Role of Home-Based Enterprises in Accra and Pretoria." *International Planning Studies* 8 (4): 253–278. doi:10.1080/1356347032000153115.

Grant, R. 2013. "Gendered Spaces Of Informal Entrepreneurship in Soweto, South Africa." *Urban Geography* 34 (1): 86-108. doi: 10.1080/02723638.2013.778640.

Greenhaus, J. H., and N. J. Beutell. 1985. "Sources of Conflict between Work and Family Roles." *Academy of Management Review* 10 (1): 76–88. doi:10.5465/amr.1985.4277352.

Hilbrecht, M. 2016. "Self-Employment and Experiences of Support in a Work–Family Context." *Journal of Small Business & Entrepreneurship* 28 (1): 75–96. doi:10.1080/08276331.2015.1117878.

IFC. 2011. Strengthening Access to Finance for Women-Owned SMEs in Developing Countries. Washington, DC: International Financial Corporation.

ILO. 2015. *World Employment and Social Outlook: Trends 2015*. Geneva, Switzerland: Internaitonal Labour Organisation.

Jennings, J. E., and C. G. Brush. 2013. "Research on Women Entrepreneurs: Challenges to (And From) the Broader Entrepreneurship Literature?" *The Academy of Management Annals* 7 (1): 663–715. doi:10.5465/19416520.2013.782190.

Jennings, J. E., and M. S. McDougald. 2007. "Work-Family Interface Experiences and Coping Strategies: Implications for Entrepreneurship Research and Practice." *Academy of Management Review* 32 (3): 747–760. doi:10.5465/amr.2007.25275510.

Kantor, P. 2009. "Women's Exclusion and Unfavorable Inclusion in Informal Employment in Lucknow, India: Barriers to Voice and Livelihood Security." *World Development* 37 (1): 194–207. doi:10.1016/j.worlddev.2008.05.002.

Kelley, D., C. G. Brush, P. Green, M. Herrington, A. Ali, and P. Kew. 2015. *GEM Special Report Women's Entrepreneurship*. Boston: Centre for Women's Leadership, Babson College.

Khavul, S., G. D. Bruton, and E. Wood. 2009. "Informal Family Business in Africa." *Entrepreneurship Theory and Practice* 33 (6): 1219–1238. doi:10.1111/etap.2009.33.issue-6.

Kirkwood, J., and B. Tootell. 2008. "Is Entrepreneurship the Answer to Achieving Work-Family Balance?" *Journal of Management and Organization* 14 (3): 285.

Mahat, I. 2003. "Women's Development in Nepal: The Myth of Empowerment'." *PRAXIS the Fletcher Journal of International Development* 18: 67-72.

McGowan, P., C. L. Redeker, S. Y. Cooper, and K. Greenan. 2012. "Female Entrepreneurship and the Management of Business and Domestic Roles: Motivations, Expectations and Realities." *Entrepreneurship & Regional Development* 24 (1–2): 53–72. doi:10.1080/08985626.2012.637351.

Minniti, M. and W. Naude. 2010. "What Do We Know About the Patterns and Determinants of Female Entrepreneurship across Countries?" *The European Journal of Development Research* 22 (3): 277–293. doi:10.1057/ejdr.2010.17.

Mitra, A. 2005. "Women in the Urban Informal Sector: Perpetuation of Meagre Earnings." *Development and Change* 36 (2): 291–316. doi:10.1111/dech.2005.36.issue-2.

Morris, M. H., N. N. Miyasaki, C. E. Watters, and S. M. Coombes. 2006. "The Dilemma of Growth: Understanding Venture Size Choices of Women Entrepreneurs." *Journal of Small Business Management* 44 (2): 221–244. doi:10.1111/jsbm.2006.44.issue-2.

Munkejord, M. C. 2017. "His or Her Work–Life Balance? Experiences of Self-Employed Immigrant Parents." *Work, Employment and Society* 31 (4): 624–639. doi:10.1177/0950017016667041.

Neves, D., and A. Du Toit. 2012. "Money and Sociality in South Africa's Informal Economy." *Africa (Roma), Quaderni* 82 (1): 131–149. doi:10.1017/S0001972011000763.

Nippert-Eng, C. 1996. Calendars and Keys: The Classification of "Home" and "Work". Paper presented at the Sociological Forum. doi:10.1007/BF02408393

Özbilgin, M. F., A. T. Beauregard, A. Tatli, and M. P. Bell. 2011. "Work–Life, Diversity and Intersectionality: A Critical Review and Research Agenda." *International Journal of Management Reviews* 13 (2): 177–198. doi:10.1111/j.1468-2370.2010.00291.x.

Ntseane, P. 2004. "Being a Female Entrepreneur in Botswana: Cultures, Values, Strategies for Success." *Gender And Development* 12 (2): 37-43.

Piszczek, M. M., and P. Berg. 2014. "Expanding the Boundaries of Boundary Theory: Regulative Institutions and Work–Family Role Management." *Human Relations* 67 (12): 1491–1512. doi:10.1177/0018726714524241.

Poggesi, S., M. Mari, and L. De Vita. 2015. "What's New in Female Entrepreneurship Research? Answers from the Literature." *International Entrepreneurship and Management Journal* 12 (3): 735–764. doi:10.1007/s11365-015-0364-5.

Powell, G. N., and K. A. Eddleston. 2013. "Linking Family-To-Business Enrichment and Support to Entrepreneurial Success: Do Female and Male Entrepreneurs Experience Different Outcomes?" *Journal of Business Venturing* 28 (2): 261–280. doi:10.1016/j.jbusvent.2012.02.007.

Pratt, M. G. 2009. "From the Editors: For the Lack of a Boilerplate: Tips on Writing up (And Reviewing) Qualitative Research." *Academy of Management Journal* 52 (5): 856–862. doi:10.5465/amj.2009.44632557.

Rehman, S., and A. M. Roomi. 2012. "Gender and Work-Life Balance: A Phenomenological Study of Women Entrepreneurs in Pakistan." *Journal of Small Business and Enterprise Development* 19 (2): 209–228. doi:10.1108/14626001211223865.

Ridgeway, C. L. 2011. *Framed by Gender: How Gender Inequality Persists in the Modern World*. Oxford: Oxford University Press.

Scalise, E. 2009. "Women's Inheritance Rights to Land and Property in South Asia: A Study of Afghanistan, Bangladesh, India, Nepal, Pakistan, and Sri Lanka." *Rural Development Institute Report for the World Justice Project*. Brandon, Canada: Rural Development Institute.

Shelton, L. M. 2006. "Female Entrepreneurs, Work–Family Conflict, and Venture Performance: New Insights into the Work–Family Interface." *Journal of Small Business Management* 44 (2): 285–297. doi:10.1111/jsbm.2006.44.issue-2.

Subedi, M. 2011. "Caste System: Theories and Practices in Nepal." *Himalayan Journal of Sociology and Anthropology* 4: 134–1

Upreti, B. C. 2006. "The Maoist Insurgency in Nepal: Nature, Growth and Impact." *South Asian Survey* 13 (1): 35-50.

Villanger, E. 2012. "*Caste Discrimination and Barriers to Microenterprise Growth in Nepal*." CMI working paper 9. Bergen, Norway: Chr. Michelsen Institute.

Viswanathan, M., R. Echambadi, S. Venugopal, and S. Sridharan. 2014. "Subsistence Entrepreneurship, Value Creation and Community Exchange Systems: a Social Capital Explanation." *Journal Of Macromarketing* 34 (2): 213-226.

Viswanathan, M., S. Gajendiran, and R. Venkatesan. 2008. "Understanding and Enabling Marketplace Literacy in Subsistence Contexts: The Development of a Consumer and Entrepreneurial Literacy Educational Program in South India." *International Journal of Educational Development* 28 (3): 300–319. doi:10.1016/j.ijedudev.2007.05.004.

Voydanoff, P. 2004. "The Effects of Work Demands and Resources on Work-to-Family Conflict and Facilitation." *Journal of Marriage and Family* 66 (2): 398–412. doi:10.1111/jomf.2004.66.issue-2.

Warren, T. 2015. "Work–Life Balance/Imbalance: The Dominance of the Middle Class and the Neglect of the Working Class." *The British Journal of Sociology* 66 (4): 691–717. doi:10.1111/1468-4446.12160.

Webb, J. W., C. G. Pryor, and F. W. Kellermans. 2015. "Household Enterprise in Base Of Pyramid Markets: The Influence Of Institutions and Family Embeddedness." *Africa Journal Of Management* 1 (2): 115-136.

Welter, F., D. Smallbone, and N. B. Isakova. 2006. *Enterprising Women in Transition Economies*. Aldershot: Ashgate Publishing.

Zahra, S. A. 2007. "Contextualizing Theory Building in Entrepreneurship Research." *Journal of Business Venturing* 22 (3): 443–452. doi:10.1016/j.jbusvent.2006.04.007.

Zhao, E. Y., and T. Wry. 2016. "Not All Inequality Is Equal: Deconstructing the Societal Logic of Patriarchy to Understand Microfinance Lending to Women." *Academy of Management Journal* 59 (6): 1994–2020. doi:10.5465/amj.2015.0476.

Embeddedness in context: understanding gender in a female entrepreneurship network

Annie Roos (iD)

ABSTRACT

In this paper I argue that through a process of embeddedness in context, a female entrepreneurship network is able to challenge gender structures. I investigate how a female entrepreneurship network is constructed and how they reinforce and possibly challenge existing gender structures. From an ethnographic study, three processes in the female entrepreneurship network were identified: *making proper entrepreneurs, building relationships* and *engaging in change*. In the different processes the women involved in the network reinforced gender structures through compliance with a masculine discourse of entrepreneurship, but also challenged gender structures through questioning this discourse. Through becoming embedded in their local community, the women entrepreneurs were able to take charge of the development of the network and challenge gender structures as a result of questioning the masculine discourse of entrepreneurship. This implies an interplay between embeddedness and gender as two separate but dependent processes. Linking together gender and embeddedness elicits a new take on the way female entrepreneurship networks are constructed and how they could advance gender equality within entrepreneurship. Consequently, this paper emphasises a need for further examination of embeddedness within gender and entrepreneurship research.

Introduction

Programmes to support women's entrepreneurship have been both recognized and questioned as important in encouraging more women to become entrepreneurs and changing the gendered entrepreneurship discourse. The programmes are important for women to be able to meet personal and economic goals (Marlow and Patton 2005). Hanson (2009) argues that a further focus on empowering women entrepreneurs within the programme will enable the women to challenge gender structures. At the same time, these programmes further complies with the masculine norm of economy, as economic measures are determined by masculine precursors and there are limited discussions on structural issues surrounding gender and entrepreneurship (Marlow and Patton 2005). Stating that women need to network more to become more successful entrepreneurs merely establishes the notion that it is women, and not the structures, that need to change (Mirchandani 1999; Hughes et al. 2012). Women are seen as unable to achieve their entrepreneurial potential without the assistance of education, support and encouragement (Marlow and McAdam 2013). Women entrepreneurs thus operate under a 'damned if you do, damned if you don't' scenario (Ahl and Marlow 2012). The women are 'damned' if they act as proper (male) entrepreneurs, since complying with the masculine norm further upholds subordination of other forms of entrepreneurship. The women are 'damned if they don't' strive to act as proper entrepreneurs, since they then lack legitimacy and are not considered proper entrepreneurs.

With the aim of contributing to understanding the processes of gendering entrepreneurship, I address the research question: How does a female entrepreneurship network reinforce and challenge gender structures? The analysis is made through applying a theoretical framework, which links gender to embeddedness in context. Applying a poststructuralist perspective, gender is presented as a structure that people, phenomena and institutions relate to (Calás and Smircich 1996). The structures are produced through a process of social situations (West and Zimmerman 1987; Martin 2003) where differences between women and men are accomplished through creating advantage and disadvantage between femininity and masculinity (Acker 1990). Similar to gender, embeddedness is a process. Becoming embedded is to acknowledge the social context, the surrounding environment in the entrepreneurship process (Jack and Anderson 2002; Korsgaard, Ferguson, and Gaddefors 2015).

Through this study I intend to advance research on gender and entrepreneurship in several ways. First, I examine how female entrepreneurship networks are constructed, how they reinforce and challenge gender structures. Second, I show how moving towards being embedded in context enabled a female entrepreneurship network to challenge gender structures. Third, I bring forth how the processes of embeddedness and gender interplay in a female entrepreneurship network.

Initially, the paper defines some key concepts through a theoretical framework. Next, the methodological approach is developed, presenting the case studied. The case and my analysis are then offered in relation to the theoretical framework. Lastly, the findings are discussed and a conclusion is made.

Theoretical framework

By acknowledging the interplay of the gender process with different social processes (Deutsch 2007), networks targeting women are affected by and affect gender structures in various ways. As this paper focuses on how these gender structures come about and are changed through reinforcement and challenging actions, the production of gender will be the basis for analyzing the relationship between a female entrepreneurship network and the gender process. The production of gender is in itself a way of creating differences (West and Zimmerman 1987) attributing characteristics of advantage and disadvantage between women and men, and femininity and masculinity (Acker 1990). Here gender springs from social situations and is continuously produced through symbols, interactions and behaviours (West and Zimmerman 1987; Martin 2003). Structures are evident that separate men and women and value them differently (Hirdman 1988). When it comes to the entrepreneurship discourse, the hierarchy in gender structures (Hirdman 1988) is seen in how a feminine perspective becomes positioned as subordinated (Ogbor 2000). Society's view of femininity simply does not fit into the mainstream view of entrepreneurship (Ahl 2006). As an example, Lewis (2006) and Korsgaard and Anderson (2011) show how within the entrepreneurship discourse, a serious business is a business that strives for economic growth; the social enabler, social context and social outcome of entrepreneurship, is thus overlooked. Then, since a stable and small business is cast as the opposite, and men are seen as owning businesses focused on growth, women are not seen as having a place within this discourse. The dividing aspect of gender structures (Hirdman 1988) is seen in how comparisons are often made between women and men, separating *women entrepreneurs* from *entrepreneurs*, by portraying women as having shortcomings and not being as entrepreneurial as men (Bruni, Gherardi, and Poggio 2004; Ahl 2006; Henry, Foss, and Ahl 2015). The actions people perform in relation to these structures could be seen as *reinforcing* or *challenging* (West and Zimmerman 1987). Following and conforming to gender structures is a reinforcement of the structures. While a challenging action is, for example when a woman runs a business (Berg 1997) or when spaces for new expressions of the successful business woman are provided (Anderson 2008).

As I show in this paper, balancing the embeddedness process within an entrepreneurship process is a way of challenging gender structures. Since there are different types of embeddedness, such as political, cultural, cognitive and social (Welter and Smallbone 2010), using a mixed embeddedness perspective (Kloosterman, Van Der Leun, and Rath 1999) means these different types are used when analyzing an entrepreneurship process. Much like gender, embeddedness is a social process. Unlike the gender process, which is a dichotomy of either reinforcing or challenging structures, embeddedness is a process of moving between two extremes. One extreme is the rational market behaviour where almost no mention is made of how social relationships effect decisions. Here social embeddedness is almost non-existent and the relationship between buyer and seller is based on price equilibrium (Uzzi 1996). Even though social relationships where gender is reproduced and challenged are not taken into account, this extreme is still linked to a reinforcement of gender structures as the economic system is framed within masculine values (Ogbor 2000). On the other extreme, we have the behaviour of over-socialization within a market, implying that the actors do not make rational economic decisions, but instead all decisions are made according to structures (Granovetter 1985), such as gender. As in rational market behaviour, a reinforcement of gender structures is apparent, as all decisions are based in the social relations that gender undermines. In between the two extremes, an entrepreneurship process embedded in the social context enables people to realise the importance of the context, become part of it, and access resources bound to the context (Jack and Anderson 2002; Korsgaard, Ferguson, and Gaddefors 2015). Context involves acknowledging the different actors included in the entrepreneurship process, and also when, where and under what institutional conditions the entrepreneurship process emerges (Welter 2011). Changing contexts can be accomplished through the social processes of interactions such as embeddedness (Vestrum 2014). Welter (2011) points to examples of when entrepreneurship has been triggered by an embeddedness in context, leading to social change within that context. At the same time, Welter together with Smallbone (2010) also shows how women embedded in an array of former Soviet institutions affect their context by, for example offering other women jobs and being positive role models. Also, Kloosterman and Rath (2001) illustrate how an embedded business owner in a neighbourhood can be part of the process of embedding customers by selling goods, and thus changing the dynamics of the neighbourhood in which they are embedded. However, who and what are not seen as separate entities in the embeddedness processes (Aldrich and Cliff 2003). Embeddedness therefore captures how different contexts interplay (Kloosterman, Van Der Leun, and Rath 1999). Context is not the background to entrepreneurship, but a foreground actor in the entrepreneurial process, indicating that people and context can only be analysed when considered together (Spedale and Watson 2014). Looking at the embeddedness process unravels the dynamics by which the institutions of who and what are connected (Aldrich and Cliff 2003). For an organization, embeddedness is associated with positive effects to a degree. However, at a certain point, a threshold is reached and embeddedness tends to be associated with the negative outcomes of over-socialization (Uzzi 1997; Waldinger 1995). To get the most out of being embedded, entrepreneurs need to balance embeddedness through negotiation with the context, being cautious not to cross this threshold (Gaddefors and Cronsell 2009; Kalantaridis and Bika 2006).

In this theoretical framework three points are highlighted. First, how gender structures can be reinforced and challenged. Second, how the extremes in embeddedness—over-socialization and rational market behaviour—reinforce gender structures. An over-socialized view of embeddedness is linked to making decisions based solely on structures such as gender, and rational market behaviour is tied to following a masculine economic discourse. Third, how balancing the embeddedness in context could potentially challenge gender structures. In this paper, these three highlighted points are the basis for investigating how a female entrepreneurship network reinforces and challenges gender structures. The next section presents how I investigated this empirically.

Methodological approach

The process studied in this paper is a female entrepreneurship network, named Q, and it acts as a paradigmatic case (Flyvbjerg 2006). To capture the complexity of the entrepreneurship process I view the network through a social constructionist perspective (Lindgren and Packendorff 2009) and with a qualitative ethnographic approach (Morgan and Smircich 1980). The environment created in an ethnographic study makes it possible for me, as a researcher, to act reflexively and continuously compare and evaluate the findings (Alvesson and Deetz 2000). As gender is easier to experience and observe than verbally describe (Martin 2003), a mix of techniques were used ranging from interviews, participation in formal and informal meetings and observations (Silverman 1993; Alvesson 2003; Czarniawska 2007; Johnstone 2007). Since social processes, such as gender, are likely to be transparent and easier to observe in a rural community, due to the well-defined rural context (Anderson 2000; Jack and Anderson 2002), the ethnographic approach explains what the women *say* they do and what the women *actually* do.

The empirical data in this paper are from an ongoing ethnographic study about gender and entrepreneurship within a rural community where I am involved in different business networks, meetings facilitated by the municipality's administrators, as well as do interviews with and observe entrepreneurs, municipality representatives and individuals performing voluntary work. The empirics for this paper are from the first 14 months, between 2015 and 2017, of the larger ethnographic study. The female entrepreneurship network formed in 2013 as part of a Swedish government programme to encourage and support entrepreneurship by women (Swedish Agency for Economic and Regional Growth 2015). The programme ran from 2007 to 2014 and by increasing the number of women developing and running businesses, the programme aimed to create growth, competitiveness and renewal in the business sector. A number of education platforms were launched that focused on enabling women to further develop a business or business idea, and women entrepreneurship networks were initiated and eligible for financial assistance. Q was started and ran for 2 years within this programme. In the middle of 2015, the funding became linked to a regional development project funded directly by the EU.

The network had approximately 30 members, of which 18 were regular members (see Table 1). The women ran different businesses varying in sector and size, and differed in years as operational, yet were similar in the fact that they (1) defined themselves as female by participating in the network, (2) all ran some sort of business and (3) they or their business were linked to the community. During the 14 months of empirical research the female entrepreneurship network had 11 meetings. At the first meeting I attended, I held a discussion about my research project and in the following meetings I participated either as a sounding board or as an observer. Between meetings I conducted individual interviews and observations with 12 of the entrepreneurs that were interested in further taking part in the study. The interviews usually took place in their working environment; either in an office, shop or at home. In the interviews we discussed their business, their lives and their relation to Q. Observations were done, for example while listening to a lecture held by one of the women entrepreneurs. As the empirical data in this paper are from a larger study, I also met the women in other business networks and meetings in the local community. This gave me the opportunity to observe the women outside of the network, allowing a more comprehensive understanding of their relationship to Q and the local community. This resulted in meeting one member 24 times during the 2 years, and others only once when they were invited to a meeting. I had no influence over who decided to participate in either Q or any other meeting; the women attended based on their personal interest. However, I did meet all of the 18 regular members at least twice. The sampling evolved through the field work (Glaser and Strauss 1967) which is typical for an ethnographic study, where the researcher has limited control over the situation and there is the potential to be more influenced by some people than others (Johnstone 2007).

Table 1. Entrepreneurs involved in the study.

		Business information				Involvement in the study		
Respondent	Activity	Employees	Years established	Joined Q	In Q	Interviews	Observations
Addison	Horses	0	11	Start	9	4	1
Alexandra	Osteopath	0	6	Start	2	2	1
Amanda	Accounting	2	5	Middle	3	0	0
Angela	Yarn shop	1	6	Middle	3	1	0
Elisabeth	Construction and manufacturing sector	4	28	Start	7	3	1
Isabella	Administrates personal assistance	400	18	Start	10	6	8
Jennifer	Wellness centre	3	17	Middle	10	1	4
Joanna	Artist	0	30	Middle	9	1	1
Juliet	Dog training	0	5	Recent	5	0	0
Katherine	Cabin rentals	0	8	Recent	2	0	0
Maria	Logistics	10–14	16	Start	10	3	1
Michelle	Furniture, with Rebecca	4	10	Recent	2	0	0
Nina	Logistics	11	20	Start	4	0	0
Rebecca	Furniture, with Michelle	4	10	Recent	3	0	0
Rose	Honey production	0	12	Middle	8	2	0
Valerie	Leadership consulting	0	25	Start	7	3	7
Vera	Property owner	0	37	Middle	4	1	1
Zoe	IT-consultant	0	2	Start	10	2	0
Janet	Flower shop	0	15	Quit	1	1	0
Lily	Project manager	–	–	–	1	1	1

When exploring the data, I used the theoretical framework with the analytical tools of gender as reinforced or challenged, and the extremes in embeddedness and their links to gender structures. Thus my evolving theoretical framework interacted with my curiosity and the evolving fieldwork, which implies a sometimes tangible movement between different analytical levels (Glaser and Strauss 1967; Alvesson and Sköldberg 2000). The transcribed interviews and field notes were organized and coded in Nvivo, where I deconstructed the data, labelling statements and observations to create an uncluttered display. The first round of coding was based on the question 'What is going on here?'. The labels were then combined and connected in multiple stages (see Table 2 for an example of how a quote went through the analysis process). Coding and combining the labels happened in conversations with peers in seminars, meetings and over coffee. In the analysis process I constructed narratives through a multitude of conversations (Czarniawska 1998). These conversations varied in time and place but are still connected through narratives (Boje 2001). A narrative carries more than verbal dialogue; it is also written texts, body language and atmosphere. When arriving at the six narratives, the material was once again evaluated and I actively searched for missing material linked to the six remaining narratives. These updated six narratives were then categorized based on whether they were reinforcing or challenging gender structures.

Table 2. An example of how a quote evolved through the analysis process.

Quote to be analysed	First round of coding (97 labels in total)	Second round of coding (56 labels in total)	Third round of coding: narratives (6 labels in total)	Does the narrative challenge or reinforce gender structure?	Process
I would rather have seen more about me and my business and less about women entrepreneurs in general. You know, we all have so different needs. Maybe the economic part of running the business is the same but the other parts were hard to implement in my own business. —Addison	* Business training * The women are not the same * Implementation problem * Business administration is the same in all businesses	* Critical towards the provided business training * Women entrepreneurs are (wrongfully) grouped together by institutions	Othering the woman entrepreneur	Reinforce gender structures in entrepreneurship	Making proper entrepreneurs

Three processes emerged from this categorization: making proper entrepreneurs, building relationships and engaging in change process. What follows now is a presentation of the empirical material analysed as narratives and processes. After the presentation the processes are discussed in relation to each other.

Empirical analysis

Six narratives emerged in the analysis of the female entrepreneurship network (see Table 3). The narratives were classified as either 'reinforcing' or 'challenging' gender structures with three processes coming out of this analysis; 'making proper entrepreneurs', 'building relationships' and 'engaging in change'.

Making proper entrepreneurs process

In the process 'making proper entrepreneurs' the focus is generally on women entrepreneurs and the process consists of the making of the women entrepreneurs as secondary to male entrepreneurs through othering, and a focus on the government's factors of success for women's entrepreneurship. Gender structures are then reinforced by the measure of success being closely linked to a masculine evaluation (Lewis 2006) of what a business is and the expressed need to form the women into this masculine view.

Othering the woman entrepreneur

The female entrepreneurship network have the subheading 'female entrepreneurship network for business development' and they are a subgroup to an entrepreneurship network, which is simply named The Entrepreneurs. Many women are a part of both groups and three women even sit on the board of The Entrepreneurs. The activities of Q are separated from the activities that The Entrepreneurs hold, and they have different funding. As Q was initially financed and organized by a national government programme, and is now funded by an EU programme, there are expectations about how the network should use their funding appropriately. For the most part, the activities are teaching moments such as lectures and courses. In the teaching moments the women are trained in business-related practices such as making a good first impression, handling social media and basic accounting. There seems to be a view that the women need these skills to be able to perform as entrepreneurs, as previuosly suggested by Marlow and McAdam (2013). Addison, reflecting upon the teaching moments, stated:

> I would rather have seen more about me and my business and less about women entrepreneurs in general. You know, we all have such different needs. Maybe the economic part of running the business is the same, but the other parts were hard to implement in my own business.

Table 3. Six narratives from the network arranged in three processes and categorized as either reinforcing or challenging gender structures when it comes to entrepreneurship.

	Process		
	Making proper entrepreneurs	*Building relationships*	*Engaging in change*
Reinforcing gender structures in entrepreneurship	Othering the woman entrepreneur Economic growth focus	The need to feel professional	
Challenging gender structures in entrepreneurship		Develop business together	Somewhere to belong Change on two fronts

For Joanna the teaching moments were too basic 'We did not get the inspiration we need when we have been in the game for a couple of years'. This statement, and the other above, reflect the difficulty in trying to educate women entrepreneurs: they are often very different but are seen as a general group. The women entrepreneurs are all viewed as being in need of basic training, no matter their previous experience. The governing bodies do not take into account the individual goals and needs of the women entrepreneurs.

Economic growth focus

As seen in the formalized goals of the network, the women entrepreneurs are expected to grow their business through their involvement in the network. This is evident in why the women joined the network in the first place. Addison joined the network based on a persistent feeling of needing to grow her business: 'I needed to grow, I just did not know how'. Similarly, Joanna saw Q as a marketing opportunity for her business when she moved to the area. Therefore, the meetings focus on increased sales, primarily between members and secondly with actors outside of the network. It is not taken into account that the women are in vastly different sectors (see Table 1 again) and that it could be difficult to engage in transactions with each other. At one of the meetings Q's vision was discussed:

Katherine: What is Q's vision?

Elisabeth: More competence development, more women entrepreneurs and more equality.

Katherine: What kind of skills are missing?

Elisabeth: General skills.

The women discuss this and end up questioning if the objective is to be more women entrepreneurs or better women entrepreneurs.

Isabella answers: We should make more business transactions through the network and think about what we can do together.

There are different views from the members of the network as to whether networking has actually led to increased business transactions and business growth. Isabella thinks the network has led to some cooperation between the women, but believes generally that it stopped at conversations. Maria is the one that have experienced a business transaction; she met a designer at one of the regional network meetings and then hired her to make some commercial materials for her company.

Referring to Table 3, the 'making proper entrepreneurs' process is further reinforcing gender structures when it comes to entrepreneurship as an element of separating women from normative entrepreneurs is evident. The women entrepreneurs are seen as weaker versions of the normative entrepreneur and in need of training and support, thus normalizing the masculine entrepreneurship discourse (Marlow and McAdam 2013). The governing bodies are trying to challenge the gender structures through empowering and involving more women in entrepreneurship, but they end up reinforcing differences between women and men (Marlow and Patton 2005; West and Zimmerman 1987). The network is, in this narrative, poorly embedded in context. This since instead of drawing on or appreciating the knowledge from the local community (Jack and Anderson 2002; Korsgaard, Ferguson, and Gaddefors 2015) the women entrepreneurs are seen as a homogenous group facing the same challenges as other women entrepreneurs across Sweden.

Building relationships process

In the 'building relationships' process there is a social aspect of the women coming together as well as a resistance towards focusing on this social aspect. Due to the resistance and continued focus on masculine perceptions of what entrepreneurship is, this process further reinforces gender structures. At the same time, business development by interactions are emphasized, which favours challenging the structures. In the 'building relationships' process there are narratives that say there is a need for the women to feel like professional entrepreneurs and that the women develop their businesses through interaction.

The need to feel professional

To be professional is not a problem in itself. The question is what professional means. Within the entrepreneurship discourse it seems that prioritizing growth and economic values are seen as professional (Lewis 2006), while focusing on other aspects of entrepreneurship, such as social features, is not (Korsgaard and Anderson 2011). Maria joined Q because of a need to talk business. She was fed up with all the men at her company and the lack of professional business conversations. After the first meeting at the network she felt:

> I wanted to meet business owners, but I also wanted to meet women. So the first time I was here [at a meeting with the network] I was quite excited and thought that 'Lord how fun to meet girls, who, on top of everything else, also think that the business stuff is exciting'.

Maria and the other women express their need to talk business as it seems they do not experience professional business exchanges in other forums. Almost all the women express at some point during the study that the network, first and foremost, is a network where they can discuss how to grow their businesses. Additionally, they express a need to push aside the network's social aspect. Elizabeth describes what they do at meetings: '…it is not to meet and small talk, it has to be developing'. There seems to be resistance towards the network having more social aspects and a discontent feeling when the small talk dominates. For Janet, the social overload was a determining factor in deciding to leave the network. She took part in one of Q's meetings but decided not to continue feeling the network was too unprofessional, and did not contain enough business discourse. In conclusion, there are different views as to whether the network is fulfiling the need from the women to feel professional.

Develop business together

Growing their businesses in economic terms through ongoing conversations between the women can be seen as challenging gender structures. Throughout the course of the network, the women have employed different techniques in choosing what to accomplish at their meetings. Influenced by what the government formalized, Elizabeth initially decided what the members would learn about. Later she started to listen to what the members wanted and made the programme according to their needs. When Elizabeth stepped down as group leader, the members started to collectively arrange meetings and collectively decide the content. This development is far from the statements made in the 'making proper entrepreneurs' process, where there is little or no individual focus. Even though the women are still funded by an institution, which formalizes what they can do, they try to incorporate an individual focus on the development of their own businesses. In contrast to the 'making proper entrepreneurs' process, the focus is not on specific learning objectives, but a more individual focus, tailored to developing their businesses through collective and ongoing conversations about growth. Elisabeth illustrates these conversations by talking about how younger and older entrepreneurs inspire each other:

> We hope that we can inspire you and then maybe you can also inspire us. Many of us have worked a long time with our businesses and it could become a bit…, maybe I should see things from another perspective? That is one of the perks with the network; we can help each other in a way that we did not see for ourselves.

Referring back to Table 3, a 'building relationships' process appears when interactions between the women in the network become evident. They find themselves using each other to a mutual benefit as they develop their views on business and what it means to be an entrepreneur. In the 'building relationships' process we move towards embeddedness into context (Jack and Anderson 2002), as the social aspect of the network draws on the local resources of the women. The narratives here are both challenging and reinforcing gender structures. On one hand, the women reinforce the structures due to a clear desire to act and develop their businesses according to a masculine entrepreneurship discourse (West and Zimmerman 1987; Lewis 2006). On the other hand, the women challenge gender structures in how they work within the network; through ongoing conversations and a more personalized focus on developing their individual businesses.

Engaging in change process

In the 'engaging in change' process a structural perspective is added to the 'making proper entrepreneurs' and 'building relationships' processes. Here the women in the network challenge the gender structures from within the structure. The 'engaging in change' process consists of the narratives that Q is seen as somewhere to belong and that the women actively empower each other and change gender structures.

Somewhere to belong

The reasons for joining and belonging to Q are not only expressed as a desire and need for business development, as expressed in the 'making proper entrepreneurs' process. In the 'making proper entrepreneurs' process the official aim of the network was discussed in terms of economic measures. Isabella has another perception of why the network is important: 'the goal is that we will have just as much say [as men entrepreneurs] and to interact together and get space'. For Michelle it was logical to join Q as she feels 'we are strong together'. In the 'making proper entrepreneurs' process Addison acknowledged that she joined Q because she felt she needed to grow her business. However, she believes the biggest value of the group is the social aspect:

> I think it's fun to get together and I think it's nice since it feels like I know someone in the community now. That's probably the biggest value; to be able to say hi to each other. I don't remember everyone's names, but it feels good that yes 'I recognize you, good to see you again just like last month'. I think it's very enjoyable. [...] Whenever we see each other in the village it's great. We say hello and such. Before I would have been in the village shopping and not said hi to anyone. So it is nice and something I have been missing.

Q is a place of belonging, somewhere where Addison does not feel that she is at the disadvantage she often feels in other situations where her business has not been seen as a 'proper business'. She feels that, 'despite my business revolving around horses', the women in Q treat her as an equal.

Change on two fronts

There is a strong focus on change within the network; change in the way the women see themselves and in the way others see them. Thus Q seems to be a force for both individual and structural change. The network can be seen as changing on two fronts: firstly, through the women empowering one another and findings strategies to operate within the structures, and secondly, by actively trying to change the structures. The women express what can be interpreted as a feminist political view of belonging to Q, as a way to discuss issues and to empower one another. Valerie talks about empowerment between the women in their roles as entrepreneurs and sees Q as 'women power'. The women express ideas such as 'we can't have a change unless we, ourselves, are driving the change' (Lily) and '...we create an added value the more people we are. If just a few of us were to sit here and talk things over again and again nothing would change' (Elisabeth). The women in Q are what Welter and Smallbone (2010) exemplify as embedded role models for other women in their local context.

Q is also platform to breed change. Isabella hopes that Q could be a driver for change within their local business community:

> I envision that in the future we can show The Entrepreneurs that Q can contribute to all entrepreneurs and not just to a small group like us. But it must be in the next turn where we, for example, might be able to expand what we do and let Q inspire all business owners who are not in Q [...]. If you do it responsibly, so that we can make sure that Q is fully accepted, it can be a small engine of some kind. Or perhaps the catalyst that can be an involved actor and fuel the other business owners. And then [our separation] is not a problem.

Isabella illustrates the slow changes in gender structures when gender is challenged through small practices (Anderson 2008). Joanna has a similar idea: 'I am interested in entrepreneurial issues. I'm interested in issues related to female entrepreneurship. I'm interested in everything that could mean development for rural areas'. As explained previously, she joined Q as a marketing strategy but has stayed within the network because she feels a need to change structures. For Joanna, Q has become a platform for enabling change within the community:

> Firstly, [Q] is a fellowship among the likeminded. Secondly, Q is a platform that gives me things I have not thought of before, and I am active in developing myself and my business. It gives new, different insights as I said. That's what it gives me; and new interactions. New people coming in [to the network] and if there is a problem I know that I can ask them if anyone knows where I should turn. And then [Q] is a reference point, I'm not just any anonymous person. I have a platform within the community's voluntary programs where I can make a difference.

The women in the network use their local context to invite new women entrepreneurs and in turn affect them through enrolling them in the programme. They are actively embedding people into their local context much like the example from Kloosterman and Rath (2001) where a shop owner sells goods to customers and embeds them in the local context. Similar to the shop owner, the network is affecting the local context by acknowledging and engaging with people in the context. In addition, Joanna expresses how 'We are not marionettes for the government' implying that the female entrepreneurship network does not comply with the reinforcing of the gender structures that are expected of them by the government. In this process, the 'engaging in change' process, we move even further towards embeddedness into context (Uzzi 1996), not reaching the threshold of over-socialization (Uzzi 1997; Waldinger 1995) where gender processes are thought to be reinforced. This move is possible since the discussions in the network are rooted in the women's perceptions of the local community. Referring back to Table 3, it is evident within the 'engaging in change' process that the network challenges the gender structures by providing a platform where the women can develop their businesses, community and feministic views. Here the focus is larger than only following a masculine entrepreneurship discourse (Ogbor 2000) as in the process 'making proper entrepreneurs'. When the women come together in challenging the gender structures they draw from their local social context. They involve more women from the community and try changing their local business community. A sense of belonging occurs with the women becoming part of their community, their local context. Here the network is not only active in challenging gender structures but also in becoming more embedded in the local context.

Discussion of findings

The programme that finances the female entrepreneurship network is reinforcing gender structures by deciding how entrepreneurship is supposed to be measured and by how the women who join the group enact this measure. However, for the women in Q the network goes beyond the government telling them they need to be better entrepreneurs. As the network is not only reinforcing gender structures, it is also a platform for the women to challenge gender structures through embedding the network in their local context. There is a flow between reinforcing and challenging gender structures when looking at the processes in the female entrepreneurship network (see Table 4). Three processes in the female entrepreneurship network were identified through the analysis (1) 'making proper entrepreneurs' where the focus is on women entrepreneurs in general, (2) 'building relationships' where there is a focus on social interactions to develop the businesses and lastly (3) 'engaging in change' where the women are simultaneously developing

Table 4. How the gender process interplay with the process of embeddedness in context, through the three processes identified in the female entrepreneurship network.

Processes	Making proper entrepreneurs	Building relationships	Engaging in change
Gender	Reinforcing		Challenging
	←————————————————————————————————————→		
Embeddedness in context	Less		More
	←————————————————————————————————————→		

their businesses, their community and their feministic views. In the processes, a reinforcement of gender structures occurs through the 'making proper entrepreneurs' process, and to some extent, through the 'building relationships' process. Both processes further comply with the masculine norm of entrepreneurship (Ogbor 2000; Ahl 2006) through normalizing the masculine entrepreneurship discourse (Ahl and Marlow 2012). However, within the 'building relationships' process there are some narratives that challenge gender structures through the women engaging in conversation about entrepreneurship. The opposition is even more evident within the 'engaging in change' process where the women are drawing on their local resources, creating a platform to challenge gender structures through empowering each other within the structures. As there is variability in gender (in)equality (Deutsch 2007), the flow between reproducing and challenging gender structures exemplifies how this variability could look.

Just as there is a flow between reinforcing and challenging gender structures within the processes, there is also movement between the processes of being more or less embedded in context (see Table 4). The embeddedness process and the gender process seem to interplay as more embeddedness in context is associated with challenging gender structures. When the women start working in the network on a more local level, with themselves and the community at the core of the conversation, they discuss structural issues of women entrepreneurs. These are the types of issues that Marlow and Patton (2005) would like to see discussed when addressing gender and entrepreneurship. Yet, it also seems to be the other way around: challenging gender structures is associated with becoming more embedded in context. As the women become more embedded in their local context they build a platform for themselves to discuss more structural issues. There seems to be a relationship within the entrepreneurship process that is mutually constitutive: the embeddedness process shapes the gender process and the gender process shapes the embeddedness process.

Conclusions

This paper illuminates the interplay between the gender process and the embeddedness process within entrepreneurship. This has theoretical implications since embeddedness then not only changes the context in which it is embedded, in this case it also changes other social processes such as gender. Consequently, this paper adds to the literature on embeddedness by showing how embeddedness interplays with other social processes and how embeddedness in context can be a way towards gender equality.

It is in this paper shown how more embeddedness in context is associated with challenging gender structures and in turn how challenging gender structures is associated with becoming more embedded in context. Three gender structure processes are identified in the female entrepreneurship network: (1) 'making proper entrepreneurs process', (2) 'building relationships process' and (3) 'engaging in change process'. Through these processes, the network is both reinforcing gender structures, through a strong focus on masculine values, and challenging gender structures, by questioning these values within their local context. The local social aspect, enables the network to add an additional dimension beyond the masculine business discourse (Ogbor 2000; Ahl 2006), which initially brought them together.

This type of study does not aim at generalizing, because generalization is not wanted (Flyvbjerg 2006). Instead, this study '…is the telling of a very small story that [I] hope resonates with others' (Calás and Smircich 1999, 666). The focus and limitations of this study are, for theoretical purposes, on the spatial context of a rural community. This raises the question of how the process of embeddedness in context leads to challenging gender structures in other contexts. Future research could further contextualize embeddedness in different spatial contexts and other contexts such as institutions. If the concept of embeddedness is further contextualized we could advance research on gender and entrepreneurship as we find new possible actors and ways of doing entrepreneurship.

How could policy support women entrepreneurship through programmes that more effectively challenge gender structures? With networks like the one in this case, there needs to be a reinforcement of gender structures to be able to challenge them. Without the reinforcing aspects that formed the group, the challenging of gender structures could not occur since there would be no group in the first place. Drawing from this case, policy could compromise, focusing programmes more on the networking between women entrepreneurs. In line with the government's objectives, the women still develop their own and others' businesses, while the social aspects enable the women to potentially challenge gender structures surrounding entrepreneurship. If the women entrepreneurs involved in these types of networks want to take matters in their own hands they can do as the network that are described in this case: focus more and more on the social aspects and engaging in their context.

However, the aspect missing in the network studied is the over-socialization of embeddedness in context. What happens when the network become to embedded in context? Theoretically, there is a threshold where gender structures, yet again, are reinforced within the female entrepreneurship network. A future research focuses on this threshold in the embeddedness process and its implications for advancing gender equality are therefore essential.

Disclosure statement

No potential conflict of interest was reported by the author.

ORCID

Annie Roos http://orcid.org/0000-0002-6603-6079

References

Acker, J. 1990. "Hierarchies, Jobs, Bodies: A Theory of Gendered Organizations." *Gender & Society* 4 (2): 139–158. doi:10.1177/089124390004002002.

Ahl, H. 2006. "Why Research on Women Entrepreneurs Needs New Directions." *Entrepreneurship Theory and Practice* 30 (5): 595–621. doi:10.1111/etap.2006.30.issue-5.

Ahl, H., and S. Marlow. 2012. "Exploring the Dynamics of Gender, Feminism and Entrepreneurship: Advancing Debate to Escape a Dead End?" *Organization* 19 (5): 543–562. doi:10.1177/1350508412448695.

Aldrich, H. E., and J. E. Cliff. 2003. "The Pervasive Effects of Family on Entrepreneurship: Toward a Family Embeddedness Perspective." *Journal of Business Venturing* 18 (5): 573–596. doi:10.1016/S0883-9026(03)00011-9.

Alvesson, M. 2003. "Beyond Neopositivists, Romantics, and Localists: A Reflexive Approach to Interviews in Organizational Research." *The Academy of Management Review* 28 (1): 13–33. doi:10.5465/amr.2003.8925191.

Alvesson, M., and S. Deetz. 2000. *Doing Critical Management Research*. London: Sage.

Alvesson, M., and K. Sköldberg. 2000. *Reflexive Methodology: New Vistas for Qualitative Research*. Los Angeles, CA: Sage.

Anderson, A. R. 2000. "Paradox in the Periphery: An Entrepreneurial Reconstruction?" *Entrepreneurship and Regional Development* 12 (2): 91–109. doi:10.1080/089856200283027.

Anderson, E. R. 2008. "'Whose Name's on the Awning?' Gender, Entrepreneurship and the American Diner." *Gender, Place and Culture* 15 (4): 395–410. doi:10.1080/09663690802155611.

Berg, N. G. 1997. "Gender, Place and Entrepreneurship." *Entrepreneurship and Regional Development* 9 (3): 259–268. doi:10.1080/08985629700000015.

Boje, D. M. 2001. *Narrative Methods for Organizational & Communication Research*. London: Sage.

Bruni, A., S. Gherardi, and B. Poggio. 2004. "Entrepreneur-Mentality, Gender and the Study of Women Entrepreneurs." *Journal of Organizational Change Management* 17 (3): 256–268. doi:10.1108/09534810410538315.

Calás, M. B., and L. Smircich. 1996. "From 'The Woman's' Point of View: Feminist Approaches to Organization Studies." In *Handbook of Organization Studies*, edited by S. R. Clegg, C. Hardy, and W. R. Nord, 218–257. London: Sage.

Calás, M. B., and L. Smircich. 1999. "Past Postmodernism? Reflections and Tentative Directions." *Academy of Management Review* 24 (4): 649–672. doi:10.5465/amr.1999.2553246.

Czarniawska, B. 1998. *A Narrative Approach to Organization Studies*. Qualitative Research Methods . Vol. 43. London: Sage.

Czarniawska, B. 2007. *Shadowing: And Other Techniques for Doing Fieldwork in Modern Societies*. Copenhagen: Liber.

Deutsch, F. M. 2007. "Undoing Gender." *Gender & Society* 21 (1): 106–127. doi:10.1177/0891243206293577.

Flyvbjerg, B. 2006. "Five Misunderstandings About Case-Study Research." *Qualitative Inquiry* 12 (2): 219–245. doi:10.1177/1077800405284363.

Gaddefors, J., and N. Cronsell. 2009. "Returnees and Local Stakeholders Co-Producing the Entrepreneurial Region." *European Planning Studies* 17 (8): 1191–1203. doi:10.1080/09654310902981045.

Glaser, B., and A. Strauss. 1967. *The Discovery of Grounded Theory: Strategies for Qualitative Research*. Chicago: Aldine.

Granovetter, M. 1985. "Economic Action and Social Structure: The Problem of Embeddedness." *American Journal of Sociology* 91 (3): 481–510. doi:10.1086/228311.

Hanson, S. 2009. "Changing Places through Women's Entrepreneurship." *Economic Geography* 85 (3): 245–267. doi:10.1111/j.1944-8287.2009.01033.x.

Henry, C., L. Foss, and H. Ahl. 2015. "Gender and Entrepreneurship Research: A Review of Methodological Approaches." *International Small Business Journal* 25 (1): 1–25.

Hirdman, Y. 1988. "Genussystemet - Reflexioner Kring Kvinnors Sociala Underordning." *Kvinnovetenskaplig Tidskrift* 3: 49–63.

Hughes, K. D., J. E. Jennings, C. Brush, S. Carter, and F. Welter. 2012. "Extending Women's Entrepreneurship Research in New Directions." *Entrepreneurship Theory and Practice* 36 (3): 429–442. doi:10.1111/j.1540-6520.2012.00504.x.

Jack, S. L., and A. R. Anderson. 2002. "The Effects of Embeddedness on the Entrepreneurial Process." *Journal of Business Venturing* 17 (5): 467–487. doi:10.1016/S0883-9026(01)00076-3.

Johnstone, B. A. 2007. "Ethnographic Methods in Entrepreneurship Research." In *Handbook of Qualitative Research Methods in Entrepreneurship*, edited by H. Neergaard and J. P. Ullhoi, 97–121. Cheltenham: Edward Elgar.

Kalantaridis, C., and Z. Bika. 2006. "In-Migrant Entrepreneurship in Rural England: Beyond Local Embeddedness." *Entrepreneurship and Regional Development* 18 (2): 109–131. doi:10.1080/08985620500510174.

Kloosterman, R., and J. Rath. 2001. "Immigrant Entrepreneurs in Advanced Economies: Mixed Embeddedness Further Explored." *Journal of Ethnic and Migration Studies* 27 (2): 189–201. doi:10.1080/13691830020041561.

Kloosterman, R., J. Van Der Leun, and J. Rath. 1999. "Mixed Embeddedness: (In)Formal Economic Activities and Immigrant Businesses in the Netherlands." *International Journal of Urban and Regional Research* 23 (2): 252–266. doi:10.1111/1468-2427.00194.

Korsgaard, S., and A. R. Anderson. 2011. "Enacting Entrepreneurship as Social Value Creation." *International Small Business Journal* 29 (2): 135–151. doi:10.1177/0266242610391936.

Korsgaard, S., R. Ferguson, and J. Gaddefors. 2015. "The Best of Both Worlds: How Rural Entrepreneurs Use Placial Embeddedness and Strategic Networks to Create Opportunities." *Entrepreneurship and Regional Development* 27 (9–10): 574–598. doi:10.1080/08985626.2015.1085100.

Lewis, P. 2006. "The Quest for Invisibility: Female Entrepreneurs and the Masculine Norm of Entrepreneurship." *Gender, Work and Organization* 13 (5): 453–469. doi:10.1111/gwao.2006.13.issue-5.

Lindgren, M., and J. Packendorff. 2009. "Social Constructionism and Entrepreneurship: Basic Assumptions and Consequences for Theory and Research." *International Journal of Entrepreneurial Behavior & Research* 15 (1): 25–47. doi:10.1108/13552550910934440.

Marlow, S., and M. McAdam. 2013. "Gender and Entrepreneurship: Advancing Debate and Challenging Myths; Exploring the Mystery of the under-Performing Female Entrepreneur." *International Journal of Entrepreneurial Behaviour & Research* 19 (1): 114–124. doi:10.1108/13552551311299288.

Marlow, S., and D. Patton. 2005. "All Credit to Men? Entrepreneurship, Finance, and Gender." *Entrepreneurship Theory and Practice* 29 (6): 717–735. doi:10.1111/(ISSN)1540-6520.

Martin, P. Y. 2003. "'Said and Done' versus 'Saying and Doing' Gendering Practices, Practicing Gender at Work." *Gender & Society* 17 (3): 342–366. doi:10.1177/0891243203017003002.

Mirchandani, K. 1999. "Feminist Insight on Gendered Work: New Directions in Research on Women and Entrepreneurship." *Gender, Work and Organization* 6 (4): 224–235. doi:10.1111/gwao.1999.6.issue-4.

Morgan, G., and L. Smircich. 1980. "The Case for Qualitative Research." *The Academy of Management Review* 5 (4): 491–500. doi:10.5465/amr.1980.4288947.

Ogbor, J. O. 2000. "Mythicizing and Reification in Entrepreneurial Discourse: Ideology-Critique of Entrepreneurial Studies." *Journal of Management Studies* 37 (5): 605–635. doi:10.1111/1467-6486.00196.

Silverman, D. 1993. *Interpreting Qualitative Data: Methods for Analysing Talk, Text and Interaction*. London: Sage.

Spedale, S., and T. J. Watson. 2014. "The Emergence of Entrepreneurial Action: At the Crossroads between Institutional Logics and Individual Life-Orientation." *International Small Business Journal* 32 (7): 759–776. doi:10.1177/0266242613480376.

Swedish Agency for Economic and Regional Growth. 2015. 8 Years of Promoting Women's Entrepreneurship in Sweden. Info 0607.

Uzzi, B. 1996. "The Sources and Consequences of Embeddedness for the Economic Performance of Organizations: The Network Effect." *American Sociological Review* 674–698. doi:10.2307/2096399.

Uzzi, B. 1997. "Social Structure and Competition in Interfirm Networks: The Paradox of Embeddedness." *Administrative Science Quarterly* 41 (1): 35–67. doi:10.2307/2393808.

Vestrum, I. 2014. "The Embedding Process of Community Ventures: Creating a Music Festival in a Rural Community." *Entrepreneurship and Regional Development* 26 (7–8): 619–644. doi:10.1080/08985626.2014.971076.

Waldinger, R. 1995. "The 'Other Side' of Embedded Ness: A Case-Study of the Interplay of Economy and Ethnicity." *Ethnic and Racial Studies* 18 (3): 555–580. doi:10.1080/01419870.1995.9993879.

Welter, F. 2011. "Contextualizing Entrepreneurship: Conceptual Challenges and Ways Forward." *Entrepreneurship Theory and Practice* 35 (1): 165–184. doi:10.1111/j.1540-6520.2010.00427.x.

Welter, F., and D. Smallbone. 2010. "The Embeddedness of Women's Entrepreneurship in a Transition Context." In *Women Entrepreneurs and the Global Environment for Growth: A Research Perspective*, edited by C. G. Brush, A. D. Bruin, E. J. Gatewood, and C. Henry, 96–117. Cheltenham: Edward Elgar.

West, C., and D. H. Zimmerman. 1987. "Doing Gender." *Gender & Society* 1 (2): 125–151. doi:10.1177/0891243287001002002.

Women's experiences of legitimacy, satisfaction and commitment as entrepreneurs: embedded in gender hierarchy and networks in private and business spheres

Ye Liu, Thomas Schøtt and Chuqing Zhang

ABSTRACT

When a woman perceives legitimacy in her job as an entrepreneur from networks that are often influenced by the gender hierarchy that grants men higher status than women, she is encouraged in her job. What are the effects of gender hierarchy and networks on the legitimacy a female entrepreneur perceives and on her satisfaction and commitment to the job? A sample of 5997 female entrepreneurs in the developing world was surveyed for Global Entrepreneurship Monitor. They were found to experience legitimacy as entrepreneurs in their networks in the private sphere and the business sphere. Gender hierarchy constrains legitimacy more in the private sphere than it does in the business sphere. Legitimacy in the business sphere can fulfil the need to feel competent and enhance job satisfaction, while legitimacy in the private sphere can fulfil the need to feel related and enhance job commitment. The account contributes to a two-level contextualization of experiences: micro-level embedding in networks that are nested in macro-level embedding in gender hierarchy.

1. Introduction: legitimacy experienced in micro- and macro-contexts

A girl playing with a doll elicits smiles from her parents, encouraging her play. If she picks up a truck, however, the smiles may turn to frowns, especially if she lives in a society that assigns females and males strictly different roles. Just as the girl pursues legitimacy in her environment by upholding her gender role, entrepreneurs pursue legitimacy in their environment (Fisher et al. 2017). However, legitimacy is a particular issue for female entrepreneurs, who must combine the role of 'woman' with the role of 'entrepreneur', roles that are frequently considered to be conflicting (McAdam, Harrison, and Leitch 2018).

An individual's legitimacy is often contextualized in networking with stakeholders. The legitimacy of a woman who enacts her role as a woman is perceived in networking with her family (Eagly, Wood, and Diekman 2000), and the legitimacy of a person who enacts the role of entrepreneur is perceived in networking with business contacts (de Clercq and Voronov 2009). But who approves of a woman as entrepreneur? Family and business contacts often approve, but their institutional logics and expectations differ, so her experiences of legitimacy may vary.

Research on individuals' legitimacy as entrepreneurs has focused on how entrepreneurs and stakeholders coproduce legitimacy and on the legitimacy of the entrepreneur and the entrepreneur's business, especially concerning financing, hiring, collaboration, supplies, resource acquisition and marketing (Fisher et al. 2017; Lounsbury and Glynn 2001). Research on women's legitimacy as entrepreneurs has focused on their networking for advice (Robinson and Stubberud 2009), on discredit in financing (Marlow and Swail 2014), on the masculine discourse of entrepreneurship (Hamilton 2013), on balancing the gender role with the entrepreneurial role (McGowan et al. 2012), on the formation of subjective norms (Terrell and Troilo 2010) and on how women's entry are shaped by social norms, notably gender hierarchy (Klyver, Nielsen, and Evald 2013), and moderated by culture (Zhang and Schøtt 2017). However, contextualizing female entrepreneurs' experiences of legitimacy remains a gap in the research.

A woman's perception of legitimacy as an entrepreneur is problematic in two ways. First, perceiving legitimacy in one's job is essential for satisfaction and commitment to the job, including when the job is entrepreneurship (Bradley and Roberts 2004). Second, legitimacy is perceived by networks of people who uphold institutions (Thornton, Ocasio, and Lounsbury 2012). The network's approval is influenced by its society's regulations, norms and beliefs such that network members are likely to approve of female entrepreneurs if rules and regulations support, rather than discriminate against, them; if the prevailing belief is that women and men are similarly endowed, rather than that women are genetically risk-averse and unfit; and if cultural values and norms favour gender-egalitarianism, rather than favouring distinct roles for women and men and a strict gender hierarchy (McAdam, Harrison, and Leitch 2018). Despite the considerable amount of research on legitimacy, institutions' effects on women's perceptions of legitimacy remain unclear (Amine and Staub 2009). As a result, research has called for contextualizing individuals' behaviour in networks and institutions, thereby investigating the influence of context on entrepreneurial actions, particularly experiences of legitimacy (Überbacher 2014).

These gaps in understanding the embeddedness of legitimacy frame our question: *What are the effects of gender hierarchy and networks on the legitimacy a female entrepreneur experiences and on her satisfaction and commitment to the job?*

Of course, while legitimacy benefits a female entrepreneur's work, gender hierarchy constrains her legitimacy as an entrepreneur. Legitimacy is perceived in diverse networks with diverse institutional logics, as Überbacher (2014) theorized and Fisher et al. (2017) researched. The present study discerns perceptions of legitimacy in distinct networks that are differently influenced by the gender hierarchy and that have different consequences for work.

This study contributes an account of legitimacy as perceived by female entrepreneurs, contextualized as embeddedness in networks and institutions (Überbacher 2014). Legitimacy's macro-level institutional embeddedness in the gender hierarchy, drawing on theory of gender roles, is combined with legitimacy's meso-level relational embeddedness in networks, with consequences for women's satisfaction and commitment to their job as entrepreneurs. This contribution draws on the theory of self-determination in the context of networking, which contextualizes well-being, enhanced by fulfilment of the need to feel competent and related (Ryan and Deci 2000).

The following sections elaborate on roles as a foundation for developing hypotheses, describe the research design, report on the analyses and conclude by pinpointing contributions, implications for policy and practice, and suggestions for further research.

2. Theoretical background and hypotheses

Female entrepreneurs combine the role of 'woman' with the role of 'entrepreneur'. The entrepreneur's task is to pursue opportunity, which distinguishes the role of entrepreneur from those of other occupations. Values and norms for the role of 'woman' differ across cultures, which generally have gender hierarchies that grant higher status to men than they do to women. Gender hierarchy is a composite of female subordination in terms of esteem, resources, authority and power, as indicated by advantages for males and prescriptions for men to be breadwinners and women to be homemakers, with higher value granted to breadwinning than to homemaking (Baughn, Chua, and Neupert 2006).

The two roles – entrepreneur and woman – often conflict (Hamilton 2013; McGowan et al. 2012; Terrell and Troilo 2010), depending on the culture. A culture with a steep gender hierarchy expects women to devote themselves to homemaking, rather than other vocations; therefore, for a woman, becoming an entrepreneur may be not only difficult but even illegitimate (Marlow and McAdam 2015). Conversely, in a more gender-egalitarian culture, entrepreneurship, homemaking and other vocations may be similarly appropriate for both women and men.

Any role carries expectations for behaviour that is necessary for approval and reward, while inappropriate behaviour is illegitimate and punished. A person experiences legitimacy, approval and rewards from others, who, in their evaluation, invoke the standards and norms that express institutions' values (Überbacher 2014). This theory of roles in networks and institutions is useful in contextualizing legitimacy as perceived by female entrepreneurs.

2.1. Gender hierarchy shaping legitimacy in business sphere and private sphere

Entrepreneurs experience legitimacy, advice and other resources from two spheres (Lounsbury and Glynn 2001; Middleton 2013): the private sphere of family and friends in their immediate surroundings, and the business sphere of business contacts and other business-related persons in the public arena (Jensen and Schøtt 2017). Advisors from each sphere influence outcomes like innovation and exportation of entrepreneur's aspirations for growth, especially those of female entrepreneurs (Schøtt and Cheraghi 2015).

In a culture with a strict gender hierarchy, gender roles shape the feasibility of entrepreneurship by rendering entry, survival and growth difficult for women. Women who occupy roles or have abilities that are atypical relative to cultural norms tend to be undervalued and discounted by their peers at work. The embedded dependence on males limits a woman's agency and prevents her from pursuing opportunities. Such circumstances also reduce women's legitimacy in male-dominated vocations like business (Blake 2006; Godwin, Stevens, and Brenner 2006). Thus, the gender hierarchy reduces female entrepreneurs' perceptions of legitimacy in their surroundings (Marlow and Swail 2014), and we hypothesize:

H1a. Strictness of gender hierarchy reduces legitimacy in the private sphere.

H1b. Strictness of gender hierarchy reduces legitimacy in the business sphere.

Legitimacy in the two spheres may differ because each sphere is dominated by a distinct logic (Fisher et al. 2017). People in the business sphere relate to a female entrepreneur primarily as an entrepreneur, and they typically invoke a business logic when considering her legitimacy (Thornton, Ocasio, and Lounsbury 2012). However, a comprehensive study of the sources of entrepreneurial ventures' legitimacy involved no consideration of gender or family (Fisher et al. 2017). In addition, although gender roles are not dominant in business logic, gender and family logic influence business and access to resources (Blake 2006; Greenwood et al. 2010; McAdam, Harrison, and Leitch 2018).

People in the private sphere tend to relate to a female entrepreneur as woman, and they typically invoke a family logic when considering her legitimacy as entrepreneur (Miller, Breton-Miller, and Lester 2011; Thornton, Ocasio, and Lounsbury 2012). They are not oblivious to her role as entrepreneur, but her role as woman is primary, especially as mother, wife, caretaker and homemaker, and the dense, strong, affective and durable family ties enhance social control and reciprocity in the private sphere (Fairclough and Micelotta 2013). If the gender hierarchy is strict, the family logic is especially dominant (Amine and Staub 2009). Therefore, a woman's legitimacy as an entrepreneur is likely to be reduced more if the gender hierarchy is steep than if the gender hierarchy is less steep:

H1c. Strictness of gender hierarchy reduces legitimacy in the private sphere more than in the business sphere.

2.2. Legitimacy's fulfilling of the need to feel competent and connected

People have needs for autonomy, competence and relatedness, and fulfilment of these needs increases well-being, according to the theory of self-determination (Ryan and Deci 2000). A female entrepreneur's need to feel competent may be fulfilled by the perception of legitimacy, which enhances the feeling of competence and increases the entrepreneur's motivation and well-being (Bradley and Roberts 2004). The need to feel related may also be fulfilled by the perception of legitimacy in the network of significant others, which manifests the relatedness that, according to the theory of self-determination, increases the entrepreneur's well-being and motivation.

Well-being in the role of entrepreneur is expressed as satisfaction with the job, while motivation in the role of entrepreneur is expressed as commitment to continue running the business. This theory of fulfilment of needs is a basis for hypothesizing the consequences of legitimacy for satisfaction in and commitment to the job.

A person's legitimacy in his or her role influences his or her motivation and performance in the role. Studies have shown that an entrepreneur's legitimacy typically increases his or her activity (Kibler and Kautonen 2014), satisfaction in performing the role of entrepreneur (Schjoedt 2009) and commitment to continue in the role (Wincent, Örtqvist, and Drnovsek 2008).

Satisfaction in a job refers to a person's satisfaction with the type of work and its autonomy, meaningfulness, income and stress level (Block and Koellinger 2009). A newcomer often lacks the familiarity and credibility that typifies interactions among incumbent players in the field. Indeed, the ability to pursue a venture may depend on the legitimacy perceived from others (de Clercq and Voronov 2009). Therefore, we expect:

H2a. Legitimacy in the business sphere promotes job satisfaction.

Family influence on a person's pursuit of a career is all but inevitable. Often a son follows in his father's footsteps, and a daughter follows her mother's (Greene, Han, and Marlow 2013). In addition, a person's well-being often depends on the ability to find a balance between work and family (Greenhaus and Allen 2011), as the family may provide emotional and social support that enables the entrepreneur to balance work and family and to be satisfied in both roles (Eddleston and Powell 2012). Perceived legitimacy from family also enhances satisfaction with entrepreneurship as a career choice, as well as satisfaction with family life. Thus:

H2b. Legitimacy in the private sphere promotes job satisfaction.

Perceptions of legitimacy in the business sphere and in the private sphere may differ in their benefits for job satisfaction. The daily work as entrepreneur is embedded more in the business sphere, with its enabling and constraining relationships with suppliers and customers, than it is in the family sphere. Therefore, H2a and H2b can be augmented:

H2c. Job satisfaction is promoted by legitimacy in the business sphere more than by legitimacy in the private sphere.

2.3. Legitimacy as a promoter of job commitment

Job commitment, which refers to the determination to stay in a job and includes a long-term orientation to goals, is a central theme in research on occupations, including entrepreneurship (Bradley and Roberts 2004; Fornes, Roccard, and Wollard 2008). The perception of one's legitimacy in the business sphere tends to enhance self-esteem and competence, which increases the effort to pursue goals. A person's legitimacy in a role often frees up cognitive resources, which facilitates the pursuit of job-related goals (Uy, Foo, and Ilies 2015). Therefore:

H3a. Legitimacy in the business sphere promotes job commitment.

Women often leave jobs because of imbalances between work and family. However, when balance is achieved, legitimacy from the private environment is enhanced, and family and friends are likely to support the career emotionally and materially (Leung 2011). Family support is also likely to enhance performance in the job and, thus, to enhance the family's income (Powell and Eddleston 2013). Therefore:

H3b. Legitimacy in the private sphere promotes job commitment.

Job commitment is a long-term orientation. The family has a stake in the long-term future, whereas business contacts are more concerned with daily operations, so H3a and H3b can be extended:

H3c. Job commitment is promoted by legitimacy in the private sphere more than by legitimacy in the business sphere.

2.4. Sphere differences in promoting job satisfaction and job commitment

Does legitimacy in a sphere affect job commitment and job satisfaction differently? Institutional logic in the business sphere is dominated by a market logic with concern for daily operations more than for long-term prospects, so we hypothesize:

H4a. Legitimacy in the business sphere promotes job satisfaction more than job commitment.

Conversely, institutional logic in the private sphere is dominated by a family logic with greater concern for long-term prospects, so we hypothesize:

H4b. Legitimacy in the private sphere promotes job commitment more than job satisfaction.

The hypotheses are represented in Figure 1, which shows the strength of the detrimental effects of gender hierarchy and the strength of the positive effects of legitimacy.

The perspective of embeddedness can be interpreted as an issue of mediation, such that the gender hierarchy reduces legitimacy, and through this reduces job satisfaction and job commitment.

3. Research design

The hypotheses are tested with data from the Global Entrepreneurship Monitor (GEM) (Bosma et al. 2012; Global Entrepreneurship Research Association 2017). Legitimacy was queried in an extended version of the common survey in 2013 in 15 developing countries: Algeria, Angola, Bosnia and

Hypothesized effects.

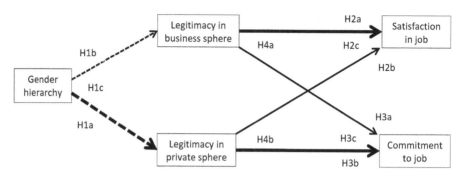

Figure 1. Hypothesized effects.

Herzegovina, Botswana, Ghana, India, Malawi, Namibia, Nigeria, Philippines, South Africa, Suriname, Turkey, Uganda and Zambia, a sample of countries that is representative of the developing world.

Adults were randomly sampled in each country, and entrepreneurs were identified as those who own and manage a starting or operating business. We analysed the responses of 5997 female entrepreneurs who reported their perceptions of legitimacy. The representativeness of sampling implies that findings can be generalized to female entrepreneurs in the developing world.

3.1. Measurements

3.1.1. Job commitment
Entrepreneurs' job commitment was measured by asking, *'Do you think you will still be an entrepreneur or business-owner in 5 years?'* Responses of No versus Yes are coded 0 and 1, respectively.

Findings show that female entrepreneurs tend to stay longer in their entrepreneurial jobs if they are motivated to start a business by seeing a business opportunity than they are if they are motivated by the necessity to make a living (Bosma et al. 2012). Therefore, our measure of job commitment correlates positively with being motivated by opportunity in contrast to being motivated by necessity. Likewise, job commitment correlates positively with both innovation and expectations of growth. These correlations indicate that our operationalization of job commitment is valid.

3.1.2. Job satisfaction
Job satisfaction was measured with questions from previous surveys (Blustein 2008). The entrepreneurs reported disagreement or agreement with five statements: *'I can decide on my own how I go about doing my work', 'The work I do is meaningful to me', 'At my work, I am not exposed to excessive stress', 'I am satisfied with my current work'* and *'I am satisfied with my current income from work'.* Disagreement versus agreement was rated on 5-point Likert scale coded −2 to 2. The five ratings are positively intercorrelated, with the factor analysis revealing one factor, with Cronbach's alpha .76. Their mean is the measure of job satisfaction.

This operationalization has been validated (Blustein 2008; Zhang and Schøtt 2017). Job satisfaction correlates positively with being motivated by opportunity, rather than necessity, indicating validity of our measurement. Job satisfaction and job commitment are correlated .1.

3.1.3. Legitimacy in private- and business-sphere networks
Perception of legitimacy was measured through the question, *'How does being an entrepreneur impact how you are treated by the following people (positively, no impact, or negatively)? Family? Friends? Business people? Suppliers? Customers?'* Negatively was coded −1, no impact was coded 0 and

positively was coded +1. Factor analysis reveals that family and friends form a group (Cronbach's alpha .71), appropriately called the private sphere, and that business people, suppliers and customers form another group (Cronbach's alpha .68), fittingly labelling the business sphere. Thus, the factor analysis matches the theorized conceptual distinction. Legitimacy in the private sphere was measured by the mean of the two ratings concerning family and friends, while legitimacy in the business sphere was measured as the mean of the ratings of business people, suppliers and customers. Legitimacy in the private sphere and legitimacy in the business sphere are correlated .4.

Legitimacy in the private sphere correlate positively with willingness to take risk, with viewing upstart opportunities as good, and with networking with advisors in the private sphere. Legitimacy in the business sphere also correlates positively with self-efficacy and with networking with advisors in the public sphere (Jensen and Schøtt 2017), indicating validity.

3.1.4. Gender hierarchy in the community

Gender hierarchy was measured on a 5-point scale (−2 to +2) on which respondents indicated their agreement with statements on three aspects of gender hierarchy: *'Where you live, it is believed that men should earn more than women'*, *'Where you live, a young woman's primary responsibility should be to start and maintain a family'* and *'Where you live, young women are disadvantaged in starting a business due to religious or cultural beliefs'*. Factor analysis revealed a single factor (Cronbach's alpha .70), so we used the mean of the three ratings to measure gender hierarchy, where a low value indicates a tendency towards gender equality, and a high value indicates that men are granted higher status.

Gender hierarchy is also measured at national level, by the Gender Inequality Index from the Human Development Program's *Human Development Report*. We use this measure to examine mediation.

3.1.5. Control variables at the micro-level

Analyses should control for conditions related to job characteristics. Entrepreneurs' job satisfaction is correlated with the entrepreneur's age and education, and the business's size (Schjoedt 2009), and with the entrepreneur's motive and the business's phase, owners and age (Jensen, Liu, and Schøtt 2017). The control variables, then, are:

- Entrepreneur's age (in years)
- Entrepreneur's education (in years)
- Business's phase (starting or operating, coded 0 and 1, respectively)
- Business's owners (number of owners, transformed logarithmically to reduce skew)
- Business's age (logged number of years since starting)
- Business's size (logged number of employees)
- Entrepreneur's motive (seeing a business opportunity or inability to find a better job, coded 1 and 0, respectively)

3.1.6. Control variables at the macro-level

Countries' wealth and culture are also controlled for. The wealth of a country is measured by the log of Gross National Income per capita, coded from the *Human Development Report*. The culture is from the World Values Survey (Inglehart and Welzel 2005), which discerns traditional versus secular-rationalistic cultures, a dimension that shapes female entrepreneurs' networking for advice (Schøtt and Cheraghi 2015). Standardized scores are coded from the homepage www.WorldValuesSurvey.org. The score is positive for a country with secular-rational culture and negative for a country with traditional culture.

3.2. Technique for analysis

Entrepreneurs are embedded within the macro-level context of their countries and have individual outcomes like satisfaction and commitment, which are affected by micro-level individual characteristics like perceived legitimacy and by macro-level contextual characteristics like their countries' wealth. Effects are appropriately ascertained by hierarchical linear regression (also called hierarchical linear modelling; Snijders and Bosker 2012), which is like linear regression but also considers that measurements are at two levels, that influences come from both levels, and that individuals in a country behave similarly. The model estimates effects of control variables that characterize entrepreneurs and their businesses and the wealth and culture of their countries. Since the countries are not of interest in themselves, they are omitted from the tables. Each numerical variable is standardized, so the model yields standardized coefficients that are comparable to each other and are essential for testing the hypotheses that compare effects. Each independent individual-level variable is centred in each country in order to better discern its effect. Effects are subtle and not strong, so coefficients are mostly small, while the estimates of macro-level conditions' effects typically are larger.

4. Results

A description of the sample with correlations and means for each country is available from the authors. Here, we report that no variable is overly skewed and no correlation is strong.

4.1. Legitimacy affected by gender hierarchy

Hypothesis 1a, that gender hierarchy reduces legitimacy in the private sphere, is tested in Model 1 in Table 1. The effect of gender hierarchy upon legitimacy in the private sphere is negative ($\beta = -.053$, $p = .0005$), providing support for Hypothesis 1a. The coefficient is larger than most coefficients for individual-level effects, and the effect is substantial.

Hypothesis 1b, that gender hierarchy reduces legitimacy in the business sphere, is tested in Model 2 in Table 1. The effect of gender hierarchy on legitimacy in the business sphere is estimated as near zero and is not significant ($\beta = .014$, $p = .35$), so Hypothesis 1b is not supported.

Hypothesis 1c is that gender hierarchy reduces legitimacy in the private sphere more than it reduces legitimacy in the business sphere. Comparing the estimated effect upon legitimacy in the private sphere, $-.053$ and the estimated effect upon legitimacy in the business sphere, .014,

Table 1. Legitimacy in private and business spheres, affected by gender hierarchy.

	Legitimacy in private sphere	Legitimacy in business sphere	Legitimacy in private sphere minus Legitimacy in business sphere
	Model 1	Model 2	Model 3
Gender hierarchy	−.053 ***	.014	−.063 ***
Age of entrepreneur	.006	.035 *	−.030
Education of entrepreneur	.019	−.004	.025
Motive: opportunity	.041 *	.076 ***	−.036 *
Phase: operating	−.028	−.028	−.006
Age of business	.026	.045	−.020
Owners of business	−.021	.025	−.044 *
Size of business	.059 *	.060 *	.000
GNI per capita	.065	−.049	.094
Secular-rational culture	.059	.069	−.009
Intercept	.045	−.080	.115
Country	Yes	Yes	Yes
N women entrepreneurs	3970	3891	3889
N countries	11	11	11

Hierarchical linear regression (including the categorical variable 'country', as indicated by 'Yes').
Each variable has been standardized.
Each independent individual-level variable has been centred within each country.
*$p < .05$, **$p < .005$, ***$p < .0005$.

suggests that gender hierarchy reduces legitimacy in the privates sphere more than in the public sphere, as expected. The hypothesis is tested by modelling the effect of gender hierarchy on the difference, as shown in Model 3 in Table 1. The negative coefficient ($\beta = -.063$, $p < .0005$) indicates that legitimacy in the private sphere is significantly more reduced than legitimacy in the business sphere, supporting Hypothesis 1c.

In short, gender hierarchy is detrimental to legitimacy in the private sphere but does not discernibly affect legitimacy in the business sphere. Whereas legitimacy is perceived by a woman entrepreneur in the business sphere irrespective of the gender hierarchy in the community, the legitimacy perceived in the private sphere is reduced by the gender hierarchy.

4.2. Legitimacy's effect on job satisfaction and job commitment

Hypothesis 2a, that job satisfaction is promoted by legitimacy in the business sphere, is tested in Model 1 in Table 2. The effect of legitimacy in the business sphere is positive ($\beta = .051$, $p < .0005$), supporting Hypothesis 2a. The coefficient is of similar magnitude as other individual-level effects and is substantial.

Hypothesis 2b, that job satisfaction is promoted by legitimacy in the private sphere, is tested in Model 1 in Table 2. The effect of legitimacy in the private sphere is positive ($\beta = .025$, $p = .04$), supporting Hypothesis 2b, although the effect is small.

Hypothesis 2c proposes that job satisfaction is promoted by legitimacy in the business sphere more than by legitimacy in the private sphere. Comparing the two coefficients, .051 and .025, respectively, suggests a greater effect of legitimacy in the business sphere than that of legitimacy in the private sphere, as expected. The hypothesis is tested by a model of job satisfaction with two independent variables: legitimacy in the business sphere and the sum of the two legitimacies, as shown in Model 2 in Table 2. In this model, the difference in effects of the two legitimacies is expressed by the coefficient for legitimacy in the business sphere. This coefficient, however, is not statistically significant ($\beta = .024$, $p = .15$), so Hypothesis 2c is not supported.

Hypothesis 3a, that job commitment is promoted by legitimacy in the business sphere, is tested in Model 3 in Table 2. The effect of legitimacy in the business sphere is positive ($\beta = .031$, $p = .02$), supporting Hypothesis 3a, but the coefficient indicates that the effect is small.

Table 2. Job satisfaction and job commitment affected by legitimacy.

	Job satisfaction		Job commitment		Job commitment minus job satisfaction
	Model 1	Model 2	Model 3	Model 4	Model 5
Legitimacy in business sphere	.051 ***	.024	.031 *		−.015
Legitimacy in private sphere	.025 *		.085 ***	.054 **	.065 **
L. in business + L. in private		.025		.031 *	
Age of entrepreneur	.064 ***	.065 ***	−.034 *	−.034 *	−.091 ***
Education of entrepreneur	.019	.019	.020	.020	−.011
Motive: opportunity	.076 ***	.075 ***	.042 **	.042 **	−.032
Phase: operating	.047 *	.047 *	.035	.035	−.008
Age of business	−.033	−.033	−.097 ***	−.097 ***	−.064 *
Owners of business	−.024	−.024	.016	.016	.029
Size of business	.021	.021	−.003	−.003	−.020
GNI per capita	.288 *	.288 *	.029	.029	−.249 *
Secular-rational culture	.156	.156	.076	.076	−.085
Intercept	.065	.065	.005	.005	−.060
Country	Yes	Yes	Yes	Yes	Yes
N women entrepreneurs	4406	4406	4927	4927	4157
N countries	15	15	15	15	15

Hierarchical linear regression (including the categorical variable 'country', as indicated by 'Yes').
Each variable has been standardized.
Each independent individual-level variable has been centred within each country.
*$p < .05$, **$p < .005$, ***$p < .0005$.

Hypothesis 3b, that job commitment is promoted by legitimacy in the private sphere, is also tested in Model 3 in Table 2. The effect of legitimacy in the business sphere is positive (β = .085, p < .0005), supporting Hypothesis 3b, and the coefficient indicates that the effect is substantial.

Hypothesis 3c proposes that job commitment is promoted by legitimacy in the private sphere more than by legitimacy in the business sphere. Comparing the two coefficients suggests a greater effect of legitimacy in the private sphere, as expected. The hypothesis is tested by a model of job satisfaction with two independent variables: legitimacy in the private sphere and the sum of the two legitimacies, as shown in Model 4 in Table 2. The positive coefficient for legitimacy in the private sphere (β = .054, p = .02) captures the differential effect of the two spheres and indicates that legitimacy in the private sphere has the greater effect, thus supporting Hypothesis 3c.

Hypothesis 4a proposes that legitimacy in the business sphere promotes job satisfaction more than it promotes job commitment. Comparing the two coefficients, .051 and .031, respectively, suggests that job satisfaction is strengthened by legitimacy in the business sphere more than job commitment is, as expected. The hypothesis is tested by modelling the effect on the difference, as shown in Model 5 in Table 2. The effect of legitimacy in the business sphere on the difference is not significant (β = −.015, p = .24), so Hypothesis 4a is not supported.

Hypothesis 4b proposes that legitimacy in the private sphere promotes job commitment more than it promotes job satisfaction. Comparing the two coefficients, .085 and .025, respectively, suggests that job commitment is promoted more than job satisfaction, as expected. The hypothesis is tested by modelling the effect on the difference, as shown in Model 5 in Table 2. The effect of legitimacy in the private sphere on the difference is as expected (β = .065, p = .002), thus supporting Hypothesis 4b.

In short, legitimacy in the business sphere promotes job satisfaction and, to some extent, also job commitment, while legitimacy in the private sphere promotes job commitment and, to some degree, also job satisfaction.

4.3. Legitimacy's mediating effects on gender hierarchy's relationships with satisfaction and commitment

The embeddedness perspective can be turned around to be an issue of mediation. We expect that gender hierarchy reduces job satisfaction and job commitment through legitimacy and examine this mediation, operationalizing gender hierarchy using the Gender Inequality Index for each of the 15 sampled countries.

As a starting point, the direct effects of gender inequality on job satisfaction and job commitment seem negative, as expected. The effects of gender inequality on legitimacy in the business sphere and on legitimacy in the private sphere seem negative, as expected, and effects of legitimacy on job satisfaction and job commitment seem positive, as expected and seen in the above analyses. Finally, some of the indirect effects of gender inequality, through legitimacy, upon job-related outcomes, seem significant. In short, the analysis indicates that legitimacy mediates negative effects of gender hierarchy on job characteristics. However, the effects of gender inequality are ascertained for only 15 countries, so this analysis of mediation is not conclusive.

5. Conclusions

Gaps in understanding the embeddedness of a woman's legitimacy as an entrepreneur framed our research question: What are the effects of gender hierarchy and networks on the legitimacy a female entrepreneur experiences and on her satisfaction and commitment to her job?

5.1. Contribution

Fisher et al. (2017) asked, *'Legitimate to whom?'* The grantors of an entrepreneur's legitimacy are diverse, they differ in their logic in granting or withholding legitimacy and the legitimacy the entrepreneur experiences affects his or her motivation and access to resources (Pollack, Rutherford, and Nagy 2012; Überbacher 2014).

The study builds a model of female entrepreneurs' legitimacy, which is conceptualized as a woman's perception of the appropriateness of her incumbency in the role of entrepreneur. Therefore, the study's focus is on the experiences of female entrepreneurs at the receiving end of legitimacy, rather than on the granting of legitimacy (Nagy et al. 2012).

The legitimacy of a female entrepreneur, as a micro-level phenomenon, is contextualized as embedded in meso-level and macro-level structures. At the meso-level, the woman experiences legitimacy in her networks. An entrepreneur's networking for advice, financing and other resources in the private sphere and in the public sphere has been found to differ as it relates to gender, its embeddedness in culture and the local community, and its effects on outcomes (Blake 2006; Jensen and Schøtt 2017). Our study broadens and complements this research on resource networks to encompass the legitimacy perceived in networks. Theoretically and empirically, we distinguish between a female entrepreneur's network in the private sphere and that in the business sphere. The distinction is informative because the two networks differ in terms of both antecedents and consequences.

Legitimacy is embedded in networks and is further embedded at the macro-level in gender hierarchy, which differs across societies in steepness and institutionalization (Yousafzai, Saeed, and Muffatto 2015). Gender hierarchy reduces legitimacy of female entrepreneurs, and the model theorizes that the steepness of gender hierarchy constrains legitimacy in the private sphere more than it does legitimacy in the business sphere.

Legitimacy in the business sphere can fulfil a need to feel competent, while legitimacy in the private sphere can fulfil a need to feel related, as described by the theory of self-determination (Ryan and Deci 2000). As expected in theorizing about diverse institutional logics (Überbacher 2014), legitimacy in the business sphere promotes job satisfaction more than legitimacy in the private sphere does, and legitimacy in the private sphere enhances job commitment more than legitimacy in the business sphere does. Of course, female entrepreneurs' satisfaction and commitment to theirs jobs are essential for inclusiveness and the development of entrepreneurship as an institution in society (Block and Koellinger 2009).

Therefore, the story of job characteristics embedded in networks that are themselves embedded in institutions can be retold as a story of mediation, of institutions that affect jobs through networks. Networks are the medium or mechanism that channels the effects of institutions on individual endeavours. The model is supported empirically with data that come mainly from Sub-Saharan Africa, where traditional gender hierarchy constrains female entrepreneurs' legitimacy (Amine and Staub 2009). The findings can be generalized to female entrepreneurs in the developing world. The model may have wider applicability, we surmise, in so far as gender hierarchy appears to operate similarly in more secular-rational culture (McAdam, Harrison, and Leitch 2018).

5.2. Relevance to policy and practice

The role of the entrepreneur is valued in nearly all societies. Most societies have policies for increasing entry into the entrepreneurial role, and several societies have policies for inclusiveness, especially of women. Women's legitimacy and devotion to the entrepreneurial job are valued and desirable for both society and women individually. Our findings indicate that legitimacy, satisfaction and commitment are enhanced by reducing the gender hierarchy. Gender hierarchies have been reduced around the world as women have entered the working world, most notably in Eastern Europe under communism, in Western Europe in the latter half of the twentieth century, and in China during recent decades. Therefore, it should be feasible to reduce gender hierarchy in the domain of self-employment and entrepreneurship in particular.

Entrepreneurial endeavours have high probability of failure, affecting entrepreneurs' personal well-being and that of their families, employees and investors. Enhancing legitimacy, and thereby satisfaction and commitment to the job, may reduce strain on the role combination required of female entrepreneurs. In a gender-hierarchical culture, women may be deviating from norms by becoming entrepreneurs, so legitimacy and support from family and the environment can reduce the stress that results from the role combination (Hmieleski and Corbett 2008).

Because women, perhaps even more than men, tend to be significantly affected by their networks, it would be especially fruitful to create environments that are friendly to female entrepreneurs at both the meso-level of networks and the macro-level of institutions. Female entrepreneurs may experience more legitimacy with more preferential policies, such as tax reductions, other kinds of government support and other kinds of support that reduce barriers to start-ups and to satisfaction and commitment. Another way to support female entrepreneurs is to offer women more opportunities for entrepreneurial training and education. Such programmes can not only help to improve their business skills but can also increase their self-efficacy and confidence, which are essential to their motivation for entrepreneurial activities and to their networking in the business sphere. Creating women-only networks has been advocated to enhance women's social capital but has also been criticized as being ineffective and causing ghettoization (McAdam, Harrison, and Leitch 2018). Partnering female entrepreneurs with men has also been advocated for enhancing legitimacy and access to resources (Godwin, Stevens, and Brenner 2006).

The gender hierarchy is especially detrimental to legitimacy in the private sphere. Women's involvement in economic life is important for development of society and for life in the private sphere, but changes in this realm are slow, as women continue to devote more time to domestic tasks than men do. Family members can offer support by sharing responsibilities among family members and by socializing and training men for family life and for supporting woman entrepreneurship. Female entrepreneurs can also practise more strategic networking with legitimating audiences (Überbacher 2014) in both the private sphere and the public sphere (Fisher et al. 2017). In addition, women entrepreneurs can collectively form a social movement advocating legitimacy.

5.3. Limitations

The limitations of this study are both methodological and substantive. A methodological limitation is that the survey is cross-sectional, so causality is assumed rather than ascertained empirically. Another methodological limitation is that concepts are operationalized with indices that are based on only few items in a questionnaire. For example, legitimacy in the private sphere is measured by a two-item index and legitimacy in the business sphere by a three-item index, and legitimacy was measured in only 15 countries. This limitation did not constrain the individual-level analyses reported in the tables, but when a national-level measure of gender hierarchy, the Gender Inequality Index, was used to analyse mediation, the small sample size reduced the power in tests of gender inequality's effects.

The study's substantive limitations concern legitimacy's embeddedness in certain contexts. The study analysed two contexts – gender hierarchy and networking in the private and business spheres. Other contexts were included as controls. Embeddedness was considered mainly in terms of the direct effects of gender hierarchy on networks, the direct effects of networking on legitimacy and the direct effects of legitimacy on job characteristics, so a limitation is that moderating effects were not considered. These substantive limitations point to opportunities for further research.

5.4. Future research

Three of the 11 hypothesized effects were not significant. The analysis did not discern an effect of gender hierarchy on legitimacy in the business sphere (Hypothesis 1b). This result is consistent with the study of sources of legitimacy, which have not revealed any influence of gender or family logics (Fisher et al. 2017). However, available evidence indicates that gender hierarchy does reduce legitimacy in the business sphere, notably in Sub-Saharan Africa, where the survey was mainly conducted (Amine and Staub 2009). While the gendering of networks is being researched, more research on legitimacy experienced in networks will be informative. Furthermore, analyses did not show that legitimacy in the business sphere promotes job satisfaction more than private sphere legitimacy does (Hypothesis 2c) or that it promotes job satisfaction more than job commitment does (Hypothesis 4a). Both non-findings would be accounted for if legitimacy in the business sphere promotes job satisfaction less than hypothesized. Conceivably, job satisfaction depends on so many other conditions that the effect of legitimacy in the business sphere is small. This suggestion calls for further research on sources of satisfaction in the job of entrepreneur (Block and Koellinger 2009; Jensen, Liu, and Schøtt 2017).

Acknowledgments

Data were collected by Global Entrepreneurship Monitor, but responsibility for interpretations rests with the authors. Analyses were supported by an award from the National Natural Science Foundation of China (grant 71603241) to Ye Liu for her research project, 'Hybrid organization in entrepreneurial universities'. Schøtt appreciates the hospitality of Tsinghua University. The article benefitted greatly from comments by the reviewers and guest-editors.

Disclosure statement

No potential conflict of interest was reported by the authors.

Funding

This work was supported by the National Natural Science Foundation of China; [71603241].

References

Amine, L. S., and K. M. Staub. 2009. "Women Entrepreneurs in sub-Saharan Africa: An Institutional Theory Analysis from a Social Marketing Point of View." *Entrepreneurship and Regional Development* 21 (2): 183–211. doi:10.1080/08985620802182144.

Baughn, C. C., B.-L. Chua, and K. E. Neupert. 2006. "The Normative Context for Women's Participation in Entrepreneurship: A Multi-Country Study." *Entrepreneurship Theory and Practice* 30 (5): 687–708. doi:10.1111/j.1540-6520.2006.00142.x.

Blake, M. K. 2006. "Gendered Lending: Gender, Context and the Rules of Business Lending." *Venture Capital* 8 (2): 183–201. doi:10.1080/13691060500433835.

Block, J., and P. Koellinger. 2009. "I Can't Get No Satisfaction – Necessity Entrepreneurship and Procedural Utility." *Kyklos* 62 (2): 191–209. doi:10.1111/kykl.2009.62.issue-2.

Blustein, D. L. 2008. "The Role of Work in Psychological Health and Well-Being." *American Psychologist* 63 (4): 228–240. doi:10.1037/0003-066X.63.4.228.

Bosma, N., A. Coduras, Y. Litovsky, and J. Seaman. 2012. *GEM Manual: A Report on the Design, Data and Quality Control of the Global Entrepreneurship Monitor*. Accessed 1 May 2017. www.gemconsortium.org.

Bradley, D. E., and J. A. Roberts. 2004. "Self-Employment and Job-Satisfaction: Investigating the Role of Self-Efficacy, Depression, and Seniority." *Journal of Small Business Management* 42 (1): 37–58. doi:10.1111/j.1540-627X.2004.00096.x.

de Clercq, D., and M. Voronov. 2009. "Toward a Practice Perspective of Entrepreneurship: Entrepreneurial Legitimacy as Habitus." *International Small Business Journal* 27 (4): 395–419. doi:10.1177/0266242609334971.

Eagly, A. H., W. Wood, and A. B. Diekman. 2000. "Social Role Theory of Sex Differences and Similarities: A Current Appraisal." In *The Developmental Social Psychology of Gender*, edited by T. Eckes and H. M. Trautner. Mahwah: Erlbaum.

Eddleston, K. A., and G. N. Powell. 2012. "Nurturing Entrepreneurs' Work–Family Balance: A Gendered Perspective." *Entrepreneurship Theory & Practice* 36 (3): 513–541. doi:10.1111/etap.2012.36.issue-3.

Fairclough, S., and E. R. Micelotta. 2013. "Beyond the Family Firm: Reasserting the Influence of the Family Institutional Logic across Organizations." In *Institutional Logics in Action, Part B*, edited by M. Lounsbury and E. Boxenbaum, 63–98, Emerald.

Fisher, G., D. F. Kuratko, J. M. Bloodgood, and J. S. Hornsby. 2017. "Legitimate to Whom? The Challenge of Audience Diversity and New Venture Legitimacy." *Journal of Business Venturing* 32: 52–71. doi:10.1016/j.jbusvent.2016.10.005.

Fornes, S., T. Roccard, and K. Wollard. 2008. "Workplace Commitment: A Conceptual Model Developed from Integrative Review of the Research." *Human Resource Development Review* 7: 339–357. doi:10.1177/1534484308318760.

Global Entrepreneurship Research Association. 2017. Accessed April 2 2017. www.gemconsortium.org

Godwin, L. N., C. E. Stevens, and N. L. Brenner. 2006. "Forced to Play by the Rules? Theorizing How Mixed-Sex Founding Teams Benefit Women Entrepreneurs in Male-Dominated Contexts." *Entrepreneurship Theory and Practice* 30 (5): 623–642. doi:10.1111/etap.2006.30.issue-5.

Greene, F. J., L. Han, and S. Marlow. 2013. "Like Mother, like Daughter? Analyzing Maternal Influences upon Women's Entrepreneurial Propensity." *Entrepreneurship Theory and Practice* 37 (4): 687–711. doi:10.1111/etap.2013.37.issue-4.

Greenhaus, J. H., and T. D. Allen. 2011. "Work-Family Balance: A Review and Extension of the Literature." In *Handbook of Occupational Health Psychology*, edited by J. C. Quick and L. E. Tetrick. Washington: American Psychological Association.

Greenwood, R., A. M. Díaz, S. X. Li, and J. C. Lorente. 2010. "The Multiplicity of Institutional Logics and the Heterogeneity of Organizational Responses." *Organization Science* 21: 521–539. doi:10.1287/orsc.1090.0453.

Hamilton, E. 2013. "The Discourse of Entrepreneurial Masculinities (and Femininities)." *Entrepreneurship & Regional Development* 25 (1–2): 90–99. doi:10.1080/08985626.2012.746879.

Hmieleski, K. M., and A. C. Corbett. 2008. "The Contrasting Interaction Effects of Improvisational Behavior with Entrepreneurial Self-Efficacy on New Venture Performance and Entrepreneur Work Satisfaction." *Journal of Business Venturing* 23 (4): 482–496. doi:10.1016/j.jbusvent.2007.04.002.

Inglehart, R., and C. Welzel. 2005. *Modernization, Cultural Change, and Democracy*. Cambridge: CUP.

Jensen, K. W., Y. Liu, and T. Schøtt. 2017. "Entrepreneurs' Innovation Bringing Job-Satisfaction with Job, Work-Family Balance, and Life-Satisfaction: In China and around the World." *International Journal of Innovation Studies* 1 (4): 193–206. doi:10.1016/j.ijis.2017.11.002.

Jensen, K. W., and T. Schøtt. 2017. "Components of the Network around an Actor." In *Encyclopedia of Social Network Analysis and Mining*, edited by R. Alhajj and J. Rokne, 2nd ed. 1 vol. New York: Springer.

Kibler, E., and T. Kautonen. 2014. "The Moral Legitimacy of Entrepreneurs: An Analysis of Early-Stage Entrepreneurship across 26 Countries." *International Small Business Journal* 34 (1): 34–50. doi:10.1177/0266242614541844.

Klyver, K., S. L. Nielsen, and M. R. Evald. 2013. "Women's Self-Employment: An Act of Institutional (Dis)Integration? A Multilevel, Cross-Country Study." *Journal of Business Venturing* 28: 474–488. doi:10.1016/j.jbusvent.2012.07.002.

Leung, A. 2011. "Motherhood and Entrepreneurship: Gender Role Identity as a Resource." *International Journal of Gender and Entrepreneurship* 3 (3): 254–264. doi:10.1108/17566261111169331.

Lounsbury, M., and M. A. Glynn. 2001. "Cultural Entrepreneurship: Stories, Legitimacy, and the Acquisition of Resources." *Strategic Management Journal* 22 (6–7): 545–564. doi:10.1002/(ISSN)1097-0266.

Marlow, S., and M. McAdam. 2015. "Incubation or Induction? Gendered Identity Work in the Context of Technology Business Incubation." *Entrepreneurship Theory and Practice* 39 (4): 791–816. doi:10.1111/etap.2015.39.issue-4.

Marlow, S., and J. Swail. 2014. "Gender, Risk and Finance: Why Can't a Woman Be More like a Man?" *Entrepreneurship & Regional Development* 26 (1–2): 80–96. doi:10.1080/08985626.2013.860484.

McAdam, M., R. T. Harrison, and C. M. Leitch. 2018. "Stories from the Field: Women's Networking as Gender Capital in Entrepreneurial Ecosystems." *Small Business Economics*. Online. doi:10.1007/s11187-018-9995-6.

McGowan, P., C. L. Redeker, S. Y. Cooper, and K. Greenan. 2012. "Female Entrepreneurship and the Management of Business and Domestic Roles: Motivations, Expectations and Realities." *Entrepreneurship & Regional Development* 24 (1–2): 53–72. doi:10.1080/08985626.2012.637351.

Middleton, K. L. W. 2013. "Becoming Entrepreneurial: Gaining Legitimacy in the Nascent Phase." *International Journal of Entrepreneurial Behavior & Research* 19 (4): 404–424. doi:10.1108/IJEBR-04-2012-0049.

Miller, D., I. L. Breton-Miller, and R. H. Lester. 2011. "Family and Lone Founder Ownership and Strategic Behavior: Social Context, Identity and Institutional Logics." *Journal of Management Studies* 48 (1): 1–25. doi:10.1111/j.1467-6486.2009.00896.x.

Nagy, B. G., J. M. Pollack, M. W. Rutherford, and F. T. Lohrke. 2012. "The Influence of Entrepreneurs' Credentials and Impression Management Behaviors on Perceptions of New Venture Legitimacy." *Entrepreneurship Theory and Practice* 36 (5): 941–965. doi:10.1111/etap.2012.36.issue-5.

Pollack, J. M., M. W. Rutherford, and B. G. Nagy. 2012. "Preparedness and Cognitive Legitimacy as Antecedents of New Venture Funding in Televised Business Pitches." *Entrepreneurship Theory and Practice* 36 (5): 915–939. doi:10.1111/etap.2012.36.issue-5.

Powell, G. N., and K. A. Eddleston. 2013. "Linking Family-To-Business Enrichment and Support to Entrepreneurial Success: Do Female and Male Entrepreneurs Experience Different Outcomes?" *Journal of Business Venturing* 28 (2): 261–280. doi:10.1016/j.jbusvent.2012.02.007.

Robinson, S., and H. A. Stubberud. 2009. "Sources of Advice in Entrepreneurship: Gender Differences in Business Owners' Social Networks." *International Journal of Entrepreneurship* 13: 83–101.

Ryan, R. M., and E. L. Deci. 2000. "Self-Determination Theory and the Facilitation of Intrinsic Motivation, Social Development, and Well-Being." *American Psychologist* 55 (1): 68–78.

Schjoedt, L. 2009. "Entrepreneurial Job Characteristics: An Examination of Their Effect on Entrepreneurial Satisfaction." *Entrepreneurship Theory and Practice* 33 (3): 619–644. doi:10.1111/etap.2009.33.issue-3.

Schøtt, T., and M. Cheraghi. 2015. "Gendering Pursuits of Innovation: Embeddedness in Networks and Culture." *International Journal of Entrepreneurship and Small Business* 24 (1): 83–116. doi:10.1504/IJESB.2015.066160.

Snijders, T., and R. J. Bosker. 2012. *Multilevel Models*. Thousand Oaks: Sage.

Terrell, K., and M. Troilo. 2010. "Values and Female Entrepreneurship." *International Journal of Gender and Entrepreneurship* 2 (3): 260–286. doi:10.1108/17566261011079242.

Thornton, P. H., W. Ocasio, and M. Lounsbury. 2012. *The Institutional Logics Perspective*. Oxford: Oxford University Press.

Überbacher, F. 2014. "Legitimation of New Ventures: A Review and Research Agenda." *Journal of Management Studies* 51 (4): 667–698. doi:10.1111/joms.12077.

Uy, M. A., M. D. Foo, and R. Ilies. 2015. "Perceived Progress Variability and Entrepreneurial Effort Intensity: The Moderating Role of Venture Goal Commitment." *Journal of Business Venturing* 30 (3): 375–389. doi:10.1016/j.jbusvent.2014.02.001.

Wincent, J., D. Örtqvist, and M. Drnovsek. 2008. "Entrepreneur's Role Stressors and Proclivity for Venture Withdrawal." *Scandinavian Journal of Management* 24: 232–246. doi:10.1016/j.scaman.2008.04.001.

Yousafzai, S., S. Saeed, and M. Muffatto. 2015. "Institutional Theory and Contextual Embeddedness of Women's Entrepreneurial Leadership: Evidence from 92 Countries." *Journal of Small Business Management* 53 (3): 587–604. doi:10.1111/jsbm.2015.53.issue-3.

Zhang, C., and T. Schøtt. 2017. "Young Employees' Job-Autonomy Promoting Intention to Become Entrepreneur: Embedded in Gender and Traditional versus Modern Culture." *International Journal of Entrepreneurship and Small Business* 30 (3): 357. doi:10.1504/IJESB.2017.081974.

Token entrepreneurs: a review of gender, capital, and context in technology entrepreneurship

Mandy Wheadon and Nathalie Duval-Couetil

ABSTRACT

This article reviews the literature on gender and entrepreneurship in technology to explore individual and contextual factors maintaining the token status of women in this field. It examines how the intersection of gender and context influences participation rates in entrepreneurship, and suggests that the deeply embedded cultural and cognitive associations that frame both technology and entrepreneurship as masculine concepts create barriers for women when these contexts overlap. It offers a framework for research and practice that aids in the analysis of complex multi-level barriers that control access to the forms of capital necessary for initial and continued participation in technology entrepreneurship. Given calls for women to participate more fully in high-growth technology ventures, it highlights the need for research to incorporate broader analytical perspectives that simultaneously examine both the barriers faced by women in these contexts and the factors that systemically sustain them.

Introduction

The future of American entrepreneurship and growth is in the hands of women. (Robb, Coleman, and Stangler 2014, 3)

It has been over 40 years since the first journal article about women in entrepreneurship was published (Schwartz 1976). In the four decades since that initial article appeared, the number of women working as entrepreneurs both globally and in the USA has grown considerably, as has the attention given to them by researchers (see Brush 1992; Gatewood et al. 2003; Sullivan and Meek 2012). It has been estimated that there were approximately 9.4 million women-owned enterprises in the USA alone in 2015 (American Express OPEN Forum 2015), and as many as 207 articles touching on women in entrepreneurship appearing in academic journals between 1976 and 2010 (Gatewood et al. 2003; Sullivan and Meek 2012). While involvement and attention to gender within entrepreneurship have increased, these are viewed by many as insufficient given economic and workforce trends and the potential that remains for women to be more fully represented in technology-related fields.

The economy has experienced significant transformations in this 40-year timeframe, increasingly shifting away from the production of material goods and towards the commercialization of knowledge, information and technological innovations (Best et al. 2016; Chandan 2015; Duderstadt, Wulf, and Zemsky 2005; Etzkowitz et al. 2000; Nye 2006; Truss et al. 2012; Walby 2011). Entrepreneurship is increasingly considered to be 'one of the most important activities of modern economic life' (Fairlie et al. 2015, 3).

Working to meet the demands of the new 'innovation economy' (Kenney and Patton 2015; Wendler et al. 2010), entrepreneurs are more conceptually linked with technology and high-tech enterprises than ever before given their role in job creation (Dohrman 2010; Hsu, Roberts, and Eesley 2007; Kenney and Patton 2015; Shartrand et al. 2010; Wendler et al. 2010; Wiens and Jackson 2015).

However, participation in the creation of high-growth, innovation- and technology-based ventures is not reflected equally across gender lines. Female entrepreneurs are underrepresented in the more profitable, faster-growing types of entrepreneurship that are increasingly valued by this new economy (GEM 2010; Kelley et al. 2012). Reports indicate that the number of women entering these fields as entrepreneurs has remained relatively unchanged since 2004 (Kelley et al. 2014). Despite extensive work done to generate female participation in entrepreneurship generally (Bygrave et al. 2013; Karimi et al. 2013; Obschonka, Schmitt-Rodermund, and Terracciano 2014; Pettersson and Lindberg 2013; Ranga and Etzkowitz 2010; Stephan and El-Ganainy 2007), and to raise awareness of gender disparities in technology entrepreneurship globally (Dautzenberg 2012; Ezzedeen and Zikic 2012; Hampton, McGowan, and Cooper 2011; Orser and Hogarth-Scott 2009; Sappleton 2009), females in highly developed economies with advanced technological infrastructures remain 'token' or minority players in what is still a fundamentally masculine field.

Persistent gender gaps suggest that our examinations of them, and/or our assumptions about which factors are contributing to gendered inequalities and disparities in participation, are insufficient. This was recognized in a recent GEM report which called for more research that incorporates the contextually significant variables that underlie and sustain gender-based disparities (Herrington and Kew 2017). Specifically, the report stated that in order to create and implement more effective strategies for overcoming persistent gender gaps in entrepreneurship, scholars must first 'acknowledge and take into account multiple perspectives and the particular context of specific economies (including the development profile, national culture, and political and social dynamic)' (Herrington and Kew 2017, 11).

In light of this, the goal of this literature review is to examine the factors that sustain persistent gender disparities in participation and success in contexts where technology and entrepreneurship intersect – i.e. in technology entrepreneurship. The rationale for examining this particular area of entrepreneurship is not that the technology sector itself is distinctive (although it is a context with unequal rates of participation by gender – see Henwood 2000; Walby 2011), it's that 'technology entrepreneurship' is a field where gendered contexts intersect or overlap (i.e. both technology AND entrepreneurship are gendered). Industry segregation patterns shows that even when women overcome the barriers of one gendered context (entrepreneurship), they tend to remain in sectors that are stereotypically female (e.g. service or retail) instead of the more lucrative sectors associated by many cultures with men and masculinity (like technology – GEM 2010; Kelley et al. 2012). Therefore, it is important to recognize the layered nature of barriers found in overlapping gendered contexts in order to increase our understanding of persistent and systemic gender gaps, and then address them more fully in initiatives focused on moving women in entrepreneurship beyond just the typically 'feminine' sectors to the more lucrative technology-based 'masculine' sectors as well.

To examine these topics, we first introduce background from existing research on the barriers faced by women in both technology and entrepreneurship contexts. Second, we present the methods used to conduct a review of the literature focused on gender in contexts where technology and entrepreneurship intersect. Third, we describe the procedures used to evaluate the articles, examine the variables found to influence participation and/or persistence of women as entrepreneurs in technology and innovation contexts, and the data-driven inductive approach used to identify patterns and explore the connections between them. Lastly, we discuss our analysis using a multi-level framework of internal and external barriers that regulate access to the various forms of capital necessary for initial and sustained participation in this context. This framework shows barriers as layered concepts that can be encountered in multiple forms, with additive or multiplicative consequences, particularly in contexts where identities intersect and stereotypes overlap. Finally, it suggests that developing long-term solutions for systemic and persistent inequalities requires expanding perspectives to recognize and address them in both research and practice.

Women and technology

If machismo is on the run in most U.S. corporate settings, then [technology] is its Alamo – a last holdout of redoubled intensity. (Hewlett et al. 2008, 23)

The concept of technology is not gender neutral (Henwood 2000; Walby 2011). Like most concepts, technology could only exist as a neutral entity if the sociocultural context and issues surrounding it were removed (Green 2002). However, 'no technology is, has been, or [ever] will be a "natural force" … Technologies are not foreign to "human nature" but inseparable from it' (Nye 2006, 19). Ultimately, technology is a social process that reflects the larger relationships and socially constructed systems of meaning that surround it (Nye 2006). As such, the deeply embedded cultural associations linking technology with men and masculinity in many contemporary Western contexts influence the 'everyday experiences of gender, historical narratives, employment practices, education, and the distribution of power across a global society in which technology is seen as the driving force of progress' (Bray 2007, 38).

On an applied level, this translates into the gendered acquisition of skills, expertise, and divisions of labour that continue to place men at the centre of technology and innovation, and frame women primarily as its passive recipients (Bilimoria, Joy, and Liang 2008; Bray 2007; Kelan 2007). Progress has been made in understanding the effects of gender stereotypes on the performance of females, especially in traditionally male-dominated contexts (Hill, Corbett, and St. Rose 2010); however, research indicates that participation rates of women in technology fields remain low despite the measures taken to fix the so-called leaky pipeline (Bilimoria, Joy, and Liang 2008; Hewlett et al. 2008). Systemic and institutionalized biases that sustain traditional divisions of labour by gender continue to impact the recruitment and retention of women into the very educational programmes and jobs that provide the skills necessary to eliminate gender gaps and reduce technology's masculine stereotypes (Godwin, Stevens, and Brenner 2006; Goel, Goktepe-Hulten, and Ram 2014; Orser and Hogarth-Scott 2009).

Women and entrepreneurship

Although a seemingly modern concept, the historical roots of entrepreneurship have been developed over the last 300 years by a long – and almost exclusively male – line of scholars and philosophers (Jones 2012; Nightingale and Coad 2011). As a field where the sex of an individual often determines perceptions about ability and access to the skills and resources needed to start and grow a business, entrepreneurship suffers from many of the same complex and culturally masculine associations that have hindered the full participation of females in technology (Bury 2011; Goss et al. 2011; Rindova, Barry, and Ketchen 2009; Zott and Nguyen Huy 2006). Over time, imbalanced distributions of skills and resources that result from greater access to education and opportunities to practice entrepreneurship have resulted in the discipline becoming implicitly associated with men and the characteristics ascribed to masculinity. Ely and Padavic (2007) sum up the self-replicating nature of this process, stating that 'the result is a hierarchal system in which the dominant group maintains control over the distribution of resources' (1128) and thereby remains deeply associated with the category and idealized as more inherently legitimate.

This conflation between stereotypically masculine traits, the skills used to define a successful entrepreneur, and the subsequently lowered expectations about the ability of women as entrepreneurs has resulted in 'covert discriminatory practices' (Kelley et al. 2012) that impact female career intent, self-efficacy, and the types of entrepreneurial ventures chosen by women in contexts such as the USA. The stereotypes framing men as more natural and more successful entrepreneurs have huge financial implications for women entrepreneurs as individuals, as well as to the growth of the national and global economies they are a part of (Jones 2012). Disproportionate levels of access to, and development of, entrepreneurial skills and careers in technology-related sectors by women have contributed to diminished business creation rates and fiscal growth, despite the growing population of well-educated women workers in the USA (Jones 2012).

Intersecting contexts and overlapping barriers

Most women expressed some variation on believing "entrepreneurs" and "support for entrepreneurs" to be for young, male entrepreneurs in the tech sector who are looking for venture capital money. (North, A. 2015, para. 8)

The term 'token' is used in this article to mean more than just minority status or a problem of numbers and momentum that will resolve itself once more members of the missing group are added to the equation (Kanter 1977). More significantly, the term is used to highlight the inadequacy of scholarship and policies that superficially address inequalities by universalizing diverse experiences into a single social group, identity category, or context to simplify the search for causal explanations and concrete solutions (Scott 1986; Zimmer 1988). For example, reasoning that assumes research on women as entrepreneurs to be generalizable for all types of women in all types of entrepreneurship is over-simplified; 'women' are not a homogeneous group any more than 'men' are (Symington 2004), and neither is 'entrepreneurship' (Bruyat and Julien 2000).

Studies that overlook context (Lansky 2000) and within-group differences (Nelson and Duffy 2010) perpetuate problematic assumptions. These include the tendency to assess gender gaps with deficit models that frame males as the standard for entrepreneurs (Byrne and Fayolle 2010; Marlow and Mcadam 2015; Mirchandani 1999), or the use of conflated categories (like 'women and minorities') that 'effectively equate "women" with "well-to-do White women,"' thereby obscuring the additional inequalities faced by female entrepreneurs of diverse backgrounds (McConnell-Ginet 2003, 70; Eckert and McConnell-Ginet 2013; Ozkazanc-Pan 2014). The opportunities, resources, and career paths available to women, as well as the types of barriers constraining them, inevitably vary in relation to the multiple layers of identity each individual embodies – such as their race, age, sexual orientation, and socioeconomic status (De Clercq and Voronov 2008; Dubrow 2008; Symington 2004). Aspects of these intersecting social categories become more or less salient in different settings (Steele, Spencer, and Aronson 2002), and the identities useful to women in one context can simultaneously disadvantage them in others (Collins 2008; Symington 2004). The overlap of more than one gendered context (e.g. combining both entrepreneurship and technology) creates barriers reinforced with 'multiple margin-alities' (Turner 2002) that are substantially more complex to navigate or overcome.

Understanding how gender, technology, and entrepreneurship intersect to form contextually unique participation barriers for women is useful for a variety of reasons. For example, the USA is celebrated as the global leader in high-tech entrepreneurship (Coy 2015; Florida 2014) and is home to four of the world's top five startup cities (Florida 2014; Herrmann et al. 2015). Yet within this context, technology-based ventures are often better known for their pervasive sexism and lack of diversity than their innovativeness in attracting the new populations needed to fuel and sustain future growth (Burleigh 2015, para.1; see also Bercovici 2015; Corbyn 2015; Dusenbery and Pasulka 2012; Gongloff 2014; Griswold 2016; Hu 2013; Kang 2015; Kasperkevic 2016; Khazan 2015; Knowles 2012; Lobo 2014; Sandberg 2013; Staff 2015; Stillman 2016; Stromberg 2015; Tasneem 2012; Vassallo et al. 2016; Williams and Dempsey 2012; Yeh 2012).

The potential exclusion of approximately half the USA population from careers considered to be the key drivers of economic growth is concerning on multiple levels (Acs and Szerb 2010; Fazio et al. 2016; Horn and Pleasance 2012; Morelix, Reedy, and Russell 2016). Those concerned about the collective economic well-being of the nation cite growing doubts about the ability of the USA to keep pace in an increasingly innovation-based global economy, unless it can also significantly increase the number and diversity of participants in its high-growth types of entrepreneurship

(Andes and Castro 2009; Fingleton 2013; Horn and Pleasance 2012; Lohr 2009; Mangelsdorf 2011; Savitz 2013). In an economic future where entrepreneurship may become the only sure way to get and keep a job (Network for Teaching Entrepreneurship 2013), overcoming the barriers that constrain diversity in the most lucrative fields of enterprise becomes an imperative if we hope to avoid further exacerbating the 'feminization [and racialization] of poverty' (Chant 2006).

Review of the literature

To conduct this literature review, procedures similar to those used in the most commonly cited, broad reviews of studies on women in entrepreneurship were used (Brush 1992; Gatewood et al. 2003, Greene et al. 2003; Sullivan and Meek 2012). Limiting the search for relevant articles on women and technology entrepreneurship to the most frequently cited entrepreneurship and small business journals (Greene et al. 2003) returned very few results. The interdisciplinary nature of this topic required searching a much broader range of publications in a variety of study areas, combined with an iterative 'snowballing' technique (i.e. reviewing bibliographies and relevant citations to identify other topically relevant articles) to assemble enough of the existing literature to produce an overview of the research that has been done on this subject.

Procedures and boundary conditions

Using an online database containing full-text, peer-reviewed journal articles, scholarly dissertations and empirical research reports, the search terms[1]: 'gender', 'female' and 'women' along with 'entrepreneurship' and 'technology' and their derivations were searched. Following the example of previous studies (Bastedo 2010; Brush et al. 2014; Goel, Goktepe-Hulten, and Ram 2014; Prowess 2007; Robb, Coleman, and Stangler 2014; Sweida and Reichard 2013; Tinkler et al. 2015; Tracy 2011), derivations for technology ventures included the terms 'high-tech', 'high-growth', 'innovation-driven', 'high-impact' and 'high-potential'; similarly, derivations for entrepreneurship included 'small-to-medium enterprise (SME)', 'venture', 'company', 'enterprise', '(small) business', 'firm', and 'startups' (Acs, Parsons, and Tracy 2008; Aulet and Murray 2013; Brush 1992; Dautzenberg 2012; Greene 2014; Greene et al. 2003; Henrekson and Johansson 2008; Nightingale and Coad 2011; Tracy 2011).

Search query results were narrowed using filters to weed out duplicates and return only peer-reviewed articles and reports written in English. Though no filters for date were set, all of the articles most relevant to this topic were published after 2001. Our original objective was to fill an existing gap in the literature by populating the review primarily with research articles on empirical studies of female populations in the USA; however, excluding research situated outside of the USA left too few peer-reviewed journal articles on this topic to conduct a comprehensive review. Consequently, articles using international samples that included the USA as well as studies done on populations in countries with economies comparable to that of the USA were included. This process resulted in a total of 50 articles containing a least two of the three key search terms ('gender', 'technology', and 'entrepreneurship').

In summary, 18 articles explicitly examined the role of gender in the field of technology entrepreneurship, and 6 more articles described studies conducted in the related subfield of academic entrepreneurship (specifically gender and patenting, technology transfer, and research commercialization in STEM-related academic settings); 12 articles discussed recent studies that looked at gender and entrepreneurship more broadly, but included technology as one of the sectors under examination; the final 14 articles described relevant studies that examined the interplay between gender and technology generally, or in STEM participation and technology-related careers specifically. The 24 articles that described empirical studies AND contained all three search terms were used as the primary basis for this literature review. These articles are summarized in the Appendix.

Content analysis and categorization

Content analysis was done with the articles selected for inclusion in this literature review using NVivo. A preliminary analysis deductively coded the content for surface data on research context, population sample, theories and methods used, independent and dependent variables examined, and key findings from each study (Appendix) (Krippendorff 2004; Stemler 2001). A second stage of analysis then inductively coded a subset of this data (factors found to be limiting participation of women in technology entrepreneurship – i.e. 'barriers') for latent content to evaluate any relationships or similarities and differences between them, and to determine any emergent patterns, dimensions or themes in the research findings (Krippendorff 2004; Shapiro and Markoff 1997; Stemler 2001). Barriers were categorized into three dimensions: location of barrier, level of barrier, and type of barrier. The properties and scope of these dimensions were developed further by adding subgroups to expand their descriptive value (Table 1), and by exploring the boundaries of the subgroups in relation to one another (Bradley 1993; Zhang and Wildemuth 2005).

As Table 1 indicates, barriers are complex phenomena, layered with a variety of multi-directional influences capable of overlapping differently in different contexts. An analysis of the intersections between barriers limiting women's participation in technology entrepreneurship identified new groupings of barriers. These were categorized in a matrix (Table 2) whereby the dimension 'type of barrier' was superimposed over the other two (e.g. overlapping the 'symbolic'/'macro' columns and the 'explicit'/'micro' columns). This resulted in four overall category quadrants, and the variables described as barriers in the literature were tested against each quadrant for fit using the descriptions in Table 2 to organize them into categories.

Organizing the data in this manner provides a more layered and contextualized view of barriers that exist simultaneously and the factors that sustain them, highlighting relationships that are often difficult to see in other ways. One such observation, for example, was that the variables identified as 'barriers' for females in technology entrepreneurship are generally the same as those described as 'resources' in descriptions of successful (male) entrepreneurs in the same context. In other words, when the context stays constant, the most noticeable difference between people with barriers and people with resources is gender. Within the context of technology entrepreneurship, the resources most often noted as barriers for women are access to financial and social capital (Robb, Coleman, and Stangler 2014).

Table 1. Barriers limiting women's participation in technology entrepreneurship by dimensions or themes identified in the research.

Location of barrier	Internal (individual)	• Situated within the individual, or focused on individual behaviours, skills, resources, or cognitive processes
	External (context)	• Situated outside of the individual, or focused on resources with access based on how the individual is perceived by others
Level of barrier	Macro (cultural)	• More identity and culture-oriented; focused more on informal structures, less visible influences, and access to intangible resources
	Micro (situational)	• More action and practice-oriented; focused more on formal structures, observable factors, and access to concrete resources
Type of barrier	Symbolic (intangible)	• Concerns implicit resources embedded in individual and collective sociocultural identities, meanings and values; may be needed to access other, more explicit types of resources
	Explicit (tangible)	• Concerns more recognizable resources that may be available but inaccessible, depending on context or the symbolic resources needed to acquire them

Table 2. Relationships between intersecting barrier dimensions /themes and their descriptions.

		Level		Type	
		Macro	Micro	Symbolic	Explicit
Location	Internal	• Individual identity and cognitive processes	• Individual actions and skill acquisition	• Shaped by culture and social influences	• Shaped by choices and access to opportunities
	External	• Social identity and cultural factors	• Formal structures and practices	• Informal processes, expectations or standards	• Related to accessibility or control of tangible assets

Capital as a framework for expanding our understanding of women in technology entrepreneurship

Contexts where the only discernible difference between those with resources and those with barriers is gender (and/or race, or ethnicity, etc.) highlight a gap in our collective understanding. It suggests the presence of less visible, more symbolic types of resources that are as influential to participation in a given context as the more explicit ones. This illustrates the need to investigate beyond the discernible barriers (described in Table 1) and examine underlying sociocultural factors and cognitive processes (like traditional gender roles, cultural influences, gendered and racial divisions of labour and resources, stereotypes, and implicit biases) that shape access to both symbolic and explicit resources and create contextually specific barriers along gender lines (Table 2). To do this requires an expanded framework that captures the research conducted to date while also extending our understanding of the role of context(s) and how it affects access to the resources and forms of capital described as barriers to women in technology entrepreneurship.

In response to these needs, we expand the conceptualization of both *resources* and *capital* beyond their traditional economic meanings and intentionally differentiate between the two in the context of this literature review. We do this to emphasize that (1) there are *explicit resources* (which are more visible and concrete) and *symbolic resources* (which are less visible and more abstract, with value and access determined by social and cultural norms and perceptions), needed by entrepreneurs in order to participate in this context; and (2) the challenges encountered by women in technology entrepreneurship involve both types of resources, meaning that barriers to 'capital' in this context go beyond financial investments or social networks. In this sense, 'capital' is actually a term that encompasses both explicit and symbolic resources (Bourdieu 1986) that impart 'power, status or authority on their holders' (Maton 2004, 37) and exists in multiple forms, including: *human capital* (or skills, experience, education, and time), *social capital* (mentors, networks, and stereotype bias), *financial capital* (access to investment money, risks assessed by lenders), and *cognitive capital* (self-efficacy, motivation, outcome expectations, and interest).

All four forms of capital are necessary for women to participate as technology entrepreneurs, and each becomes a barrier to participation when inaccessible. Therefore, a broader framework is needed to analyse each form of capital as a complex barrier consisting of multiple layers of explicit and symbolic resources. To do this, we use the data from the literature review to develop a *capital framework* (Figure 1) to represent the multi-faceted barriers and intersecting layers of context involved in technology entrepreneurship as it relates to gender. The sections below summarize the findings of the literature review within this framework to provide a more comprehensive view of the barriers at play. We align the research in this way to demonstrate the relevance of each form of capital as well as the interconnectedness of the layered individual, sociocultural, and contextual factors maintaining the token status of women in this field.

Human capital

Human capital in the context of entrepreneurship is best described as the *potential* or *capacity* of an individual to start a venture in any particular area. Comprised of the accumulated education, skills, knowledge, abilities, training, and technical work experiences in an industry or sector, human capital represents the raw individual resources a potential entrepreneur can transfer into an enterprise (Bourdieu 1986; Ezzedeen and Zikic 2012; Gatewood et al. 2003; Klyver and Terjesen 2007; Manolova, Brush, and Edelman 2007; Marlow and McAdam 2013; Robinson and Stubberud 2009; Terjesen 2005; Thebaud 2015b).

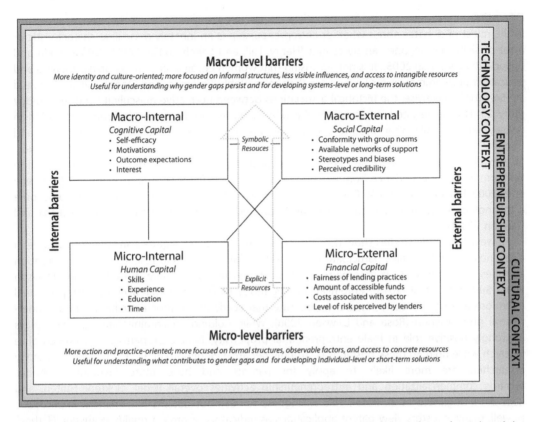

Figure 1. A capital framework of analysis for examining complex gender barriers and access to forms of capital needed to participate in overlapping contexts.

Nature vs. nurture

One of the biggest barriers preventing many women from seeking to develop the skills used by entrepreneurs are biologically based arguments that claim men are more genetically pre-disposed to have the personality characteristics, or 'basic talent', needed for entrepreneurship and new venture creation (Lazear 2004; Obschonka, Silbereisen, and Schmitt-Rodermund 2011, 2012). This reflects 'one of the oldest questions in entrepreneurship research, namely, whether an entrepreneurial mindset is the result of development and experiences or whether it is a talent some people have and others do not' (Stuetzer, Obschonka, and Schmitt-Rodermund 2012, 97). One research study in 2014 reported that entrepreneurship requires 'a special type of individual' with particular, inherent personality traits (Miller 2014, 2). Other scholars report that successful entrepreneurs have higher testosterone levels than non-entrepreneurs (Miller 2014; Mitchell, Randolph-Seng, and Mitchell 2011; Rauch and Frese 2007), and explain that an 'intrinsic barrier [for women becoming entrepreneurs] is the natural female disinclination to rivalry and competition' (Polkowska 2013, 160).

A feminist theoretical perspective suggests that many of the characteristics typically used to explain lower rates of female entrepreneurship – such as risk-aversion (Fox and Xiao 2013; Sugimoto et al. 2015; Tan 2008) – are likely less a consequence of biology and more the result of socialized gender roles (Agnete Alsos, Ljunggren, and Hytti 2013; Blickenstaff 2005; Gatewood et al. 2003; Gundry and Welsch 2001; Jome, Donahue, and Siegel 2006; Sullivan and Meek 2012; Sweida and Reichard 2013). Similarly, research on differences in interest, ability, and performance levels in math, science, and technology between males and females shows these skills to be learned and not innately tied to sex (Dweck 2008; Hill, Corbett, and St. Rose 2010; Yeager and Dweck 2012).

Education

In the midst of debates about whether entrepreneurship is an innately masculine characteristic or a set of skills that anyone can be taught (Henry, Hill, and Leitch 2005a, 2005b, 2005c; Klein and Bullock 2006; Kuratko 2005), it is not surprising that women enroll in entrepreneurship training and education programmes at far lower rates than men (Robb, Coleman, and Stangler 2014; Thebaud 2015a, 2015b). Likewise, the historical associations between normative masculinity and technology (Bury 2011) have resulted in women in the USA being less likely to pursue formal education in fields where the skills often used to start technology ventures are acquired (BarNir 2012; Gill and Ganesh 2007; Hill, Corbett, and St. Rose 2010; Orser, Riding, and Manley 2006; Ranga and Etzkowitz 2010; Williams 2013), and are subsequently less likely to acquire any additional human capital in the form of career experience from working in technological fields later on (Bastedo 2010; Greene et al. 2003; Hill, Corbett, and St. Rose 2010). In other words, a woman is much less likely to become a technology entrepreneur if she is less likely to study technology in the first place (Rosa and Dawson 2006).

However, multiple studies show that among women who have acquired an advanced degree in a technology field, females participate in less technology transfer and research commercialization activities than their male counterparts (Goel, Goktepe-Hulten, and Ram 2014; Rosa and Dawson 2006; Sugimoto et al. 2015). Empirical investigations of gender differences in entrepreneurial intentions among university researchers indicate that academic entrepreneurship is not a gender-neutral phenomenon (Rosa and Dawson 2006). While holding an administrative position plays a strongly positive role in male entrepreneurial propensity, female propensity to commercialize research while holding these positions is strongly negative (Sugimoto et al. 2015). Male technology researchers are more likely to apply for patents and have more favorable attitudes towards commercialization and entrepreneurship activities overall (Goel, Goktepe-Hulten, and Ram 2014; Sugimoto et al. 2015). This willingness to seek out patents has financial implications as well; many investors view patent applications as indicators of project quality (Haussler, Harhoff, and Mueller 2012) and reports state that 76% of venture capitalists consider patents in funding decisions (Graham et al. 2009). However, studies that evaluate patenting as an actual measure of 'innovative output' show that although female scientists participate less in commercialization activities and produce less patents as primary inventors (Delixus Inc 2012; Milli et al. 2016; U.S. Patent and Trademark Office 2016), 'the quality and impact of their patents is equal to or better than that of male scientists' (Whittington and Smith-Doerr 2005, 365; see also Ashcraft and Breitzman 2012).

Work experience

Since both men and women are more likely to establish businesses in sectors with which they have gained some familiarity during employment (Koeber and Wright 2006; Ljunggren and Kolvereid 1996), and there are more than 10 times the number of men-owned as women-owned firms in the science, engineering, and technology sectors (Prowess 2007), many explanations for gender gaps in high-tech entrepreneurship are centred around the lack of female work experience in technology (Greene et al. 2003; Simard et al. 2008). Research shows a negative association between industry experience and enterprise failure rate, as well as a positive relationship between technology-related work experience and venture growth (Colombo and Grilli 2007). Technology-related work experience is also associated with increased contacts within the technology industry and more elaborate networks – the types of vital social capital found to facilitate the creation and growth of new ventures (Thebaud 2015a, 2015b; Tinkler et al. 2015). However, some research indicates that this connection between technology work experience and the intention to pursue technology entrepreneurship may not be the same for everyone. A study by BarNir (2012) found that while industry experience and a background in technology occupations are significant positive predictors for the startup decision for men in IT, they are actually *negative* predictors for women.

Social capital

In addition to human capital, the number and quality of an individual's social connections can also influence intentions to become an entrepreneur and the types of ventures created (Baron 2007). An entrepreneur's social capital is often defined as the benefits that can be extracted from their social structures, networks, and relationships (Baron 2007; Ogzen and Baron 2007). These benefits can either take the form of physical resources (like investors or collaborators), or less tangible assets such as mentorship, support, advice, introductions, and access to valuable information, opportunities, or partnerships (Sappleton 2009; Sullivan and Meek 2012).

Mentors and role models

Evidence regarding the importance of same-gendered mentors is mixed for entrepreneurs, though female entrepreneurs in high-tech industries cited a 'lack of available advisors' (4) to be one of their top challenges in a 2014 survey (Robb, Coleman, and Stangler 2014). Several studies indicate that same-gender mentoring relationships may have some advantages over cross-gender ones (Agnete Alsos, Ljunggren, and Hytti 2013; Ezzedeen and Zikic 2012; Marlow and Mcadam 2015). For example, mentors in same-gender dyads have been reported to provide more psychosocial support (Agnete Alsos, Ljunggren, and Hytti 2013; Lockwood 2006). Gender demographics in both the entrepreneurship and technology fields, however, have resulted in male mentors being more readily available than female mentors (Martin et al. 2015; Polkowska 2013; Ranga 2008; Stephan and Levin 2005). Additionally, cross-gender mentorships may allow women to leverage some of the legitimacy (Godwin, Stevens, and Brenner 2006; Sappleton 2009) and broader network connections that are typically more accessible to males in technology as a result of their gender (Etzkowitz et al. 2000; Ranga and Etzkowitz 2010; Sullivan and Meek 2012). Providing more access to mentors (of any gender) may prove to be an important strategy for encouraging women to start and run successful high-growth companies (Bastedo 2010; Coleman and Robb 2014; Dabic et al. 2012; Kirkwood 2009; Robb, Coleman, and Stangler 2014).

Networks

Research findings on gender differences in networking practices between men and women in technology entrepreneurship show mixed results. It has been suggested that women network and form professional relationships differently than men in business settings (Dabic et al. 2012; Gatewood et al. 2009; Marlow and Carter 2004), and their tendency to primarily befriend other women hinders their advancement in male-dominated fields (BarNir 2012; Lounsbury and Glynn 2001; Navis and Glynn 2011). Studies of academic technology commercialization find that men and women in academia experience different 'network pathways' to the commercial realm – women form concentrated, close ties while men form more diffuse referral networks (Goel, Goktepe-Hulten, and Ram 2014; Polkowska 2013; Sugimoto et al. 2015). Diffuse networks are believed to advantage men in this area because the majority of spinout companies created from the commercialization of academic research are catalyzed by external interest from investors and potential industry partners. Senior academics in technology departments are most likely to be approached by external investors with opportunities for commercialization activities and, proportionally, most senior researchers in these departments are male (Rosa and Dawson 2006).

Other studies have found that although the gender composition of individuals in the networks of male and female entrepreneurs is different, the ways in which they network are not, and gender composition has little bearing on the effectiveness of the network (Baker, Aldrich, and Nina 1997; Tan 2008). Though some researchers suggest that the most successful female entrepreneurs in the technology sector are those who 'accept the established male models of doing business [in order to] gain acceptance and credibility' (Martin et al. 2015, 548), many report that when it comes to the establishment and leveraging of their networks, women and men appear to behave in largely similar ways (Foss 2010; Neergaard, Shaw, and Carter 2005) and have similar network composition and quality (Hampton, Cooper, and McGowan 2009; Rutashobya, Allan, and Nilsson 2009), especially as the venture becomes more established (Hampton, Cooper, and McGowan 2009; Klyver and Terjesen 2007).

Financial capital

Both real and perceived barriers to obtaining financial capital and sustained investor interest are common explanations for the lack of women in technology entrepreneurship (Avnimelech and Teubal 2006; BarNir 2012; Brooks et al. 2014; Brush et al. 2014; Gatewood et al. 2003; Holmquist and Wetter 2010; Klotz et al. 2014; Menzies, Diochon, and Gasse 2004; Tinkler et al. 2015; Zimmerman and Zeitz 2002). Female entrepreneurs are generally perceived as 'riskier' investments than men when it comes to venture financing (Gatewood et al. 2003), although explicit evidence of discriminatory lending practices towards women remains mixed (Coleman and Robb 2014; Kenney and Patton 2015; Marlow and McAdam 2013; Orser, Riding, and Manley 2006). Venture capital, often seen as being critical to growth in technology and innovation sectors, remains 'notoriously difficult for women to access' (Ezzedeen and Zikic 2012, p.46). Female entrepreneurs who believe that they will not get credit often do not even contact a bank or apply for a loan when starting a venture (Holmquist and Wetter 2010).

In addition, research shows that the uncertainty factor that accompanies innovative ventures has a greater negative impact on the ability of female entrepreneurs to receive investment money than it does for males (Orser, Riding, and Manley 2006; Thebaud 2015a, 2015b; Tinkler et al. 2015). Entrepreneurial ventures that pitch new technologies and innovations are considered to be riskier by potential investors than their more traditional counterparts (Thebaud 2015b; Verheul, Uhlaner, and Thurik 2005). Considering this along with the stereotypes about women being less capable in technical areas and implicit expectations that men will be better entrepreneurs, decisions about women seeking financing for innovative technology ventures are coloured by multiple cognitive biases as potential investors calculate risks (Coleman and Robb 2014; Gatewood et al. 2003; Orser, Riding, and Manley 2006).

Overall, it has been found that female entrepreneurs are substantially less likely to receive private investment funding compared to male entrepreneurs with similar levels of experience (Tinkler et al. 2015). The National Center for Women and Information Technology reports that female-owned businesses rely primarily on internal sources of start-up capital, while male-owned businesses have greater access to external sources (Aspray and Cohoon 2006). The ultimate consequences of the gender disparities in access to investment money is that female entrepreneurs are required to start new businesses with lower amounts of start-up capital, are typically unable to create enterprises in fields with higher levels of startup costs, and are unable to match the growth of better-funded firms (Avnimelech and Teubal 2006; Coleman and Robb 2014; Gatewood et al. 2003; Robb and Coleman 2009).

Cognitive capital

The accumulation of cognitive or psychological capital – which can be conceptualized as the desire or intent to participate, self-efficacy, confidence, outcome expectations, and motivation – is shaped by both implicit and explicit factors (Ahl 2002, 2006; Ahl and Nelson 2010; Eagly, Beall, and Sternberg 2004). Many women are currently acting as entrepreneurs, yet they continue to be dismissed by the larger culture as a type of 'peripheral' or 'secondary' entrepreneur (Ahl 2006; Byrne and Fayolle 2010; Mohanty 2003; Perrin Moore 2012). Lower expectations about women's ability as entrepreneurs lead to what the 2012 Global Entrepreneurship Monitor report calls 'covert discriminatory practices' that 'are subtle, and sometimes not even recognized by entrepreneurs, in that they have to do with status expectations or gendered roles. It is expected that men will be venture capitalists or fast growth high-tech entrepreneurs, but less expected that women will be in these roles' (Kelley et al. 2012, 7). Ultimately, actual or perceived career barriers, stereotypes, and beliefs about entrepreneurship are 'shaped by subtle but pervasive cognitive and social input from the environment' (Walton and Banaji 2004, 193) and influence access to opportunity, improved social status, and economic well-being.

Willingness to participate

Much of the research on female entrepreneurship over the past four decades has focused on how they compare to male entrepreneurs (Brush 1992; Greene et al. 2003; Sullivan and Meek 2012), and has often framed females as deficient or 'handicapped' (Bates 2002; Ezzedeen and Zikic 2012; Foss 2010) by various factors as both potential and practicing entrepreneurs (Goss et al. 2011; Karimi et al. 2013; Marlow and McAdam 2013; Mitchelmore and Rowley 2010; Shao-Hui, Ping, and Peng-Peng 2011). Research shows a strong link between women's perceptions about entrepreneurship and their rates of participation as entrepreneurs (GEM 2010; Kelley et al. 2014, 2012). 'Where women believed there were good opportunities for starting businesses, and where they had confidence, ability and spirit for this activity, there were typically higher female entrepreneurship rates' (Kelley et al. 2012, 42). Doubly impacted by the masculine stereotypes surrounding both technology and entrepreneurship, women who do become entrepreneurs are overwhelmingly found in the less-profitable consumer, retail, and service industries, while males continue to dominate the more profitable and faster-growing manufacturing and technology sectors (GEM 2010; Kelley et al. 2012).

Self-efficacy

Gender differences in skill level and confidence are frequently observed in fields stereotypically associated with male characteristics (Chen and Latham 2014; Dohrman 2010; Fox and Xiao 2013; Pathak, Goltz, and Buche 2013; Sappleton 2009; Smith et al. 2013; Smith 2009), and women are more likely than men to limit their career choices in male-dominated fields because they believe they lack the necessary abilities – regardless of their academic achievements in these areas (Bandura 1993; Kay and Shipman 2014; Wilson, Kickul, and Marlino 2007). Actual skill levels appear to matter less than self-perceptions of those skills (Bandura 2001), especially when those self-perceptions are reinforced by gender stereotypes (Wilson, Kickul, and Marlino 2007). Research by Kickul and D'Intino (2005) demonstrates a direct relationship between self-efficacy and entrepreneurial intentions in female students, supporting the need for educational initiatives that address both entrepreneurial knowledge and self-efficacy.

Motivations

Even though motivation is a complex process and notoriously difficult to assess (Bloch 1979; Margison and Brown 2007), the motives for becoming self-employed, starting a new enterprise, or taking a risk on a venture with uncertain outcomes are frequently topics of examination in entrepreneurship research (Barakat, Boddington, and Vyakarnam 2014; Baron 2007; Chandan 2015; Petridou, Sarri, and Kyrgidou 2009). The cognitive processes that form our intentions rarely occur deliberately; instead, motivations are usually developed unconsciously and shaped by a tangle of external influences and internal resources (like past experiences, biases, perceptions, expectations and a variety of other inextricable social, contextual, and cognitive factors) that most individuals never examine or become consciously aware of. Since motivations are abstract and unobservable they are usually assessed using self-reports, although people tend to be more confident than accurate when asked to introspectively determine the reasons for their own behaviours (Gopnik 1993; Johansson et al. 2005; Pronin 2009; Steele, Spencer, and Aronson 2002; Wilson and Bar-Anan 2008) .

In spite of this, opinions are divided about the role that gender plays in shaping motivations for becoming an entrepreneur, as well as the outcomes or goals entrepreneurship is intended to achieve (Heydari, Madani, and Rostami 2013; Mitchelmore and Rowley 2010; Orser and Hogarth-Scott 2009; Rindova, Barry, and Ketchen 2009). While venture creation in the technology sector and high-growth enterprises are commonly described as *opportunity-motivated* entrepreneurship, *necessity-driven* motivations for entrepreneurship are often associated with smaller, less growth-oriented enterprises (Avnimelech and Teubal 2006; Loscocco and Bird 2012; Moore and Buttner 1997; Morris et al. 2006) that are less attractive to investors (Gatewood et al. 2003; Sappleton 2009; Zimmerman and Zeitz 2002) and must be started with less capital (Brush et al. 2014; Orser, Riding, and Manley 2006) – all of which increases their vulnerability to the economic risks associated with entrepreneurship and decreases their likelihood of success (Mcgrath 1999; Watson 2003).

Female entrepreneurs are more likely than their male counterparts to be found in ventures associated with necessity-driven entrepreneurship (Brush et al. 2014; DeTienne and Chandler 2007; Fletcher 2006; Gedeon 2010; Kelley et al. 2014; Zeyen et al. 2012). However, it is likely that assessments of motivation tell us more about cultural expectations and the unconscious biases that shape intentions than they do about actual motivation (Margison and Brown 2007). This may account for newer research demonstrating that entrepreneurial motives for men and women are the same much more often than they are different (Thebaud 2015a), and that the differences that get emphasized are likely far better reflections of gendered access to resources and how society frames the work done by women than they are of actual motivational dissimilarities (Green and Cohen 1995; Hughes 2003; Jennings and Brush 2013; Loscocco and Bird 2012; Mattis 2004; Moore and Buttner 1997; Reynolds and Renzulli 2005).

Contrary to what is portrayed about entrepreneurs in the media, entrepreneurship is far more likely to be prompted by economic necessity than by opportunities to get rich quick or commercialize a new idea – for both men and women (GEM 2010; Rindova, Barry, and Ketchen 2009; Scott and Vincent-Lancrin 2014). Yet in cultures with social norms that define certain responsibilities as more feminine or more masculine than others, inequalities in the amount of time these tasks require and the resources received in return can divide access to need- and opportunity-driven pursuits by gender (Jacobs and Gerson 2004; Thebaud 2015a). Females are also more likely than their male partners to be faced with balancing outside work requirements with a full load of domestic and family obligations, but the ventures they start are not likely to be depicted as opportunity-motivated ways to overcome these challenges or even as entrepreneurship at all; instead, working from home and business ownership are often framed simply as female 'coping strategies' (Aaltio and Wang 2015; Dohrman 2010; Marlow 1997) for women who want more flexibility in how they manage the competing demands on their time (Alonso-Galicia et al. 2015; Ben 2007; Brush 1992; Ranga and Etzkowitz 2010).

Discussion and implications for future research

Despite the persistent notion of entrepreneurship as a meritocratic and equally accessible field of gender-neutral opportunities, research conducted to date suggests otherwise. The masculinity embedded in the concept of entrepreneurship, historically and culturally, have made it difficult for women to symbolically and logistically claim the position of 'entrepreneur' (Ahl 2006; Ahl and Nelson 2010; Calas, Smircich, and Bourne 2009; Marlow and Mcadam 2015; Watson and Newby 2005), and this is particularly true when situated within the context of technology (Fisher 2010; Lounsbury and Glynn 2001; Marlow and McAdam 2013; Navis and Glynn 2011; Zimmerman and Zeitz 2002). As seen in efforts to encourage more women to participate in STEM fields, gender gaps are systemic and influenced in numerous ways by culture, cognition, choices and contexts (Hill, Corbett, and St. Rose 2010). These become increasingly complex where identities and contexts overlap, and where access to explicit and symbolic resources is tied implicitly to category expectations, social roles and perceptions about fit or belonging (Nina Gunnerud 1997; Symington 2004).

A review of the individual and contextual factors maintaining the token status of women in technology entrepreneurship indicates the need to consider broader frameworks to understand the barriers associated with access and participation. Access to financial and social capital are insufficient for explaining these barriers. If research and practice continues to focus primarily on resources women lack, and the improvement of 'female deficits', it may be inadequate for driving significant increases in participation and retention.

Other forms of 'capital', including cognitive attributes and human capital, provide a useful framework for broadening our research and programming around inclusivity in entrepreneurship and technology. Framing capital more broadly allows us to extend beyond the explicit resources required to examine sociocultural factors and cognitive processes as embedded symbolic resources. Further, it allows us to examine how these are contextually determined. Interestingly, these forms are capital are fairly well-studied in the more general research on entrepreneurs, particularly in relation to entrepreneurship education, but appear to take a secondary role in discussions around women's involvement in technology entrepreneurship. Changing the status of women from token players to full participants in technology entrepreneurship requires examining layers of overlapping barriers on multiple fronts and shifting our approaches to research and practice to create more context-specific solutions.

Yet there are significant challenges associated with moving in this direction, which may explain the limited literature in this field. Small and dispersed populations impede efforts to conduct new streams of empirical research and generalizable recommendations. The research required to understand systemic issues, as described in this article, is complex. Variables are influenced by multiple individual and environmental factors, many of which cannot be manipulated in research settings, and may not even be recognized by scholars without interdisciplinary training. These factors encompass early socialization, culture, educational experiences, and access to/acquisition of both entrepreneurship and technology skills, not to mention the influence of society, culture, and understanding of how cognitive biases are formed and interrupted.

As an example, this synthesis of research represents the tradeoffs between depth and breadth of analyses that result from resource constraints (e.g. time, funding, faculty expertise), as well as contextual boundaries (e.g. geographic focus, cultural barriers, language). It was challenging to extend the scope beyond simply 'women' in technology entrepreneurship to include an examination of differences in female participation rates across the many industry sectors that encompass 'technology'. Further, it was not logistically possible to address how each additional intersection (such as race, class and gender) may impose new barriers. Every additional intersection means there are less participants available to study. The inability to 1) adequately address specific barriers and intersections beyond gender, technology, and entrepreneurship, and 2) avoid using 'women' as an oversimplified social category, were noticeable tradeoffs made in order to compile enough articles for a comprehensive review of the literature.

It is quite possible that the best way to overcome these challenges is to change tactics. As a discipline, we need to shift from a 'fixed-mindset' of inherent, between-sex differences and gendered personality traits to a 'growth-mindset' (Dweck 1999) that emphasizes learnable skills that differ according to context, not gender. As researchers, we need to shift our methods to include more multi-level analyses that explore how social practices and cultural discourses shape access to both explicit and symbolic resources and contribute to the underrepresentation of skilled and innovative women. This means research approaches may need to shift from sampling convenient but homogenous populations because they are large enough to study, to doing more in-depth examinations of marginalized populations to understand how to decrease barriers, and subsequently increase participation enough for more generalizable studies. The objectives of these studies must also shift from the development of short-term strategies to help women overcome existing barriers to longer-term approaches that focus on discovering how to prevent gendered barriers from being created in the first place.

This may require scholars who are willing to apply more macro-level sociocultural methods traditionally found outside of the discipline – such as discourse analysis, media content studies, and rhetorical framing analysis – to entrepreneurship research. This would require that academic departments shift their faculty selection criteria to cultivate and/or value more disciplinary diversity, and that these types of research methods be acceptable for inclusion in top business and entrepreneurship journals. Most importantly, new approaches to research in this area must be recognized with research funding and be valued in promotion and tenure decisions. Finally, when it comes to the assessment of programmes and policies already in place to enhance the participation rates of women in both entrepreneurship and technology, such as female startup incubators, we should consider including broader frameworks such as those presented in this manuscript, as opposed to measurements based on stereotypical forms of masculinity as embedded yardsticks of success.

Conclusion

Involvement in and attention to gender within the fields of entrepreneurship and technology have increased over the years, yet are viewed by many as being insufficient given shifts in demographic, economic and workforce trends. This manuscript provides the most current review of the literature on gender and technology entrepreneurship, underscoring the token-nature of women in the research and practice associated with the field. The proposed framework extends the concept of the 'capital' required for participation technology entrepreneurship beyond that of financial investment and social networks, to human capital and cognitive capital, thereby providing a more comprehensive and descriptive approach to measure the influence of embedded individual and contextual factors influencing intent, outcome, and participation. This approach responds to the need for more integrated, multilevel analytical frameworks in the research on women in technology entrepreneurship.

Note

1. There is a general lack of disciplinary consensus about what types of ventures specifically qualify as 'technology entrepreneurship'. We operationally defined both 'entrepreneurship' and 'technology' in this context somewhat broadly to encompass many of the diverse terms that frequently appear with them in the literature.

Disclosure statement

No potential conflict of interest was reported by the authors.

References

Aaltio, I., and Q. Wang. 2015. "Entrepreneurship Education as Learning to Form Identities: Cross-Cultural Perspective." In *Entrepreneurship Education and Training*, edited by J. Sanchez-Garcia, 201–224. www.intechopen.com.

Acs, Z. J., and L. Szerb. 2010. "The Global Entrepreneurship Index (GEINDEX)." *Foundations and Trends in Entrepreneurship* 5 (5): 341–435.

Acs, Z. J., W. Parsons, and S. L. Tracy. 2008. *High-Impact Firms: Gazelles Revisited*. Washington, DC: Small Business Administration Office of Advocacy.

Agnete Alsos, G., E. Ljunggren, and U. Hytti. 2013. "Gender and Innovation: State of the Art and a Research Agenda." *International Journal of Gender and Entrepreneurship* 5 (3): 236–256.

Ahl, H. 2002. "The Construction of the Female Entrepreneur as the Other." In *Management, Organizations and Society– Casting the Other: Theproduction and Maintenance of Inequalities in Work Organizations*, edited by B. Czarniawska and H. Höpfl, 52–67. London, England: Routledge.

Ahl, H. 2006. "Why Research on Women Entrepreneurs Needs New Directions." *Entrepreneurship Theory and Practice* 30 (5): 595–621.

Ahl, H., and T. Nelson. 2010. "Moving Forward: Institutional Perspectives on Gender and Entrepreneurship." *International Journal of Gender and Entrepreneurship* 2 (1): 5–9.

Alonso-Galicia, P. E. P. E., V. Fernández-Pérez, L. Rodríguez-Ariza, and M. D. M. Fuentes-Fuentes. 2015. "Entrepreneurial Cognitions in Academia: Exploring Gender Differences." *Journal of Managerial Psychology* 30 (6): 630–644.

American Express OPEN Forum. 2015. *The State of Women-Owned Businesses: A Summary of Important Trends 1997–2015*. American Express. https://about.americanexpress.com/sites/americanexpress.newshq.businesswire.com/files/doc_library/file/2017_SWOB_Report_-FINAL.pdf.

Andes, S., and D. Castro. 2009. "The World Is Digital." *IEEE INternet Computing* 13 (Nov/Dec): 88–91.

Ashcraft, Catherine, and Anthony Breitzman Sr. "Who Invents IT? Women's participation in information technology patenting, 2012 update". (2012).

Aspray, W., and J. M. Cohoon. 2006. *Access to Financial Capital: A Review of Research Literature on Women's Entrepreneurship in the Information Technology Field*. Cambridge, MA: The MIT Press.

Aulet, B., and F. Murray. 2013. "A Tale of Two Entrepreneurs: Understanding Differences in the Types of Entrepreneurship in the Economy." *Kauffman Foundation Papers*. http://www.kauffman.org/uploadedFiles/DownLoadableResources/a-tale-of-two-entrepreneurs.pdf.

Avnimelech, G., and M. Teubal. 2006. "Creating Venture Capital Industries that Co-Evolve with High Tech: Insights from an Extended Industry Life Cycle Perspective of the Israeli Experience." *Research Policy* 35: 1477–1498.

Baker, T. E., H. Aldrich, and L. Nina. 1997. "Invisible Entrepreneurs: The Neglect of Women Business Owners by Mass Media and Scholarly Journals in the USA." *Entrepreneurship & Regional Development* 9 (3): 221–238.

Bandura, A. 1993. "Perceived Self-Efficacy in Cognitive Development and Functioning." *Educational Psychologist* 28 (2): 117–148.

Bandura, Albert. 2001. "Social Cognitive Theory: An Agentic Perspective." *Annual Review Of Psychology* 52: 1–26.

Barakat, S., M. Boddington, and S. Vyakarnam. 2014. "Measuring Entrepreneurial Self-Efficacy to Understand the Impact of Creative Activities for Learning Innovation." *International Journal of Management Education* 12 (3): 456–468.

BarNir, A. 2012. "Starting Technologically Innovative Ventures: Reasons, Human Capital, and Gender." *Management Decision* 50 (3): 399–419.

Baron, R. A. 2007. "Behavioral and Cognitive Factors in Entrepreneurship: Entrepreneurs as the Active Element in New Venture Creation." *Strategic Entrepreneurship Journal* 1 (1–2): 167–182.

Bastedo, R. 2010. "Q & A. Why Is There a Dearth of Women on High-Growth Technology Startup Teams?" *Open Source Business Resource*. https://timreview.ca/article/456.

Bates, T. 2002. "Restricted Access to Markets Characterizes Women-Owned Businesses." *Journal of Business Venturing* 17 (4): 313–324.

Ben, E. R. 2007. "Development while Doing Gender." *Gender, Work and OrganizationWork* 14 (4): 312–332.

Bercovici, J. 2015. "What it's Like Raising Money as a Woman in Silicon Valley." Accessed June 30 2016. http://www.forbes.com/sites/jeffbercovici/2014/08/07/what-its-like-raising-money-as-a-woman-in-tech/2/#33cfcdc94ae2

Best, K., A. Sinell, M. L. Heidingsfelder, and M. Schraudner. 2016. "The Gender Dimension in Knowledge and Technology Transfer: The German Case." *European Journal of Innovation Management* 19 (1): 2–25.

Bilimoria, D., S. Joy, and X. Liang. 2008. "Breaking Barriers and Creating Inclusiveness: Lessons of Organizational Transformation to Advance Women Faculty in Academic Science and Engineering." *Human Resource Management Review* 47 (3): 423–441.

Blickenstaff, J. C. 2005. "Women and Science Careers: Leaky Pipeline or Gender Filter?" *Gender and Education* 17 (4): 369–386.

Bloch, S. 1979. "Assessment of Patients for Psychotherapy." *The British Journal of Psychiatry* 135 (3): 193–208.

Bourdieu, P. 1986. "The Forms of Capital." In *Handbook of Theory and Research for the Sociology of Education*, edited by J. Richardson, 241–258. New York: Greenwood.

Bradley, J. 1993. "Methodological Issues and Practices in Qualitative Research." *Library Quarterly* 63 (4): 431–449.

Bray, F. 2007. "Gender and Technology." *Annual Review of Anthropology* 36: 37–53.

Brooks, A. W., L. Huang, S. W. Kearney, and F. E. Murray. 2014. "Investors Prefer Entrepreneurial Ventures Pitched by Attractive Men." *Proceedings of the National Academy of Sciences of the United States of America* 111(12): 4427–4431. doi:10.1073/pnas.1321202111.

Brush, C. G. 1992. "Research on Women Business Owners: Past Trends, a New Perspective and Future Directions." *Entrepreneurship Theory and Practice* 16 (4): 5–26.

Brush, C. G., P. G. Greene, L. Balachandra, and A. E. Davis. 2014. *Diana Report Women Entrepreneurs 2014: Bridging the Gender Gap in Venture Capital*. Boston, MA: Babson College.

Bruyat, C., and P.-A. Julien. 2000. "Defining the Field of Research in Entrepreneurship." *Journal of Business Venturing* 16: 165–180.

Burleigh, N. 2015. "What Silicon Valley Thinks of Women; the Sexism in Silicon Valley Is Sordid and Systemic." *It's Going to Take a Revolution to Bring it Down–or a Woman's Touch*. Accessed October 5 2016. http://www.newsweek.com/2015/02/06/what-silicon-valley-thinks-women-302821.htmlage/MagazinesDetailsWindow?failOverType=&query=&prodId=OVIC&windowstate=normal&contentModules=&display-query=&mode=view&displayGroupName=Magazines&limiter=&u=purdue_main&currPa

Bury, R. 2011. "She's Geeky: The Performance of Identity among Women Working in IT." *International Journal of Gender, Science and Technology* 3 (1): 34–53.

Bygrave, W. D., K. Healey, M. Lee, B. Barefoot, M. Fetters, and P. Greene. 2013. *Global Entrepreneurship Monitor: National Entrepreneurial Assessment for the United States of America*. https://www.gemconsortium.org/.

Byrne, J., and A. Fayolle. 2010. "A Feminist Inquiry into Entrepreneurship Training." In *The Theory and Practice of Entrepreneurship: Frontiers in European Entrepreneurship Research*, edited by D. Smallbone, J. Leitao, M. Raposo, and F. Welter, 76–100. Northampton, MA: Edward Elgar Publishing.

Calas, M. B., L. Smircich, and K. A. Bourne. 2009. "Extending the Boundaries: Reframing "Entrepreneurship as Social Change" through Feminist Perspectives." *Academy of Management Review* 34 (3): 552–569.

Chandan, H. C. 2015. "Motivations and Challenges of Female Entrepreneurship in Developing and Developed Countries." In *Handbook of Research on Entrepreneurship in the Contemporary Knowledge-Based Global Economy*, edited by N. Baporikar, 260–286. IGI Global, 2016.

Chant, S. 2006. "Re-thinking The "Feminization Of Poverty" in Relation to Aggregate Gender Indices." *Journal Of Human Development* 7 (2): 201–220.

Chen, X., and G. P. Latham. 2014. "The Effect of Priming Learning Vs. Performance Goals on a Complex Task." *Organizational Behavior and Human Decision Processes* 125 (2): 88–97.

Coleman, S., and A. Robb. 2014. *Access to Capital by High-Growth Women-Owned Businesses*, 1–32. Washington DC: National Women's Business Council.

Collins, P. H. 2008. *Black Feminist Thought: Knowledge, Consciousness, and the Politics of Empowerment*. 3rd ed. New York, NY: Routledge.

Colombo, M. G., and L. Grilli. 2007. "Funding Gaps? Access to Bank Loans by High-Tech Start-Ups. 29." *Small Business Economics* 29: 25–46.

Corbyn, Z. 2015. "Silicon Valley is Cool and Powerful." *But Where are the Women?* Accessed June 30 2016. https://www. theguardian.com/technology/2015/mar/08/sexism-silicon-valley-women

Coy, P. 2015. "The 2015 Bloomberg Innovation Index." Accessed February 3 2017. https://www.bloomberg.com/ graphics/2015-innovative-countries/

Dabic, M., T. Daim, E. Bayraktaroglu, I. Novak, and M. Basic. 2012. "Exploring Gender Differences in Attitudes of University Students Towards Entrepreneurship: An International Survey." *International Journal of Gender and Entrepreneurship* 4 (3): 316–336.

Dautzenberg, K. 2012. "Gender Differences of Business Owners in Technology-Based Firms." *International Journal of Gender and Entrepreneurship* 4: 79–98. doi:10.1108/17566261211202990.

De Clercq, D. C., and M. Voronov. 2008. "The Role of Cultural and Symbolic Capital in Entrepreneurial Legitimacy." *Frontiers of …* 28 (16): 398–420.

Delixus Inc. 2012. *Intellectual Property and Women Entrepreneurs: Quantitative Analysis.* Washington DC: Delixus, Inc. and National Women's Business Council. http://nwbc.gov/sites/default/files/IP%20&%20Women%20Entrepreneurs.pdf.

DeTienne, D. R., and G. N. Chandler. 2007. "The Role of Gender in Opportunity Recognition." *Entrepreneurship Theory & Practice,* 31(3): 365–387.

Dohrman, R. 2010. *Making Sense of High-Tech Entrepreneurial Careers: The Meaning(S) and Materialities of Work for Young Adults.* West Lafayette, IN: Purdue University.

Dubrow, J. K. 2008. "How Can We Account for Intersectionality in Quantitative Analysis of Survey Sata? Empirical Illustration of Central and Eastern Europe." *ASK: Society, Research, Methods* 17: 85–102.

Duderstadt, J., W. Wulf, and R. Zemsky. 2005. "Envisioning a Transformed University." *Issues in Science and Technology* 22 (1): 35–42.

Dusenbery, M., and N. Pasulka. 2012. ""Gangbang Interviews" and "Bikini Shots": Silicon Valley's Brogrammer Problem." Accessed June 30 2016. http://www.motherjones.com/media/2012/04/silicon-valley-brogrammer-culture-sexist-sxsw? page=3

Dweck, C. S. 1999. *Self-Theories: Their Role in Motivation, Personality, and Development.* Philadelphia: Psychology Press.

Dweck, C. S. 2008. "Can Personality Be Changed? The Role of Beliefs in Personality and Change." *Current Directions in Psychological Science* 17 (6): 391–394.

Eagly, A. H., A. E. Beall, and R. J. Sternberg. 2004. *The Psychology of Gender.* 2nd ed. New York, NY: Guilford Press.

Eckert, P., and S. McConnell-Ginet. 2013. *Language and Gender.* 2nd ed. Cambridge, MA: Cambridge University Press.

Ely, R. J., and I. Padavic. 2007. "A Feminist Analysis of Organizational Research on Sex Differences." *Academy of Management Review* 32 (4): 1121–1143.

Etzkowitz, H., A. Webster, C. Gebhardt, and B. Terra. 2000. "The Future of the University and the University of the Future: Evolution of Ivory Tower to Entrepreneurial Paradigm." *Research Policy* 29 (2): 313–330.

Ezzedeen, S. R., and J. Zikic. 2012. "Entrepreneurial Experiences of Women in Canadian High Technology." *International Journal of Gender and Entrepreneurship* 4 (1): 44–64.

Fairlie, R. W., A. Morelix, E. J. Reedy, and J. Russell. 2015. *The Kauffman Index of StartUp Activity: National Trends 2015.* doi:10.2139/ssrn.2613479

Fazio, C., J. Guzman, F. Murray, and S. Stern. 2016. *A New View of the Skew: A Quantitiative Assessment of the Quality of American Entrepreneurship.* Kanas, MO: Kauffman Foundation New Entrepreneurial Growth.

Fingleton, E. 2013. "America the Innovative?" *The New York Times,* March 30. http://www.nytimes.com/2013/03/31/ sunday-review/america-the-innovative.html.

Fisher, G. C. 2010. "Who Has the Right to Be an Entrepreneur? The Theoretical Foundations of Entrepreneurial Legitimacy (Summary)." *Frontiers of Entrepreneurship Research* 30 (5). Art 6. http://digitalknowledge.babson.edu/ fer/vol30/iss5/6.

Fletcher, D. E. 2006. "Entrepreneurial Processes and the Social Construction of Opportunity." *Entrepreneurship and Regional Development* 18 (5): 421–440.

Florida, R. 2014. "The Creaive Class and Economic Development." *Economic Development Quarterly* 28 (3): 196–205.

Foss, L. 2010. "Research on Entrepreneur Networks: The Case for a Constructionist Feminist Theory Perspective." *International Journal of Gender and Entrepreneurship* 2 (1): 83–102.

Fox, M. F., and W. Xiao. 2013. "Perceived Chances for Promotion among Women Associate Professors in Computing: Individual, Departmental, and Entrepreneurial Factors." *Journal of Technology Transfer* 38 (2): 135–152.

Gatewood, E. J., C. G. Brush, N. M. Carter, P. G. Greene, and M. M. Hart. 2009. "Diana: A Symbol of Women Entrepreneurs' Hunt for Knowledge, Money, and the Rewards of Entrepreneurship." *Small Business Economics* 32 (2): 129–144.

Gatewood, E. J., N. M. Carter, C. G. Brush, P. G. Greene, and M. M. Hart. 2003. *Women Entrepreneurs, Their Ventures, and the Venture Capital Industry: An Annotated Bibliography.* Stockholm: ESBRI.

Gedeon, S. 2010. "What Is Entrepreneurship?" *Entrepreneurial Practive Review* 1 (3): 16–35.

GEM. 2010. *Global Enrepreneurship Monitor 2010 Women's Report.* www.gemconsortium.org.

Gicheva, D. and A. Link, 2015. "The Gender Gap in Federal and Private Support for Entrepreneurship," UNCG Economics Working Papers 15-5, University of North Carolina at Greensboro, Department of Economics. https:// ideas.repec.org/p/ris/uncgec/2015_005.html

Gill, R., and S. Ganesh. 2007. "Empowerment, Constraint, and the Entrepreneurial Self: A Study of White Women Entrepreneurs." *Journal of Applied Communication Research* 35 (3): 268–293.

Godwin, L. N., C. E. Stevens, and N. L. Brenner. 2006. "Forced to Play by the Rules? Theorizing How Mixed-Sex Founding Teams Benefit Women Entrepreneurs in Male-Dominated Contexts." *Entrepreneurship Theory and Practice* 30 (5): 623–642.

Goel, R. K., D. Goktepe-Hulten, and R. Ram. 2014. "Academics' Entrepreneurship Propensities and Gender Differences." *Journal of Technology Transfer* 40: 161–177.

Gongloff, M. 2014. "We Know Tech Companies Are Sexist, But This Is Horrifying." Accessed June 30 2016. http://www.huffingtonpost.com/2014/02/05/silicon-valley-sexist_n_4731151.html

Gopnik, A. 1993. "How We Know Our Own Minds: The Illusion of First-Person Knowledge of Intentionality." In *Readings in Philosophy and Cognitive Science*. 2nd ed., edited by A. I. Goldman, 315–346. Cambridge, MA: MIT Press.

Goss, D., R. Jones, M. Betta, and J. Latham. 2011. "Power as Practice: A Micro-Sociological Analysis of the Dynamics of Emancipatory Entrepreneurship." *Organization Studies* 32 (2): 211–229.

Graham, S. J. H., R. P. Merges, P. Samuelson, and T. Sichelman. 2009. "High Technology Entrepreneurs and the Patent System: Results of the 2008 Berkeley Patent Survey." *Berkeley Technology Law Journal* 24 (4): 255–327.

Green, E., and L. Cohen. 1995. "Women's Business: Are Women Entrepreneurs Breaking New Ground or Simply Balancing the Demands of Women's Work in a New Way?" *Journal of Gender Studies* 4: 297–314.

Green, L. 2002. *Technoculture: From Alphabet to Cybersex*. Sydney: Allen & Unwin.

Greene, P. G. 2014. *Stimulating small business growth: Progress report on Goldman Sachs "10,000 Small Businesses"*. Goldman Sachs. https://www.goldmansachs.com/citizenship/10000-small-businesses/US/news-and-events/10ksb-impact-report-2014/program-report.pdf

Greene, P. G., Hart, M. M., Gatewood, E. J., Brush, C. G., and Carter, N. M. 2003. "Women entrepreneurs: Moving front and center: An overview of research and theory." *USASBE White Papers*.

Griswold, A. 2016. "When it Comes to Diversity in Tech, Companies Find Safety in Numbers." Accessed June 30 2016. http://www.inc.com/alison-griswold/diversity-in-tech-data-facebbok-google-yahoo.html

Gundry, L. K., and H. P. Welsch. 2001. "The Ambitious Entrepreneur: High Growth Strategies of Enterprises." *Journal of Business Venturing* 16 (312): 453–470.

Hampton, A., P. McGowan, and S. Cooper. 2011. "Developing Quality in Female High-Technology Entrepreneurs' Networks." *International Journal of Entrepreneurial Behaviour & Research* 17 (6): 588–606.

Hampton, A., S. Cooper, and P. McGowan. 2009. "Female Entrepreneurial Networks and Networking Activity in Technology Based Ventures." *International Small Business Journal* 27 (2): 193–214.

Haussler, C., D. Harhoff, and E. Mueller. 2012. "To Be Financed or not...The Role of Patents for Venture Capital Financing (SSRN Scholarly Papers No. ID 1393725)." Rochester, NY.

Henrekson, M., and D. Johansson. 2008. "Gazelles as Job Creators: A Survey and Interpretation of the Evidence (No. 733)." *IFN Working Paper Series*.

Henry, C., F. Hill, and C. Leitch. 2005b. "Can Entrepreneurship Be Taught? Part I." *Education and Training* 47 (2): 98–111.

Henry, C., F. Hill, and C. Leitch. 2005c. "Can Entrepreneurship Be Taught? Part II." *Education and Training* 47 (3): 158–169.

Henry, C., F. Hill, and C. M. Leitch. 2005a. "Entrepreneurship Education and Training: Can Entrepreneurship Be Taught?" *Education + Training* 48 (2): 98–111.

Henwood, F. 2000. "From the Woman Question in Technology to the Technology Question in Feminism: Rethinking Gender Equality in IT Education." *European Journal of Women's Studies* 7 (2): 209–227.

Herrington, M., and P. Kew. 2017. *2016–2017 Global Entrepreneurship Monitor*. London : Global Entrepreneurship Research Association (GERA)

Herrmann, B. L., J. F. Gauthier, D. Holtschke, R. Berman, and M. Marmer. 2015. *The Global Startup Ecosystem Ranking 2015*. Oakland, CA : Startup Genome

Hewlett, S. A., C. B. Luce, L. J. Servon, L. Sherbin, P. Shiller, E. Sosnovich, and K. Sumberg. 2008. *The Athena Factor: Reversing the Brain Drain in Science, Engineering, and Technology*. New York, NY: Center for Work-Life Policy.

Heydari, H., D. Madani, and M. Rostami. 2013. "The Study of the Relationships between Achievement Motive, Innovation, Ambiguity Tolerance, Self-Efficacy, Self-Esteem, and Self- Actualization, with the Orientation of Entrepreneurship in the Islamic Azad University of Khomein Students." *Procedia - Social and Behavioral Sciences* 84: 820–826.

Hill, C., C. Corbett, and A. St. Rose. 2010. *Why so Few? Women in Science, Technology, Engineering, and Mathmatics*. Washington, DC: American Association of University Women (AAUW).

Holmquist, C., and E. Wetter. 2010. "Stereotype Spillover: Does Gender Impact Perceived Venture Risk and Viability? (Summary)." *Frontiers of Entrepreneurship Research* 30 (8): 12–13.

Horn, J., and D. Pleasance. 2012. "Restarting the Small-Susiness Growth Engine." *McKinsey Quarterly*, November.

Hsu, D. H., E. B. Roberts, and C. E. Eesley. 2007. "Entrepreneurs from Technology-Based Universities: Evidence from MIT." *Research Policy* 36 (5): 768–788.

Hu, E. 2013. "Sexism in the Tech Industry Takes Center Stage." Accessed June 30 2016. http://www.npr.org/sections/alltechconsidered/2013/09/11/221052414/sexism-in-the-tech-industry-takes-center-stage?ft=1&f=1001

Hughes, K. D. 2003. "Pushed or Pulled? Women's Entry into Self-Employment and Small Business Ownership." *Gender, Work and Organization* 10: 433–454.

Jacobs, J. A., and K. Gerson. 2004. *The Time Divide: Work, Family, and Gender Inequality*. Cambridge, MA: Harvard University Press.

Jennings, J. E., and C. G. Brush. 2013. "Research on Women Entrepreneurs: Challenges to (And From) the Broader Entrepreneurship Literature?" *Academy of Management Annals* 7: 661–713.

Johansson, P., L. Hall, S. Sikstro, and A. Olsson. 2005. "Failure to Detect Mismatches between Intention and Outcome in a Simple Decision Task." *Science* 213 (5745): 116–119.

Jome, L. M., M. P. Donahue, and L. A. Siegel. 2006. "Working in the Uncharted Technology Frontier: Characteristics of Women Web Entrepreneurs." *Journal of Business and Psychology* 21 (1): 127–147.

Jones, S. 2012. "Gendered Discourses of Entrepreneurship in UK Higher Education: The Fictive Entrepreneur and the Fictive Student." *International Small Business Journal* 32 (3): 237–258.

Kang, C. 2015. "Obama's Top Tech Adviser Takes Fight for Silicon Valley Diversity to Washington." *The Washington Post*, July 9. https://www.washingtonpost.com/news/the-switch/wp/2015/07/09/obamas-top-tech-adviser-explains-why-silicon-valley-is-so-bad-at-diversity/.

Kanter, R. M. 1977. *Men and Women of the Corporation*. New York: Basic Books.

Karimi, S., H. J. A. Biemans, T. Lans, M. Chizari, M. Mulder, and K. N. Mahdei. 2013. "Understanding Role Models and Gender Influences on Entrepreneurial Intentions among College Students." *Procedia - Social and Behavioral Sciences* 93: 204–214.

Kasperkevic, J. 2016. "Sexism Valley: 60% of Women in Silicon Valley Experience Harassment." Accessed June 30 2016. https://www.theguardian.com/technology/2016/jan/12/silicon-valley-women-harassment-gender-discrimination

Kay, K., and C. Shipman. 2014. *The Confidence Code: The Science and Art of Self-Assurance—What Women Should Know*. New York, NY: HarperCollins.

Kelan, E. K. 2007. ""I Don"T Know Why': Accounting for the Scarcity of Women in ICT Work." *Women's Studies International Forum* 30 (6): 499–511.

Kelley, D. J., A. Ali, C. Brush, A. C. Corbett, C. Daniels, P. H. Kim, T. S. Lyons, M. Majbouri, and E. G. Rogoff.2014. *2014 United States Report National Entrepreneurial Assessment for the United States of America*.London : Global Entrepreneurship Research Association (GERA)

Kelley, D. J., C. G. Brush, P. G. Greene, and Y. Litovsky. 2012. *2012 Global Entrepreneurship Monitor Women's Report*. London : Global Entrepreneurship Research Association (GERA)

Kenney, M., and D. Patton. 2015. "Gender, Ethnicity and Entrepreneurship in Initial Public Offerings: Illustrations from an Open Database." *Research Policy* 44 (9): 1773–1784.

Khazan, O. 2015. "The Sexism of Startup Land: Is the Road to Success More Difficult for Female Entrepreneurs?" Accessed June 30 2016. http://www.theatlantic.com/business/archive/2015/03/the-sexism-of-startup-land/387184/

Kickul, J., and R.S. D'Intino. 2005. "Measure for Measure: Modeling Entrepreneurial Self-Efficacy onto Instrumental Tasks within the New Venture Creation Process." *New England Journal of Entrepreneurship* 8(2): 39–47. doi: 10.1108/ NEJE-08-02-2005-B005.

Kirkwood, J. 2009. "Is a Lack of Self-Confidence Hindering Women Entrepreneurs?" *International Journal of Gender and Entrepreneurship* 1 (2): 118–133.

Klein, P. G., and J. B. Bullock. 2006. "Can Entrepreneurship Be Taught?" *Journal of Agricultural and Applied Economics* 38 (2): 429–439.

Klotz, A., K. Hmieleski, B. Bradley, and L. Busenitz. 2014. "New Venture Teams a Review of the Literature and Roadmap for Future Research." *Journal of Management* 40 (1): 226–255.

Klyver, K., and S. Terjesen. 2007. "Entrepreneurial Network Composition: An Analysis across Venture Development Stage and Gender." *Women in Management Review* 22 (8): 682–688.

Knowles, J. 2012. "Sqoot Loses Sponsors following Misogynistic Description of Their API Jam Event." Accessed June 30 2016. http://thenextweb.com/us/2012/03/20/sqoot-loses-sponsors-following-misogynistic-description-of-their-api-jam-event/

Knowlton, K., B. Ozkazanc-Pan, S. Clark Muntean, and Y. Motoyama. 2015. *Support Organizations and Remediating the Gender Gap in Entrepreneurial Ecosystems: A Case Study of St. Louis*. Saint Louis, MO: Social Science Research Network. doi:10.2139/ssrn.2685116.

Koeber, C., and D. W. Wright. 2006. "Gender Differences in the Reemployment Status of Displaced Workers Human Capital as Signals that Mitigate Effects of Bias." *Journal of SocioEconomics* 35 (5): 780–796.

Krippendorff, K. 2004. *Content Analysis: An Introduction to Its Methodology*. Thousand Oaks, CA: Sage.

Kuratko, D. F. 2005. "The Emergence of Entrepreneurship Education: Development, Trends, and Challenges." *Entrepreneurship Theory and Practice* 29 (5): 577–597.

Lansky, M. 2000. "Gender, Women and the Rest Part 1." *International Labour Review* 139 (4): 481–505.

Lazear, E. P. 2004. "Balanced Skills and Entrepreneurship." *American Economic Review* 94: 208–211.

Ljunggren, E., and L. Kolvereid. 1996. "New Business Formation: Does Gender Make a Difference?" *Women In Management Review* 11 (4): 3–12.

Lobo, R. 2014. "Silicon Valley's Sexist Brogrammer Culture Is Locking Women Out of Tech." Accessed June 30 2016. http://www.theneweconomy.com/technology/silicons-sexist-brogrammer-culture-is-locking-women-out-of-tech

Lockwood, P. 2006. "Someone like Me Can Be Successfull": Do College Students Need Same-Gender Role Models?" *Psychology of Women Quarterly* 30 (1): 36–46.

Lohr, S. 2009. "In Innovation, U.S. Said to Be Losing Competitive Edge." *The New York Times*, February 25. B9. http://www.nytimes.com/2009/02/25/technology/25innovate.html.

Loscocco, K., and S. R. Bird. 2012. "Gendered Paths: Why Women Lag behind Men in Small Business Success." *Work and Occupations* 39: 183–219.

Lounsbury, M., and M. A. Glynn. 2001. "Cultural Entrepreneurship: Stories, Legitimacy, and the Acquisition of Resources." *Strategic Management Journal* 22 (6–7): 545–564.

Mangelsdorf, M. E. 2011. "Is the U.S. Losing Its Innovation Edge?" Accessed February 3 2017. http://sloanreview.mit.edu/article/is-the-us-losing-its-innovation-edge/

Manolova, T. S., C. G. Brush, and L. F. Edelman. 2007. "What Do Women (And Men) Want? Entrepreneurial Expectancies of Women and Men Nascent Entrepreneurs." Babson College Entrepreneurship Research Conference (BCERC) 2007; Frontiers of Entrepreneurship Research 2007; Babson College Center for Entrepreneurship Research Paper No. 2008-01. Available at SSRN: https://ssrn.com/abstract=1060241 or http://dx.doi.org/10.2139/ssrn.1060241.

Margison, F., and P. Brown. 2007. "Assessment in Psychotherapy." In *Seminars in the Psychotherapies*, edited by J. Naismith and S. Grant, 1–27. London : The Royal College of Psychiatrists

Marlow, S. 1997. "Self-Employed Women: New Opportunities, Old Challenges?" *Entrepreneurship & Regional Development* 9 (3): 199–210.

Marlow, S., and M. Mcadam. 2015. "Incubation or Induction? Gendered Identity Work in the Context of Technology Business Incubation." *Entrepreneurship Theory & PracticeTheory and Practice* 39 (4): 791–816.

Marlow, S., and M. McAdam. 2013. "Gender and Entrepreneurship: Advancing Debate and Challenging Myths; Exploring the Mystery of the Underperforming Female Entrepreneur." *International Journal of Entrepreneurial Behavior & Research* 19 (1): 114–124.

Marlow, S., and S. Carter. 2004. "Accounting for Change: Professional Status, Gender Disadvantage and Self-Employment." *Women in Management Review* 19 (1): 5–16.

Martin, L.M. and Wright, L.T. (2005) "No gender in cyberspace?: Empowering entrepreneurship and innovation in female-run ICT small firms", International Journal of Entrepreneurial Behavior & Research, 11(2) : 162–178, https://doi.org/10.1108/13552550510590563

Martin, L., L. Wright, Z. Beaven, and H. Matlay. 2015. "An Unusual Job for a Woman? Female Entrepreneurs in Scientific, Engineering and Technology Sectors." *International Journal of Entrepreneurial Behavior & Research* 21 (4): 539–556.

Maton, K. 2004. *The Field of Higher Education: A Sociology of Reproduction, Transformation, Change and the Conditions of Emergence for Cultural Studies*. Cambridge: University of Cambridge. http://acriticalengagement.com/wp-content/uploads/2016/02/he-Field-of-Higher-Education-A-sociology-of-reproduction-transformation-change-and-the-conditions-of-emergence-for-cultural-studies.pdf

Mattis, M. C. 2004. "Women Entrepreneurs: Out from under the Glass Ceiling." *Women in Management Review* 19: 154–163.

Mayer, H., 2008. Segmentation and Segregation Patterns of Women-Owned High-Tech Firms in Four Metropolitan Regions in the United States. Regional Studies, 42(10): 1357–1383. Routledge, Taylor & Francis Group 10.1080/00343400701654194

McConnell-Ginet, S. 2003. "What's in a Name? Social Labeling and Gender Practices." In *The Handbook of Language and Gender*, edited by J. Holmes and M. Meyerhoff, 69–97, Malden, MA: Blackwell.

McGrath, Cohoon, J. 2011. "Which Gender Differences Matter for High Tech Entrepreneurship?" *Technology Innovation Management Review*, July 2011. https://timreview.ca/article/454

Mcgrath, R. G. 1999. "Falling Forward: Real Options Reasoning and Entrepreneurial Failure." *The Academy of Management Review* 24 (1): 13–30.

McQuaid, J., L. Smith-Doerr, and D. J. Monti. "Expanding Entrepreneurship: Female and Foreign-Born Founders of New England Biotechnology Firms." American Behavioral Scientist 53, no. 7 (March 2010): 1045–63. doi:10.1177/0002764209356238.

Menzies, T. V., M. Diochon, and Y. Gasse. 2004. "Examining Venture-Related Myths Concerning Women Entrepreneurs." *Journal of Developmental Entrepreneurship* 9: 89–107.

Miller, D. 2014. "A Downside to the Entrepreneurial Personality?" *Entrepreneurship Theory and Practice* 38 (5): 1–8.

Milli, J., B. Gault, E. Williams-Barron, J. Xia, and M. Berlan. 2016. "The Gender Patenting Gap (IWPR Briefing Papers No. C440)." Washington, DC.

Mirchandani, K. 1999. "Feminist Insight into Gendered Work: New Directions in Research on Female and Entrepreneurship." *Gender, Work and Organisations* 6 (4): 224–235.

Mitchell, R. K., B. Randolph-Seng, and J. R. Mitchell. 2011. "Socially Situated Cognition : Imagining New Opportunities for Entrepreneurship Research." *Academy of Management Review* 36 (4): 774–777.

Mitchelmore, S., and J. Rowley. 2010. "Entrepreneurial Competencies: A Literature Review and Development Agenda." *International Journal of Entrepreneurial Behaviour & Research* 16 (2): 92–111.

Mohanty, C. T. 2003. *Feminism without Borders: Decolonizing Theory, Practicing Solidarity*. Durham, NC: Duke University Press.

Moore, D. P. 2012. *WomenPreneurs: 21st Century Success Strategies*. New York, NY: Routledge.

Moore, D. P., and E. H. Buttner. 1997. *Women Entrepreneurs: Moving beyond the Glass Ceiling*. Thousand Oaks, CA: Sage.

Morelix, A., E. J. Reedy, and J. Russell. 2016. "Kauffman Index: Growth Entrepreneurship National Trends." https://ssrn.com/abstract=2783817

Morris, M. H., N. N. Miyasaki, C. E. Watters, and S. M. Coombes. 2006. "The Dilemma of Growth : Understanding Venture Size Choices of Women Entrepreneurs." *Journal of Small Business Management* 44 (2): 221–244.

Navis, C., and M. Glynn. 2011. "Legitimate Distinctiveness and the Entrepreneurial Identity: Influence on Investor Judgments of New Venture Plausibility." *Academy of Management Review* 36 (3): 479–499.

Neergaard, H., E. Shaw, and S. Carter. 2005. "The Impact of Gender, Social Capital and Networks on Business Ownership: A Research Agenda." *International Journal of Entrepreneurial Behaviour & Research* 11 (5): 338–357.

Nelson, T., and S. Duffy. 2010. "Entrepreneurship Education: Women, Men, Sex and Gender." In *Handbook of Research in Entrepreneurship Education*, edited by A. Fayolle. Vol. 3,153–165. UK/USA: Edward Elgar Publishing.

Network for Teaching Entrepreneurship. 2013. *Grow the Global Economy: Entrepreneurship Education for All Youth*. New York: Network for Teaching Entrepreneurship (NFTE).

Nightingale, P., and A. Coad. 2011. *MUPPETS and GAZELLES: Rooting Out Ideological and Methodological Biases in Entrepreneurship Research*. Milton Keynes: Finance, Innovation & Growth (FINNOV). http://www.finnov-fp7.eu/publications.html.

Nina Gunnerud, B. 1997. "Gender, Place and Entrepreneurship." *Entrepreneurship & Regional Development* 9 (3): 259–268.

North, A. 2015. "Innovating the Innovation Community: Strategies to Include Women Entrepreneurs." Ewing Marion Kauffman Foundation Website. 2015. https://www.kauffman.org/currents/2015/11/innovating-the-innovation-community-strategies-to-include-women-entrepreneurs.

Nye, D. E. 2006. *Technology Matters: Questions to Live With*. Cambridge, MA: MIT Press.

Obschonka, M., E. Schmitt-Rodermund, and A. Terracciano. 2014. "Personality and the Gender Gap in Self-Employment: A Multi-Nation Study." *PloS One* 9 (8): e103805. https://doi.org/10.1371/journal.pone.0103805.

Obschonka, M., R. K. Silbereisen, and E. Schmitt-Rodermund. 2011. "Successful Entrepreneurship as Developmental Outcome: A Path Model from A Lifespan Perspective of Human Development." *European Psychologist* 16 (3): 174–186.

Obschonka, M., R. K. Silbereisen, and E. Schmitt-Rodermund. 2012. "Explaining Entrepreneurial Behavior: Dispositional Personality Traits, Growth of Personal Entrepreneurial Resources, and Business Idea Generation." *The Career Development Quarterly* 60 (2): 178–190.

Ogzen, E., and R. A. Baron. 2007. "Social Sources of Information in Opportunity Recognition: Effects of Mentors, Industry Networks, and Professional Forums." *Journal of Business Venturing* 22: 174–192.

Orser, B., A. Riding, and J. Stanley. 2012. "Perceived Career Challenges and Response Strategies Of Women in The Advanced Technology Sector." *Entrepreneurship & Regional Development* 24 (1–2): 73–93. doi:10.1080/08985626.2012.637355.

Orser, B., A. Riding, and K. Manley. 2006. "Women Entrepreneurs and Financial Capital." *Entrepreneurship Theory & Practice* 30 (5): 643–665.

Orser, B., and S. Hogarth-Scott. 2009. "Opting for Growth: Gender Dimensions of Choosing Enterprise Development." *Canadian Journal of Administrative Sciences* 19 (3): 284–300.

Ozkazanc-Pan, B. 2014. "Postcolonial Feminist Analysis of High-Technology Entrepreneuring." *International Journal of Entrepreneurial Behaviour & Research* 20 (2): 155–172.

Pathak, S., S. Goltz, and M. W. Buche. 2013. "Influences of Gendered Institutions on Women's Entry into Entrepreneurship." *International Journal of Entrepreneurial Behaviour & Research* 19 (5): 478–502.

Petridou, E., A. Sarri, and L. P. Kyrgidou. 2009. "Entrepreneurship Education in Higher Educational Institutions: The Gender Dimension." *Gender in Management: an International Journal* 24 (4): 286–309.

Pettersson, K., and M. Lindberg. 2013. "Paradoxical Spaces of Feminist Resistance: Mapping the Margin to the Masculinist Innovation Discourse." *International Journal of Gender and Entrepreneurship* 5 (3): 323–341.

Polkowska, D. 2013. "Women Scientists in the Leaking Pipeline: Barriers to the Commercialisation of Scientific Knowledge by Women." *Journal of Technology Management and Innovation* 8 (2): 156–165.

Pronin, E. 2009. "The Introspection Illusion." In *Advances in Experimental Social Psychology*, edited by M. P. Zanna, 1–67, Cambridge, MA: Academic Press.

Prowess. 2007. *Under the Microscope: Female Entrepreneurs in Science, Engineering, Construction and Technology (SECT)*. Norwich, UK: Prowess Ltd. http://www.prowess.org.uk/wp-content/uploads/2011/10/UndertheMicroscope_0002.pdf.

Ranga, M. 2008. "Gender Patterns in Technology Transfer: Social Innovation in the Making?" *Research Global*, 4–5. http://www.academia.edu/18734359/Gender_Patterns_in_Technology_Transfer_Social_innovation_in_the_making

Ranga, M., and H. Etzkowitz. 2010. "Athena in the World of Techne: The Gender Dimension of Technology, Innovation and Entrepreneurship." *Journal of Technology Management and Innovation* 5 (1): 1–12.

Rauch, A., and M. Frese. 2007. "Let's Put the Person Back into Entrepreneurship Research: A Meta-Analysis on the Relationship between Business Owners' Personality Traits, Business Creation, and Success." *European Journal of Work and Organizational Psychology* 16 (4): 353–385.

Reynolds, J., and L. A. Renzulli. 2005. "Economic Freedom or Self-Imposed Strife: Work–Life Conflict, Gender, and Self-Employment." In *Research in the Sociology of Work*, edited by L. A. Keister, 33–60. Bingley, UK: Emerald Group.

Rindova, V., D. Barry, and D. J. Ketchen Jr. 2009. "Entrepreneuring as Emancipation." *Academy of Management Review* 34 (3): 477–491.

Robb, A., S. Coleman, and D. Stangler. 2014. *Sources of Economic Hope: Women's Entrepreneurship*. Kansas, MO: Ewing Marion Kauffman Foundation. https://www.kauffman.org/what-we-do/research/2014/11/sources-of-economic-hope-womens-entrepreneurship.

Robb, A. M., and S. Coleman. 2009. *Sources of Financing for New Technology Firms: A Comparison by Gender*. Kansas, MO: Ewing Marion Kauffman Foundation. https://doi.org/10.2139/ssrn.1352601.

Robinson, S., and H. A. Stubberud. 2009. "Sources of Advice in Entrepreneurship: Gender Differences in Business Owners' Social Networks." *International Journal of Entrepreneurship* 13: 83–101.

Rosa, P., and A. Dawson. 2006. "Gender and the Commercialization of University Science: Academic Founders of Spinout Companies." *Entrepreneurship & Regional Development* 18 (4): 341–366.

Rutashobya, L. K., I. S. Allan, and K. Nilsson. 2009. "Gender, Social Networks and Entrepreneurial Outcomes in Tanzania." *Journal of African Business* 12: 67–83.

Sandberg, S. 2013. *Lean In: Women, Work, and the Will to Lead*. New York: Alfred A. Knopf.

Sappleton, N. 2009. "Women Non-Traditional Entrepreneurs and Social Capital." *International Journal of Gender and Entrepreneurship* 1 (3): 192–218.

Savitz, E. 2013. "Is The U.S. Really Losing Its Innovative Edge?" *Forbes*, January. https://www.forbes.com/sites/ciocentral/2013/01/02/is-the-u-s-really-losing-its-innovative-edge/#69411a674c78.

Schwartz, E. B. 1976. "Entrepreneurship: A New Female Frontier." *Journal of Contemporary Business* 5 (1): 47–76.

Scott, J. W. 1986. "Gender : A Useful Category of Historical Analysis." *The American Historical Review* 91 (5): 1053–1075.

Scott, R., and S. Vincent-Lancrin. 2014. *The Global Innovation Index 2014: The Human Factor in Innovation (Ch. 3– Educating Innovators and Entrepreneurs)*. Geneva: World Intellectual Property Organization (WIPO). https://www.wipo.int/edocs/pubdocs/en/wipo_pub_gii_2014-chapter3.pdf.

Shao-Hui, L., L. Ping, and F. Peng-Peng. 2011. "Mediation and Moderated Mediation in the Relationship among Entrepreneurial Self-Efficacy, Entrepreneurial Intention, Entrepreneurial Attitude and Role Models." In *International Conference on Management Science and Engineering - Annual Conference Proceedings*, edited by LAN Hua, 129–134. Piscataway, NJ: IEEE. doi: 10.1109/ICMSE.2011.6069954

Shapiro, G., and J. Markoff. 1997. "A Matter of Definition." In *Text Analysis for the Social Sciences: Methods for Drawing Statistical Inferences from Texts and Transcripts*, edited by C. W. Roberts. Mahwah, 9–33. NJ: Lawrence Erlbaum Associates.

Shartrand, A., P. Weilerstein, M. Besterfield-Sacre, and K. Golding. 2010. "Technology Entrepreneurship Programs in U.S. Engineering Schools: An Analysis of Programs as the Undergraduate Level." Paper presented at 2010 Annual Conference & Exposition, Louisville, Kentucky. https://peer.asee.org/16057.

Simard, C., H. D. Henderson, S. K. Gilmartin, L. Shiebinger, and T. Whitney. 2008. *Climbing the Technical Ladder: Obstacles and Solutions for Mid-Level Women in Technology*. Stanford, CA: The Michelle R. Clayman Institute for Gender Research (Stanford University) and the Anita Borg Institute for Women and Technology. https://gender.stanford.edu/publications/climbing-technical-ladder-obstacles-and-solutions-mid-level-women-technology

Smith, J. L., K. L. Lewis, L. Hawthorne, and S. D. Hodges. 2013. "When Trying Hard Isn't Natural: Women's Belonging with and Motivation for Male-Dominated STEM Fields as a Function of Effort Expenditure Concerns." *Personality & Social Psychology Bulletin* 39 (2): 131–143.

Smith, R. 2009. "The Diva Storyline: An Alternative Social Construction of Female Entrepreneurship." *International Journal of Gender and Entrepreneurship* 1 (2): 148–163.

Staff. 2015. "Valley of the Dudes: Tech Firms Can Banish Sexism without Sacrificing the Culture that Made Them Successful." Accessed June 30 2012. http://www.economist.com/news/business/21647611-tech-firms-can-banish-sexism-without-sacrificing-culture-made-them-successful-valley

Steele, C. M., S. J. Spencer, and J. Aronson. 2002. "Contending with Images of One's Group: The Psychology of Stereotype and Social Identity Threat." *Advances in Experimental Social Psychology* 34: 379–440.

Stemler, S. 2001. "An Overview of Content Analysis." *Practical Assessment, Research & Evaluation* 7 (17): 1–6. https://pareonline.net/getvn.asp?v=7&n=17.

Stephan, P. E., and A. El-Ganainy. 2007. "The Entrepreneurial Puzzle: Explaining the Gender Gap." *Journal of Technology Transfer* 32 (5): 475–487.

Stephan, P. E., and S. G. Levin. 2005. "Leaving Careers in IT: Differences in Retention by Gender and Minority Status." *Computer* 30: 383–396.

Stillman, J. 2016. "New Report: Sexism in Silicon Valley Is Really Pretty Awful." Accessed June 30 2016. http://www.inc.com/jessica-stillman/new-report-sexism-in-silicon-valley-is-really-pretty-awful.html

Stromberg, L. 2015. "Problem with Women in Tech? The Pipeline or the Revolving Door." Accessed June 30 2016. http://www.huffingtonpost.com/lisen-stromberg/problem-with-women-in-tech-the-pipeline-or-the-revolving-door_b_6992522.html

Stuetzer, M., M. Obschonka, and E. Schmitt-Rodermund. 2012. "Balanced Skills among Nascent Entrepreneurs." *Small Business Economics* 41 (1): 93–114.

Sugimoto, C. R., C. Ni, J. D. West, and V. Larivière. 2015. "The Academic Advantage: Gender Disparities in Patenting." *PloS One* 10 (5): e012800. doi:10.1371/journal.pone.0128000.

Sullivan, D. M., and W. R. Meek. 2012. "Gender and Entrepreneurship: A Review and Process Model." *Journal of Managerial Psychology* 27: 428–458.

Sweida, G. L., and R. J. Reichard. 2013. "Gender Stereotyping Effects on Entrepreneurial Self-Efficacy and High-Growth Entrepreneurial Intention." *Journal of Small Business and Enterprise Development* 20 (2): 296–313.

Symington, A. 2004. "Intersectionality: A Tool for Gender and Economic Justice." *Women's Rights and Economic Change* 9 (August): 1–8.

Tan, J. 2008. "Breaking the "Bamboo Curtain" and the "Glass Ceiling": The Experience of Women Entrepreneurs in High-Tech Industries in an Emerging Market." *Journal of Business Ethics* 80 (3): 547–564.

Tasneem, R. 2012. "The Rise of the Brogrammer: Can Silicon Valley Solve Its Sexism Problem?" Accessed June 30 2016. https://storify.com/motherjones/sexism-in-tech

Terjesen, S. 2005. "Senior Women Managers' Transition to Entrepreneurship." *Career Development International* 10 (3): 246–262.

Thebaud, S. 2015a. "Business as Plan B: Institutional Foundations of Gender Inequality in Entrepreneurship across 24 Industrialized Countries." *Administrative Science Quarterly* 60 (4): 671–711.

Thebaud, S. 2015b. "Status Beliefs and the Spirit of Capitalism: Accounting for Gender Biases in Entrepreneurship and Innovation." *Social Forces* 94 (1): 61–86.

Tinkler, J. E., K. Bunker Whittington, M. C. Ku, and A. R. Davies. 2015. "Gender and Venture Capital Decision-Making: The Effects of Technical Background and Social Capital on Entrepreneurial Evaluations." *Social Science Research* 51: 1–16.

Tracy, S. L.2011. *Accelerating Job Creation in America: The Promise of High-Impact Companies. Small Business and Job Creation: Analyses and Implications.* Washington, DC. Retrieved from https://www.sba.gov/content/high-impact-firms-gazelles-revisited.

Truss, C., E. Conway, A. D'Amato, G. Kelly, K. Monks, E. Hannon, and P. C. Flood. 2012. "Knowledge Work: Gender-Blind or Gender-Biased?" *Work, Employment & Society* 26 (5): 735–754.

Turner, C. S. V. 2002. "Women of Color in Academe: Living with Multiple Marginality." *The Journal of Higher Education* 73 (1): 74–93.

U.S. Patent and Trademark Office. 2016. U.S. Patent Statistics Chart: Calendar years 1963–2015. Accessed November 7 2016. http://www.uspto.gov/web/offices/ac/ido/oeip/taf/us_stat.htm.

Vassallo, T., E. Levy, M. Madansky, H. Mickell, B. Porter, M. Leas, and J. Oberweis. 2016. "Elephant in the Valley." Accessed June 30 2016. http://www.elephantinthevalley.com/

Verheul, I., L. Uhlaner, and R. Thurik. 2005. "Business Accomplishments, Gender and Entrepreneurial Self-Image." *Journal of Business Venturing* 20. 483–518.

Walby, S. 2011. "Is the Knowledge Society Gendered?" *Gender, Work and Organization* 18 (1): 1–29.

Walton, G. M., and M. R. Banaji. 2004. "Being What You Say: The Effect of Essentialist Linguistic Labels on Preferences." *Social Cognition* 22 (2): 193–213.

Watson, J. 2003. "Failure Rates for Female-Controlled Businesses: Are They Any Different?" *Journal of Small Business Management* 41 (3): 262–277.

Watson, J., and R. Newby. 2005. "Biological Sex, Stereotypical Sex-Roles, and SME Owner Characteristics." *International Journal of Entrepreneurial Behaviour & Research* 11 (2): 129–143.

Wendler, C., B. Bridgeman, F. Cline, C. Millett, J. Rock, N. Bell, and P. McAllister. 2010. *The Path Forward: The Future of Graduate Education in the United States.* Princeton, NJ: Educational Testing Service.

Whittington, K. B., and L. Smith-Doerr. 2005. "Gender and Commercial Science: Women's Patenting in the Life Sciences." *Journal of Technology Transfer* 30 (4): 355–370.

Wiens, J., and C. Jackson. 2015. "The Importance of Young Firms for Economic Growth (An Educational Policy Brief from the Ewing Marion Kauffman Foundation)." Accessed February 4 2017. https://tinyurl.com/mprssnm or http://www.kauffman.org/what-we-do/resources/entrepreneurship-policy-digest/the-importance-of-young-firms-for-economic-growth

Williams, J., and R. Dempsey. 2012. "The "Uppity Women" of Silicon Valley." Accessed June 30 2016. http://www.huffingtonpost.com/joan-williams/silicon-valley-sexism_b_1569784.html

Williams, K. 2013. "Tackling the Tech Gap." *IEEE Women in Engineering Magazine*, 18–20.

Wilson, F., J. Kickul, and D. Marlino. 2007. "Gender, Entrepreneurial Self-Efficacy, and Entrepreneurial Career Intentions: Implications for Entrepreneurship Education." *Entrepreneurship Theory and Practice* 31 (3): 387–406.

Wilson, T. D., and Y. Bar-Anan. 2008. "The Unseen Mind." *Science* 321 (5892): 1046–1047.

Yeager, D. S., and C. S. Dweck. 2012. "Mindsets that Promote Resilience: When Students Believe that Personal Characteristics Can Be Developed." *Educational Psychologist* 47: 302–314. February 2015.

Yeh, C. 2012. "Speak Up, Silicon Valley." Accessed June 30 2016. http://chrisyeh.blogspot.com/2012/04/speak-up-silicon-valley.html

Zeyen, A., M. Beckmann, S. Mueller, J. G. Dees, D. Khanin, and N. Krueger. 2012. "Social Entrepreneurship and Broader Theories : Shedding New Light on the "Bigger Picture"." *Journal of Social Entrepreneurship* 3 (1): 1–20.

Zhang, Y., and B. M. Wildemuth. 2005. "Qualitative Analysis of Content." *Analysis* 1 (2): 1–12.

Zimmer, L. 1988. "Tokenism and Women in the Workplace: The Limits of Gender-Neurtral Theory." *Social Problems* 35 (1): 64–77.

Zimmerman, M. A., and G. J. Zeitz. 2002. "Beyond Survival: Achieving New Venture Growth by Building Legitimacy." *The Academy of Management Review* 27 (3): 414–431.

Zott, C., and Q. Nguyen Huy. 2006. How entrepreneurs use symbolic management to acquire resources: *Administrative Science Quarterly* 52(1): 70–105. doi:10.2189/asqu.52.1.70.

Appendix

Summary of women and technology entrepreneurship articles

Citation/Journal	Independent variables (IV)	-Dependent variable(s) (DV)	Population sample	Theory	Methods	Key findings
Cohoon and Mcgrath (2011) *Open Source Business Resource (OSBR) (now Technology Innovation Management Review (TIM Review))*	Gender	Highest degree earned; interest in becoming an entrepreneur; family educational and entrepreneurial history; motivations for starting business(es); sources of funding; importance of various factors for startup success; challenges faced, professional networks	Founders of high-tech enterprises	None stated	Email surveys ($n = 542$; 41 female/501 male)	When the gender distribution of a trait was similar in both groups, it was not likely to be a cause of women's underrepresentation among successful high-tech entrepreneurs. Motivation by desire for wealth, importance of knowledge gained from experience, and access to social networks including mentors and advisors could all contribute to the gender imbalance among successful high-tech entrepreneurs
Dautzenberg (2012) *International Journal of Gender and Entrepreneurship*	Gender of founder (m/f/ mixed teams)	Firm size; number of employees; revenue	German technology firms	Social constructivism	Secondary data analysis ($n = 6301$ firms); comparison of temporal cohorts using binary logistic regression	While firm characteristics such as firm size, number of employees, and revenues are correlated to gender, firm success appears to be independent of these
Dohrman (2010) *Dissertation*	Gender; age	Perceptions of entrepreneurship/ entrepreneurial work	Young high-tech entrepreneurs (mostly students)	Social constructionism; Discourse theory; Organizational communication theory	Discourse analysis of mainstream media; thematic analyses of interviews with young entrepreneurs ($n = 50$) and focus groups with members of the Millennial Generation ($n = 57$); secondary data analysis of the Global Entrepreneurship Monitor (GEM) data	Offers collective sense-making as an complement to the individual traits-based model of understanding entrepreneurial work: perceived meaningfulness of one's work may lessen the negative impacts of the enterprising self and ideal worker ideologies

(Continued)

(Continued).

Citation/Journal	Independent variables (IV)	Dependent variable(s) (DV)	Population sample	Theory	Methods	Key findings
Ezzedeen and Zikic (2012) *International Journal of Gender and Entrepreneurship*	Gender	Experiences of entrepreneurship within the technology field	Canadian female high-tech entrepreneurs	Role congruity theory	Interpretive phenomenological approach; in-depth interviews ($n = 12$)	Subjects encountered persistent gender stereotypes, a lack of female role models, resistance from associates within and outside of their organizations, and societal pressures to maintain appropriate levels of work-family balance
Gicheva, Dora; Link, Albert N. (2015) *Small Business Economics*	Gender of firm owner	Relative probability of attracting private investments to fund commercialization of technology to market	Participants in NIH small business programme (tech sector)	Network theory	Survey responses ($n = 323$)	Women-owned firms are much less likely to attract private investment dollars compared to male-owned firms; women-owned firms that received larger awards performed substantially better
Hampton, McGowan, and Cooper (2011) *International Journal of Entrepreneurial Behaviour & Research*	Gender of entrepreneur	Network type and composition; nature and frequency of engagement; changes in network composition and networking activities through the business lifecycle	Female entrepreneurs operating STEM-based ventures in Northern Ireland	None stated	In-depth interviews ($n = 18$)	Women and men behave in largely similar ways in the establishment and utilization of their networks, and have similar network composition and quality, especially as the venture becomes more established
Martin and Wright (2005) *International Journal of Entrepreneurial Behaviour & Research*	Personal background and motivation; personal contacts; networking practices	Access to resources; firm outcomes	Owners and other staff in tech companies run by female entrepreneurs	None stated	Semi-structured interviews ($n = 10$ firms) and thematic grid analysis to form a major part of text analysis	The types of companies set up and the way in which they were run inevitably relates to the gender of the entrepreneur, where deliberate choices have to be made to combine home and work needs

(Continued)

(Continued).

Citation/Journal	Independent variables (IV)	Dependent variable(s) (DV)	Population sample	Theory	Methods	Key findings
Martin et al. (2015) *International Journal of Entrepreneurial Behavior & Research*	Perceptions and experiences of the STEM context for female entrepreneurs; experiences of business start-up	Strategies for managing gender-based discrimination	Female STEM entrepreneurs with businesses that had progressed beyond the initial start-up phase	Identity construction theory	Semi-structured interviews (n = 15) and documentary records analysis using both manual and software-based thematic review	Taking a longitudinal approach which covers different stages in the development of the firm, might show how women engage with STEM start-up, growth and exit to help policymakers provide the right kind of support environments to female entrepreneurs at different stages of their business development
Mayer and Heike (2008) *Regional Studies*	Gender of entrepreneur; geographic location; prior experience & education	Type of venture/industry sector; firm longevity & performance	Records for women-owned high-tech firms in four regions (Silicon Valley, Boston, Washington, DC, Portland)	Labour market segmentation theories (including neoclassical, institutional and feminist frameworks)	Secondary data analysis (n = 11,772 records) using ANOVA	Although women are entering non-traditional sectors, female entrepreneurs tend to own businesses in female-typed high-tech sectors (management consulting services, computer systems design services, software and Internet/telecommunication services). Female-typed high-tech firms have on average fewer employees, smaller sales volume and are younger than their male-typed counterparts. Male-typed and female-typed women-owned high-tech firms differ significantly in terms of sectoral and spatial segmentation regardless of firm age
McQuaid, Smith-Doerr, and Monti (2010) *American Behavioral Scientist*	Founder gender; countries of origin	Firm revenue; industry specialty area	Biotech firms located in Massachusetts and New England	Social capital theory	Survey (n = 261 firms)	Female life scientists are underrepresented in founding roles in biotech firms; immigrant men have better success in entrepreneurship than do female scientists

(*Continued*)

(Continued).

Citation/Journal	Independent variables (IV)	-Dependent variable(s) (DV)	Population sample	Theory	Methods	Key findings
Orser, Barbara; Riding, Allan; Stanley, Joanne (2012) *Entrepreneurship & Regional Development*	Gender of entrepreneur	Sector; perceived barriers to career advancement in technology; challenge resolution strategies	Entrepreneur members of Canadian Women in Technology	Gender schema theory	Analysis of qualitative data from an online survey using Nvivo	Respondents attributed a high proportion of the challenges they encountered to gender; respondents were most likely to resolve challenges through personal solutions with few firm or industry-related support structures cited; lack of mentorship opportunities is particularly acute for women entrepreneurs
Robb and Coleman (2009) *Kauffman Foundation Report*	Gender of entrepreneur	Sources of financing for new tech firms	New businesses in the USA, partitioned into sampling strata defined by industrial technology categories	Life cycle of ventures theory	Longitudinal survey	Women entrepreneurs raised significantly smaller amounts of financial capital at startup than men did; women high-tech entrepreneurs were significantly less likely to use external equity
Sappleton (2009) *International Journal of Gender and Entrepreneurship*	Business owner gender; firm sector	Level of social capital	Male and female business owners in Europe	Gender stereotypes theory; social networks theory	Secondary data analysis of subsets of the 2006 European Social Survey (ESS); regression analysis of four sub-samples: females in female-dominated industries ($n = 283$); females in male-dominated industries ($n = 337$); males in male-dominated industries ($n = 1476$) and males in female-dominated industries ($n = 118$)	Women who operate firms in traditionally female sectors are found to have the highest levels of social capital. Men and women working in traditionally male sectors exhibit lower levels of social capital, measured in terms of trust, community engagement and social networks. Self-employment in a gender traditional or non-traditional sector is found to be a significant predictor of social capital

(Continued)

(Continued).

Citation/Journal	Independent variables (IV)	-Dependent variable(s) (DV)	Population sample	Theory	Methods	Key findings
Sweida and Reichard (2013) *Journal of Small Business and Enterprise Development*	Conceptual paper	Conceptual paper	N/A	Stereotype activation theory	N/A	By decreasing the masculine stereotype-related barriers associated with high-growth entrepreneurship and increasing women's HGE self-efficacy it should be possible to increase women's intention to engage in high-growth venture creation
Tan (2008) *Journal of Business Ethics*	Gender of entrepreneur	Entrepreneurial intention; venture performance	Male and female entrepreneurs in the Chinese tech sector	Institutional theory; entrepreneurial orientation theory	Survey ($n = 43$; 18 female) with ANOVA; Randomly selected interviews for triangulation	Women entrepreneurs can be driven by opportunities rather just necessity. This is a departure from findings from a large scale global study of entrepreneurs from 27 countries, which reports that men are more likely than women to pursue opportunity entrepreneurship, while women are more likely to pursue necessity entrepreneurship
Thebaud (2015a) *Social Forces*	Gender of the entrepreneur; innovativeness of the business plan	Perceived competence of entrepreneur, how skilled they were, and how committed they were to the venture; perceived quality of the business proposal and likelihood of participant investing in it	University students in the UK and the USA	Social psychology of gender; gender status beliefs theory	Three experimental studies using 2×2 mixed factorial design. Study 1 evaluated the effects of gender status beliefs and innovation in a UK setting. Study 2 evaluated these effects in a US setting for a cross-cultural comparison to Study 1. Study 3 evaluated these effects in a high-tech industry setting in the US to provide a comparison to Study 2 (total participants $n = 178$; 86 males/92 females; $n = 21$–41 per condition)	Gender status beliefs disadvantage women entrepreneurs when compared to their male counterparts, but innovation in a business model has a stronger and more positive impact on ratings of women's entrepreneurial ability and overall support for their business ideas than it does for men's. However, the strength of these patterns varies significantly depending on the societal and industry context of the new venture in question

(Continued)

(Continued).

Citation/Journal	Independent variables (IV)	-Dependent variable(s) (DV)	Population sample	Theory	Methods	Key findings
Thebaud (2015b) *Administrative Science Quarterly*	Institutional work–family practices; gender; industry sector	Business start-up and ownership rates	Male and female business owners from 24 countries over the span of eight years	Institutional theory of gender inequalities in business start-up, ownership, and growth orientation	Multilevel secondary analyses of GEM survey data	Institutionally embedded incentives that lead people towards entrepreneurship may operate quite differently for different groups of people, namely men and women; women's disadvantages in entrepreneurship are deeply rooted in the organizational structures, norms, and practices that tend to disadvantage them in wage and salary jobs
Tinkler et al. (2015) *Social Science Research*	Gender of entrepreneur; technical background of entrepreneur (history major with no software engineering work experience/computer science major with some software engineering experience); closeness of social tie between entrepreneur and VC	Evaluation of entrepreneur's leadership capability, competence, and sociability; evaluation about venture's potential for success, uniqueness, and amount they would be willing to invest; importance of perceived level of social capital on decision-making	Male MBA students from the Stanford Graduate School of Business Entrepreneur Club	Status characteristics theory and its applications to gender	Online survey design: study participants ($n = 114$) evaluated an executive summary of a business plan	The gender of the entrepreneur influences evaluations most when the person, rather than the venture, is the target of evaluation. Technical background qualifications moderate the influence of gendered expectations, and women receive more of a payoff than men from having a close contact to the evaluating VC

Index

Note: Page numbers in **bold** refer to tables, and in *italics* refer to figures.

For Product Safety Concerns and Information please contact our
EU representative GPSR@taylorandfrancis.com Taylor & Francis
Verlag GmbH, Kaufingerstraße 24, 80331 München, Germany